2026

브랜드 만족 1위

9급 공무원 영어 시험대비

# 박문각 공무원
## 문제집

합격까지 함께

공무원 영어 만점 독해 문제집

실전문제+기출문제 완벽 분석

독해 유형별 풀이해법 제시

김세현 편저

# 김세현
## 영어
### 전혀 다른 개념 독해

동영상 강의 www.pmg.co.kr

# PREFACE

## 이 책의 머리말

### 공무원 시험을 준비하는 공시생들에게 영어는 가장 좋은 과목입니다.

지금까지 공시생들의 대다수는 영어 때문에 불합격했고 영어 때문에 괴로워하고 영어 때문에 시험을 그만 둘까?라는 생각을 끊임없이 해 왔습니다. 하지만 지금부터는 다릅니다. 인사혁신처의 9급 공무원시험 영어 과목의 출제기조 전환 발표 이후 영어가 쉬워졌습니다. 이는 조금만 영어에 관심을 갖고 최소한의 시간을 들이면 영어가 합격을 위한 가장 좋은 과목이 될 수 있다는 것을 의미합니다. 영어 때문에 고민했던 모든 수험생 여러분 한 번 도전해 보세요. 틀림없이 영어가 가장 효자과목이 될 겁니다.

### 쉬운 영어에 대한 가장 경제적이고 효율적인 방향성을 제시합니다.

김세현 영어는 가장 효율적이고 경제적인 방향을 제시하려 합니다. 여기에서 효율적이고 경제적이라 함은 단기간의 시간 투자로 합격할 수 있는 방향성과 거기에 맞는 학습 과정(curriculum)의 구성을 의미합니다. 공무원 시험에 합격하기 위한 영어 공부는 영어를 학문적으로 연구하며 공부하는 것이 아니라 오직 합격만을 위해 존재해야 한다고 생각합니다. 따라서 김세현 영어는 시험에 꼭 나올 것만을 다루고 문제를 풀 수 있는 방법론에 초점을 맞춘 교재입니다.

### 쉬운 영어로 전환되었기에 이제부터는 독해가 관건입니다.

2회에 걸친 영어 예시문제를 분석한 결과 가장 큰 특징은 독해에 변별력을 준 것입니다. 물론 독해에도 새로운 유형(글의 목적과 안내문)이 추가되었지만 이 새로운 유형은 변별력 없이 어느 정도의 기본 소양을 갖춘 수험생이라면 문제를 해결하는 데 큰 어려움은 없을 겁니다. 하지만 기존 유형에서 빈칸 완성이나 삽입, 배열은 예년에 비해 좀 더 어려운 수준으로 출제되었습니다. 이에 전혀 다른 개념 독해는 가장 충실한 대비책이 될 겁니다. 기본이론을 다시 한 번 정리하고 고난도의 다양한 문제풀이를 통해 어려워진 독해의 가장 확실한 해결책을 마련했습니다.

### 수험생 여러분께 경의를 표합니다.

끊임없는 치열한 경쟁 속에서 오직 하나의 목표를 위해 지금 이 책을 마주하고 있는 여러분의 궁극적 목표는 이번 공무원 시험에서의 합격일 것입니다. 그 합격을 위해 작은 마음을 보태고자 합니다. 모두 다 합격할 수는 없습니다. 단, 스스로를 잘 관리한다면 그리고 최선을 다한다면 그 합격의 영광은 여러분들에게 반드시 돌아올 것입니다. 힘내시고 김세현 영어와 함께합시다. 합격의 영광을 곧 맞이하게 될 여러분께 경의를 표합니다.

### 모든 분들께 감사드립니다.

이 교재가 나오기까지 많은 힘을 실어 주신 박용 회장님께 깊은 감사를 드립니다. 또한 우리 연구실 직원들에게도 고마움을 표합니다. 마지막으로 주말을 반납하면서 애써주신 박문각 출판팀의 노고에 깊은 감사 말씀을 전합니다.

2025년 10월
수험생 여러분의 건승을 기원하며 노량진 연구실에서

# ANALYSIS

## 이 책의 구성과 특징

### 독해

**① 유형별 풀이 해법 제시**

공무원 독해 시험을 유형별로 분류해서 각 유형별 풀이 해법을 제시하였다. 또한 그 풀이 해법을 예제 문제의 분석을 통해 완벽하게 이해할 수 있게 하였다. 물론 새로운 시험체계에 대비하여 다양한 신유형 독해문제도 추가시켰다.

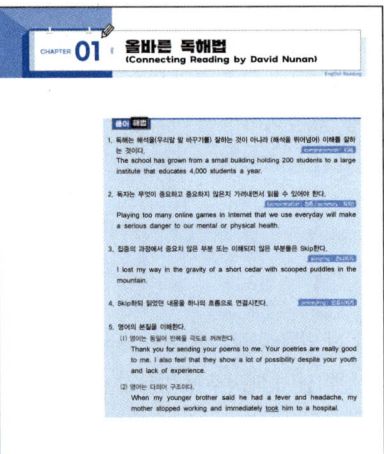

**② 실전문제 + 기출문제**

유형별 풀이 해법을 실전문제를 통해 다시 한 번 점검할 수 있게 하였다. 특히, 올바른 독해법을 토대로 글을 정확하고 빠르게 이해할 수 있도록 방법을 제시함으로써 수험생 여러분들의 독해 문제에 최적화된 최신 기출문제를 엄선하여 수록하였다.

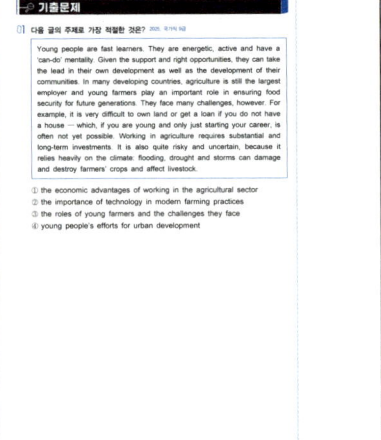

# 김세현 영어 전혀 다른 개념 독해

### 3 독해 한 번 더

독해지문을 해설에 한 번 더 수록해서 수업시간에 들었던 내용을 토대로 독해를 한 번 더 할 수 있다. 정답의 단서를 표시해 둔 원문을 다시 한 번 더 보게 하여 복습에 상당 부분 도움이 될 수 있게 하였다.

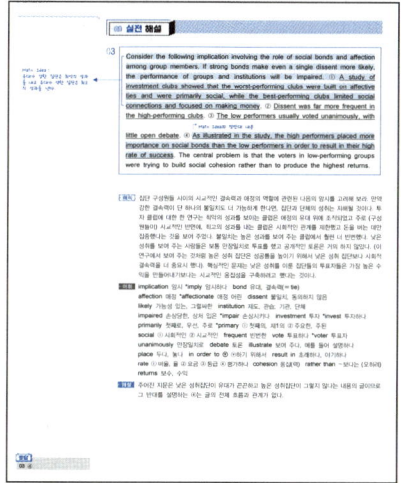

### 4 자세한 해설

독해지문과 해설, 해석이 분리되어있는 기존의 해설서와는 달리 단서가 표시된 원문을 보면서 동시에 해설, 해석, 어휘를 볼 수 있게 하였다. 이런 식으로 복습을 함으로써 시간 효율성을 극대화할 수 있는 이점을 제공하였다.

## CONTENTS

## 이 책의
# 차례

| PART 01 | 올바른 독해법 | 10 |
| PART 02 | 주제, 제목, 요지 | 18 |
| PART 03 | 통일성 | 48 |
| PART 04 | 단락의 전개 방식 | 76 |
| PART 05 | 일관성 | 188 |
| PART 06 | 빈칸 완성 | 264 |

김세현
영어 전혀 다른 개념 독해

김세현 영어 전혀 다른 개념 독해

PART

# 01

# 올바른 독해법

# PART 01 올바른 독해법
## (Connecting Reading by David Nunan)

### 풀이 해법

1. 독해는 해석을(우리말 말 바꾸기를) 잘하는 것이 아니라 (해석을 뛰어넘어) 이해를 잘하는 것이다.

   *comprehension : 이해*

   The school has grown from a small building holding 200 students to a large institute that educates 4,000 students a year.

2. 독자는 무엇이 중요하고 중요하지 않은지 가려내면서 읽을 수 있어야 한다.

   *(concentration : 집중 / summary : 요약)*

   Playing too many online games in Internet that we use everyday will make a serious danger to our mental or physical health.

3. 집중의 과정에서 중요치 않은 부분 또는 이해되지 않은 부분들은 Skip한다.

   *skipping : 건너뛰기*

   I lost my way in the gravity of a short cedar with scooped puddles in the mountain.

4. Skip하되 읽었던 내용을 하나의 흐름으로 연결시킨다.

   *connecting : 연결시키기*

5. 영어의 본질을 이해한다.

   (1) 영어는 동일어 반복을 극도로 꺼려한다.

   Thank you for sending your poems to me. Your poetries are really good to me. I also feel that they show a lot of possibility despite your youth and lack of experience.

   (2) 영어는 다의어 구조이다.

   When my younger brother said he had a fever and headache, my mother stopped working and immediately <u>took</u> him to a hospital.

전혀 다른 **개념 독해**

## 연습문제

**EX 1** 다음 글의 주제로 가장 적절한 것은?

Even though it's the fact that most people like to talk about themselves and their lives, just remember it's important to concentrate on the other person and their interests rather than your own. For example, at a party, you may see an attractive woman with whom you'd like to strike up a conversation. Perhaps that woman is wearing a T-shirt emblazoned with a "Save the Whales" logo. You may begin with something like "Excuse me, I noticed your shirt — a friend of mine is really into environmental issues, but I don't know a lot about the whales thing…" These types of conversation starters are sure to make her spit her knowledge out in no time.

① closing a conversation wisely
② importance of quick conversation
③ common errors in a conversation
④ becoming a good conversationalist

## 연습해설

### EX 1

Even though it's the fact that most people like to talk about themselves and their lives, just remember it's important to concentrate on the other person and their interests rather than your own. For example, at a party, you may see an attractive woman with whom you'd like to strike up a conversation. Perhaps that woman is wearing a T-shirt emblazoned with a "Save the Whales" logo. You may begin with something like "Excuse me, I noticed your shirt — a friend of mine is really into environmental issues, but I don't know a lot about the whales thing…" These types of conversation starters are sure to make her spit her knowledge out in no time.

**해석** 비록 대부분의 사람들이 자기 자신이나 자신들의 삶에 대해 이야기하기를 좋아할지라도 타인과 그들의 관심에 집중하는 것이 중요하다는 것을 단지 기억하라. 예를 들어서 당신이 파티에서 이야기를 하고 싶은 매력적인 여성을 본다. 아마도 그 여성은 "고래를 구하자"라는 로고가 새겨진 티셔츠를 입고 있다. 당신은 "실례지만 제가 당신의 셔츠를 봤는데 사실, 내 친구는 환경문제에 관여하고 있지만 전 그것에 대해 많이 몰라서요…"라고 이야기를 시작할 수 있을 것이다. 이런 식으로 대화를 시작하는 사람은 분명히 그녀로 하여금 지체 없이 자신의 지식을 쏟아 낼 것이다.
① 대화를 현명하게 끝내기
② 빠른 대화의 중요성
③ 대화에서의 보편적인 실수
④ 좋은 대화자가 되기

**어휘** even though 비록 ~일지라도(= even if, though, although, however, no matter how, if)
concentrate on 집중하다   attractive 매력적인   would like to ⓥ ⓥ하고 싶다
strike up ~을 시작하다   emblazon (상징, 문구 등을) 선명하게 새기다, 장식하다
notice ① 알아차리다 ② 보다   spit (주로, 침을) 뱉다, 내뱉다   in no time 지체 없이
close ① 닫다 ② 가까운

**해설** 주어진 지문은 대화를 시작할 때 상대방의 관심에 집중해서 시작해야 한다는 내용의 글이므로 이 글의 주제로 가장 적절한 것은 ④ '좋은 대화자가 되기'이다.

정답
01 ④

## 연습문제

**EX 2** 밑줄 친 부분에 들어갈 말로 가장 적절한 것을 고르시오.  *2025. 지방직 9급*

> A gazelle on the African savanna is trying not to be eaten by cheetahs, but it is also trying to outrun other gazelles when a cheetah attacks. What matters to the gazelle is being faster than other gazelles, not being faster than cheetahs. In the same way, psychologists sometimes wonder why people are endowed with the ability to learn the part of Hamlet or understand calculus when neither skill was of much use to mankind in the primitive conditions where his intellect was shaped. Einstein also would probably have been as hopeless as anybody in working out how to catch a woolly rhinoceros. Nicholas Humphrey, a Cambridge psychologist, was the first to see clearly the solution to this puzzle. We use our intellects not to solve practical problems but to outwit each other. Deceiving people, detecting deceit, understanding people's motives, manipulating people—these are what intellect is used for. So what matters is _____.
>
> *calculus : 미적분

① not how clever and crafty you are but how much more clever and craftier you are than other people
② that individuals act according to their collective interest rather than their own personal interest
③ to design a society where members cooperate to find optimal solutions to benefit themselves
④ coming up with the best solution to practical problems in a given condition

### 연습해설

**EX 2**

A gazelle on the African savanna is trying not to be eaten by cheetahs, but it is also trying to outrun other gazelles when a cheetah attacks. What matters to the gazelle is being faster than other gazelles, not being faster than cheetahs. In the same way, psychologists sometimes wonder why people are endowed with the ability to learn the part of Hamlet or understand calculus when neither skill was of much use to mankind in the primitive conditions where his intellect was shaped. Einstein also would probably have been as hopeless as anybody in working out how to catch a woolly rhinoceros. Nicholas Humphrey, a Cambridge psychologist, was the first to see clearly the solution to this puzzle. We use our intellects not to solve practical problems but to outwit each other. Deceiving people, detecting deceit, understanding people's motives, manipulating people—these are what intellect is used for. So what matters is _____.

*calculus : 미적분

**해설** 주어진 지문은 가젤이 치타보다 빠를 수는 없지만 다른 가젤보다 빨라야 살아남듯 인간이 지능을 발달시킨 이유가 실질적인 생존 문제를 해결하기 위해서가 아니라 다른 사람들보다 앞서기 위해서라는 내용의 글이므로 빈칸에 들어갈 말로 가장 적절한 것은 ① '당신이 얼마나 영리하고 교활한가가 아니라 다른 사람들보다 얼마나 더 영리하고 교활한가'이다.

**해석** 아프리카 사바나의 가젤은 치타에게 잡아먹히지 않으려 노력하지만, 치타가 공격할 때 다른 가젤들보다 더 빨리 달리려 노력하기도 한다. 가젤에게 중요한 것은 치타보다 빠른 것이 아니라 다른 가젤들보다 빠른 것이다. 마찬가지로, 심리학자들은 때때로 사람들이 Hamlet의 대사를 외우거나 미적분을 이해하는 능력을, 둘 중 어느 기술도 지능이 형성되던 원시적 환경에서 인류에게 별로 쓸모없었는데도 타고난 이유를 궁금해 한다. Einstein 또한 아마 털 코뿔소를 잡는 방법을 알아내는 데는 여느 사람 못지않게 형편없었을 것이다. Cambridge의 심리학자 Nicholas Humphrey는 이 수수께끼의 해답을 처음으로 명확하게 알아냈다. 우리는 우리의 지능을 현실적인 문제를 해결하기 위해서가 아니라 서로보다 한 수 앞서기 위해 사용한다. 사람들을 속이고, 속임수를 간파하고, 사람들의 동기를 이해하고, 사람들을 조종하는 것이 바로 지능이 사용되는 목적이다. 그러므로 중요한 것은 <u>당신이 얼마나 영리하고 교활한가가 아니라 다른 사람들보다 얼마나 더 영리하고 교활한가</u>이다.

① 당신이 얼마나 영리하고 교활한 가가 아니라 다른 사람들보다 얼마나 더 영리하고 교활한가
② 개인이 자신만의 개인적 이익보다는 집단의 이익에 따라 행동하는 것
③ 구성원들이 협력하여 자신에게 이익이 되는 최적의 해결책을 찾는 사회를 설계하는 것
④ 주어진 조건 내에서 현실적인 문제에 대한 최선의 해결책을 생각해 내는 것

**정답**
02 ①

**어휘** gazelle 가젤  savanna 사바나  outrun ~보다 빨리 달리다  matter 중요하다  psychologist 심리학자  wonder 궁금해하다  endow 부여하다  part (극 중의) 역할  calculus 미적분  neither 어느 것도 ~아니다  mankind 인류  primitive 원시의  intellect 지능  shape 형성하다  hopeless 희망 없는, 서툰, 가망이 없는  work out 해결하다  woolly 털이 많은  rhinoceros 코뿔소  practical 실용적인  outwit 이기다, 한 수 위를 가다, 계략으로 앞서다  deceive 속이다  deceit 속임수  motive 동기  manipulate 조종하다  crafty 교활한  collective 공동의  interest 이익  rather than ~보다는  cooperate 협력하다  optimal 최적의  come up with ~을 떠올리다  given 주어진

김세현 영어 전혀 다른 개념 독해

PART

# 02

# 주제, 제목, 요지

# PART 02 주제, 제목, 요지

English Reading

### 출제 유형

1. 다음 글의 주제는?
2. 다음 글의 제목은?
3. 다음 글의 요지는?
4. 다음 글에서 필자가 주장하는 바는?

### 풀이 해법

[주제, 제목, 요지 공통]

1. 선택지(보기)부터 먼저 읽는다.

2. 올바른 독해법에 맞추어 글을 읽고 정답을 유도한다.

3. 너무 광범위하지 않은 또는 너무 세부적이지 않은 정답을 유도한다.
   (Not too general or Not too specific)

4. 정답을 선택할 때 선택지의 재진술(Restatement)에 유의한다.

## 연습문제

**EX 1** 다음 글의 주제로 가장 적절한 것을 고르시오.

The population growth of Mexico City is issuing pretty quickly. In 1970, the city had about 9 million people. Now it has over 17 million. All these people are causing problems for the city. There are not enough jobs. Also, there is not enough housing. Large families have to live together in small homes. Many homes do not have water. They also do not have bathrooms or electricity. The Mexican government is worried about all these problems. It is working hard to make life better in the city. But, it's not easy.

① problems of Mexico
② consensus in Mexico
③ plights of Mexico City
④ large families in Mexico City

## 연습해설

### EX 1

▢ : 집중해야 할 정보

The population growth of Mexico City is issuing pretty quickly. In 1970, the city had about 9 million people. Now it has over 17 million. All these people are causing problems for the city. There are not enough jobs. Also, there is not enough housing. Large families have to live together in small homes. Many homes do not have water. They also do not have bathrooms or electricity. The Mexican government is worried about all these problems. It is working hard to make life better in the city. But, it's not easy.

**해석** 멕시코시티의 인구 성장은 매우 빠르게 진행되고 있다. 1970년 도시에는 약 900만 명의 사람들이 있었다. 지금은 1,700만 명이 넘는다. 이 모든 사람들이 그 도시의 문제들을 야기시킨다. 일자리가 충분하지 않다. 또한 집도 충분하지 않다. 대가족이 작은 집에서 함께 살아야 한다. 많은 집에 물이 나오지 않는다. 그들은 또한 욕실이나 전기도 없다. 멕시코 정부는 이런 모든 문제들에 대해 걱정이 된다. 정부는 도시에서의 삶을 더 낫게 만들기 위해 열심히 일하고 있다. 하지만 쉽지 않다.
① 멕시코의 문제점
② 멕시코에서의 합의
③ 멕시코시티의 골칫거리
④ 멕시코시티의 대가족

**어휘** population 인구  issue ① 발표하다 ② 쟁점 ③ 문제 ④ (잡지의) 호  cause 야기하다, 초래하다
electricity 전기  consensus 합의, 일치  plight 어려움, 골칫거리

**해설** 주어진 지문은 멕시코시티의 인구 증가로 인한 문제점을 설명하는 글이므로 ③이 정답이 된다. 참고로 멕시코 전체의 문제가 아니라 멕시코시티만의 문제를 말하고 있으므로 ①은 정답이 될 수 없다.

**정답**
01 ③

## 연습문제

**EX 2** 다음 글의 주제로 가장 적절한 것을 고르시오.

During the population explosion of the 20th century, the demand for water rose dramatically. Construction of numerous engineering projects designed to control floods and protect water supplies brought great benefits to many people. Vast cities incapable of surviving on their local resources have bloomed in the desert with water brought from hundreds of miles away. Food production has kept pace with soaring populations mainly because of the expansion of artificial irrigation systems that make possible the growth of 40 percent of the world's food.

① a population explosion of the world
② the development of water resources
③ the problem in securing water resources
④ agriculture growth with population explosion

## 연습해설

### EX 2

> During the population explosion of the 20th century, the demand for water rose dramatically. Construction of numerous engineering projects designed to control floods and protect water supplies brought great benefits to many people. Vast cities incapable of surviving on their local resources have bloomed in the desert with water brought from hundreds of miles away. Food production has kept pace with soaring populations mainly because of the expansion of artificial irrigation systems that make possible the growth of 40 percent of the world's food.

 : 집중해야 할 정보

- 해석 ] 20세기 인구 폭발(갑작스러운 인구 증가) 동안에 물에 대한 수요가 급격하게 늘어났다. 홍수를 조절하고 물의 공급을 보호(원활히)하기 위해서 고안된 무수히 많은 공학 프로젝트의 건설이 많은 사람들에게 이점을 가져다주었다. 그 지역 내 자원으로는 생존이 불가능했던 거대한 도시들이 수백 마일 떨어진 곳에서 물을 끌어올 수 있게 되어서 사막에서도 꽃피울 수 있게(성장할 수 있게) 되었다. 세계 음식 생산의 40% 성장을 가능하게 해 준 인공 관개 시설 덕분에 농업 생산성은 대체로 치솟는 인구와 보조를 맞출 수 있게 되었다.
  ① 세상의 인구 폭발
  ② 수자원 개발
  ③ 수자원 확보의 문제점
  ④ 인구폭발로 인한 농업성장

- 어휘 ] explosion 폭발  demand 요구  dramatically 극적으로, 급격하게  construction 건설
  numerous (상당히) 많은  control 통제하다  flood ① 홍수 ② 흘러넘치다
  supply ① 공급 ② 공급하다 ③ 보급품  vast 거대한  bloom ① 꽃 피우다 ② 꽃  desert 사막
  keep pace with ~와 보조를 맞추다  soar 치솟다  expansion 팽창  artificial 인공의
  irrigation 관개  secure 확보하다  agriculture 농업

- 해설 ] 주어진 지문은 물을 통제하고 특히 사막지역에서도 물을 공급할 수 있는 기술개발에 관한 내용의 글이므로 이 글의 주제로 가장 적절한 것은 ② '수자원 개발'이다.

정답
02 ②

## 실전문제

**01** 다음 글의 주제로 가장 적절한 것을 고르시오.

> There is a strong view that holds that success is a myth, and ambition therefore a sham. Does this mean that success does not really exist? That achievement is at bottom empty? That the efforts of men and women are of no significance alongside the force of movements and events? Now not all success, obviously, is worth esteeming, nor all ambition worth cultivating. Which are and which are not is something one soon enough learns on one's own. But even the most cynical secretly admit that success exists; that achievement counts for a great deal; and that the true myth is that the actions of men and women are useless. To believe otherwise is to take on a point of view that is likely to be deranging. It is, in its implications, to remove all motive for competence, interest in attainment, and regard for posterity.

① causes of a myth and a sham on ambition
② importance of cultivating virtues on one's own
③ maintaining virtues of ambition and success
④ comparison of true myth and true success

## 실전 해설

**01**

　　　　　　　　　　　　　　　　　　　　：집중해야 할 정보

There is a strong view that holds that success is a myth, and ambition therefore a sham. Does this mean that success does not really exist? That achievement is at bottom empty? That the efforts of men and women are of no significance alongside the force of movements and events? Now not all success, obviously, is worth esteeming, nor all ambition worth cultivating. Which are and which are not is something one soon enough learns on one's own. But even the most cynical secretly admit that success exists; that achievement counts for a great deal; and that the true myth is that the actions of men and women are useless. To believe otherwise is to take on a point of view that is likely to be deranging. It is, in its implications, to remove all motive for competence, interest in attainment, and regard for posterity.

**해석** 성공은 근거 없는 믿음이고 야망도 허위라고 주장(hold)하는 강력한 견해가 있다. 이는 성공이 진정 존재하지 않는다는 것을 의미하는가? 인간이 이룬 업적은 실제로 하찮은 것이란 의미인가? 모든 움직임과 사건과 함께 (전개되는) 인간 남녀의 노력 역시 아무 의미가 없다는 말인가? 분명 모든 성공을 다 높게 평가할 수는 없으며, 모든 야망을 다 이룰 수 있다고도 할 수 없다. 어느 것이 그런지 그렇지 않은지는 우리가 이내 곧 스스로 배우게 될 것이다. 하지만 가장 냉소적인 사람조차 성공이 존재한다는 것과 성취 또한 중요하다는 것을 은밀하게 인정한다. 또한 인간의 행위가 아무런 쓸모가 없다라고 주장하는 것이야 말로 진정한 근거 없는 믿음임을 인정한다. 그렇지 않음을 믿는 것은 사람을 혼란에 빠트릴 수 있는 관점을 취하게 한다. 그러한 관점에서 보면, 이는 할 수 있다는 능력에 대한 모든 동기를, 무엇을 달성하기에 대한 모든 관심을, 그리고 후대에 대한 모든 배려를 없애버리는 것과 같은 의미가 된다.

① 야망에 대한 허구와 거짓의 원인
② 자기 자신만의 덕목을 배양하는 중요성
③ 야망과 성공의 덕목을 유지하기
④ 진정한 허구와 진정한 성공의 비교

**어휘** view 견해, 관점　myth ① 신화 ② 근거 없는 믿음, 허구　ambition 야망, 야심
sham 가짜, 엉터리, 허위　exist 존재하다　at bottom 실제로
of no significance 중요치 않은, 하찮은 *significance 중요(함)
alongside ① ~ 옆에, 나란히 ② ~와 함께　esteem 존경하다, 존중하다 *self-esteem 자존감
cultivate 배양하다, 경작하다; 재배하다, 기르다　cynical 냉소적인
secretly 비밀스럽게, 은밀하게　admit 인정[시인]하다　count ① 세다 ② 중요하다
a great deal 많이　useless 쓸모없는　otherwise (만약) 그렇지 않으면[않았다면]
take on 떠맡다; 취하다　deranging 미치게 하는, 어지럽히는　perspective ① 관점, 시각 ② 원근법
remove 없애다, 제거하다　motive 동기 *motivation 동기 부여
competence 능력 *competent 능력 있는　attainment ① 달성, 성취 ② 학식
regard ① 간주하다, 여기다 ② 관심, 배려　posterity 후대, 후세　virtue 덕, 덕목

**해설** 주어진 지문은 성공의 덕목은 존재하는 것이고 이를 부인하는 것이 허구라는 내용의 글이므로 이 글의 주제로 가장 적절한 것은 ③ '야망과 성공의 덕목을 유지하기'이다.

**정답**
01 ③

## 실전문제

**02** 다음 글의 제목으로 가장 적절한 것을 고르시오.

Certainly no creature in the sea is odder than the sea cucumber. All living creatures, including human beings, have their characters, but everything about the sea cucumber seems very unusual. The most peculiar thing about the sea cucumber is the way it defends itself. Its major enemies are fish and crabs, and when threatened, it sends out all of its internal organs into the water. It also casts off attached structures such as tentacles. If attacked or even touched, the sea cucumber may let out its inside organs and later regenerate those parts lost in the process. Sea cucumber is thought to be the only creature knowing giving itself up is surviving.

\* tentacle : 촉수

① The Adaptability of the Sea Cucumber
② The Characters Found in Sea Cucumber
③ How Sea Cucumber Defend Its Enemies
④ Releasing Sea Cucumber's Parts for Defense

## 실전 해설

**02**

: 집중해야 할 정보

Certainly no creature in the sea is odder than the sea cucumber. All living creatures, including human beings, have their characters, but everything about the sea cucumber seems very unusual. The most peculiar thing about the sea cucumber is the way it defends itself. Its major enemies are fish and crabs, and when threatened, it sends out all of its internal organs into the water. It also casts off attached structures such as tentacles. If attacked or even touched, the sea cucumber may let out its inside organs and later regenerate those parts lost in the process. Sea cucumber is thought to be the only creature knowing giving itself up is surviving.

\* tentacle : 촉수

**해석** 분명히 해삼보다 더 이상한 바다 생물은 없을 것이다. 인간을 포함한 모든 살아있는 생물들은 독특한 특성을 지니고 있으나, 해삼은 모든 면에서 아주 이상한 것 같다. 해삼에 관한 가장 독특한 점은 해삼이 자신을 방어하는 방법이다. 해삼의 주요 천적은 물고기와 게인데 해삼은 위협을 받게 되면, 자신의 모든 내장을 물에 내놓는다. 해삼은 또한 촉수와 같은 몸에 붙어 있는 조직들을 포기해 버린다. 해삼은 공격을 당하거나 만지기만 해도 자신의 내장을 내보내며 나중에 그러한 과정에서 손상된 부분들을 재생한다. 해삼이야 말로 자신을 버려서 살아남을 수 있다는 것을 생각하게 해 준다.
① 공격이 항상 최상의 방어이다.
② 해삼에서 발견되는 특성
③ 어떻게 해삼이 자신의 적을 방어하는가
④ 방어를 위하여 해삼의 장기를 내보내기

**어휘** certainly 분명히, 확실히  creature 생물  odd 이상한, 낯선
sea cucumber 해삼 \*cucumber 오이  human being 인간  character ① 특성 ② 등장인물
seem ~인 것 같다  defend 방어하다  peculiar 독특한  major 주된, 주요한  threaten 위협하다
send out (밖으로) 내보내다  internal 내부의  organ 장기, 기관  cast ① 던지다 ② (의료) 깁스
attach 붙이다  structure 구조  such as (가령, 예를 들어서) ~와 같은, ~처럼  attack 공격하다
let out (밖으로) 내보내다  regenerate 재생시키다, 다시 만들다  process 과정  only 유일한
give up 포기하다  adaptability 적응(성)  enemy 적  release 내보내다, 방출하다

**해설** 주어진 지문은 해삼이 공격을 당하면 자신의 장기를 밖으로 내보내 스스로 살아남는 생존 본능에 관한 내용의 글이므로 이 글의 제목으로 가장 적절한 것은 ④ '방어를 위하여 해삼의 장기를 내보내기'이다. 참고로 ②와 ③은 너무 개괄적인(too general)선택지이다.

정답
02 ④

## 실전문제

**03** 다음 글의 제목으로 가장 적절한 것을 고르시오.

A few years ago we purchased a brand-new camper van. Not long after we bought our camper, a friend of ours asked if her family could borrow it for house guests. We were not too interested in loaning out our spotless camper, so we declined. This happened in the fall, and we stored the camper in our backyard all that winter. In the spring my husband and I were setting it up to prepare for a trip to visit some relatives. Imagine our surprise to find that we had left cookie boxes in the camper over the winter! We'd moved and had a baby that previous summer and fall, and cleaning out the camper had been overlooked. That in itself wouldn't have been so bad had it not been for the mice. Mice were attracted by the food and they destroyed all the curtains, screens, and cushions. Had we let the friend borrow the camper, she would have discovered the boxes before the mice did.

① It Pays Off to Share
② Sharing: Pros and Cons?
③ Shared Loss Leads to Friendship
④ Virtue of Sharing: Not Always Good

## 실전 해설

**03**

: 집중해야 할 정보

A few years ago we purchased a brand-new camper van. Not long after we bought our camper, a friend of ours asked if her family could borrow it for house guests. We were not too interested in loaning out our spotless camper, so we declined. This happened in the fall, and we stored the camper in our backyard all that winter. In the spring my husband and I were setting it up to prepare for a trip to visit some relatives. Imagine our surprise to find that we had left cookie boxes in the camper over the winter! We'd moved and had a baby that previous summer and fall, and cleaning out the camper had been overlooked. That in itself wouldn't have been so bad had it not been for the mice. Mice were attracted by the food and they destroyed all the curtains, screens, and cushions. Had we let the friend borrow the camper, she would have discovered the boxes before the mice did.

**해석** 몇 년 전 우리는 최신형 캠핑카를 구입했다. 우리가 캠핑카를 구입한 지 얼마 지나지 않아 친구가 손님들을 위해 자기 가족이 그것을 빌릴 수 있는지 물어보았다. 우리는 한 점의 얼룩도 없는 캠핑카를 별로 빌려주고 싶지 않았기 때문에 거절했다. 이것은 가을에 일어난 일이고, 우리는 그 캠핑카를 겨울 내내 뒷마당에 두었다. 봄에 남편과 나는 친척을 방문할 여행 준비를 위해 그것을 정리하고 있었다. 겨우내 그 캠핑카에 과자 상자를 놔두었다는 것을 발견하고서 우리가 놀란 것을 상상해 보라! 우리는 그 전 해의 여름과 가을에 이사를 하고 아기를 낳아서 캠핑카를 깨끗이 청소하는 것을 간과했던 것이다. 쥐만 없더라면, 그것은 그 자체로 그렇게 나쁘지 않았을 것이다. 음식 때문에 쥐가 꾀었고, 쥐는 모든 커튼, 스크린 및 쿠션을 조각조각으로 찢어 놓았다. 친구가 캠핑카를 빌리도록 했다면 그녀는 쥐보다 먼저 그 상자들을 발견했을 것이다.

① 공유하는 것이 이익이다
② 공유: 찬성하나 반대하나?
③ 공유된 손실이 우정을 이끈다
④ 공유의 덕목: 항상 좋은 것은 아니다

**어휘** camper van 캠핑카  not too 별로 ~하지 않는
be interested in -ing ~하는 데 흥미를 가지다  loan out 빌려주다  spotless 얼룩 없는
decline 거절하다  relative 친척  overlook 빠뜨리다, 간과하다
shred (쥐 등이) 쏠아서 조각조각으로 찢다  pay off 성공하다; 이익이 되다
pros and cons 찬반  virtue 덕, 덕목

**해설** 주어진 지문은 자기 것만 챙기는 것보다는 공유하는 것이 더 이익이라는 내용의 글이므로 이 글의 제목으로 가장 적절한 것은 ① '공유하는 것이 이익이다'이다.

**정답**
03 ①

## 실전문제

**04** 다음 글의 주제로 가장 적절한 것을 고르시오.

In monkey colonies, where strict dominance hierarchies exist, beneficial innovations do not spread quickly through the group unless they are taught first to a dominant animal. When a lower animal is taught the new concept first, the rest of the colony remains mostly unaware of its value. One study on the introduction of new food tastes to Japanese monkeys furnishes a nice illustration. In one troop, a taste for caramels was developed by introducing this new food into the diet of young minors, low on the status ladder. The taste for caramels inched slowly up the ranks: A year and a half later, only 51 percent of the colony had acquired it, and still none of the leaders. Contrast this with what happened in a second troop where wheat was introduced first to the leader: Wheat eating — to this point unknown to these monkeys — spread through the whole colony within four hours.

① monkeys' learning ability through imitation
② strict dominance hierarchies in monkey colonies
③ the difference between higher and lower monkeys in learning
④ monkeys' honor to authority in adapting themselves to new things

## 실전 해설

**04**

: 집중해야 할 정보

In monkey colonies, where strict dominance hierarchies exist, beneficial innovations do not spread quickly through the group unless they are taught first to a dominant animal. When a lower animal is taught the new concept first, the rest of the colony remains mostly unaware of its value. One study on the introduction of new food tastes to Japanese monkeys furnishes a nice illustration. In one troop, a taste for caramels was developed by introducing this new food into the diet of young minors, low on the status ladder. The taste for caramels inched slowly up the ranks: A year and a half later, only 51 percent of the colony had acquired it, and still none of the leaders. Contrast this with what happened in a second troop where wheat was introduced first to the leader: Wheat eating — to this point unknown to these monkeys — spread through the whole colony within four hours.

**해석** 원숭이 군집에서는 엄격한 지배 서열이 존재하는데, 유익하고 획기적인 것들이 우월한 지위의 원숭이에게 먼저 가르쳐지지 않으면 무리 전체로 빠르게 퍼져나가지 않는다. 서열이 낮은 원숭이가 새로운 개념을 먼저 배우게 되면, 군집에 있는 나머지는 대개 그것의 가치에 대해 여전히 모르는 상태로 남게 된다. 일본 원숭이에게 새로운 음식 맛을 처음 접하게 한 것에 대한 연구는 좋은 실례를 제공한다. 한 무리에서, 캐러멜 맛보기는 이 새로운 음식을 지위 계층상 낮은, 어린 원숭이들의 식단에 처음 선보임으로써 전개되었다. 캐러멜 맛보기는 조금씩 서서히 계층 위쪽으로 움직여 나갔다. 일 년 반이 지난 후에, 그 군집의 단지 51%만이 캐러멜 맛을 알게 되었고, 여전히 우두머리 원숭이들은 어느 누구도 캐러멜의 맛을 알지 못했다. 이것을 밀이 우두머리에게 먼저 소개되었던 두 번째 무리에서 있었던 일과 대조해 보라. 밀 섭취는 이때까지는 이 원숭이들에게 알려지지 않았으나, 네 시간 만에 무리 전체로 퍼져 나갔다.

① 모방을 통한 원숭이들의 학습 능력
② 원숭이 군집의 엄격한 지배 서열
③ 학습에 있어서 높고 낮은 원숭이 서열의 차이점
④ 새로운 것에 적응하는 데 있어서 원숭이들의 권위에 대한 존중

**어휘** colony ① 군집, 무리 ② 식민지, 거주지   strict 엄격한   dominance 지배, 우월성
hierarchy 서열, 계급   exist 존재하다   beneficial 유익한, 이로운
innovation 획기적인 것, 혁신, 쇄신   unless 만약 ~하지 않으면   dominant 지배적인, 우월한
lower ① 더 낮은 ② 아래쪽의   unaware 모르는, 알지 못하는   furnish 주다, 제공하다
illustration ① 삽화, 도해 ② 실례, 예   troop ① 군대, 병력 ② 무리
develop ① 발전하다 ② 전개시키다   diet 음식, 식단   status 지위, 신분
ladder 사다리 *status ladder 지위 계층   inch 조금씩 (서서히) 움직이다   acquire 얻다, 획득하다
contrast A with B A와 B를 대조하다, 대비시키다   wheat 밀   whole 전체의
capacity 수용력, 능력   imitation 모방   honor 명예, 존중   authority 권위
adapt A to B A를 B에 적응시키다

**해설** 주어진 지문은 엄격한 지배 서열이 존재하는 원숭이 군집에서는 새로운 것이 우월한 지위의 원숭이에게 먼저 가르쳐야 무리 전체로 빠르게 퍼져나간다는 내용의 글이므로 이글의 주제로 가장 적절한 것은 ④ '새로운 것에 적응하는 데 있어서 원숭이들의 권위에 대한 존중'이다.

**정답**
04 ④

## 실전문제

**05** 다음 글의 제목으로 가장 적절한 것을 고르시오.

> Over the past 50 years, researchers who study human judgment have realized that we depend on emotions to make decisions about risk. As we can't possibly mull over every new piece of data our brains collect, our emotions give us shortcuts, helping us make split-second judgments about that information. The more uncertainty, the more shortcuts we use. This is a good thing. People who have suffered brain damage from an operation that removes emotions cannot function. They can't make decisions, even simple ones. So we need our emotions to make sense of the world. But our emotions can lead us astray, particularly when we encounter an exception to a lifetime's worth of rules. The brain's shortcuts accompany certain predictable biases. Researchers assume people reliably overestimate the chances of something happening if they can vividly imagine it. If we see something new, we are supposed to try to fit it into a box that we understand. That's the very reason.
>
> \* mull over : 심사숙고하다

① Reason over Emotion in Decision-Making
② Importance of Emotion When We Make Decisions
③ How Many Risks There Are in the Information Age
④ Intuition: Way of Leading us to Lifetime's Worth of Rules

## 실전 해설

**05**

: 집중해야 할 정보

Over the past 50 years, researchers who study human judgment have realized that we depend on emotions to make decisions about risk. As we can't possibly mull over every new piece of data our brains collect, our emotions give us shortcuts, helping us make split-second judgments about that information. The more uncertainty, the more shortcuts we use. This is a good thing. People who have suffered brain damage from an operation that removes emotions cannot function. They can't make decisions, even simple ones. So we need our emotions to make sense of the world. But our emotions can lead us astray, particularly when we encounter an exception to a lifetime's worth of rules. The brain's shortcuts accompany certain predictable biases. Researchers assume people reliably overestimate the chances of something happening if they can vividly imagine it. If we see something new, we are supposed to try to fit it into a box that we understand. That's the very reason.

\* mull over : 심사숙고하다

**해석** 지난 50년 동안 인간의 판단을 연구하는 연구자들은 우리가 위험에 관한 결정을 하는 데 감정에 의존한다는 것을 알게 되었다. 우리는 도저히 두뇌가 모으는 모든 새로운 자료를 심사숙고할 수 없기 때문에 우리의 감정이 우리에게 지름길을 제공하면서 그 정보에 관한 순간적인 판단을 내리도록 도와준다. 불확실성이 더 많을수록 우리는 더 많은 지름길을 사용한다. 이것은 좋은 일이다. 감정을 제거하는 수술로 뇌 손상을 입는 사람들은 제대로 기능할 수 없다. 그들은 단순한 것조차도 결정을 내리지 못한다. 따라서 우리가 세상을 이해하기 위해서는 감정을 필요로 한다. 하지만 우리가 평생의 가치 있는 규칙의 예외에 해당하는 일을 만날 때에 특히 감정은 우리의 길을 잃게 할 수도 있다. 두뇌의 지름길은 확실한 예측 가능한 편견을 수반한다. 연구자들은 사람들이 일어날 어떤 것을 생생하게 상상할 수 있다면 그들은 그 가능성을 확실히 과대평가한다고 추정한다. 하지만, 우리가 새로운 어떤 것을 보게 된다면 우리는 그것을 우리가 이해하고 있는 박스 안으로 맞추려고 노력해야 한다. 그것이 바로 이성이다.

① 의사 결정 시 감정보다는 이성
② 의사 결정 시 감정의 중요성
③ 정보화 시대에 얼마나 많은 위험이 있는가
④ 직관: 우리를 인생의 규칙에 관한 가치로 이끄는 방식

**어휘** over ~동안에  judgment 판단  realize 깨닫다, 알아차리다
depend on ① ~에 의존하다 ② ~에 달려있다  make decision 결정하다  possibly 도저히
mull over ~에 대해 숙고하다, 곰곰이 생각하다  shortcut 지름길, 손쉬운 방법
split-second 순간적인  uncertainty 불확실성  brain damage 뇌손상  remove 제거하다
function 기능하다  make sense of ~을 이해하다  lead 이끌다, ~하게 하다
astray 길을 잃은, 길에서 벗어난  particular 특히  encounter (우연히) 마주치다, 만나다
exception 예외  accompany ① 수반[동반]하다 ② 동행하다  certain ① 확실한, 분명한 ② 어떤
predictable 예측 가능한, 예측할 수 있는  bias 편견  assume 추정하다, 생각하다
reliably 확실히, 분명히  overestimate 과대평가하다  chance 기회, 가능성  vividly 생생하게
fit 맞추다, 끼워 넣다  reason 이성  decision-making 의사결정  intuition 직관

**해설** 주어진 지문은 도입부에서는 의사 결정 시 감정에 의존한다는 내용이고 본문 중반부부터는 감정에 의존하는 것이 적절하지 않다고 했으므로 이 글의 제목으로 가장 적절한 것은 ① '의사 결정 시 감정보다는 이성'이다.

**정답**
05 ①

## 실전문제

**06** 다음 글의 제목으로 가장 적절한 것은?

> Milton was a poet of great promise in 1640, but spent twenty useless years in the eventful atmosphere of the Puritan revolution. He achieved his great promise when the revolution was dead, and he was in solitary disgrace. Cellini was one of the mysterious, larger-than-life figures of the Italian Renaissance: a celebrated sculptor, goldsmith, author and soldier, but also hooligan and even avenging killer. His exciting life kept him from becoming the great artist he could have been. As a Renaissance Man, Machiavelli was a diplomat, political philosopher, musician, poet and playwright, but foremost, he was a Civil writer of the Florentine Republic. It is reasonable to doubt whether Machiavelli would have written his great books had he been allowed to continue in the diplomatic service of Florence and had he gone on interesting missions.

① Loneliness Bears Great Fruits
② Many Talents Make Life Great
③ Just Release Your Creative Flow
④ Various Life Leads to Masterpiece

# 실전 해설

**06**

> : 집중해야 할 정보

Milton was a poet of great promise in 1640, but spent twenty useless years in the eventful atmosphere of the Puritan revolution. He achieved his great promise when the revolution was dead, and he was in solitary disgrace. Cellini was one of the mysterious, larger-than-life figures of the Italian Renaissance: a celebrated sculptor, goldsmith, author and soldier, but also hooligan and even avenging killer. His exciting life kept him from becoming the great artist he could have been. As a Renaissance Man, Machiavelli was a diplomat, political philosopher, musician, poet and playwright, but foremost, he was a Civil writer of the Florentine Republic. It is reasonable to doubt whether Machiavelli would have written his great books had he been allowed to continue in the diplomatic service of Florence and had he gone on interesting missions.

**해석** Milton은 1640년에는 가장 전도유망한 시인이었지만, 청교도 혁명의 다사다난한 분위기 속에서 20여년을 허송세월로 보냈다. 혁명이 끝나고, 외로운 불명예 속에 살고 있을 때에, 그는 그의 진가를 발휘하였다. Cellini는 이탈리아 르네상스의 신비스러우며 전설적인 인물 중의 하나였는데, 저명한 조각가, 금세공인, 저자이며 군인이기도 했지만, 또한 불량배이며 복수심에 찬 살인자였다. 그의 현란한 삶이 훌륭한 화가로서의 그의 가능성을 막고 말았다. 르네상스 인물로서 Machiavelli는 외교관, 정치철학자, 음악가, 시인, 그리고 극작가이기도 했지만, 무엇보다도 그는 플로렌스의 외교 업무를 수행할 수 있게 되고 재미있는 임무들에 계속 종사했더라면 그가 그의 위대한 저서들을 쓸 수 있었을지는 꽤 회의적이다.

① 고독이 위대한 과실을 맺는다
② 많은 재능이 삶을 위대하게 만든다
③ 단지 당신의 창의적 흐름을 내보내라
④ 다양한 삶이 걸작을 이끈다

**어휘** poet of great promise 장래가 촉망되는 시인  useless 쓸모없는  eventful 다사다난한
atmosphere ① 대기 ② 분위기  revolution 혁명  solitary 고독한  disgrace 불명예
larger-than-life 전설적인  figure 인물  hooligan (운동경기의) 난동꾼
avenging 복수심에 가득 찬  diplomat 외교관  playwright (연극) 작가
reasonable 이치에 맞는, 합리적인, 이성적인  diplomatic 외교의  civil servant 공무원
loneliness 고독, 외로움  bear 낳다  release 내보내다, 석방하다  masterpiece 걸작
invention 발명

**해설** 주어진 지문은 너무 많은 일을 하게 되면 오히려 아무 일도 이룰 수 없다는 내용의 글이므로 이 글의 제목으로 가장 적절한 것은 ① '고독이 위대한 과실을 맺는다'이다.

**정답**
06 ①

## 기출문제

**01** 다음 글의 주제로 가장 적절한 것은? 2025. 국가직 9급

> Young people are fast learners. They are energetic, active and have a 'can-do' mentality. Given the support and right opportunities, they can take the lead in their own development as well as the development of their communities. In many developing countries, agriculture is still the largest employer and young farmers play an important role in ensuring food security for future generations. They face many challenges, however. For example, it is very difficult to own land or get a loan if you do not have a house — which, if you are young and only just starting your career, is often not yet possible. Working in agriculture requires substantial and long-term investments. It is also quite risky and uncertain, because it relies heavily on the climate: flooding, drought and storms can damage and destroy farmers' crops and affect livestock.

① the economic advantages of working in the agricultural sector
② the importance of technology in modern farming practices
③ the roles of young farmers and the challenges they face
④ young people's efforts for urban development

## 기출 분석

**01**

> Young people are fast learners. They are energetic, active and have a 'can-do' mentality. Given the support and right opportunities, they can take the lead in their own development as well as the development of their communities. In many developing countries, agriculture is still the largest employer and young farmers play an important role in ensuring food security for future generations. They face many challenges, however. For example, it is very difficult to own land or get a loan if you do not have a house — which, if you are young and only just starting your career, is often not yet possible. Working in agriculture requires substantial and long-term investments. It is also quite risky and uncertain, because it relies heavily on the climate: flooding, drought and storms can damage and destroy farmers' crops and affect livestock.

**해석** 젊은이들은 배우는 속도가 빠르다. 그들은 에너지가 넘치고 활동적이며, '할 수 있다'는 태도를 가지고 있다. 적절한 지원과 기회만 주어진다면, 그들은 자기 자신뿐만 아니라 지역사회의 발전에서도 주도적인 역할을 할 수 있다. 많은 개발도상국에서 농업은 여전히 가장 큰 고용 분야이며, 젊은 농부들은 미래 세대를 위한 식량 안보를 보장하는 데 중요한 역할을 한다. 하지만 이들은 많은 어려움에 직면해 있다. 예를 들어, 집이 없다면 토지를 소유하거나 대출을 받는 것이 매우 어렵다. 그런데 젊고 이제 막 경력을 시작한 경우에는 집을 마련하는 것이 아직 불가능한 경우가 많다. 농업 분야에서 일하는 것은 상당한 장기 투자를 필요로 한다. 또한 기후에 크게 의존하기 때문에 위험성과 불확실성이 크다. 홍수, 가뭄, 폭풍 등은 농작물을 해치거나 파괴할 수 있고, 가축에도 영향을 줄 수 있다.

① 농업 분야에서 일하는 경제적 이점
② 현대농업을 실천하는 데 있어서 기술의 중요성
③ 젊은 농부들의 역할과 그들이 직면한 어려움
④ 도시 개발을 위한 젊은이들의 노력

**어휘** can-do 할 수 있다는, 적극적인 mentality 정신, 태도 take the lead 이끌다, 선두에 서다 developing country 개발도상국 agriculture 농업 role 역할 ensure 보장하다, 확실하게 하다 food security 식량 안보 generation 세대 face 직면하다 own 소유하다 loan 대출 require 요구하다 substantial 상당한, 꽤 많은 long-term 장기적인 investment 투자 quite 아주, 매우, 꽤 risky 위험한 uncertain 불확실한 rely on ~에 의존하다, 의지하다 drought 가뭄 crop 작물 livestock 가축 sector 분야, 부문 practice 관행, 실행, 실천 urban 도시의

**해설** 단락의 도입부에서 젊은 농부들의 중요한 역할을 설명하다가 중반부에 However를 기준으로 그들이 직면한 어려움을 언급하고 있으므로 주어진 글의 주제로 가장 적절한 것은 ③ '젊은 농부들의 역할과 그들이 직면한 어려움'이다.

**정답**
01 ③

## 기출문제

**02** 다음 글의 주제로 가장 적절한 것은? 2025. 국가직 9급

> The reason artificial blue light in devices can be so harmful in the evening is that it mimics the sun's natural blue light—which confuses the body's circadian clock. A study showed that viewing artificial blue light in the evening will push sleep-inducing melatonin hormones down drastically, disrupting bedtimes and affecting daytime behavior. But getting that same blue light from the sun, which contains a health-boosting full spectrum of light, does the opposite. According to the study, the more daytime blue light a person gets, the better defense they have against the harms of evening blue light from screens. Thus, packing the day with sunshine creates a blue-light build-up that helps counteract the consequences of that artificial light at night. In other words, the more sunlight exposure a child gets during the day, the better their brain can build a wall against the harms of artificial blue light later.

① Sunlight's help in fighting artificial blue light effects
② The dangers of using devices during the day
③ How screens affect children's sleep cycles
④ Why melatonin levels drop in the evening

## 기출 분석

**02**

: 집중해야 할 정보

The reason artificial blue light in devices can be so harmful in the evening is that it mimics the sun's natural blue light—which confuses the body's circadian clock. A study showed that viewing artificial blue light in the evening will push sleep-inducing melatonin hormones down drastically, disrupting bedtimes and affecting daytime behavior. But getting that same blue light from the sun, which contains a health-boosting full spectrum of light, does the opposite. According to the study, the more daytime blue light a person gets, the better defense they have against the harms of evening blue light from screens. Thus, packing the day with sunshine creates a blue-light build-up that helps counteract the consequences of that artificial light at night. In other words, the more sunlight exposure a child gets during the day, the better their brain can build a wall against the harms of artificial blue light later.

**해석** 기기의 인공 청색광이 저녁에 매우 해로울 수 있는 이유는 그것이 태양의 자연 청색광을 흉내 내기 때문인데, 이는 몸의 생체 시계를 혼란스럽게 만든다. 한 연구는 저녁에 인공 청색광을 보는 것이 수면을 유도하는 멜라토닌 호르몬을 급격히 감소시켜 취침 시간을 방해하고 낮 동안의 행동에 영향을 끼칠 것을 보여 주었다. 그러나 건강을 증진하는 전체 스펙트럼의 빛을 포함하는 태양으로부터 동일한 청색광을 받는 것은 반대의 효과를 낸다. 연구에 따르면 사람은 낮 청색광을 더 많이 받을수록 화면에서 나오는 저녁 청색광의 해로움에 대한 방어력이 더 높아진다. 따라서 하루를 햇빛으로 채우는 것은 청색광의 축적을 만들어 내어 밤에 그 인공 청색광이 주는 영향을 상쇄하는 데 도움이 된다. 다시 말해, 아이가 낮동안 햇빛에 더 많이 노출될수록, 아이의 뇌는 나중에 인공 청색광의 해로움을 막는 장벽을 더 잘 구축할 수 있다.

① 인공 청색광의 영향에 대항하는 데 있어 햇빛의 도움
② 낮 동안 기기를 사용하는 것의 위험
③ 화면이 아이들의 수면 주기에 영향을 미치는 방식
④ 저녁에 멜라토닌 수치가 떨어지는 이유

**어휘** artificial 인공의  blue light 블루라이트, 청색광  device 장치, 기기  harm 해를 끼치다  mimic 모방하다  confuse 혼란스럽게 하다  circadian 생체의  clock 시계, 주기  view 보다  push 밀어내다  melatonin 멜라토닌 (수면 호르몬)  hormone 호르몬  drastically 급격히  disrupt 방해하다  affect 영향을 주다  contain 포함하다  boost 향상시키다  spectrum 스펙트럼  opposite 반대  defense 방어  wall 벽  level 수준, 정도, 수치

**해설** 주어진 지문은 화면에서 나오는 인공 청색광이 수면에 부정적인 영향을 미치고, 반면에 낮 동안 햇빛의 자연 청색광은 그 해로움을 줄이는 데 도움이 된다는 내용의 글이므로 이 글의 주제로 가장 적절한 것은 ① '인공 청색광의 영향에 대항하는 데 있어 햇빛의 도움'이다.

**정답**
02 ①

## 기출문제

**03** 다음 글의 주제로 적절한 것은? 2024. 지방직 9급

> In recent years Latin America has made huge strides in exploiting its incredible wind, solar, geothermal and biofuel energy resources. Latin America's electricity sector has already begun to gradually decrease its dependence on oil. Latin America is expected to almost double its electricity output between 2015 and 2040. Practically none of Latin America's new large-scale power plants will be oil-fueled, which opens up the field for different technologies. Countries in Central America and the Caribbean, which traditionally imported oil, were the first to move away from oil-based power plants, after suffering a decade of high and volatile prices at the start of the century.

① booming oil industry in Latin America
② declining electricity business in Latin America
③ advancement of renewable energy in Latin America
④ aggressive exploitation of oil-based resources in Latin America

## 기출 분석

**03**

: 집중해야 할 정보

In recent years Latin America has made huge strides in exploiting its incredible wind, solar, geothermal and biofuel energy resources. Latin America's electricity sector has already begun to gradually decrease its dependence on oil. Latin America is expected to almost double its electricity output between 2015 and 2040. Practically none of Latin America's new large-scale power plants will be oil-fueled, which opens up the field for different technologies. Countries in Central America and the Caribbean, which traditionally imported oil, were the first to move away from oil-based power plants, after suffering a decade of high and volatile prices at the start of the century.

**해석** 최근 몇 년 동안 라틴 아메리카는 믿을 수 없을 정도로 풍력, 태양열, 지열 및 바이오 연료 에너지 자원을 이용하는 데 큰 성과를 이루었다. 라틴 아메리카의 전력 부문은 이미 석유에 대한 의존을 점진적으로 낮추기 시작했다. 라틴 아메리카는 2015년에서 2040년 사이에 전력 생산량을 거의 두 배로 늘릴 것으로 예상된다. 실제로 라틴 아메리카의 새로운 대규모 발전소 중 석유를 연료로 사용하는 발전소는 거의 없을 것이며, 이는 다양한 기술들의 장을 열어줄 것이다. 전통적으로 석유를 수입했던 중앙아메리카와 카리브해 지역의 국가들은 (21)세기 초 10년간의 높고 변덕스러운 (석유)가격을 겪은 후 가장 먼저 석유 기반 발전소로부터 벗어났다.

① 라틴 아메리카의 석유 산업 호황
② 라틴 아메리카의 전력 사업 감소
③ 라틴 아메리카의 재생 에너지 발전
④ 라틴 아메리카의 공격적인 석유 기반 자원 이용

**어휘** huge 거대한  stride ① 발전, 진전, 성과 ② (성큼성큼 걷는) 걸음, 발걸음 ③ 성큼성큼 걷다
exploit ① 이용하다, 활용하다 ② 착취하다  incredible 믿을 수 없는, 놀랄 정도의
geothermal 지열의  biofuel 바이오 연료  sector 부문, 영역  gradually 점차로, 점진적으로
electricity 전기, 전력  dependence 의존  expect 기대하다  almost 거의
double 두 배(가 되다)  output 생산량, 산출량  practically 실제로  large-scale 대규모
power plant 발전소  oil-fueled 기름을 연료로 사용하는  open up the field 장을 열다
traditionally 전통적으로  import 수입하다  move away from ~에서 벗어나다
oil-based 석유 기반의  suffer 겪다, 경험하다  volatile 변덕스러운, 변동이 심한
booming 호황  decline 감소하다  advancement 진보, 발전  aggressive 공격적인
exploitation ① 이용, 활용 ② 착취

**해설** 주어진 지문은 라틴 아메리카가 최근 재생에너지 분야에서 큰 발전을 이루어 전력 생산에 대한 석유 의존도를 줄였다는 내용의 글이므로 이 글의 주제로 가장 적절한 것은 ③ '라틴 아메리카의 재생 에너지 발전'이다.

**정답**
03 ③

## 기출문제

**04** 다음 글의 제목으로 적절한 것은? 2024. 지방직 9급

Every organization has resources that it can use to perform its mission. How well your organization does its job is partly a function of how many of those resources you have, but mostly it is a function of how well you use the resources you have, such as people and money. You as the organization's leader can always make the use of those resources more efficient and effective, provided that you have control of the organization's personnel and agenda, a condition that does not occur automatically. By managing your people and your money carefully, by treating the most important things as the most important, by making good decisions, and by solving the problems that you encounter, you can get the most out of what you have available to you.

① Exchanging Resources in an Organization
② Leaders' Ability to Set up External Control
③ Making the Most of the Resources: A Leader's Way
④ Technical Capacity of an Organization: A Barrier to Its Success

## 기출 분석

**04**

: 집중해야 할 정보

Every organization has resources that it can use to perform its mission. How well your organization does its job is partly a function of how many of those resources you have, but mostly it is a function of how well you use the resources you have, such as people and money. You as the organization's leader can always make the use of those resources more efficient and effective, provided that you have control of the organization's personnel and agenda, a condition that does not occur automatically. By managing your people and your money carefully, by treating the most important things as the most important, by making good decisions, and by solving the problems that you encounter, you can get the most out of what you have available to you.

**해석** 모든 조직에는 임무를 수행하는 데 사용할 수 있는 자원을 가지고 있다. 당신의 조직이 얼마나 일을 잘 수행하는지는 부분적으로는 당신이 그 자원을 얼마나 많이 보유하고 있는지에 달려있지만, 대개는 당신이 갖고 있는 자원 즉, 사람과 돈을 당신이 얼마나 잘 활용하느냐에 달려있다. 만약 당신이 조직의 직원들과 안건에 대한 통제력을 가지고 있다면 조직의 리더로서 당신은 언제든지 그 자원들을 더 효율적이고 효과적으로 사용할 수 있지만 이는 자동으로 발생하는 조건이 아니다. 당신의 사람들과 자금을 신중하게 관리함으로써, 가장 중요한 것을 가장 중요한 것으로 처리함으로써, 좋은 결정을 내림으로써, 그리고 당신이 직면한 문제를 해결함으로써 당신은 당신에게 이용 가능한 것들을 최대한 활용할 수 있다.

① 조직 내 자원 교환하기
② 외부 통제를 설정하는 리더의 능력
③ 자원을 최대한 활용하기: 리더의 길
④ 조직의 기술적 능력: 성공의 장애물

**어휘** organization 조직  resource 자원  perform 수행하다  mission 임무  partly 부분적으로
be a function of ~에 달려있다  mostly 주로, 대개는  make the use of ~을 이용하다
efficient 능률적인, 효율적인  effective 효과적인  provided (that) 만약 ~라면
personnel 직원들  agenda 안건  condition 조건  occur 일어나다, 발생하다  manage 관리하다
treat 다루다, 취급하다  make decision 결정하다  encounter 마주치다, 직면하다
available 이용 가능한  exchange 교환하다  set up 설정하다, 설치하다  external 외부의
make the most of ~을 최대한 활용하다  capacity 능력, 역량  barrier 장벽, 장애물

**해설** 주어진 지문은 좋은 리더는 조직 내에 주어진 자원을 효과적이고 효율적으로 활용할 수 있어야 한다는 내용의 글이므로 이 글의 제목으로 가장 적절한 것은 ③ '자원을 최대한 활용하기: 리더의 길'이다.

**정답**
04 ③

## 기출문제

**05** 다음 글의 주제로 적절한 것은? 2024. 국가직 9급

> It seems incredible that one man could be responsible for opening our eyes to an entire culture, but until British archaeologist Arthur Evans successfully excavated the ruins of the palace of Knossos on the island of Crete, the great Minoan culture of the Mediterranean was more legend than fact. Indeed its most famed resident was a creature of mythology: the half-man, half-bull Minotaur, said to have lived under the palace of mythical King Minos. But as Evans proved, this realm was no myth. In a series of excavations in the early years of the 20th century, Evans found a trove of artifacts from the Minoan age, which reached its height from 1900 to 1450 B.C.: jewelry, carvings, pottery, altars shaped like bull's horns, and wall paintings showing Minoan life.

① King Minos' successful excavations
② Appreciating artifacts from the Minoan age
③ Magnificence of the palace on the island of Crete
④ Bringing the Minoan culture to the realm of reality

## 기출 분석

**05.**

> : 집중해야 할 정보
>
> It seems incredible that one man could be responsible for opening our eyes to an entire culture, but until British archaeologist Arthur Evans successfully excavated the ruins of the palace of Knossos on the island of Crete, the great Minoan culture of the Mediterranean was more legend than fact. Indeed its most famed resident was a creature of mythology: the half-man, half-bull Minotaur, said to have lived under the palace of mythical King Minos. But as Evans proved, this realm was no myth. In a series of excavations in the early years of the 20th century, Evans found a trove of artifacts from the Minoan age, which reached its height from 1900 to 1450 B.C.: jewelry, carvings, pottery, altars shaped like bull's horns, and wall paintings showing Minoan life.

- **해석** 한 사람이 어떤 문화 전체에 대한 우리의 눈을 뜨게 해줄 수 있다는 것은 믿기지 않지만, 영국의 고고학자 Arthur Evans가 크레타섬의 크노소스 궁전의 유적을 성공적으로 발굴하기 전까지 지중해의 위대한 미노스 문화는 사실보다는 전설에 가까웠다. 실제로 그 문명에서 가장 유명한 것은 신화 속에 나오는 Minos 왕의 궁전 아래에 살았다고 전해지는 반인반수의 미노타우로스라는 신화 속 생물이었다. 그러나 Evans가 증명했던 것처럼 이 왕국은 신화가 아니었다. 20세기 초 일련의 발굴을 통해 Evans는 보석, 조각, 도자기, 황소 뿔 모양의 제단, 미노스의 삶을 보여 주는 벽화 등 기원전 1900년부터 1450년까지 절정에 다다른 미노스 시대의 귀중한 인공물들을 발견했다.
  ① Minos 왕의 성공적인 발굴
  ② 미노스시대의 인공물 감상하기
  ③ 크레타섬 궁전의 웅장함
  ④ 미노스 문명을 사실의 영역으로 가져오기

- **어휘** incredible 믿기 어려운, 믿을 수 없는  responsible 책임지는  entire 전체의, 전반적인  archaeologist 고고학자  excavate 발굴하다  ruins 유적, 유물  palace 궁전  island 섬  Mediterranean 지중해  legend 전설  famed 유명한  resident 거주자  creature 생물  mythology 신화  half-man, half-bull 반인반수(半人半獸)  *bull 황소  mythical 신화 속에 나오는  prove 증명하다, 입증하다  excavation 발굴  a trove of 소중한, 귀중한  artifact 인공물  reach ~에 이르다, 다다르다  height ① 높이 ② 키 ③ 정점, 절정  jewelry 보석  carving 조각  pottery 도자기  altar 제단  horn 뿔  wall painting 벽화  appreciate 감상하다  magnificence 장엄함, 웅장함  reality 현실, 사실

- **해설** 주어진 지문은 미노스 시대의 유물을 발굴함으로써 신화로만 여겨졌던 미노스 문화가 사실로 판명되었다는 내용의 글이므로 이 글의 주제로 가장 적절한 것은 ④ '미노스 문명을 사실의 영역으로 가져오기'이다.

05 ④

MEMO

김세현 영어 전혀 다른 개념 독해

PART

03

통일성

# PART 03 통일성

## 출제 유형

다음 글의 흐름상 어색한 문장은?

## 풀이 해법

1. **단락의 도입부에서 무엇에 관한 글인지 살펴본다.**
   정답을 구하려 하지 말고 처음 3~4줄 정도 읽어가면서 Main Idea(중심 소재 ⊕ 작가의 견해)를 떠올린다. 이 과정에서 작가의 견해가 ⊕인지 ⊖인지 살펴본다.

2. **무엇에 관한 글인지가 대충 파악이 됐으면 이제 정답을 찾으러 간다.**
   Main Idea를 염두에 두면서 글의 흐름을 방해하는(논리의 비약) 부분을 찾는다.

3. **문장과 문장 간 논리파악이 필요하다.**
   어색한 문장을 고를 때 새로운 정보가 등장할 수 있다. 이 새로운 정보가 다음 문장과 연결성이 있는지 확인해 본다. 만약 연결성이 없다고 판단되면 그것이 정답이 된다.

4. **패턴과 시그널도 이용할 수 있어야 한다.**

## 연습문제

**EX 1** 다음 글의 흐름상 어색한 문장은?

Movies and cartoons sometimes portray scientists as loners in white lab coats, working in isolated labs. In reality, science is an intensely social activity. Most scientists work in teams, which often include both graduate and undergraduate students. And to succeed in science, it helps to be a good communicator. ① Research results have no impact until shared with a community of peers through seminars, publications, and websites. ② But the communication of scientific knowledge does not automatically lead to a problem solution unless it is translated into effective public policies and citizen action. ③ And, in fact, research papers aren't published until they are vetted by colleagues in what is called the "peer review" process. ④ Most of the examples of scientific inquiry described in science textbooks for college students, for instance, have all been published in peer-reviewed journals.

vet : 심사하다

## 연습해설

### EX 1

Movies and cartoons sometimes portray scientists as loners in white lab coats, working in isolated labs. In reality, science is an intensely social activity. Most scientists work in teams, which often include both graduate and undergraduate students. And to succeed in science, it helps to be a good communicator. ① Research results have no impact until shared with a community of peers through seminars, publications, and websites. ② But the communication of scientific knowledge does not automatically lead to a problem solution unless it is translated into effective public policies and citizen action. ③ And, in fact, research papers aren't published until they are vetted by colleagues in what is called the "peer review" process. ④ Most of the examples of scientific inquiry described in science textbooks for college students, for instance, have all been published in peer-reviewed journals.

vet : 심사하다

**해석** 영화와 만화는 때로 과학자를 흰색 실험실 가운을 입고 외딴 실험실에서 일하는 외톨이로 묘사한다. 실제로 과학은 매우 사회적인 활동이다. 대부분의 과학자는 팀을 이루어 일하는데, 팀은 흔히 대학원생과 학부생을 모두 포함한다. 그리고 과학에서 성공하기 위해서는 의사소통을 잘하는 것이 도움이 된다. 연구 결과는 세미나, 출판물, 웹 사이트를 통해 동료 집단과 공유되고 나서야 비로소 영향을 미친다. (그러나 과학 지식이 효과적인 공공 정책과 시민 행동으로 전환되지 않으면, 그 과학 지식의 전달이 자동적으로 문제 해결로 이어지지는 않는다.) 그리고 사실 연구 논문은 '동료 심사' 과정이라고 불리는 것으로 동료들에 의해 심사를 받고 나서야 비로소 발표된다. 예를 들어 대학생용 과학 교재에 기술된 과학 연구 사례의 대부분은 모두 동료 심사를 받는 학술지에 발표되었다.

**어휘** portray 묘사하다  loner 외톨이  lab coat 실험실 가운  isolated 외딴, 격리된, 고립된
in reality 사실상  intensely 강력하게, 매우, 아주  graduate student 대학원생
undergraduate student 학부생  impact 영향(력)  peer 동료, 또래
publication 출판(물)  *publish 출판하다, 발표하다  translate A into B A를 B로 전환하다[바꾸다]
effective 효과적인  policy 정책  citizen 시민  publish 출판하다  case 사례  inquiry 연구, 조사
describe 묘사하다, 기술하다  journal 학술지, 저널

**해설** 주어진 지문은 과학자들의 연구 활동은 다른 사람과의 의사소통이 수반되는 사회적인 활동이며, '동료 심사'라 불리는 과정을 거쳐 결과가 공유된다는 내용의 글이다. 따라서 과학 지식을 효과적인 공공 정책과 시민 행동으로 전환해야 과학 지식의 전달이 문제 해결로 이어진다는 ②는 글의 전체 흐름과 관계가 없다.

**정답**
01 ②

## 연습문제

**EX 2** 다음 글의 흐름상 어색한 문장은?

The immune system is the body's defense against foreign invaders such as bacteria. The immune system protects and preserves the body's integrity, and it does this by developing antibodies to attack hostile invaders. ① We know that the immune system begins to decline after adolescence, and the weakening of immune function is linked to age-related vulnerability. ② According to the autoimmune theory of aging, the system may eventually become defective and no longer distinguish the body's own tissues from foreign tissues. ③ Human tissue repair after injury and in disease and the development of effective treatments are the focus of all biomedical research. ④ The body may then begin to attack itself, as suggested by the rising incidence of autoimmune diseases with advancing age.

## 연습해설

### EX 2

The immune system is the body's defense against foreign invaders such as bacteria. The immune system protects and preserves the body's integrity, and it does this by developing antibodies to attack hostile invaders. ① We know that the immune system begins to decline after adolescence, and the weakening of immune function is linked to age-related vulnerability. ② According to the autoimmune theory of aging, the system may eventually become defective and no longer distinguish the body's own tissues from foreign tissues over time. ③ Human tissue repair after injury and in disease and the development of effective treatments are the focus of all biomedical research. ④ The body may then begin to attack itself, as suggested by the rising incidence of autoimmune diseases with advancing age.

**해석** 면역 체계는 박테리아와 같은 외래 침입자에 대한 신체의 방어 수단이다. 면역 체계는 신체의 완전한 상태를 보호하고 보존하는데 그것은 적대적인 침입자를 공격할 항체를 생성함으로써 이 일을 한다. 우리는 면역 체계가 청소년기 이후에 쇠퇴하기 시작하며, 면역 기능의 약화는 나이와 관련된 취약성과 연관되어 있음을 알고 있다. 노화의 자가 면역 이론에 따르면, 시간이 흐르면서 면역 체계에 결국 결함이 생겨 더 이상 자기 신체의 세포 조직을 외래 조직과 구분하지 못할 수가 있다. (부상 후나 질병 중 인체 세포 조직의 복구와 효과적인 치료의 개발은 모든 생체 의학 연구의 초점이다.) 그러면 나이가 들면서 증가하는 자가 면역질환 발병률이 보여 주듯이 신체는 자기 스스로를 공격하기 시작할지도 모른다.

**어휘** immune 면역(성)의  defense 방어  foreign 외래의, 이질적인  invader 침입자  preserve 보존하다
integrity 완전한 상태, 온전함  by ~ing ~함으로써  antibody 항체  hostile 적대적인
decline 쇠퇴하다, 감소하다  adolescence 청소년기  weakening 약화  function 기능
be linked to ~에 연관되다, ~와 관련이 있다  age-related 나이와 관련된  vulnerability 취약성
autoimmune 자가 면역의  aging 노화  eventually 결국, 궁극적으로  defective 결함이 있는
no longer 더 이상 ~가 아닌  distinguish A from B A와 B를 구별하다, 식별하다
tissue (세포들로 이루어진) 조직  repair 수리하다, 고치다  injury 부상, 상처  disease 질병, 질환
treatment 치료(법)  biomedical 생체[생물]의학의  incidence 발병률, 발생률

**해설** 주어진 지문은 노화와 함께 면역 체계가 약화되고 결함이 생겨 자기 신체의 조직을 외래 조직과 구분하지 못하고 스스로를 공격할지도 모른다는 자가 면역질환에 대한 글이므로, 세포 조직의 회복과 치료가 생체 의학 연구의 초점이라는 ③은 이 글의 전체 흐름과 관계가 없다.

**정답**
02 ③

## 실전문제

**01** 다음 글의 흐름상 어색한 문장은?

One of the little understood paradoxes in communication is that the more difficult the word, the more concise the explanation. ① <u>The more meaning you can pack into a single word, the fewer words are needed to get the idea across</u>. Complex words are resented by persons who don't understand them and, of course, very often they are used to confuse rather than clarify. ② <u>But this is not the fault of language</u>. That is, it is the arrogance of the individual who misuses the tools of communication. ③ <u>The best reason for acquiring a large vocabulary is that it keeps you from being simple</u>. A genuinely educated person can express himself briefly. ④ <u>For example, if you don't know, or use, the word 'imbricate,' you have to say to someone, 'having the edges overlapping in a regular arrangement like tiles on a roof, scales on a fish, or sepals on a plant.'</u> More than 20 words to say what can be said in one.

## 실전 해설

**01**

> ▶ Main Idea : 단어가 어려울수록 설명이 쉬워진다.
>
> One of the little understood paradoxes in communication is that the more difficult the word, the more concise the explanation. ① The more meaning you can pack into a single word, the fewer words are needed to get the idea across. Complex words are resented by persons who don't understand them and, of course, very often they are used to confuse rather than clarify. ② But this is not the fault of language. That is, it is the arrogance of the individual who misuses the tools of communication. ③ ▶ Main Idea와 정반대 내용
> The best reason for acquiring a large vocabulary is that it keeps you from being simple. A genuinely educated person can express himself briefly. ④ For example, if you don't know, or use, the word 'imbricate,' you have to say to someone, 'having the edges overlapping in a regular arrangement like tiles on a roof, scales on a fish, or sepals on a plant.' More than 20 words to say what can be said in one.

**[해석]** 의사소통에 있어서 거의 잘 이해되지 않는 역설 중의 하나는 단어가 어려우면 어려울수록 설명은 더욱 더 간결해진다는 것이다. 한 단어에 더욱 더 많은 의미를 집어넣을수록 그 생각이 전달되게 하는 데는 더욱더 적은 단어가 필요하게 된다. 어려운 말을 이해하지 못하는 사람들은 그 말에 대해 분개하고, 물론 그 말은 아주 종종 명료하게 하기보다는 혼란스러움을 조장하게 된다. 그러나 이것은 언어의 잘못이 아니다. 그것은 의사소통 도구를 잘못 사용하는 사람의 거만함이다. (풍부한 어휘를 습득하는 가장 좋은 이유는 그것으로 인해 당신이 간결해지는 것을 막게 하는 것이다.) 진정으로 교육을 받은 사람이라면 간결하고 깔끔하게 자신을 표현할 수 있다. 예를 들어, 만약 당신이 'imbricate'라는 단어를 모르거나 사용하지 않는다면, '지붕위의 타일, 물고기의 비늘 혹은 꽃받침처럼 규칙적으로 배열된, 부분적으로 겹친 모서리가 있는'이라고 누군가에게 말해야 한다. 한 단어로 될 수 있는 것을 말하기 위해 스무 개 이상의 단어를 쓰게 된다.

**[어휘]** paradox 역설, 패러독스  concise 간결한  explanation 설명
get A across A를 이해시키다, A를 전달하다  complex 복잡한, 어려운
resent 분개하게 하다, 몹시 화나게 하다  clarify 분명[명료]하게 하다  acquire 얻다, 습득하다
arrogance 오만, 거만함  misuse 잘못 사용하다, 오용하다  genuinely 진실로
educated 교육받은  express 표현하다  briefly 간결하게, 간단하게
imbricate 비늘(기와) 모양으로 겹쳐진  edge 모서리  overlap 중첩되다[부분적으로 겹치다]
arrangement 배열, 배치  scale (물고기) 비늘  sepal 꽃받침

**[해설]** 주어진 지문은 어려운 단어를 사용함으로써 표현이 더 간결해 질 수 있다는 내용의 글이므로 어려운 단어의 습득이 간결함을 피할 수 있다는 내용의 ③은 이 글의 전체 흐름과 무관하다.

01 ③

## 실전문제

**02** 다음 글의 흐름상 어색한 문장은?

In recent decades, territories that had lost their mainstay activities under the impact of transformations in energy, technology and economy have been arranging their cultural resources to explore new paths of development and thereby affirm their determination to survive. ① For example, some American cities that were hollowed out by recessions have been restoring their heritage buildings and setting up cultural districts devoted to audiovisual production. ② Many regional tourist boards of the U.K. are working to promote cultural tourism, which can help to subsidize the expensive process of conserving heritage sites and create revenue for local residents and shops. ③ Many rural areas around the Mediterranean have sought to derive tourism benefits from more careful conservation of their distinctive popular heritage and their landscapes. ④ North African countries bordering the Mediterranean Sea are more attractive tourist destinations, due to their natural landscapes and regional situations. And today, many countries are longing for using cultural tourism to meet their financial needs.

## 실전 해설

**02**

In recent decades, territories that had lost their mainstay activities under the impact of transformations in energy, technology and economy have been arranging their cultural resources to explore new paths of development and thereby affirm their
↳ Main Idea : 지역들이 발전하기 위해 문화적 자원을 개발하고 있다.
determination to survive. ① For example, some American cities that were hollowed out by recessions have been restoring their heritage buildings and setting up cultural districts devoted to audiovisual production. ② Many regional tourist boards of the U.K. are working to promote cultural tourism, which can help to subsidize the expensive process of conserving heritage sites and create revenue for local residents and shops. ③ Many rural areas around the Mediterranean have sought to derive tourism benefits from more careful conservation of their distinctive popular
⌐ Main Idea와 무관한 문장
heritage and their landscapes. ④ North African countries bordering the Mediterranean Sea are more attractive tourist destinations, due to their natural landscapes and regional situations. And today, many countries are longing for using cultural tourism to meet their financial needs.

**해석** 최근 수십 년 동안 에너지, 기술, 그리고 경제 상황의 변화의 영향으로 주요 생업 활동을 상실한 지역들은 새로운 발전의 길을 탐구하고 그로 인해 생존 결의를 확인하기 위해 그들의 문화적 자원을 준비하고 있다. 예를 들어 경기 침체로 텅 비게 된 몇몇 미국의 도시들은 그들의 문화재 건축물을 복원하고 시청각 자료 제작에 전념하는 문화 구역을 설정해 왔다. 영국의 많은 지역 관광청은 문화 관광을 촉진시키기 위해 일하고 있는데, 그것은 유적지를 보존하는 값비싼 과정에 자금을 보조하고 지역 주민들과 상점들의 수입을 창출하는 데 도움이 될 수 있다. 지중해 주변에 있는 많은 시골 지역들은 그들의 독특하고 인기 있는 유산들과 경관들을 보다 세심하게 보존함으로써 관광 산업의 혜택을 끌어 모으기 위해 노력해 왔다. (지중해와 접하고 있는 북아프리카의 국가들은 그 나라들의 자연 경관과 지역적 상황 때문에 관광 중심지로서의 매력이 더 높아지고 있다.) 그리고 오늘날에는 많은 나라들이 그들의 재정적 필요를 충족시키기 위해 문화관광을 사용하기를 갈망하고 있다.

**어휘** territory 영토, 지역, 영역  mainstay ① 주축, 기둥 ② 주요생업
impact ① 영향(력); ② 충격, 충돌(하다)  transformation 변형, 변화
arrange ① 정리[정돈]하다 ② 준비[마련]하다 ③ 배치[배열]하다  resource 자원
explore 탐험하다 *exploration 탐험  path 길, 통로  thereby 그로 인해  confirm 확인하다
determination 결정, 결심  hollow ① (속이) 텅 비게 하다 ② 텅 비어 있는
recession 불황, 경기침체  restore 복원하다  heritage 유산, 유적
devote to ~에 전념[몰두]하다  audiovisual 시청각의  regional 지역의
board ① (관서의) 부, 청 ② 이사회  promote ① 승진하다 ② 발전하다 ③ 홍보하다
subsidize 보조금을 주다, 지원하다  conserve 보존하다 *conservative 보수적인
**conservation 보존  revenue 소득, 수입원  resident 거주자  rural 시골의
Mediterranean sea 지중해  derive 얻다, 획득하다  distinctive 뚜렷이 구별되는, 차별화된
landscape 경치, 풍경  border ① 국경, 경계 ② ~에 접하다, ~을 둘러싸다
tourist destination 관광 명소 *destination 목적지  due to ~ 때문에
long for 갈망하다, 열망하다  financial 재정적인, 재정상의

**정답** 02 ④

**해설** 주어진 지문은 많은 도시들이 문화유산을 이용해 관광지로 개발한다는 내용의 글이므로 북아프리카 국가들이 자연경관으로 인해 관광중심지가 된다는 ④는 이 글의 전체 흐름과 관계가 없다.

## 실전문제

**03** 다음 글의 흐름상 어색한 문장은?

Consider the following implication involving the role of social bonds and affection among group members. If strong bonds make even a single dissent more likely, the performance of groups and institutions will be impaired. ① A study of investment clubs showed that the worst-performing clubs were built on affective ties and were primarily social, while the best-performing clubs limited social connections and focused on making money. ② Dissent was far more frequent in the high-performing clubs. ③ The low performers usually voted unanimously, with little open debate. ④ As illustrated in the study, the high performers placed more importance on social bonds than the low performers in order to result in their high rate of success. The central problem is that the voters in low-performing groups were trying to build social cohesion rather than to produce the highest returns.

## 실전 해설

**Main Idea :**
유대가 강한 집단은 최악의 성과를 내고 유대가 약한 집단은 최고의 성과를 낸다.

**03** Consider the following implication involving the role of social bonds and affection among group members. If strong bonds make even a single dissent more likely, the performance of groups and institutions will be impaired. ① A study of investment clubs showed that the worst-performing clubs were built on affective ties and were primarily social, while the best-performing clubs limited social connections and focused on making money. ② Dissent was far more frequent in the high-performing clubs. ③ The low performers usually voted unanimously, with little open debate. ④ As illustrated in the study, the high performers placed more importance on social bonds than the low performers in order to result in their high rate of success. The central problem is that the voters in low-performing groups were trying to build social cohesion rather than to produce the highest returns.

↑ Main Idea와 정반대 내용

**해석** 집단 구성원들 사이의 사교적인 결속력과 애정의 역할에 관련된 다음의 암시를 고려해 보라. 만약 강한 결속력이 단 하나의 불일치도 더 가능하게 한다면, 집단과 단체의 성취는 저해될 것이다. 투자 클럽에 대한 한 연구는 최악의 성과를 보이는 클럽은 애정의 유대 위에 조직되었고 주로 (구성원들이) 사교적인 반면에, 최고의 성과를 내는 클럽은 사회적인 관계를 제한했고 돈을 버는 데만 집중했다는 것을 보여 주었다. 불일치는 높은 성과를 보여 주는 클럽에서 훨씬 더 빈번했다. 낮은 성취를 보여 주는 사람들은 보통 만장일치로 투표를 했고 공개적인 토론은 거의 하지 않았다. (이 연구에서 보여 주는 것처럼 높은 성취 집단은 성공률을 높이기 위해서 낮은 성취 집단보다 사회적 결속력을 더 중요시 했다). 핵심적인 문제는 낮은 성취를 이룬 집단들의 투표자들은 가장 높은 수익을 만들어내기보다는 사교적인 응집성을 구축하려고 했다는 것이다.

**어휘** implication 암시 *imply 암시하다   bond 유대, 결속력(= tie)
affection 애정 *affectionate 애정 어린   dissent 불일치, 동의하지 않음
likely 가능성 있는, 그럴싸한   institution 제도, 관습; 기관, 단체
impaired 손상당한, 상처 입은 *impair 손상시키다   investment 투자 *invest 투자하다
primarily 첫째로, 우선, 주로 *primary ① 첫째의, 제1의 ② 주요한, 주된
social ① 사회적인 ② 사교적인   frequent 빈번한   vote 투표하다 *voter 투표자
unanimously 만장일치로   debate 토론   illustrate 보여 주다, 예를 들어 설명하다
place 두다, 놓다   in order to ⓥ ⓥ하기 위해서   result in 초래하다, 야기하다
rate ① 비율, 율 ② 요금 ③ 등급 ④ 평가하다   cohesion 응집(력)   rather than ~보다는 (오히려)
returns 보수, 수익

**해설** 주어진 지문은 낮은 성취집단이 유대가 끈끈하고 높은 성취집단이 그렇지 않다는 내용의 글이므로 그 반대를 설명하는 ④는 글의 전체 흐름과 관계가 없다.

**정답**
03 ④

## 실전문제

**04** 다음 글의 흐름상 어색한 문장은?

Scientific experiments should be designed to show that your hypothesis is wrong and should be conducted completely objectively with no possible subjective influence on the outcome. ① Unfortunately few, if any, scientists are truly objective as they have often decided long before the experiment is begun what the result would be like. ② This means that very often bias is (unintentionally) introduced into the experiment, the experimental procedure or the interpretation of results. ③ It is all too easy to justify to yourself why an experiment which does not fit with your expectations should be ignored, and why one which provides the results you 'hoped for' is the right one. ④ As a result, it is important to draw a meaningful result from premise that your hypothesis is right one rather than false. This can be partly avoided by conducting experiments 'blinded' and by asking others to check your data or repeat experiments.

## 실전 해설

**04**

> Main Idea : 과학적 실험은 객관적이고 당신의 가설이 틀렸다는 전제여야 한다.

Scientific experiments should be designed to show that your hypothesis is wrong and should be conducted completely objectively with no possible subjective influence on the outcome. ① Unfortunately few, if any, scientists are truly objective as they have often decided long before the experiment is begun what the result would be like. ② This means that very often bias is (unintentionally) introduced into the experiment, the experimental procedure or the interpretation of results. ③ It is all too easy to justify to yourself why an experiment which does not fit with your expectations should be ignored, and why one which provides the results you 'hoped for' is the right one. ④ As a result, it is important to draw a meaningful result from premise that your hypothesis is right one rather than false. This can be
↳ Main Idea와 정반대 개념

partly avoided by conducting experiments 'blinded' and by asking others to check your data or repeat experiments.

**해석** 과학 실험은 자신의 가설이 틀렸다는 것을 보여 주도록 설계되어야 하고, 결과에 대해 있을 법한 그 어떤 주관적 영향도 없이 완벽하게 객관적으로 수행되어야 한다. 유감스럽게도 있다 하더라도 진정으로 객관적인 과학자는 거의 없는데 이는 그들이 흔히 실험이 시작되기 오래전에 결과가 어떨지 결정했기 때문이다. 이것은 매우 빈번히 편견이 실험, 실험 절차 혹은 결과의 해석에 (무심코) 더해진다는 것을 의미한다. 자신의 기대와 어긋나는 실험이 왜 무시되어야 하는지, 그리고 자신이 '기대했던' 결과를 가져다주는 실험이 왜 옳은 것인지를 자신에게 정당화하기는 너무나 쉽다. (당신의 가설이 잘못됐다기보다 옳다는 전제로부터 의미 있는 결과를 도출하는 것이 중요하다). 이것은 당신이 '눈 먼 상태(미리 예측하지 않은 상태)에서' 실험을 하고 다른 사람들에게 당신의 데이터를 점검하거나 실험을 되풀이해 보라고 요청함으로써 어느 정도 피할 수 있다.

**어휘** experiment 실험  hypothesis 가설  wrong 틀린  conduct 수행하다, 실행하다
objectively 객관적으로  subjective 주관적인  outcome 결과  bias 편견, 편향
unintentionally 무심코  procedure 과정, 절차  interpretation 해석  justify 정당화하다
fit ① ~에 맞다[맞추다] ② ~에 적절하다, 적절하게 하다  ignore 무시하다  hope for 기대하다
draw 잡아당기다, 끌어내다  premise 전제  conduct 행하다  blind ① 눈먼 ② 눈멀게 하다
by ~ing ~함으로써  repeat 반복하다

**해설** 주어진 지문은 과학실험은 자신의 가설이 틀렸다는 전제로 설계되어야 한다는 내용의 글이므로 당신의 가설이 옳다는 전제로 결과를 도출해야한다는 ④는 글의 전체 흐름과 관계가 없다.

**정답**
04 ④

## 기출문제

**01** 다음 글의 흐름상 어색한 문장은? 2025. 국가직 9급

As OECD countries prepare for an AI revolution, underscored by rapid advancements in generative AI and an increased availability of AI-skilled workers, the landscape of employment is poised for significant change. ① To navigate this shift, it's critical to prioritise training and education to equip both current and future workers with the necessary skills, and to support displaced workers with adequate social protection. ② Additionally, safeguarding workers' rights in the face of AI integration and ensuring inclusive labour markets become paramount. ③ Social dialogue will also be key to success in this new era. ④ Many experts believe that AI will completely replace all human jobs within the next decade. Together, these actions will ensure that the AI revolution benefits all, transforming potential risks into opportunities for growth and innovation.

## 기출 분석

**01** As OECD countries prepare for an AI revolution, underscored by rapid advancements in generative AI and an increased availability of AI-skilled workers, the landscape of employment is poised for significant change. ① To navigate this shift, it's critical to prioritise training and education to equip both current and future workers with the necessary skills, and to support displaced workers with adequate social protection. ② Additionally, safeguarding workers' rights in the face of AI integration and ensuring inclusive labour markets become paramount. ③ Social dialogue will also be key to success in this new era. ④ Many experts believe that AI will completely replace all human jobs within the next decade. Together, these actions will ensure that the AI revolution benefits all, transforming potential risks into opportunities for growth and innovation.

↳ ④는 Main Idea와 정반대 내용

**해석** OECD 국가들이 생성형 AI의 급속한 발전과 AI기술을 갖춘 노동자들의 증가로 강조되는 AI혁명에 대비하면서, 고용 환경은 상당한 변화를 맞이할 것으로 보인다. 이러한 변화에 잘 적응하기 위해서는 현재와 미래의 노동자가 필요한 기술을 갖추도록 훈련과 교육을 우선시하고, 일자리를 잃은 노동자들에게 적절한 사회적 보호를 제공하는 것이 매우 중요하다. 또한, AI가 통합되는 과정에서 노동자의 권리를 보호하고 포용적인 노동시장을 보장하는 것도 최우선 과제가 된다. 새로운 시대에 성공하기 위해서는 사회적 대화도 핵심적인 역할을 할 것이다. (앞으로 10년 이내에 AI가 인간의 모든 일자리를 완전히 대체할 것이라고 많은 전문가들은 믿고 있다.) 이러한 조치들이 함께 이루어지면 AI혁명이 모두에게 이익이 되도록 보장하여 잠재적 위험을 성장과 혁신의 기회로 전환하도록 할 것이다.

**어휘** prepare for ~에 대비하다  revolution 혁명  underscore 강조하다  rapid 빠른
advancement 진보, 발전  generative 생성의, 생성형의  availability 이용 가능성, 유효성
AI-skilled AI 기술을 갖춘  landscape (특정 분야의) 환경, 정세, 판도
be poised for ~을 맞이하다, ~할 태세를 갖추다  significant 상당한
navigate shift 변화에 잘 적응하다  critical 중요한, 결정적인
prioritise(prioritize) 우선시하다, 우선순위를 정하다  equip A with B A에게 B를 갖추게 하다
displaced 실직한, 쫓겨난  adequate 적절한, 알맞은, 충분한  additionally 게다가
safeguard 보호하다, 지키다  right 권리  in the face of ~에 직면하여  integration 통합, 융합
action 행동, 조치  ensure 보장하다, 확실하게 하다  inclusive 포용적인, 포함하는
paramount 가장 중요한  era 시대, 시기  expert 전문가  replace 대체하다
benefit 이익을 주다  transform 변형시키다  potential 잠재적인  innovation 혁신

**해설** 주어진 지문은 AI 시대를 맞아 고용 환경의 변화와 이에 대한 대응 방안에 관한 글이므로 'AI가 인간의 모든 일자리를 대체할 것'이라는 ④는 전체 글의 흐름상 어색한 문장이다.

**정답**
01 ④

## 기출문제

**02** 다음 글의 흐름상 어색한 문장은? 2025. 지방직 9급

> Scientists in the UK grew special tomatoes with extra vitamin D, which is important for people's health. Vitamin D deficiency affects about one billion people worldwide. ① Tomatoes naturally contain a substance that gets converted into vitamin D. ② The team altered the genes of the tomato plants, breeding them to have more of this substance than usual. ③ Each tomato came to have about as much vitamin D as two medium-sized eggs. ④ Moreover, tomatoes are commonly eaten raw in salads and served as a cooked vegetable. The scientists think the technique could be used with other foods, too.

## 기출 분석

**02**

Scientists in the UK grew special tomatoes with extra vitamin D, which is important for people's health. Vitamin D deficiency affects about one billion people worldwide. ① Tomatoes naturally contain a substance that gets converted into vitamin D. ② The team altered the genes of the tomato plants, breeding them to have more of this substance than usual. ③ Each tomato came to have about as much vitamin D as two medium-sized eggs. ④ Moreover, tomatoes are commonly eaten raw in salads and served as a cooked vegetable. The scientists think the technique could be used with other foods, too.

↳ ④는 Main Idea와 무관한 내용

**해석** 영국의 과학자들은 사람들의 건강에 중요한 비타민 D가 추가된 특별한 토마토를 재배했다. 비타민 D 결핍은 전 세계적으로 약 10억 명에게 영향을 미친다. 토마토는 자연적으로 비타민 D로 전환되는 물질을 함유하고 있다. 그 (연구)팀은 토마토 식물의 유전자를 변형하여, 이 물질을 평소보다 더 많이 함유하도록 재배했다. 각 토마토는 중간 크기 달걀 두 개와 비슷한 양의 비타민 D를 갖게 되었다. (게다가 토마토는 일반적으로 샐러드에서 생으로 먹거나 익힌 채소로 제공된다.) 과학자들은 이 기술이 다른 식품에도 활용될 수 있다고 생각한다.

**어휘** deficiency 결핍  affect 영향을 주다  billion 10억  worldwide 전 세계적으로  contain 포함하다  substance 물질  convert 전환하다  alter 바꾸다  gene 유전자  plant 식물  breed 교배하다, 품종 개량하다  come to ~하게 되다  medium-sized 중간 크기의  moreover 게다가  raw 날것의, 생으로 된

**해설** 주어진 지문은 비타민 D로 전환되는 물질을 더 많이 함유하도록 유전자를 변형한 토마토를 재배한 사례에 관한 것이므로, 글의 흐름상 어색한 문장은 토마토의 일반적인 섭취 방법을 소개하는 내용의 ④이다. 주어진 지문의 Main Idea는 토마토의 유전자 변형을 통해 비타민 D 함량을 높인 과학적 성과를 설명하는 것이므로 단순히 '토마토의 일반적인 섭취 방식(샐러드나 조리된 채소로 먹는 것)'을 설명하는 ④는 전체 글의 흐름과 무관하다.

**정답**
02 ④

## 기출문제

**03** 다음 글의 흐름상 어색한 문장은? 2024. 지방직 9급

Critical thinking sounds like an unemotional process but it can engage emotions and even passionate responses. In particular, we may not like evidence that contradicts our own opinions or beliefs. ① If the evidence points in a direction that is challenging, that can rouse unexpected feelings of anger, frustration or anxiety. ② The academic world traditionally likes to consider itself as logical and free of emotions, so if feelings do emerge, this can be especially difficult. ③ For example, looking at the same information from several points of view is not important. ④ Being able to manage your emotions under such circumstances is a useful skill. If you can remain calm, and present your reasons logically, you will be better able to argue your point of view in a convincing way.

## 기출 분석

**03**

> Main Idea : 비판적 사고는 감정과 관련이 있다.
>
> Critical thinking sounds like an unemotional process but **it can engage emotions and even passionate responses**. In particular, we may not like evidence that contradicts our own opinions or beliefs. ① <u>If the evidence points in a direction that is challenging, that can rouse unexpected feelings of anger, frustration or anxiety.</u> ② <u>The academic world traditionally likes to consider itself as logical and free of emotions, so if feelings do emerge, this can be especially difficult.</u> ③ <u>For example, looking at the same information from several points of view is not important.</u>
> └→ Main Idea와 무관한 문장
> ④ <u>Being able to manage your emotions under such circumstances is a useful skill.</u> If you can remain calm, and present your reasons logically, you will be better able to argue your point of view in a convincing way.

**해석** 비판적 사고는 감정과 무관한 과정처럼 들리지만, 감정 그리고 심지어는 격렬한 반응과 관계를 맺을 수 있다. 특히, 우리는 자신의 의견이나 믿음에 모순되는 증거를 좋아하지 않을지도 모른다. 만약 증거가 도전적인 방향을 가리키면 그것은 예상치 못한 분노나 좌절 또는 불안감을 불러일으킬 수 있다. 학계는 전통적으로 자신을 논리적이고 감정적이지 않다고 여기고 싶어 한다. 그래서 만약 감정이 발생하면 이는 특히나 어려울 수 있다. (예를 들어, 같은 정보를 여러 관점에서 바라보는 것은 중요하지 않다.) 그러한 상황에서 당신의 감정을 관리할 수 있는 것은 유용한 기술이다. 만약 당신이 침착함을 유지하고 근거를 논리적으로 제공할 수 있다면, 당신은 자신의 관점을 설득력 있는 방식으로 더 잘 주장할 수 있을 것이다.

**어휘** critical 비판적인   sound like ~처럼 들리다   unemotional 비감정적인, 감정과 무관한
process 과정, 절차   engage ~와 관계를 맺다   passionate 열정적인   response 반응
in particular 특히   evidence 증거   contradict 모순되다   belief 믿음
point in a direction that ~한 방향을 가리키다   *point 가리키다   **direction 방향
rouse 깨우다, 각성하다, 불러일으키다   unexpected 예상치 못한   anger 분노   frustration 좌절(감)
anxiety 불안, 걱정   consider A as B A를 B로 여기다, 간주하다   logical 논리적인
free of ~이 없는   emerge 나오다, 나타나다   especially 특히   manage 관리하다
circumstance 상황   calm 고요한, 침착한   present 주다, 제공하다
reason ① 근거 ② 이유 ③ 이성   argue 주장하다, 논쟁하다   point of view 관점
convincing 설득력 있는

**해설** 주어진 지문은 비판적 사고라 하더라도 감정에 치우칠 수 있으므로 감정을 잘 관리하여 자신의 의견을 설득력 있게 주장해야 한다는 내용의 글이다. 따라서 비판적 사고나 감정과 관계없는 설명을 하고 있는 ③은 전체 글의 흐름상 어색하다.

**정답**
03 ③

## 기출문제

**04** 다음 글의 흐름상 어색한 문장은? 2024. 국가직 9급

In spite of all evidence to the contrary, there are people who seriously believe that NASA's Apollo space program never really landed men on the moon. These people claim that the moon landings were nothing more than a huge conspiracy, perpetuated by a government desperately in competition with the Russians and fearful of losing face. ① These conspiracy theorists claim that the United States knew it couldn't compete with the Russians in the space race and was therefore forced to fake a series of successful moon landings. ② Advocates of a conspiracy cite several pieces of what they consider evidence. ③ Crucial to their case is the claim that astronauts never could have safely passed through the Van Allen belt, a region of radiation trapped in Earth's magnetic field. ④ They also point to the fact that the metal coverings of the spaceship were designed to block radiation. If the astronauts had truly gone through the belt, say conspiracy theorists, they would have died.

## 기출 분석

**04**

In spite of all evidence to the contrary, there are people who seriously believe that NASA's Apollo space program never really landed men on the moon. These people claim that the moon landings were nothing more than a huge conspiracy,
↳ Main Idea : 달 착륙은 거대한 음모이다.

perpetuated by a government desperately in competition with the Russians and fearful of losing face. ① These conspiracy theorists claim that the United States knew it couldn't compete with the Russians in the space race and was therefore forced to fake a series of successful moon landings. ② Advocates of a conspiracy cite several pieces of what they consider evidence. ③ Crucial to their case is the claim that astronauts never could have safely passed through the Van Allen belt, a region of radiation trapped in Earth's magnetic field. ④ They also point to the fact that the metal coverings of the spaceship were designed to block radiation. If the
↳ Main Idea와 무관한 문장

astronauts had truly gone through the belt, say conspiracy theorists, they would have died.

**해석** 반대되는 모든 증거에도 불구하고 NASA의 아폴로 우주 프로그램이 실제로 결코 사람들을 달에 착륙시킨 적이 없다고 진지하게 믿는 사람들이 있다. 이 사람들은 달 착륙이 러시아와 필사적으로 경쟁하고 체면을 잃을까 두려워한 정부가 영속화시킨 거대한 음모론에 지나지 않는다고 주장한다. 이러한 음모론자들은 미국이 우주 경쟁에서 러시아와 경쟁할 수 없다는 것을 알았고, 따라서 일련의 성공적인 달 착륙을 조작하도록 강요를 받았다고 주장한다. 음모론 옹호자들은 그들이 증거로 여기는 몇 가지들을 인용한다. 우주비행사들이 지구 자기장에 갇힌 방사선 지역인 밴 앨런 벨트를 결코 안전하게 통과할 수 없었을 것이라는 주장이 그들의 사례에 결정적이다. (그들은 또한 그 우주선의 금속 덮개가 방사선을 차단하도록 설계되었다는 사실도 지적한다.) 우주비행사들이 정말 이 벨트를 통과했다면 그들은 사망했을 것이라고 음모론자들은 말한다.

**어휘**
in spite of ~에도 불구하고  evidence 증거  to the contrary 반대되는
seriously 진지하게, 심각하게  land 착륙하다, 착륙시키다  *landing 착륙  claim 주장하다
nothing more than ~에 지나지 않는, ~에 불과한  huge 거대한  conspiracy 음모, 음모론
perpetuate 영속시키다, 영속화하다  desperately 필사적으로  competition 경쟁  fearful 두려운
lose face 체면을 잃다  theorist 이론가  fake ① 가짜의, 위조의 ② 위조[조작]하다
advocate 옹호자  cite 인용하다  crucial 결정적인, 중요한  case 사례, 경우
astronaut 우주비행사  safely 안전하게  pass through ~을 통과하다  region 지역, 영역
radiation 방사능, 방사선  trap 가두다  magnetic field 자기장  point to ~을 지적하다
metal 금속  covering 덮개  spaceship 우주선  block 차단하다, 막다
go through ~을 통과하다

**해설** 주어진 지문은 미국의 달 착륙을 미국 정부가 가짜로 꾸며낸 음모론이라고 믿는 사람들과 그 근거에 관한 내용의 글이므로 '우주선의 금속 덮개가 방사선을 차단한다'는 ④는 전체 글의 흐름상 어색하다.

04 ④

## 기출문제

**05** 다음 글의 흐름상 어색한 문장은? 2023. 지방직 9급

I once took a course in short-story writing and during that course a renowned editor of a leading magazine talked to our class. ① He said he could pick up any one of the dozens of stories that came to his desk every day and after reading a few paragraphs he could feel whether or not the author liked people. ② "If the author doesn't like people," he said, "people won't like his or her stories." ③ The editor kept stressing the importance of being interested in people during his talk on fiction writing. ④ Thurston, a great magician, said that every time he went on stage he said to himself, "I am grateful because I'm successful." At the end of the talk, he concluded, "Let me tell you again. You have to be interested in people if you want to be a successful writer of stories."

### 기출 분석

**05**

I once took a course in short-story writing and during that course a renowned editor of a leading magazine talked to our class. ① He said he could pick up any one of the dozens of stories that came to his desk every day and after reading a few paragraphs he could feel whether or not the author liked people. ② "If the author doesn't like people," he said, "people won't like his or her stories." ③ The editor kept stressing the importance of being interested in people during his talk on fiction writing. ④ Thurston, a great magician, said that every time he went on stage he said to himself, "I am grateful because I'm successful." At the end of the talk, he concluded, "Let me tell you again. You have to be interested in people if you want to be a successful writer of stories."

**Main Idea:** 좋은 소설가가 되려면 사람에게 관심을 가져야 한다.

↑ Main Idea와 무관한 문장

**해석** 나는 한때 단편 소설 쓰기 강좌를 들었는데, 그 강좌 중에 한 주도적인 잡지의 유명한 편집장이 우리 수업에서 이야기를 했다. 그는 매일 자신의 책상에 올라오는 수십 개의 이야기 중 어느 하나든 골라 몇 단락만 읽으면 그 소설을 쓴 작가가 사람들을 좋아하는지 아닌지를 느낄 수 있다고 말했다. "만약 그 작가가 사람들을 좋아하지 않는다면 사람들은 그 작가의 소설을 좋아하지 않을 것"이라고 그는 말했다. 그 편집장은 소설 쓰기에 대한 강연 내내 사람에게 관심을 갖는 것의 중요성을 계속해서 강조했다. (위대한 마술사 Thurston은 그가 무대에 올라갈 때마다 자기 자신에게 "나는 성공했기 때문에 감사하다"라고 말했다고 했다.) 강연이 끝날 때쯤, 그는 "다시 한 번 말씀드리지만 성공적인 소설 작가가 되고 싶다면 사람들에게 관심을 가져야 합니다."라며 끝맺었다.

**어휘** once 한때, 한 번  take a course in ~ 강의를 듣다  short-story 단편소설  renowned 유명한  editor 편집장, 편집자  dozens of 수십 개의  paragraph 단락  stress 강조하다  magician 마법사  every time S + V ~할 때마다  grateful 감사하는, 고마워하는

**해설** 주어진 지문은 좋은 소설가가 되려면 사람에게 관심을 가져야 한다는 내용의 글이므로 '어떤 마술사가 무대에 오를 때마다 스스로에게 하는 말을 언급하는' 내용의 ④는 전체 글의 흐름상 어색하다. 따라서 정답은 ④이다.

**정답**
05 ④

## 기출문제

**06** 다음 글의 흐름상 어색한 문장은? 2023. 국가직 9급

In our monthly surveys of 5,000 American workers and 500 U.S. employers, a huge shift to hybrid work is abundantly clear for office and knowledge workers. ① An emerging norm is three days a week in the office and two at home, cutting days on site by 30 % or more. You might think this cutback would bring a huge drop in the demand for office space. ② But our survey data suggests cuts in office space of 1 % to 2 % on average, implying big reductions in density not space. We can understand why. High density at the office is uncomfortable and many workers dislike crowds around their desks. ③ Most employees want to work from home on Mondays and Fridays. Discomfort with density extends to lobbies, kitchens, and especially elevators. ④ The only sure-fire way to reduce density is to cut days on site without cutting square footage as much. Discomfort with density is here to stay according to our survey evidence.

## 기출 분석

Main Idea : 하이브리드 근무방식으로 사무실에서 근무하는 일수가 줄어들고 있다.

**06**

In our monthly surveys of 5,000 American workers and 500 U.S. employers, a huge shift to hybrid work is abundantly clear for office and knowledge workers. ① <u>An emerging norm is three days a week in the office and two at home, cutting days on site by 30 % or more</u>. You might think this cutback would bring a huge drop in the demand for office space. ② <u>But our survey data suggests cuts in office space of 1 % to 2 % on average, implying big reductions in density not space</u>. We can understand why. High density at the office is uncomfortable and many workers dislike crowds around their desks. ③ <u>Most employees want to work from home on Mondays and Fridays</u>. ← Main Idea와 무관한 문장  Discomfort with density extends to lobbies, kitchens, and especially elevators. ④ <u>The only sure-fire way to reduce density is to cut days on site without cutting square footage as much</u>. Discomfort with density is here to stay according to our survey evidence.

**해석** 미국인 근로자 5,000명과 미국 고용주 500명을 대상으로 실시한 우리의 월간 설문조사에 따르면, 사무직 및 지식 근로자에 대한 하이브리드 근무로의 대규모 전환이 매우 뚜렷하다. 주 3일은 사무실에서 2일은 집에서 근무하는 것이 새로운 표준으로 자리 잡으면서 현장 근무 일수가 30% 이상 단축되었다. 당신은 이러한 단축으로 인해 사무실 공간에 대한 수요가 크게 감소할 것이라고 생각할 수도 있다. 하지만 우리의 설문조사 데이터는 평균적으로 사무실 공간의 1~2%의 감소를 보여주는데, 이는 공간이 아닌 밀도의 큰 감소를 의미한다. 우리는 그 이유를 이해할 수 있다. 사무실의 높은 밀도는 불편하며 많은 근로자들은 그들 책상 주변에 사람이 붐비는 것을 싫어한다. (대부분의 직원은 월요일과 금요일에 재택근무를 원한다.) 밀도에 대한 불편함은 로비, 주방, 특히 엘리베이터에까지 적용된다. 밀도를 낮출 수 있는 유일하고 확실한 방법은 현장 근무일을 줄이면서 그만큼 평방피트를 줄이지 않는 것이다. 우리의 조사 증거에 따르면, 밀도에 대한 불편함은 계속 남아 있다.

**어휘** huge 거대한, 어마어마한   shift 이동, 이전   hybrid 하이브리드의, 혼합형의
abundantly 풍부하게, 충분히, 매우, 아주   clear 뚜렷한, 분명한   cutback 감축, 삭감, 단축
emerging 새롭게 나타나는   norm 규범, 기준   on site 현장에서   imply 의미하다, 암시하다
reduction 감소, 축소   density 밀도   uncomfortable 불편한   discomfort 불쾌감, 불편함
especially 특히, 특별히   square footage 면적

**해설** 주어진 지문은 하이브리드 근무 방식이 점점 늘어남에 따라 사무실에서 근무하는 일수가 줄어들어 사무실 공간의 밀도가 감소했다는 내용의 글이므로 '대부분의 직원들은 월요일과 금요일에 재택근무를 원한다'는 ③은 전체 글의 흐름상 어색하다.

정답
06 ③

MEMO

김세현 영어 전혀 다른 개념 독해

PART

# 04

# 단락의 전개 방식

# PART 04 단락의 전개 방식
## (Pattern and Signal)

English Reading

### 풀이 해법

**1. 나열(Listing)의 전개 방식**

나열의 Signal words

| | | | | |
|---|---|---|---|---|
| • many<br>많은 | • several<br>몇몇의 | • various<br>다양한 | • a few<br>몇몇의 | • some<br>몇몇의 |
| • first(of all)<br>첫 번째(무엇보다도, 우선) | • second<br>두 번째 | • third<br>세 번째 | • one<br>하나 | • also<br>또한 | • another<br>또 다른 |

• moreover(= in addition, additionally, besides, furthermore, further, what's more)
더욱이, 게다가

• for example(instance)          • finally(= lastly)
예를 들어서                          마지막으로

### 연습문제

**EX 1** 나열의 Signal 찾기

Over the recent ten years, scientists have found several new fuels to replace gasoline for automobiles. One of these fuels is methanol, a form of wood alcohol. It can be used in many cars in almost the same way that gasoline is used. Natural gas is another alternative fuel for cars. However, cars that burn this fuel must be equipped with special tanks of natural gas. A third alternative is electricity. Cars fueled by electricity have no engine at all, though they do have to carry large batteries. Finally, a new energy source, and perhaps the most promising, is the hydrogen fuel cell. Hydrogen is available in large quantities, but the fuel cell's only emission is a small amount of water.

## 연습해설

### EX 1

Over the recent ten years, scientists have found **several** new fuels to replace gasoline for automobiles. **One** of these fuels is methanol, a form of wood alcohol. It can be used in many cars in almost the same way that gasoline is used. Natural gas is **another** alternative fuel for cars. However, cars that burn this fuel must be equipped with special tanks of natural gas. A **third** alternative is electricity. Cars fueled by electricity have no engine at all, though they do have to carry large batteries. **Finally**, a new energy source, and perhaps the most promising, is the hydrogen fuel cell. Hydrogen is available in large quantities, but the fuel cell's only emission is a small amount of water.

**해석** 최근 10년 동안 과학자들은 자동차에 사용하는 휘발유를 대체할 몇 가지 새로운 연료를 발견했다. 이 연료 중에 하나가 메탄올, 즉 나무 알코올의 한 형태이다. 메탄올은 휘발유가 사용되는 것과 거의 똑같은 방식으로 많은 자동차에 사용될 수 있다. 천연 가스는 자동차의 또 다른 대체 연료이다. 하지만 이 연료를 사용하는 차는 특별한 천연 가스통을 갖추어야 한다. 세 번째 대체 연료는 전기이다. 전기로 연료를 공급받는 차는 비록 커다란 배터리를 가지고 다녀야 하지만 엔진은 필요 없다. 마지막으로 새로운 에너지원이자 가장 유망한 것은 수소 연료 전지이다. 수소는 거대한 양이 필요하지만 수소전지의 유일한 배출은 아주 소량의 물뿐이다.

**어휘** fuel 연료 replace 대체하다 automobile 자동차 alternative 대체의, 대안의 be equipped with ~을 갖추고 있다 carry 운반하다, 나르다 promising 유망한, 전도양양한 hydrogen 수소 available 이용 가능한 in large quantities 많은 양으로 *quantity 양 emission 배출

**정답** several / one / another / A third / Finally

## 연습문제

**EX 2** 나열의 Signal 찾기

Computer language can be funny in a few reasons. For example, we say computers have a "memory." We do not believe they really remember or think. We still use "memory", though. Also, computer programs have a term of "menus." Of course, we are not talking about restaurants or food. This is a different kind of menu, one for choosing a program or section of the memory. Moreover, the really ridiculous term is "mouse" in the computer. It can be hard not to think about a real mouse when you hear the word. But there are no little gray animals in the machine. Lastly, some programs of a computer use the word "paste which associates flour."

## 연습해설

### EX 2

Computer language can be funny in **a few** reasons. ↑나열의 시작점  **For example**, ↑첫 번째 나열 we say computers have a "memory." We do not believe they really remember or think. We still use "memory", though. **Also**, ↑두 번째 나열 computer programs have a term of "menus." Of course, we are not talking about restaurants or food. This is a different kind of menu, one for choosing a program or section of the memory. **Moreover**, ↑세 번째 나열 the really ridiculous term is "mouse" in the computer. It can be hard not to think about a real mouse when you hear the word. But there are no little gray animals in the machine. **Lastly**, ↳마지막 나열 some programs of a computer use the word "paste which associates flour."

**[해석]** 지난 몇 년 동안 컴퓨터 용어는 몇 가지 이유로 재미있다. 예를 들어서, 우리는 컴퓨터가 '메모리'를 가진다고 말한다. 우리는 컴퓨터가 진정으로 기억하거나 생각한다고 믿지는 않는다. 하지만 우리는 여전히 '메모리'를 사용한다. 또한, 컴퓨터 프로그램은 '메뉴'라는 용어를 가진다. 물론 우리는 식당이나 음식에 대한 이야기를 하는 것은 아니다. 이것은 다른 종류의 메뉴인데 즉, 프로그램 중 하나를 선택하거나 메모리의 한 영역이다. 게다가, 컴퓨터에서 진짜 우스꽝스러운 용어가 '마우스'이다. 당신이 그 단어를 들을 때 진정한 쥐를 생각 할 수도 있다. 그러나 컴퓨터에는 회색동물은 있을 수 없다. 마지막으로 컴퓨터의 몇몇 프로그램은 밀가루를 연상시키는 '반죽'이라는 단어를 사용한다.

**[어휘]** though ① 비록 ~일지라도 ② 그러나  term 용어  ridiculous 우스꽝스러운, 터무니없는  paste 반죽(하다)  associate ① 연상시키다 ② 관계[관련]시키다  flour 밀가루

**[정답]** a few / For example / Also / Moreover / Lastly

## 실전문제

**01** 다음 글의 주제로 가장 적절한 것은?

Geologists have proposed many hypotheses to account for ice ages. One idea is that the amount of heat energy given off by the sun changes. Ice ages may have occurred during periods when energy from the sun is less. Or the amount of energy reaching Earth might have changed due to volcanic dust in the atmosphere. Another possibility is that during periods of mountain building, more of Earth's land area lay above the snow line. That situation can have changed the climate enough for an ice age to begin. The third hypothesis can be related with the former position of continents on Earth's surface. If continents used to be in the way of currents between oceans, they may have prevented the mixing of cold and warm water. Without mixing between oceans, areas of Earth might have become cold enough to start an ice age. Each of these causes has its weak and strong points. Recent research has added to knowledge about the times and durations of ice ages. Scientists have discovered evidence of many more glacial climates in the distant past, though.

① pros and cons of hypotheses of ice ages
② characteristics of glacial climates
③ causes of glacial climates
④ effects of ice ages

## 실전 해설

**01**

↱ 나열의 시작점 　　　　　　　　　　↱ 첫 번째 나열

Geologists have proposed many hypotheses to account for ice ages. One idea is that the amount of heat energy given off by the sun changes. Ice ages may have occurred during periods when energy from the sun is less. Or the amount of energy reaching Earth might have changed due to volcanic dust in the atmosphere.

↱ 두 번째 나열

Another possibility is that during periods of mountain building, more of Earth's land area lay above the snow line. That situation can have changed the climate enough

↱ 세 번째 나열

for an ice age to begin. The third hypothesis can be related with the former position of continents on Earth's surface. If continents used to be in the way of currents between oceans, they may have prevented the mixing of cold and warm water. Without mixing between oceans, areas of Earth might have become cold enough to start an ice age. Each of these causes has its weak and strong points. Recent research has added to knowledge about the times and durations of ice ages. Scientists have discovered evidence of many more glacial climates in the distant past, though.

**해석** 지질학자들은 빙하기를 설명하기 위한 많은 가설을 내놓았다. 하나의 가설은 태양에 의해 방출된 열에너지의 양이 변한다는 것이다. 빙하기는 태양으로부터의 에너지가 적은 기간에 발생했을지도 모른다. 또는 지구에 도달하는 에너지의 양은 대기의 화산 분진으로 인해 바뀔 수도 있었을 것이다. 또 다른 가능성은 산이 만들어지는 시기에 더 많은 지구의 땅이 설선(만년설의 최저경계선) 위에 있었다는 것이다. 그러한 상황이 빙하기가 시작되기에 충분히 기후를 변화시켰을지도 모른다. 세 번째 가설은 지구의 표면에 있는 대륙의 이전 위치와 관련이 있을 수 있다. 만일 대륙이 대양사이의 해류의 흐름을 방해했다면 그들은 차가운 물과 따뜻한 물이 섞이는 것을 막을 수 있었을지도 모른다. 대양 사이에 바닷물이 섞이지 않으면 지구의 지역이 빙하기를 시작하기에 충분히 추울 수 있었을 것이다. 이 가설들 각각은 약점과 강점을 가지고 있다. 최근 연구는 빙하기의 시간과 지속 기간에 대한 지식을 추가했다. 하지만, 과학자들은 먼 과거에 더 많은 빙하기가 있었음을 알려주는 증거를 발견해왔다.

① 빙하기 가설의 찬반
② 빙하기후의 특성
③ 빙하기후의 원인
④ 빙하기의 결과

**어휘** geologist 지질학자　hypothesis 가설　*hypotheses 가설들　account for 설명하다
give off (냄새·열·빛 등을) 내보내다[발하다]　occur 발생하다, 일어나다　due to ~때문에
volcanic 화산의　*volcanic dust 화산재　relate 관계시키다, 관련시키다　former 이전의
continent 대륙　be in the way of ~의 방해가 되다　current 해류　duration 지속기간
distant 거리가 먼　pros and cons 찬반　glacial 빙하기의, 빙하의

**해설** 주어진 지문은 빙하기의 원인을 나열의 전개방식으로 구성했으므로 이 글의 주제로 가장 적절한 것은 ③ '빙하기후의 원인'이다.

**정답**
01 ③

## 실전문제

**02** 다음 글의 흐름으로 보아 주어진 문장이 들어가기에 가장 적절한 곳은?

> The Indians' bodies have adapted in several ways.

The Indians of the Andes Mountains, on the west coast of South America, have developed bodies which are different from ours in order to survive where they live. ( ① ) At 17,000 feet above sea level, where these Indians live, we would find it very hard to breathe, but they do not. ( ② ) For example, their lungs have grown bigger than ours, which means they can inhale and exhale more air with each breath. ( ③ ) And they also have about two quarts more blood in their systems than we do. ( ④ ) They have bigger red corpuscles to carry the oxygen and their hearts are 20% bigger than ours, too. The Indians also have shorter arms and legs to give the heart less distance to pump the blood, and smaller hands and feet, resulting in less of an area to be exposed to the cold.

## 실전 해설

**02**

> ┌ 나열의 시작점
> The Indians' bodies have adapted in several ways.

The Indians of the Andes Mountains, on the west coast of South America, have developed bodies which are different from ours in order to survive where they live. ( ① ) At 17,000 feet above sea level, where these Indians live, we would find it very hard to breathe, but they do not. ( ② ) For example, their lungs have grown bigger than ours, which means they can inhale and exhale more air with each breath. ( ③ ) And they also have about two quarts more blood in their systems than we do. ( ④ ) They have bigger red corpuscles to carry the oxygen and their hearts are 20% bigger than ours, too. The Indians also have shorter arms and legs to give the heart less distance to pump the blood, and smaller hands and feet, resulting in less of an area to be exposed to the cold.

**해석** 남아메리카 서쪽 해안에 있는 안데스 산맥의 인디언들은 그들이 사는 곳에서 생존하기 위해 우리의 신체와 다른 신체를 발전시켰다. 이 인디언들이 사는 해발 17,000피트에서 우리는 숨을 쉬는 것이 아주 힘들다는 것을 알 것이다. 그러나 그들은 그렇지 않다. <u>그 인디언들의 신체는 여러 가지 방식으로 적응해왔다.</u> 예를 들어서, 그들의 폐는 우리의 폐보다 훨씬 더 크게 자랐는데 그것은 그들이 숨을 쉴 때마다 더 많은 공기를 마시고 내쉴 수 있다는 것을 의미한다. 그리고 그들은 또한 우리보다 약 2쿼트 더 많은 피를 그들의 몸에 갖고 있다. 그들은 또한 산소를 운반하는 더 큰 적혈구를 갖고 있고 그들의 심장은 우리 심장보다 20%가 더 크다. 그 인디언들은 또한 심장이 피를 펌프질할 더 적은 거리를 갖기 위해 더 짧은 팔과 다리를 갖고 있고 더 작은 손과 발을 갖고 있어서, 그 결과 추위에 노출될 면적이 더 적다.

**어휘** adapt ①적응시키다 ②조정하다   coast 해안   sea level 해수면
breathe 숨 쉬다, 호흡하다 *breath 숨, 호흡   lung 폐, 허파
inhale 숨을 들이마시다(≠ exhale 숨을 내쉬다)   quart 쿼트 (액량의 단위)
red corpuscle 적혈구 *corpuscle 혈구   result in 야기하다, 초래하다
expose 드러내다, 노출시키다

**해설** 나열의 signal을 이용해서 주어진 문장이 들어가기에 가장 적절한 곳을 찾아야 한다. 주어진 문장에 several이 있고 ②부터 첫 번째 나열의 signal인 For example이 시작되고 ③에 also ④에 too 그리고 마지막 문장에 also가 있으므로 주어진 문장이 들어가기에 가장 적절한 곳은 ②이다.

**정답**
02 ②

## 실전문제

**03** 다음 글의 흐름상 어색한 문장은?

Soil management is the application of specific techniques to increase soil productivity in order to preserve soil resources. The most common practices are fertilization, irrigation, and drainage. ① Fertilizers are utilized in 'poor' soils in which continuous crops have depleted the nutrients in the soil or in which plant nutrients are present in very small quantities due to natural processes. ② Irrigation has allowed the production of two or more harvests from any piece of land by applying through different methods the amount of water necessary for a crop in dry periods. ③ If you want the soil to be rich, especially in dry season, you would rather provide fertilizers at the right moment than give an amount of water to it. ④ Drainage is used in places where excessive water makes growing crops very difficult; adequate drainage enhances the amount of land available for agriculture. If well applied, these practices will tend to increase productivity without deterioration of soil resources.

## 실전 해설

**03**

Soil management is the application of specific techniques to increase soil productivity in order to preserve soil resources. The most common practices are fertilization, irrigation, and drainage. ① Fertilizers are utilized in 'poor' soils in which continuous crops have depleted the nutrients in the soil or in which plant nutrients are present in very small quantities due to natural processes. ② Irrigation has allowed the production of two or more harvests from any piece of land by applying through different methods the amount of water necessary for a crop in dry periods. ③ If you want the soil to be rich, especially in dry season, you would rather provide fertilizers at the right moment than give an amount of water to it. ④ Drainage is used in places where excessive water makes growing crops very difficult; adequate drainage enhances the amount of land available for agriculture. If well applied, these practices will tend to increase productivity without deterioration of soil resources.

(A: fertilization, B: irrigation, C: drainage)
※ ③ 나열의 전개방식상 fertilization(A)이 다시 언급될 수 없다.

**해석** 토양 관리란 특정한 기법을 적용하여 토지 생산성을 향상시켜 토양 자원을 보존하려는 것이다. 가장 흔한 방법으로는 (토지) 비옥화와 관개 그리고 배수다. 비료는 토양에서 지속적인 수확으로 토양 내 양분이 고갈된 척박한 자연적인 과정으로 토양이나 식물의 양분이 매우 적은 수량만 남은 토양에 사용된다. 관개로 인하여 건기에 작물에 필요한 물의 양의 다른 방법들을 적용을 통해서 어떤 토지에서나 이모작 이상의 생산을 가능하게 해 주었다. (당신이 특히, 건기에 토양이 비옥해지기를 원한다면 많은 물을 주기보다는 적절한 시기에 비료를 주는 것이 더 좋다.) 배수는 과도한 수량으로 작물 재배가 매우 힘든 곳에 이용된다. 즉 충분한 배수가 농작에 이용할 수 있는 토지의 양을 향상시킨다. 잘만 적용된다면, 이런 방법들은 토양 자원을 저하시키지 않고 생산성을 높여 주는 경향이 있게 된다.

**어휘** soil 토양, 토지 application 적용, 응용 specific 특정한, 특별한, 명확한 productivity 생성 preserve 보존하다 resource 자원, 원천 practice 실천, 실행; 방법; 관습 fertilization 비옥화 irrigation 관개 drainage 배수 utilize 이용하다, 활용하다 crop 작물, 수확(량) deplete 고갈시키다 nutrient 영양분 present 존재하는, 있는 due to ~ 때문에 harvest 수확, 추수 excessive 지나친, 과도한 adequate 적절한, 충분한 enhance 향상시키다 deterioration 황폐화, 저하

**해설** 단락의 도입부에 토지 생산성을 높이기 위한 세 가지 방법을 제시하고 순서대로 그 세 가지 방법을 나열하고 있다. 토지의 관개에 대해 이야기하고 있는데 비료에 대한 이야기가 나오는 ③은 전체 글의 흐름과 무관한 문장이 된다.

**정답**
03 ③

## 실전문제

**04** 다음 주어진 글 다음에 이어질 글의 순서로 가장 적절한 것은?

> Ralph was asked to work on the citizens' general dissatisfaction with the effectiveness of city government. After spending some time with people in the city, he found one of the problems was the performance of the city planning department.

(A) Another one said, "The most important thing is that we've learned how to coordinate". Ralph saw that the immediate, short-term payoff for the planning department was to become more responsive to the community and its growth.

(B) Ralph determined that the citizens' complaints were justified, so he trained the city planners in setting objectives, selecting alternatives, data analysis, and coordination. At the end of the training, one of them said, "We'll use this in the future. I'm not going to be drawing boxes any more".

(C) Citizens complained that many planners were experts at 'drawing pictures' that is, physical planning and design, but did nothing to coordinate what they were doing.

① (A) – (C) – (B)
② (B) – (A) – (C)
③ (B) – (C) – (A)
④ (C) – (B) – (A)

## 실전 해설

**04**

Ralph was asked to work on the citizens' general dissatisfaction with the effectiveness of city government. After spending some time with people in the city, he found one of the problems was the performance of the city planning department.

(A) 두 번째 나열
Another one said, "The most important thing is that we've learned how to coordinate". Ralph saw that the immediate, short-term payoff for the planning department was to become more responsive to the community and its growth.

(B) Ralph determined that the citizens' complaints were justified, so he trained the city planners in setting objectives, selecting alternatives, data analysis, and coordination. At the end of the training, 첫 번째 나열 one of them said, "We'll use this in the future. I'm not going to be drawing boxes any more".

(C) 나열의 시작점
Citizens complained that many planners were experts at 'drawing pictures' that is, physical planning and design, but did nothing to coordinate what they were doing.

**해석** Ralph는 시 정부의 효율성에 대한 시민들이 가진 보편적인 불만족을 해결해 보라는 요청을 받았다. 도시의 사람들과 얼마간의 시간을 보낸 후, 그는 문제들 중 하나는 도시계획과의 업무 수행이라는 것을 알아냈다.

(C) 시민들은 많은 기획자들이 '그림을 그리는 것', 즉 물리적인 계획과 디자인에는 전문가들이지만 그들이 하고 있는 일을 조정하기 위해서는 아무 일도 하지 않았다고 불평했다.

(B) Ralph는 시민들의 불평이 정당하다는 결정을 내렸고, 도시 계획 입안자들이 목표를 설정하고, 대안을 선택하며, 데이터를 분석하고, 조정하는 훈련을 시켰다. 훈련이 끝날 무렵에 그들 중 한 사람은 "앞으로는 우리는 이 방법을 사용할 것입니다. 저는 더 이상 박스나 그리고 있지는 않을 겁니다."라고 말했다.

(A) 또 다른 사람은 "가장 중요한 것은 우리가 조정하는 것을 배웠다는 것입니다."라고 말했다. Ralph는 도시계획과에 즉각적이고 단기적으로 이득이 되는 일이란 지역사회와 지역사회의 성장에 더 많은 관심을 기울이는 것임을 확실히 했다.

**어휘** ask ① 요구하다, 요청하다 ② 묻다  work on ~을 해결하다
general ① 일반적인, 보편적인 ② 장군  dissatisfaction 불만족  effectiveness 효율성
performance 업무 수행  department 부서  complain 불평하다  *complaint 불평
expert 전문가  that is 즉, 다시 말해서  coordinate 조정하다  determine 결정하다
justify 정당화하다  objective ① 객관적인 ② 목표  select 선택하다
alternative ① 대안(의) ② 양자택일, 선택  analysis 분석  coordination 조정
short-term 단기간의  payoff 이익, 이점  *pay off ① 성과를 내다, 성공하다 ② 해고하다
responsive 반응을 보이는, 대응하는

**해설** (C)에 나열의 시작을 알리는 many planners가 있고 (B)에 첫 번째 나열을 알리는 one of them이 있으므로 (C) 다음에는 (B)가 이어져야 하고 또한 (A)에 두 번째 나열의 another가 있으므로 (B) 다음 (A)가 이어져야 한다. 따라서 주어진 문장 다음 이어질 글의 순서로 가장 적절한 것은 ④ (C) - (B) - (A)이다.

**정답**
04 ④

## 풀이 해법

### 2. 시간 순서(Time order)의 전개 방식

**시간 순서의 Signal words**

| | | | | |
|---|---|---|---|---|
| • first<br>첫 번째 | • first of all<br>무엇보다도, 우선 | • to begin with<br>우선, 먼저 | • the first step<br>첫 번째 단계 | |
| • second<br>두 번째 | • next<br>그 다음에는 | • then<br>그러고 나서, 그 당시에는 | • later<br>그 후에 | • after(that)<br>그런 다음에 |
| • finally<br>마지막으로 | | • lastly<br>마지막으로 | • the last step<br>마지막 단계 | |
| • ago<br>전에 | | • before<br>전에 | • meanwhile<br>그러는 동안에 | |
| • in the meantime<br>그러는 동안에 | | • soon<br>곧 | • one day<br>(과거의) 어느 날 | |

• chronological order(연대순): in 2022 … two years later … in 2024

## 연습문제

### EX 1  시간 순서의 Signal 찾기

Albert Einstein was born in 1879 in Ulm, Germany. He graduated from the University of Zurich in Switzerland at the age of 26. In 1905 he also did some of his most important research in physics. Sixteen years later he won the Nobel Prize for physics. Between 1924 and 1933 he lived in Germany. In the meantime he traveled a lot to discuss other scientists. Then he had to leave Germany because of Hitler and the Nazi party. Soon he emigrated to the United States. Later, he lived in Princeton, New Jersey. He passed away April 18, 1955.

## 연습해설

### EX 1

시간 순서의 시작점

Albert Einstein was born in 1879 in Ulm, Germany. He graduated from the University of Zurich in Switzerland at the age of 26. In 1905 he also did some of his most important research in physics. Sixteen years later he won the Nobel Prize for physics. Between 1924 and 1933 he lived in Germany. In the meantime he traveled a lot to discuss other scientists. Then he had to leave Germany because of Hitler and the Nazi party. Soon he emigrated to the United States. Later, he lived in Princeton, New Jersey. He passed away April 18, 1955.

**해석** Albert Einstein는 1879년에 독일 Ulm에서 태어났다. 그는 26세의 나이에 스위스에 있는 취리히 대학을 졸업했다. 1905년에 그는 또한 물리학에서 몇몇 중요한 연구를 했다. 16년 후에 그는 물리학에서 노벨상을 탔다. 1924년에서 1933년에 그는 독일에서 살았다. 그러는 동안에 그는 다른 과학자들과 토론을 위해 여행을 했다. 그러고 나서 그는 히틀러와 나치당 때문에 독일을 떠났다. 곧 그는 미국으로 이민을 갔다. 그 후에 그는 뉴저지에 있는 프린스톤에서 살았다. 그는 1955 4월 18일에 죽었다.

**어휘** physics 물리학  emigrate 이민가다  pass away 죽다, 돌아가시다

**정답**

in 1879 / at the age of 26 / In 1905 / Sixteen years later / Between 1924 and 1933 / in the meantime / Then / Soon / Later / April 18, 1955

### 연습문제

**EX 2** 시간 순서의 Signal 찾기

It is not difficult to make a good cup of tea. Just the following steps. First of all, boil some water. Next put some hot water in the tea pot to warm it. After that, pour the water out of the pot and then put some tea leaves in it. You may add one teaspoon of tea leaves for each cup of tea if you want. Later, pour the boiling water into the tea pot. Finally, cover the pot and wait for a few minutes. Now are you ready to drink a nice cup of tea?

## 연습해설

### EX 2

It is not difficult to make a good cup of tea. Just the following steps. First of all, boil some water. Next put some hot water in the tea pot to warm it. After that, pour the water out of the pot and then put some tea leaves in it. You may add one teaspoon of tea leaves for each cup of tea if you want. Later, pour the boiling water into the tea pot. Finally, cover the pot and wait for a few minutes. Now are you ready to drink a nice cup of tea?

*시간 순서의 시작점*

**해석** 좋은 차 한 잔을 만드는 것은 어렵지 않다. 단순히 다음과 같은 과정을 따르면 된다. 우선, 약간의 물을 끓여라. 그 다음 차 주전자를 데우기 위해서 뜨거운 물을 주전자에 부어라. 그리고 나서 찻잎을 주전자에 넣어라. 원한다면 당신은 각각의 찻잔에 찻잎 한 숟가락씩을 추가해도 좋다. 그 다음 끓는 물을 차 주전자에 부어라. 마지막으로 차 주전자의 뚜껑을 덮고 몇 분간 기다려라. 자 이제 당신은 멋진 차 한 잔을 마실 준비가 되었는가?

**어휘** boil 끓다, 끓이다   pour (쏟아) 붓다, 퍼 붓다   leaf 나뭇잎 *leaves 나뭇잎들

**정답**
First of all / Next /
After that / and then /
Later / Finally / Now

## 실전문제

**01** 다음 주어진 글 다음에 이어질 글의 순서로 가장 적절한 것은?

> The practice of capital punishment is as old as government itself. For most of history, it has not been considered controversial.

> (A) However, in the mid-18th century, social commentators in Europe began to emphasize the worth of the individual and to criticize government practices they considered unjust, including capital punishment.
>
> (B) The controversy and debate over whether governments should utilize the death penalty continue today. We will continue to trace the history of these controversies.
>
> (C) Since ancient times most governments have punished a wide variety of crimes by death and have conducted executions as a routine part of the administration of criminal law.

① (A) − (C) − (B)
② (B) − (A) − (C)
③ (C) − (A) − (B)
④ (C) − (B) − (A)

## 실전 해설

**01**

The practice of capital punishment is as old as government itself. For most of history, it has not been considered controversial.

(A) However, in the mid-18th century, social commentators in Europe began to emphasize the worth of the individual and to criticize government practices they considered unjust, including capital punishment.
　　↑ 시간 순서의 중간 시점

(B) The controversy and debate over whether governments should utilize the death penalty continue today. We will continue to trace the history of these controversies.
　　↳ 시간 순서의 마지막 시점

　　↑ 시간 순서의 시작점
(C) Since ancient times most governments have punished a wide variety of crimes by death and have conducted executions as a routine part of the administration of criminal law.

**해석** 사형의 관행은 통치 그 자체만큼 오래 되었다. 역사적으로 대부분의 시기 동안 그것은 논쟁거리로 여겨지지지 않았다.
(C) 고대부터 대부분의 정부들이 죽음으로 여러 종류의 범죄를 처벌해 왔고, 형법을 집행하는 관행의 일부로 사형 집행을 행해왔다.
(A) 그러나 18세기 중반, 유럽의 사회 비평가들이 개인의 가치를 강조하며, 사형을 포함한, 자신들이 옳지 않다고 생각하는 정부의 여러 관행들을 비판하기 시작했다.
(B) 정부가 사형 제도를 사용해야 하는지에 대한 논쟁과 토론은 오늘날에도 계속된다. 우리는 이 논쟁의 역사를 계속해서 추적할 것이다.

**어휘** practice 관행, 관습　capital punishment 사형 제도　controversial 논란이 되는
commentator 비평가　emphasize 강조하다　criticize 비판하다　unjust 공정하지[옳지] 않은
controversy 논란　debate 논쟁(하다)　trace 추적하다　conduct 행하다, 실행하다
execution ① 실행, 집행 ② 사형집행　administration 행정부

**해설** 시간 순서 전개방식을 이용해야 한다. 주어진 문장에 역사성을 언급하고 있고 (C)에 ancient가 있으므로 시간 순서상 제일 먼저 시작되어야 하고 (A)에 mid-18th century 그리고 (B)에 today가 있으므로 주어진 문장 다음 글의 순서로 가장 적절한 것은 ③ (C) − (A) − (B)이다.

**정답**
01 ③

## 실전문제

**02** 글의 흐름으로 보아, 주어진 문장이 들어가기에 가장 적절한 것은?

> However, that was too much for the young system to absorb, and the computer crashed, killing the connection after all.

In 1969, Charley Kline was working as a programmer at UCLA and participating in a project at Stanford University. He was asked to arrange the first computer-to-computer message through an ordinary telephone line. ( ① ) After successfully connecting the two computers, Kline began to type *login*. ( ② ) He typed *l* and got the echo from Stanford confirming that the letter had been received. ( ③ ) He proceeded with *o* and again received the appropriate echo. Then he ventured to *g*. ( ④ ) The connection was quickly reestablished, and after the UCLA and Stanford nodes were firmly in place, many others joined in.

## 실전 해설

**02**

However, that was too much for the young system to absorb, and the computer crashed, killing the connection after all.

> 시간 순서의 시작점
> In 1969, Charley Kline was working as a programmer at UCLA and participating in a project at Stanford University. He was asked to arrange the first computer-to-computer message through an ordinary telephone line. ( ① ) After successfully connecting the two computers, Kline began to type *login*. ( ② ) He typed *l* and got the echo from Stanford confirming that the letter had been received. ( ③ ) He proceeded with *o* and again received the appropriate echo. Then he ventured to *g*. ( ④ ) The connection was quickly reestablished, and after the UCLA and Stanford nodes were firmly in place, many others joined in.

※ 시간 순서의 흐름
1. 두 컴퓨터 연결
2. login 타이핑 시작
3. l 타이핑 함
4. o 타이핑 함
5. g 타이핑 함
6. 연결 끊김
7. 다시 연결

**해석** 1969년도에 Charley Kline은 UCLA에서 프로그래머로서 일하면서 Stanford 대학에서 한 프로젝트에 참여하고 있었다. 그는 일반 전화선을 통해 최초의 컴퓨터와 컴퓨터 간 메시지를 전달하라는 요구를 받았다. 성공적으로 두 컴퓨터를 연결한 후, Kline은 'login'이라는 단어를 치기 시작했다. 그는 'l'을 치고 Stanford로부터 그 문자가 수신되었다고 확인해 주는 응답을 받았다. 그는 'o'를 이어서 쳤고 다시 적절한 응답을 받았다. 그런 후 그는 'g'에 도전했다. 그러나 이 새로운 시스템이 받아들이기에 그것은 너무 많은 양이었고 컴퓨터가 기능을 멈추어 연결이 완전히 끊어져버렸다. 연결은 속히 복구되었으며, UCLA와 Stanford의 연결이 확고히 제자리를 잡게 되자 다른 대학들도 동참하였다.

**어휘** absorb ① 흡수하다 ② 몰두하다  crash 충돌하다(= collide)
participate in ~ 에 참여하다(= take part in ~)
arrange ① 처리하다, 다루다 ② 정리하다, 정돈하다 ③ 배열[배치] 하다
ordinary 보통의, 일반적인  confirm 확인하다
appropriate 적당한, 적절한(= suitable, adequate)
reestablish 다시 세우다[설립하다]  *establish 세우다, 설립하다
node ① 마디 ② (연결망의) 교점, 접점, 연결  firmly 견고하게, 단호하게

**해설** ④ 뒤에서 논리의 공백이 생겼다. ②, ③, ④에서 각각 한 글자씩 타이핑하고 그 응답을 기다렸는데 갑자기 ④ 뒤에 연결이 다시 이루어졌다는 내용이 나올 수 없으므로 주어진 제시문은 ④에 들어가는 것이 가장 적절하다.

**정답**
02 ④

## 실전문제

**03** 다음 글의 제목으로 가장 적절한 것은?

In the spring of 2015, a team of scientists decided to prepare for a large-scale reforestation project in the northern highlands. The experts in the field first collected thousands of seeds from native tree species and carefully sorted them according to region and altitude. Each batch was cleaned and treated to prevent fungal diseases that could threaten the seedlings. And then, the planting process began in early summer, when soil temperatures had risen enough to support root growth. They were placed in cold storage until the weather conditions were right for planting. After that, Volunteers hiked for hours carrying boxes of saplings and placed each one by hand into pre-dug holes. By the end of the season, over 50,000 new trees had taken root, marking a major success in ecosystem restoration.

*batch : 묶음 **sapling : 묘목

① The Plans of Large-Scale Reforestation
② The Efforts of Broad Reforestation Success
③ The Process of Extensive Reforestation Project
④ The Steps of Selecting and Classifying Saplings

## 실전 해설

**03**

In the spring of 2015, a team of scientists decided to prepare for a large-scale reforestation project in the northern highlands. The experts in the field first collected thousands of seeds from native tree species and carefully sorted them according to region and altitude. Each batch was cleaned and treated to prevent fungal diseases that could threaten the seedlings. And then, the planting process began in early summer, when soil temperatures had risen enough to support root growth. They were placed in cold storage until the weather conditions were right for planting. After that, Volunteers hiked for hours carrying boxes of saplings and placed each one by hand into pre-dug holes. By the end of the season, over 50,000 new trees had taken root, marking a major success in ecosystem restoration.

*batch : 묶음 **sapling : 묘목

**해석** 2015년 봄, 과학자들로 이루어진 한 팀이 북부 고지대에서 대규모 산림복원 프로젝트를 준비하기로 결정했다. 그 분야의 전문가들은 먼저, 자생 나무 종에서 수천 개의 씨앗을 채취하고, 지역과 고도에 따라 조심스럽게 분류했다. 각 묶음은 곰팡이 질병을 막기 위해 세척되고 처리되었다. 그러고 나서 그것들은 날씨 조건이 심기에 적합해질 때까지 냉장 보관되었다. 그런 다음 자원봉사자들은 상자에 담긴 묘목을 들고 수 시간 동안 산길을 걸어 올라가, 미리 파 놓은 구덩이에 하나하나 직접 심었다. 그 해가 끝날 무렵, 5만 그루가 넘는 새 나무들이 뿌리를 내렸고, 생태계 복원의 큰 성공을 알렸다.

① 대규모 산림복원의 계획들
② 광범위한 산림복원 성공의 노력들
③ 광범위한 산림복원 프로젝트의 과정
④ 묘목을 선별하고 분류하는 단계들

**어휘** prepare 준비하다 reforestation 산림 복원 sort 분류하다 according to ~에 따라 region 지역 altitude 고도 clean 세척하다 treat 처리하다 prevent 예방하다 fungal 곰팡이의 disease 질병 threaten 위협하다 seedling 묘목 place 두다, 놓다 storage 저장 right 적절한 plant 심다 process 과정 soil 토양 hike 도보 여행하다 dig 파다 hole 구멍 mark 표시하다 major 주요한 restoration 복원

**해설** 시간순서 전개방식을 이용해야 한다. 주어진 지문은 산림복원 프로젝트 준비에 대한 과정, 절차를 소개하는 내용의 글이므로 이 글의 제목으로 가장 적절한 것은 ③ '광범위한 산림복원 프로젝트의 과정'이다.

03 ③

## 실전문제

**04** 글의 흐름으로 보아, 주어진 문장이 들어가기에 가장 적절한 것은?

> From there they were taken to Arizona and were reassembled by workers in the Arizona desert.

In the early 1960s, London Bridge was in trouble. Cars, trucks, and buses were too heavy for it, and the bridge was sinking into the Thames river. London city officials wanted to build a new bridge, and a businessman named Robert McCulloch decided to buy the old bridge and move it to Arizona. ( ① ) Workers took apart the bridge in 1968, numbering the bricks, and sent them to Los Angeles. ( ② ) The bridge was finally got done in 1971. ( ③ ) However, McCulloch knew he needed more than a famous bridge to lure people to Lake Havasu City, so he created an English village with typical English shops and restaurants. ( ④ ) Today, London Bridge is one of Arizona's biggest attractions.

## 실전 해설

**04**

From there they were taken to Arizona and were reassembled by workers in the Arizona desert.

┌─ 시간 순서의 시작점
In the early 1960s, London Bridge was in trouble. Cars, trucks, and buses were too heavy for it, and the bridge was sinking into the Thames river. London city officials wanted to build a new bridge, and a businessman named Robert McCulloch decided to buy the old bridge and move it to Arizona. ( ① ) Workers took apart the bridge in 1968, numbering the bricks, and sent them to Los Angeles. ( ② ) The bridge was finally got done in 1971. ( ③ ) However, McCulloch knew he needed more than a famous bridge to lure people to Lake Havasu City, so he created an English village with typical English shops and restaurants. ( ④ ) Today, London Bridge is one of Arizona's biggest attractions.

※ 시간 순서의 흐름
1. 1968년 다시 해체
2. 재조립
3. 완성
4. 영국식 마을 형성
5. 오늘날 관광명소가 됨

**해석** 1960년대 초에 London Bridge는 곤경에 처해 있었다. 자동차, 트럭, 그리고 버스가 지나치게 많이 다녀서 그 다리는 템스강 속으로 가라앉고 있었다. 런던의 시공무원들이 새로운 다리의 건설을 원하자, Robert McCulloch라는 이름의 사업가는 그 낡은 다리를 사들여서 그것을 애리조나로 옮기기로 결정했다. 1968년에 작업인부들이 그 다리를 분해하여 벽돌마다 번호를 매긴 후 그 벽돌들을 로스앤젤레스로 보냈다. 그곳으로부터 그 벽돌들은 애리조나로 옮겨졌고 애리조나의 사막에서 작업인부들에 의해 재조립되었다. 그 다리는 마침내 1971년에 완성되었다. 그러나 McCulloch는 Lake Havasu City로 사람들을 유혹하기 위해서는 유명한 다리 이상의 것이 필요하다는 것을 알고, 전형적인 영국의 상점과 식당이 있는 영국식 마을을 만들어냈다. 오늘날 London Bridge는 애리조나의 최고의 명소 중 하나이다.

**어휘** in trouble 곤경에 처한   sink 가라앉다, 침몰시키다   take apart 분해하다
number 숫자를 적다, 수를 세다   brick 벽돌   get done 끝내다, 마치다   lure 유혹하다, 매혹하다
reassemble 재조립하다   *assemble 조립하다   typical 전형적인   attraction 인기거리, 명소

**해설** 시간 순서 전개 방식이므로 다리를 분해한 뒤 재조립하는 과정이 있어야 하고 dismantled 뒤에 reassembled가 이어져야 한다. 또한 재조립 후 완성된 것이므로 reassembled 다음에 got done이 이어져야 한다. 또한 주어진 문장의 there는 로스앤젤레스를 가리킨다. 이상을 종합할 때, 주어진 문장은 ②에 위치해야 함을 알 수 있다.

**정답**
04 ②

## 풀이 해법

### 3. 비교(Comparison) / 반대/대조(Contrast)의 전개 방식

비교(Comparison)의 Signal words

- (a)like ~처럼(같은)
- similar 비슷한
- both 둘 다(= the two A and B)
- similarly 마찬가지로(= likewise, in the same way)
- same 같은

## 연습문제

**EX 1** 비교의 Signal 찾기

There are some similarities between the food in India and one in China. First of all, in both countries, rice is a very important food. It is served at almost every meal in India and China. Both Indian and Chinese dish can be very spicy. Especially, India is famous for *Spicy curry* and China is noted as *Marasango*, Sacheon regional cooking. And also, India and China alike use many different kinds of vegetables. Finally, because India and China are very large countries with long histories, the two include many sorts of cooking style. In India and China, each part of the country has its own favorite kinds of food and way of cooking.

## 연습해설

### EX 1

There are some similarities between the food in India and one in China. First of all, in both countries, rice is a very important food. It is served at almost every meal in India and China. Both Indian and Chinese dish can be very spicy. Especially, India is famous for *Spicy curry* and China is noted as *Marasango*, Sacheon regional cooking. And also, India and China alike use many different kinds of vegetables. Finally, because India and China are very large countries with long histories, the two include many sorts of cooking style. In India and China, each part of the country has its own favorite kinds of food and way of cooking.

**해석** 인도와 중국 음식 사이에는 몇몇 유사점이 있다. 무엇보다도 두 나라에서는 쌀이 중요한 음식이다. 쌀은 인도와 중국의 거의 모든 식사에 제공된다. 인도와 중국 요리 둘 다 아주 매울 수 있다. 특히, 인도는 <매운 카레>로 유명하고 중국은 사천지역 요리인 <마라상궈>로 주목받는다. 그리고 또한 두 나라 모두 많은 종류의 야채를 사용한다. 마지막으로 두 나라는 오랜 역사와 넓은 땅을 가진 나라이기에 다양한 종류의 요리 방법이 있다. 인도와 중국에서는 각 지역마다 좋아하는 요리의 종류와 요리법이 있다.

**어휘** similarity 유사점  serve 제공하다  dish 요리  spicy 매운, 양념된  note 주목하다  regional 지역의  sort 종류

**정답**
similarities / both / and / both / and / alike / and / the two / and

### 풀이 해법

**반대/대조(Contrast)의 Signal words**

- but 그러나
- however 그러나(= though, still)
- in contrast 대조적으로(= against that)
- unlike ~와 달리
- more(less) than 비교급
- past / present (today) 과거 / 현재
- the former / the latter 전자 / 후자
- some / other (s) 몇몇 / 나머지는
- nevertheless 그럼에도 불구하고(= nonetheless, even so)
- (and) yet 그렇지만
- then 그러나
- conversely 반대로, 거꾸로(= on the contrary)
- different (from) 다른
- while 반면에(= whereas, on the other hand)
- formerly (= previously) / now 이전에는 / 지금
- one / the other 하나 / 나머지 하나
- fortunately / unfortunately 운 좋게도 / 불행히도
- (al)though, even though, even if, however (no matter how), despite 비록 ~일지라도

### 연습문제

**EX 2** 반대/대조의 Signal 찾기

The University of Bologna in northern Italy is different from most North American universities. One important difference is its age. Founded in the tenth century, it is the oldest university in Europe. Its ancient halls give students a strong sense of history. This is in sharp contrast to the usual attitude of American students who study in newer surroundings. The University of Bologna is different, as well, because of its location. While North American universities are often located outside the city center, Bologna's campus is in the heart of the city. Unlike the American university campus, there are no trees or open spaces near this old Italian institution. Instead, students meet on the streets, in cafes, and in the courtyards of the historic buildings.

## 연습해설

### EX 2

The University of Bologna in northern Italy is **different** from most North American universities. One important **difference** is its age. Founded in the tenth century, it is the oldest university in Europe. Its ancient halls give students a strong sense of history. This is in sharp **contrast** to the usual attitude of American students who study in newer surroundings. The University of Bologna is **different**, as well, because of its location. **While** North American universities are often located outside the city center, Bologna's campus is in the heart of the city. **Unlike** the American university campus, there are no trees or open spaces near this old Italian institution. **Instead**, students meet on the streets, in cafes, and in the courtyards of the historic buildings.

**해석** 이탈리아 북부에 있는 볼로냐 대학은 북미의 대학들과는 다르다. 한 가지 중요한 차이는 그것의 나이이다. 10세기에 설립된 볼로냐 대학은 유럽에서 가장 오래 되었다. 그 대학의 오래된 홀들은 학생들에게 역사의 강한 느낌을 준다. 이것은 좀 더 새로운 주위 환경 속에서 공부하는 미국 학생들의 보통의 태도와 뚜렷이 대조가 된다. 또한 볼로냐 대학은 위치 때문에 다르다. 북미 대학들이 종종 도시 중심부 외곽에 위치해 있는 반면에, 볼로냐의 부지는 도시 중심부에 위치하고 있다. 미국 대학 부지와는 달리 이 오래된 이탈리아 학교 근처에는 나무도 없고, 넓은 공간도 없다. 대신 학생들은 거리에서, 카페에서, 그리고 역사적 건물의 안뜰에서 만난다.

**어휘** be different from ~와 다르다　found 설립하다　sharp 뚜렷한, 선명한　attitude 자세, 태도　surroundings 주변(의 상황), 환경　as well 뿐만 아니라　courtyard (건물이나 담으로 둘러싸인) 안뜰　historic 역사적인

**정답**
different / difference / contrast / different / While / Unlike / Instead

## 실전문제

**01** 글의 흐름으로 보아, 주어진 문장이 들어가기에 가장 적절한 것은?

Likewise, a tiny crack in a dam's structure can eventually bring down the entire wall.

Human-made structures sometimes fail when exposed to even small amounts of repeated stress over time. ( ① ) A hairline fracture in the wing of a flying craft, if left undetected during a routine maintenance inspection, can ultimately result in catastrophic structural failure during flight. ( ② ) Nature has evolved built-in mechanisms that help absorb, redistribute, and neutralize pressure across the entire system, though. ( ③ ) Coral reefs in tropical oceans, for instance, can recover from partial damage caused by severe storms, rising temperatures, or predatory fish species. ( ④ ) Over time and with favorable environmental conditions, the damaged sections gradually regenerate, and the overall ecological system continues to thrive and expand.

\*catastrophic : 치명적인

## 실전 해설

**01**

> Likewise, a tiny crack in a dam's structure can eventually bring down the entire wall.

Human-made structures sometimes fail when exposed to even small amounts of repeated stress over time. ( ① ) A hairline fracture in the wing of a flying craft, if left undetected during a routine maintenance inspection, can ultimately result in catastrophic structural failure during flight. ( ② ) Nature has evolved built-in mechanisms that help absorb, redistribute, and neutralize pressure across the entire system, though. ( ③ ) Coral reefs in tropical oceans, for instance, can recover from partial damage caused by severe storms, rising temperatures, or predatory fish species. ( ④ ) Over time and with favorable environmental conditions, the damaged sections gradually regenerate, and the overall ecological system continues to thrive and expand.

\*catastrophic : 치명적인

**해석** 인간이 만든 구조물은 시간이 지나면서 반복되는 소량의 스트레스에도 쉽게 무너질 수 있다. 비행 중 점검되지 않은 상태로 남겨진 비행 기체의 날개에 있는 아주 미세한 균열은 결국 치명적인 구조적 고장으로 이어질 수 있다. 마찬가지로, 댐 구조에 생긴 아주 작은 균열도 결국 전체 벽을 무너뜨릴 수 있다. 하지만 자연은 전체 시스템에 걸쳐 압력을 흡수하고 재분산시키며 중화하는 내재적 메커니즘을 진화시켜왔다. 예를 들어, 열대 바다의 산호초는 강력한 폭풍, 상승하는 수온, 혹은 포식성 어류들로 인한 부분적인 피해로부터 회복할 수 있다. 시간이 흐르고 환경 조건이 좋아지면 손상된 부분은 서서히 재생되며 전체 생태계는 계속해서 번성하고 확장된다.

**어휘** structure 구조물  expose 노출시키다  amount 양  repeated 반복되는  hairline 아주 가는  fracture 균열  wing 날개  craft 기체  leave 남기다  undetected 감지되지 않은  routine 일상적인  maintenance 정비  inspection 점검  ultimately 결국  structural 구조적인  failure 고장, 실패  likewise 마찬가지로  tiny 매우 작은  crack 균열  eventually 결국  bring down 무너뜨리다  entire 전체의  contrast 대조하다  evolve 진화하다  absorb 흡수하다  redistribute 재분산시키다, 재분배하다  neutralize 중화하다  pressure 압력  across ~전체에 걸쳐  coral 산호  reef 암초  \*coral reef 산호초  tropical 열대의  partial 부분적인  damage 손상  cause 초래하다  severe 심한  predatory 포식성의  favorable 유리한  gradually 점차  regenerate 재생하다  overall 전체의, 전반적인  ecological 생태학적  thrive 번성하다  expand 확장하다

**해설** 주어진 문장의 Likewise를 기준으로 비교대상 (서로 다른 소재) [비교대상: a tiny crack in a dam's structure vs. A hairline fracture in an airplane wing]에 대한 유사점(작은 균열에도 전체가 망가짐)을 설명하고 있으므로 주어진 문장이 들어가기에 가장 적절한 곳은 ②이다.

**정답**
01 ②

## 실전문제

**02** 다음 빈칸에 들어갈 말로 가장 적절한 것은?

> Why do some ice cubes come out cloudy and others come out clear? Dr. John Hallet, of the Atmospheric Ice Laboratory of the Desert Research Institute in Reno, Nevada, states that the key factor in cloud formations is the temperature of the freezer. When ice forms slowly, it tends to freeze first at one edge. Air bubbles or water residuals found in a solution in the water have time to _____. As a result, ice cubers become transparent. However, when water freezes rapidly, freezing starts at more than one end, and water residuals are trapped in the middle of the cube, preventing bubble loss. Consequently, the trapped bubbles make the cube appear cloudy. After all, the clouds in ice cubes are the result of air bubbles formed as ice is freezing.
>
> *residual : 잔류물, 나머지

① get stuck
② rise and escape
③ grow and increase
④ move into the middle of the cube

## 실전 해설

**02**

Why do some ice cubes come out cloudy and others come out clear? Dr. John Hallet, of the Atmospheric Ice Laboratory of the Desert Research Institute in Reno, Nevada, states that the key factor in cloud formations is the temperature of the freezer. When ice forms slowly, it tends to freeze first at one edge. Air bubbles or water residuals found in a solution in the water have time to _____.

*However를 기준으로 반대/대조의 논리가 필요하다.*

As a result, ice cubers become transparent. However, when water freezes rapidly, freezing starts at more than one end, and water residuals are trapped in the middle of the cube, preventing bubble loss. Consequently, the trapped bubbles make the cube appear cloudy. After all, the clouds in ice cubes are the result of air bubbles formed as ice is freezing.

\* residual 잔류물, 나머지

**해석** 왜 어떤 얼음덩이는 탁하게 나오고 또 어떤 것들은 맑게 나오는가? 네바다 주 Reno에 있는 사막 연구소 대기 얼음 실험실의 John Hallet 박사는 탁한 형성물의 핵심 요소는 '냉동고'의 온도라고 말한다. 천천히 형성될 때는 얼음은 한쪽 가장자리부터 먼저 어는 경향이 있다. (얼음으로 형성되어 가는) 물속의 용액에서 발견되는 공기 방울이나 물의 잔류물은 상승하여 탈출할 시간이 있다. 그 결과, 얼음덩이는 투명해진다. 하지만, 물이 빠르게 얼 때 냉동은 한쪽 끝보다 더 많은 곳에서 시작하고, 물의 잔류물은 (얼음)덩이 가운데 갇혀, 공기 방울의 소실을 막는다. 결과적으로, 갇힌 공기 방울은 얼음덩이가 탁해 보이게 한다. 결국, 얼음덩이의 탁한 부분은 얼음이 얼 때 형성되는 공기 방울의 결과이다.

① 움직일 수 없게 될
② 상승하여 탈출할
③ 성장하고 증가할
④ 얼음덩이 가운데로 이동할

**어휘** ice cube 얼음덩이  cloudy 탁한; 흐린  laboratory 실험실  formation 형성물, 구조물  edge 가장자리  bubble 방울  solution 용액  rapidly 빠르게  trap 가두다  loss 소실, 상실  stuck 움직일 수 없는, 고정된  escape 탈출하다

**해설** Hoverer를 기준으로 얼음이 빠르게 얼 때에는 물의 잔여물이 얼음덩이 속에 갇혀 탁해 보인다는 내용과는 대조적으로 공기 방울이나 물의 잔여물이 얼음덩이 속에 남지 않아야 얼음덩이가 투명하게 보일 수 있다고 했으므로, 빈칸에 들어갈 말로 가장 적절한 것은 ② '상승하여 탈출할'이다.

**정답**
02 ②

## 실전문제

**03** 다음 글의 흐름으로 보아, 주어진 문장이 들어가기에 가장 적절한 곳은?

There is no single philosophical method that all philosophers share. In fact, philosophers have long disagreed so deeply about the best or proper way to do philosophy that sometimes they even claim that their own particular philosophical method produces the only real philosophy; the rest is either worthless or belongs to some other discipline. Contemporary philosophers of many kinds (traditional, postmodern, feminist, and others) debate what on earth kind of philosophy is worth doing best. Similarly, neither do all feminists in general nor feminist philosophers in particular _____. Although consciousness raising is extremely valuable for feminists (even sometimes considered to be the core of feminist method), it is rarely used alone in feminist scholarship. Instead, it is combined with numerous disciplinary approaches. In addition, feminist philosophers have various methodological preferences within philosophical traditions.

① have various viewpoints
② agree on a single method
③ pursue diverse areas of interest
④ expand ways of thinking widely

## 실전 해설

03
There is no single philosophical method that all philosophers share. In fact, philosophers have long disagreed so deeply about the best or proper way to do philosophy that sometimes they even claim that their own particular philosophical method produces the only real philosophy; the rest is either worthless or belongs to some other discipline. Contemporary philosophers of many kinds (traditional, postmodern, feminist, and others) debate what on earth kind of philosophy is worth doing best. Similarly, neither do all feminists in general nor feminist philosophers in particular _____. Although consciousness raising is extremely valuable for feminists (even sometimes considered to be the core of feminist method), it is rarely used alone in feminist scholarship. Instead, it is combined with numerous disciplinary approaches. In addition, feminist philosophers have various methodological preferences within philosophical traditions.

**해석** 모든 철학자가 공유하는 하나의 철학적 방법론은 없다. 사실, 철학자들은 철학을 하는 가장 좋은 또는 올바른 방법에 관해 오랫동안 매우 극심하게 뜻이 맞지 않아서 가끔은 심지어 그들 자신의 특정한 철학적 방법론이 유일한 '진짜 철학'을 낳으며, 나머지는 가치 없거나, 다른 어떤 학문 분야에 속한다고 주장하기도 한다. 많은 종류(전통, 포스트모던, 페미니스트 등)의 현대 철학자들은 도대체 어떤 종류의 철학이 가장 할 가치가 있는지를 논쟁한다. 마찬가지로, 대개의 경우 모든 페미니스트나 특별히 페미니스트 철학자들은 <u>한 가지 방법에만 합의하지</u> 않는다. 비록 페미니스트에게는 의식 고양이 매우 유용하지만(심지어 때로는 페미니스트 방법론의 핵심으로 여겨지기도 함), 그것이 페미니스트 학문에서 단독으로 사용되는 경우는 거의 없다. 그 대신에, 그것은 다수의 학문적 방법과 결합된다. 게다가, 페미니스트 철학자들은 철학적 전통 내에서 방법론적인 선호가 각양각색이다.

① 다양한 견해를 갖지
② 한 가지 방법에만 합의하지
③ 다양한 관심 분야를 추구하지
④ 사고방식을 폭 넓게 확장시키지

**어휘** philosophical 철학적인  worthless 무가치한  discipline ① 규율 ② 훈련 ③ 분야  contemporary ① 동시대의 ② 현대적인  on earth 도대체  in general 일반적으로, 대체로, 대개  consciousness 의식, 자각  in particular 특별히, 특별하게  extremely 극도로  core 핵심  scholarship ① 장학금 ② 학문  combine 섞다  numerous 무수히 많은  disciplinary 학문적인  methodological 방법론적인  preference 선호(도)

**해설** 빈칸 앞에 Similarly를 기준으로 비교대상(서로 다른 소재)[비교대상: contemporary philosophers vs. feminists or feminist philosophers]에 대한 유사점[어떤 종류의 철학이 가장 좋을까에 대한 토론 vs. 한 가지 방법에만 동의하지 않음]을 파악해야 하므로 빈칸에 들어가기에 가장 적절한 것은 ② '한 가지 방법에만 합의하지'이다.

**정답**
03 ②

## 실전문제

**04** 다음 빈칸에 들어갈 말로 가장 적절한 것을 고르시오.

> In recent years, the world has made tremendous advances in fields ranging from biology to information technology, especially artificial intelligence, and yet _____. Thus, our goal is to help apply science and technology to the problems of the neediest people. Too often, the poorest communities are left out of the conversation when new technologies are developed. This gap between innovation and accessibility has only widened the inequality across nations and within societies. To address this, we must rethink how science is shared and implemented across different socioeconomic settings. Collaborating with local communities, understanding their needs, and designing solutions accordingly are crucial steps. Only then can scientific progress truly serve as a tool for global equity and human dignity.

① it keeps everyone from benefiting these innovations
② advantages from the progress have been enjoyed by all people
③ there no longer remain demerits to be made in the near future
④ deprived people have been the primary beneficiaries of developments

## 실전 해설

**04**

In recent years, the world has made tremendous advances in fields ranging from biology to information technology, especially artificial intelligence, and yet _____. Thus, our goal is to help apply science and technology to the problems of the neediest people. Too often, the poorest communities are left out of the conversation when new technologies are developed. This gap between innovation and accessibility has only widened the inequality across nations and within societies. To address this, we must rethink how science is shared and implemented across different socioeconomic settings. Collaborating with local communities, understanding their needs, and designing solutions accordingly are crucial steps. Only then can scientific progress truly serve as a tool for global equity and human dignity.

**해석** 최근 몇 년 동안, 세계는 생물학에서 정보 기술, 특히 인공지능에 이르는 분야에서 거대한 진보를 이루었다. 그러나 아직 <u>모든 사람들이 이러한 혁신으로부터 혜택을 받고 있는 것을 막는다</u>. 따라서 우리의 목표는 과학과 기술을 가장 어려운 사람들의 문제에 적용하도록 도움을 주는 것이다. 신기술이 개발될 때, 가장 가난한 공동체는 종종 논의에서 배제되곤 한다. 이러한 혁신과 접근성 사이의 간극은 국가 간은 물론 사회 내부의 불평등을 더욱 심화시켜 왔다. 이를 해결하기 위해서는 과학이 다양한 사회경제적 환경에 어떻게 공유되고 적용되는지를 다시 고민해야 한다. 지역 공동체와 협력하고, 그들의 필요를 이해하며, 그에 맞는 해결책을 설계하는 것이 필수적인 과정이다. 그래야만 과학적 진보가 진정으로 전 세계적인 평등과 인간 존엄을 위한 도구가 될 수 있다.

① 모든 사람들이 이러한 혁신으로부터 혜택을 받고 있는 것을 막는다
② 진보로부터의 이점을 모든 이가 즐길 수 있다
③ 가까운 미래에 만들어질 더 이상의 단점은 없다
④ 궁핍한 사람들이 발전의 최고의 수혜자이다

**어휘** tremendous 엄청난, 대단한, 거대한  field 들, 밭; 분야  range from A to B A에서 B에 이르다  apply 적용(응용)하다  deprive 빼앗다  beneficiary 수혜자  no longer 더 이상 ~않다  demerit 단점, 약점  innovation 개혁, 혁신  leave out 생략하다, 빠뜨리다  accessibility 접근성  widen 넓히다  inequality 불평등  across 전반에 걸쳐  address 해결하다  implement 실행하다  collaborate 협력하다  accordingly 따라서  crucial 중요한, 결정적인  progress 진보, 발전  serve as ~로서 역할을 하다  equity 공정, 평등  dignity 존엄(성)

**해설** 빈칸 앞에 and yet을 기준으로 반대/대조의 내용이 있어야 한다. 빈칸 앞에 advance(⊕)가 있으므로 빈칸 뒤에는 (⊖)가 있어야 한다. 따라서 정답은 ① '모든 사람들이 이러한 혁신으로부터 혜택을 받고 있는 것을 막는다'이다.

**정답**
04 ①

## 실전문제

**05** 다음 빈칸에 들어갈 말로 가장 적절한 것을 고르시오.

Periodically, one or another dance organization, to promote mutual understanding, will stage a choreographers-meet-the-critics symposium. At such gatherings someone always asks the critics whether, when they set out to review something, they bother to find out what the artist is trying to do, what his or her intention is. I take this to be a very naive question, and very demeaning to choreographers, as if their work were so obscure and incomplete that it needed to carry a statement of intent. Worse, it implies that the truth of a dance _____; the real event is the intellectual process that supposedly underlies it. But the truths of dance are not on the other side. They are in the very bones of the dance, which our bones know how to read, if we let them.

\* choreographer : 안무가

① is not on the other side in itself
② is difficult for critics themselves to find
③ lies somewhere other than in the dance
④ must not be in itself real but intellectual

## 실전 해설

**05**

Periodically, one or another dance organization, to promote mutual understanding, will stage a choreographers-meet-the-critics symposium. At such gatherings someone always asks the critics whether, when they set out to review something, they bother to find out what the artist is trying to do, what his or her intention is. I take this to be a very naive question, and very demeaning to choreographers, as if their work were so obscure and incomplete that it needed to carry a statement of intent. Worse, it implies that the truth of a dance _____; the real event is the intellectual process that supposedly underlies it. But the truths of dance are not on the other side. They are in the very bones of the dance, which our bones know how to read, if we let them.

\* choreographer : 안무가

*But을 기준으로 반대/대조의 내용이 빈칸에 있어야 한다.*

**해석** 정기적으로 이런저런 무용 기관들은 안무가와 비평가의 상호 이해를 증진시키기 위해 두 집단이 만나는 심포지엄을 개최한다. 그러한 모임에서 항상 어떤 사람들은 비평가들에게 어떤 작품의 비평을 시작할 때 예술가가 하려는 것이 무엇인지, 그 예술가의 의도가 무엇인지 찾아내려고 애쓰는지 물어 본다. 나는 이것이 마치 안무가의 작품이 너무 모호하고 완성 되지 않아서 그 의도를 말로 꼭 설명해줄 필요가 있다는 것 같아서, 이 질문이 매우 어설프며 안무가에게는 매우 모욕적이라고 생각한다. 더군다나 춤의 진리는 <u>춤 이외의 다른 곳에 있고</u>, 진정한 이벤트는 춤 이면에 있는 지적 과정이라는 의미를 내포하고 있다. 그러나 춤의 진리는 다른 곳에 있지 않다. 춤의 진리는 춤의 바로 중심에 있으며, 우리의 본능을 그대로 놓아두면, 우리의 본능은 어떻게 그것을 읽어내는지 알고 있다.

① 본질적으로 다른 곳에 있지 않다
② 비평가 자신들이 찾기에는 어렵다
③ 춤 이외의 다른 곳에 있다
④ 본질적으로 사실적인 것이 아니라 지적이어야 한다

**어휘** periodically 정기적으로  promote 촉진하다, 승진시키다  mutual 상호간의, 서로의
stage 개최하다, 연출하다  choreographers-meet-the-critics 안무가와 비평가들이 만나는
\*choreographer 안무가  \*critic 비평가, 평론가  symposium 심포지엄, 학술토론회
gathering 모임  set out 시작하다, 착수하다  naive 순진한, 경험이 없는
demeaning 비하하는, 모욕적인  obscure 이해하기 힘든, 모호한  statement 진술, 언급
intent 의도  imply 암시하다, 의미하다  intellectual 지적인  supposedly 아마, 아마도
underlie ~의 아래에 있다, ~의 기초가 되다  bone 뼈, 본능  in itself 본질적으로
lie somewhere 어딘가에 있다

**해설** 반대/대조의 연결사 but을 이용하는 문제이다. But 다음 춤의 진실은 다른 곳에 있지 않다고 했으므로 빈칸에 들어가기에 가장 적절한 것은 ③ '춤 이외의 다른 곳에 있다'이다.

**정답**
05 ③

## 풀이 해법

4. 공간 순서(Spatial Order)의 전개 방식
1) 나열의 공간 개념

### 연습문제

**EX 1** 다음 글의 흐름으로 보아, 주어진 문장이 들어가기에 가장 적절한 곳은?

Vaccines have also significantly reduced the occurrence of a number of other diseases.

Some positive effects of vaccinations are simply undeniable because immunizations have eliminated altogether diseases that killed or severely disabled thousands every year. ( ① ) For example, vaccines have completely eliminated polio. ( ② ) They also exterminated smallpox, which 10 million people used to contract every year as late as the 1960s. ( ③ ) Measles used to infect about 4 million children per year, but in 1997, there were only 138 cases of measles in the United States. ( ④ ) In sum, the vast majority of healthcare professionals believe that the benefits of immunization far outnumber their few risks.

\* polio : 소아마비  \*\* smallpox : 천연두
\*\*\* measles : 홍역

## 연습해설

### EX 1

Vaccines have also significantly reduced the occurrence of a number of other diseases.

Some positive effects of vaccinations are simply undeniable because immunizations have eliminated altogether diseases that killed or severely disabled thousands every year. ( ① ) For example, vaccines have completely eliminated polio. ( ② ) They also exterminated smallpox, which 10 million people used to contract every year as late as the 1960s. ( ③ ) Measles used to infect about 4 million children per year, but in 1997, there were only 138 cases of measles in the United States. ( ④ ) In sum, the vast majority of healthcare professionals believe that the benefits of immunization far outnumber their few risks.

\* polio : 소아마비 \*\* smallpox : 천연두
\*\*\* measles : 홍역

**해석** 예방 주사는 해마다 수천 명을 죽이거나 심각하게 불구로 만들 수 있는 질병을 모두 없애 주었기 때문에 예방접종의 몇몇 긍정적 효과는 단순히 부인할 수 없다. 예를 들어서 백신은 완전히 소아마비를 제거시켰다. 백신은 또한 1960년대 약 천만 명이 걸렸던 천연두도 전멸시켰다. 백신은 또한 많은 다른 질병들의 발생을 상당히 감소시켰다. 홍역은 해마다 4백만 명의 아이들을 감염시키곤 했지만 1997년에는 미국에서 단지 138건만 있었다. 결론적으로 방대한 다수의 의료 전문가들은 예방 접종의 이점이 몇 가지 위험을 훨씬 더 능가할 수 있다고 믿는다.

**어휘** significantly 상당히, 현저하게  reduce 줄이다  occurrence 발생  a number of 많은
disease 질병  vaccination 예방접종  undeniable 부인[거부]할 수 없는  immunization 예방 주사
eliminate 없애다, 제거하다  severely 심각하게  exterminate 전멸시키다, 전멸하다
contract (병에) 걸리다  infect 감염시키다  in sum 요약해보면, 결론적으로  vast 거대한
majority 다수  outnumber ~보다 수가 많다, ~을 능가하다

**해설** 나열의 공간개념을 이용해야 한다(제시문의 also를 이용해야 한다). ①의 첫 번째 나열을 알리는 For example부터 시작해서 백신의 긍정적 요소들이 나열되고 있다. 그 첫 번째로 소아마비의 퇴치 그리고 두 번째로 천연두 퇴치가 나열되고 있으므로 주어진 문장은 ③에 들어가는 것이 가장 적절하다.

01 ③

## 풀이 해법

2) 반대/대조의 공간의 개념

### 연습문제

**EX 2** 밑줄 친 부분에 들어갈 말로 가장 적절한 것은? 2017. 하반기 지방직 9급

In a famous essay on Tolstoy, the liberal philosopher Sir Isaiah Berlin distinguished between two kinds of thinkers by harking back to an ancient saying attributed to the Greek lyric poet Archilochus (seventh century BC): "The fox knows many things, but the hedgehog knows one big thing." Hedgehogs have one central idea and see the world exclusively through the prism of that idea. They overlook complications and exceptions, or mold them to fit into their world view. There is one true answer that fits at all times and all circumstances. Foxes, for whom Berlin had greater sympathy, have a variegated take on the world, which keeps them from _____. They are skeptical of grand theories as they feel the world's complexity prevents generalizations. Berlin thought Dante was a hedgehog while Shakespeare was a fox.

① grasping the complications of the world
② articulating one big slogan
③ finding multiple solutions
④ behaving rationally

## 연습해설

### EX 2

In a famous essay on Tolstoy, the liberal philosopher Sir Isaiah Berlin distinguished between two kinds of thinkers by harking back to an ancient saying attributed to the Greek lyric poet Archilochus (seventh century BC): "The fox knows many things, but the hedgehog knows one big thing." Hedgehogs have one central idea and see the world exclusively through the prism of that idea. They overlook complications and exceptions, or mold them to fit into their world view. There is one true answer that fits at all times and all circumstances. Foxes, for whom Berlin had greater sympathy, have a variegated take on the world, which keeps them from _____. They are skeptical of grand theories as they feel the world's complexity prevents generalizations. Berlin thought Dante was a hedgehog while Shakespeare was a fox.

**해석** Tolstoy에 관한 유명한 수필에서, 진보적인 철학자 Isaiah Berlin 경은 그리스 서정시인 Archilochus(BC 7세기)의 말로 여겨지는 오래된 속담을 상기시킴으로써, 두 종류의 사상가들을 구분하였다. "여우는 많은 것을 아는 반면, 고슴도치는 큰 한 가지만 안다." 고슴도치들은 하나의 중심 사상을 가지고 세상을 오직 그 사상의 프리즘을 통해서만 본다. 그들은 복잡성과 예외들을 간과하거나, 그것들을 틀에 넣어 그들의 세계관에 맞춘다. (그들에게는) 모든 시기와 모든 상황에 맞는 하나의 진정한 답만 있다. Berlin이 더 크게 공감했는데, 여우들은 세상에 대한 더 다양한 의견을 가지고 있어, 그들이 <u>하나의 큰 구호만을 표현하는 것</u>을 못하게 했다. 그들은 세상의 복잡성이 일반화를 막는다고 느끼기 때문에 거대한 이야기에 회의적이다. Berlin은 Dante를 고슴도치로, 반면에 Shakespeare를 여우로 생각했다.
① 세계의 복잡성을 파악하는 것을
② 하나의 큰 구호만을 표현하는 것을
③ 다양한 해법을 찾아내는 것을
④ 합리적으로 행동하는 것을

**어휘** liberal 진보적인, 자유로운  philosopher 철학가  hark back to ~를 상기시키다[떠올리다]  attribute ① ~의 탓으로 돌리다[여기다] ② ~라고 여기다  lyric ① 서정적인 ② 서정시  hedgehog 고슴도치, 호저  exclusively ① 단지, 다만, 오직 ② 독점적으로, 배타적으로  overlook 간과하다  mold ① 틀 ② 틀에 넣어 만들다[주조하다] ③ 곰팡이  exception 예외  take 의견, 생각  skeptical 회의적인  grasp ① 이해하다, 파악하다 ② 잡다, 쥐다  complication 복잡한, 복잡성  articulate 분명하게 표현하다[설명하다]  slogan 구호, 슬로건  multiple 많은, 다수의, 다양한  rationally 이성적으로, 합리적으로

**해설** 빈칸 완성은 Two 개념(반대/대조의 공간개념)을 이용할 수 있어야 한다. 이 글은 두 종류의 사상가(Fox vs. Hedgehog)에 관한 글이고, 빈칸에는 Fox에 관한 설명이 있어야 한다. Fox는 많은 것을 아는 유형인데, 빈칸 앞에 prevent(부정어)가 있으므로 빈칸에는 '많은 것을 아는'과 반대/대조의 내용이 있어야 하므로 빈칸에 가장 적절한 것은 ②이다.

02 ②

## 실전문제

**01** 다음 빈칸에 들어갈 말로 가장 적절한 것을 고르시오..

> There are two distinct mind-sets that dramatically influence how we react to failure. A fixed mind-set is grounded in the belief that talent is genetic. The fixed mind-set believes it is entitled to success without much effort and regards failure as a personal insult. When things get tough, it is quick to blame, withdraw, and avoid future challenge or risk. Conversely, a growth mind-set assumes that no talent is entirely _____ and that effort and learning make everything possible. The growth mind-set sees failure as opportunity rather than insult. When challenged, it is quick to reassess, adjust, and try again. In fact, it relishes this process. We are all born with growth mind-sets. So with many little things we can guarantee that our kids or our students never get discouraged by failure. In school, instead of saying "You're so smart", praise effort or strategy by saying "I'm proud of your persistence." At the dinner table, instead of "How was your day?", ask "What did you learn today?"

① experienced
② heaven-sent
③ obtained
④ worthy

## 실전 해설

**01**

> Two 개념: ① fixed mind-set 재능은 선천적 ② growth mind-set 재능은 후천적

There are two distinct mind-sets that dramatically influence how we react to failure.

> 개념 ①

A fixed mind-set is grounded in the belief that talent is genetic. The fixed mind-set believes it is entitled to success without much effort and regards failure as a personal insult. When things get tough, it is quick to blame, withdraw, and avoid future challenge or risk.

> 이와는 반대로   개념 ②

Conversely, a growth mind-set assumes that no talent is entirely _____ and that effort and learning make everything possible. The growth mind-set sees failure as opportunity rather than insult. When challenged, it is quick to reassess, adjust, and try again. In fact, it relishes this process. We are all born with growth mind-sets. So with many little things we can guarantee that our kids or our students never get discouraged by failure. In school, instead of saying "You're so smart", praise effort or strategy by saying "I'm proud of your persistence." At the dinner table, instead of "How was your day?", ask "What did you learn today?"

**[해석]** 우리가 어떻게 실패에 반응하는가에 대해 극적으로 영향을 주는 두개의 뚜렷이 다른 사고방식이 있다. 고정된 사고방식은 재능이란 유전적인(타고난) 것이라는 믿음을 기반으로 한다. 이 고정된 사고방식은 많은 노력을 하지 않고도 성공할 자격이 있다고 믿으며 실패를 개인적 치욕으로 여긴다. 상황이 어려워지면, 재빨리 남 탓을 하고, 물러나며, 미래의 도전이나 위기를 피하려 한다. 반대로, 성장형 사고방식은 전적으로 하늘이 내려준(타고난) 재능은 없다고 생각하고, 노력과 배움으로 모든 것을 가능하게 한다고 생각한다. 성장형 사고방식은 실패를 치욕이라기보다는 기회로 여긴다. 어려움이 닥치면, 재빨리 재평가하고, 조정하고, 다시 시도한다. 사실, 이 사고방식은 이런 과정을 즐긴다. 우리 모두는 성장형 사고방식을 가지고 태어났다. 그래서 많은 사소한 일들로 우리의 자녀나 학생들이 결코 실패에 좌절하지 않을 것이라 우리는 확신할 수 있다. 학교에서 "넌 참 똑똑해"라는 말 대신, "난 너의 끈기가 자랑스러워"라 말하며 노력이나 계획을 칭찬해주어라. 저녁 식사시간에 "오늘 어땠니?" 대신, "오늘 무엇을 배웠니?"라고 물어보아라.
① 경험된 ② 하늘이 내려준(타고난) ③ 습득된 ④ 가치 있는

**[어휘]** distinct (뚜렷이) 다른, 구별되는   mind-set 사고방식   react to ~에 반응하다   failure 실패
fixed 고정된   be grounded in ~을 기반으로 하다, ~에 근거를 두다   talent 재능
genetic 유전적인   be entitled to ~을 받을 자격이 있다
regard A as B A를 B로 여기다, 간주하다   insult 모욕(하다)   tough 힘든, 어려운
blame 비난하다, 남 탓을 하다   withdraw 물러나다, 후퇴하다, 철수하다   conversely 반대로
assume 추정하다, 생각하다, 가정하다   entirely 전적으로
see A as B A를 B로 여기다, 간주하다   opportunity 기회   reassess 재평가하다, 다시 평가하다
adjust 조정하다, 적응하다   relish 즐기다, 음미하다   guarantee 보장하다, 확신하다
instead of ~대신에   praise 칭찬하다   strategy 전략   persistence 끈기, 불굴의 의지
obtain 얻다, 습득하다

**[해설]** two 개념을 이용해야 한다. 주어진 지문은 두 가지 서로 다른 사고방식을 설명하고 있다. 빈칸에 있는 Conversely를 기준으로 앞에는 재능이란 유전적(타고난)이라는 고정된 사고방식과 뒤에는 이와 반대되는 내용인 재능은 후천적이라는 성장형 사고방식에 대한 설명이 이어지고 있다. 다만, 빈칸이 있는 문장에 부정어 no가 있으므로 빈칸에는 성장형 사고방식과 반대되는 내용이 있어야 한다. 따라서 빈칸에 들어가기에 가장 적절한 것은 ② '하늘이 내려준(타고난)'이다.

**[정답]**
01 ②

## 실전문제

**02** 다음 빈칸에 들어갈 말로 가장 적절한 것을 고르시오.

> Participating in sports is quite different from watching sports. Yet in sport studies, these two activities are often lumped together statistically and anecdotally. Combining them only adds to the confusion of the value of each and interferes with the assessment of the overall influence of sports. For example, many people would rate tackle football as the most popular sport in the United States. Based on observer interest, this is a rational conclusion. But if we look at participation, football is popular only through high school and only with boys. Beyond the age of 18, tackle football is not a reasonable option due to the number of players required, deficiency of equipment, and risk of injury. Therefore, it is more accurate to say that football is the most popular _____ sport in the United States but rates far down the list in terms of taking part in.
> 
> \* lumped together : 함께 묶다

① spectating
② irrational
③ interesting
④ participating

## 실전 해설

**02**

> ┌ Two 개념: ① Participating ② Spectating → 차이점 설명
>
> Participating in sports is quite different from watching sports. Yet in sport studies, these two activities are often lumped together statistically and anecdotally. Combining them only adds to the confusion of the value of each and interferes with the assessment of the overall influence of sports. For example, many people would rate tackle football as the most popular sport in the United States. Based on observer interest, this is a rational conclusion. But if we look at participation, football is popular only through high school and only with boys. Beyond the age of 18, tackle football is not a reasonable option due to the number of players required, deficiency of equipment, and risk of injury. Therefore, it is more accurate to say that football is the most popular _____ sport in the United States but rates far down the list in terms of taking part in.
>
> * lumped together : 함께 묶다

**해석** 스포츠에 참여하는 것은 스포츠를 관람하는 것과 매우 다르다. 그러나 스포츠 연구에서는 이 두 활동이 종종 통계적으로, 그리고 일화적으로 함께 묶여진다. 이 두 활동을 합치는 것은 각각의 가치에 대해 혼동을 가중시키고, 스포츠에 대한 전반적 영향을 평가하는 것을 방해한다. 예를 들어 많은 사람들이 태클 풋볼을 미국에서 가장 인기 있는 스포츠라고 평가할 것이다. 관중의 관심도로 본다면 이것은 합리적인 결론이다. 그러나 참여 면에서 본다면, 풋볼은 고등학생들까지, 그리고 남학생들한테만 인기가 있다. 18세가 넘으면 태클 풋볼은 경기에 필요한 인원수, 장비의 부족, 부상의 위험 때문에 합리적인 선택이 아니다. 그러므로 풋볼은 미국에서 가장 인기 있는 관람 스포츠이지만 참가한다는 관점에서는 아주 하위 순위로 평가된다고 말하는 것이 더 정확하다.

① 관람의
② 비이성적인
③ 흥미로운
④ 참여하는

**어휘** participate in ~에 참여하다  lump 함께 묶다  statistically 통계적으로, 통계상으로
combine 결합하다  add to ~에 더하다, ~을 가중시키다  confusion 혼란, 혼동
interfere with ~을 방해하다  assessment 평가  overall 전반적인
rate 평가하다[되다], 순위를 매기다  tackle ① 태클을 걸다, 씨름하다 ② 태클
observer 관찰자, 관중  rational 이성적인(= reasonable)  conclusion 결론
participation 참여  option 선택  due to ~ 때문에  deficiency 부족, 결핍
equipment ① 장비 ② 준비  injury 부상  accurate 정확한  in terms of ~의 관점에서
involve 관련[관계]시키다, 참여시키다  spectate 관람하다, 구경하다  irrational 비이성적인

**해설** two 개념을 이용해야 한다. 주어진 지문은 스포츠에 참여하는 것과 스포츠를 관람하는 것은 다르다는 내용의 글이고 또한 미국에서는 태클 풋볼이 가장 인기 있는 관람스포츠이지만 여러 가지 이유로 참여 면에서는 그렇지 않다고 설명하고 있으므로 빈칸에 들어가기에 가장 적절한 것은 참여의 반대되는 내용인 ① '관람의'이다.

02 ①

## 실전문제

**03** 다음 주어진 문장이 들어가기에 가장 적절한 곳은?

> Against that, the construction of wind farms is not welcomed everywhere due to their visual impact.

Although wind power provides less than one percent of global energy needs (as of 2009), it is currently one of the fastest growing renewable energy sources, with global installed wind power capacity increasing at a rate of over 15 percent annually. ( ① ) In many respects, wind power typifies both the benefits and some of the short-term drawbacks of renewables. ( ② ) As a power source, wind energy is highly fascinating because it is plentiful, widespread, clean, and produces no greenhouse gas emissions. ( ③ ) In addition, the expense of installing them is soaring: a wind farm with a capacity of about 100 megawatts typically costs hundreds of millions of dollars to set up — more if offshore — although the costs are coming down. ( ④ ) The energy provided by wind farms is also sporadic; the period of peak demand (the winter months) rarely corresponds with the period of peak supply — unlike solar power, for example.

# 실전 해설

03

> 반대/대조의 시그널 Against that을 기준으로 ⊕ / ⊖ 개념이 이어지고 있다.
> Against that, the construction of wind farms is not welcomed everywhere due to their visual impact.
> └ ⊖ 개념

Although wind power provides less than one percent of global energy needs (as of 2009), it is currently one of the fastest growing renewable energy sources, with global installed wind power capacity increasing at a rate of over 15 percent annually. ( ① ) In many respects, wind power typifies both the benefits and some of the short-term drawbacks of renewables. ( ② ) As a power source, wind energy is highly fascinating because it is plentiful, widespread, clean, and produces no greenhouse gas emissions. ( ③ ) In addition, the expense of installing them is soaring: a wind farm with a capacity of about 100 megawatts typically costs hundreds of millions of dollars to set up — more if offshore — although the costs are coming down. ( ④ ) The energy provided by wind farms is also sporadic; the period of peak demand (the winter months) rarely corresponds with the period of peak supply — unlike solar power, for example.

**해석** 풍력 발전은 (2009년 현재) 세계 에너지 수요의 1퍼센트 미만을 제공하지만, 현재 가장 빠르게 성장하는 재생 가능 에너지 자원 중의 하나로 세계 풍력 발전 설비 용량이 매년 15퍼센트가 넘는 속도로 증가하고 있다. 많은 측면에서 풍력 발전은 재생 가능 에너지의 이점과 몇몇 단기 결점을 모두 전형적으로 보여준다. 동력 자원으로서 풍력 에너지는 풍부하고, 널리 퍼져 있고, 깨끗하며, 온실가스를 방출하지 않기 때문에 매우 매력적이다. <u>그에 반해, 풍력 발전 단지의 건설은 그것들의 경관 영향으로 인해 모든 곳에서 환영받지는 못한다.</u> 게다가, 그것들을 설치하는 비용이 치솟고 있다. 비용이 내려가고 있기는 하지만, 대략 100메가와트 용량을 가진 풍력 발전 단지를 설치하는 데 보통 수억 달러의 비용이 들고, 앞바다에서라면 비용이 더 많이 든다. 풍력 발전 단지가 제공하는 에너지는 또한 간헐적이다. 예를 들어서, 태양광 발전과는 달리 (겨울철) 절정 수요의 시기가 일반적으로 절정 공급의 시기와 거의 일치하지 않는다.

**어휘** construction 건설  wind farm 풍력 발전 단지  visual impact 경관 영향
renewable energy 재생 가능 에너지  installed capacity 설비 용량  annually 매년
typify 전형적으로 보여주다  short-term 단기의  drawback 결점  fascinating 매력적인, 매혹적인
plentiful 풍부한  widespread 널리 퍼진  emission 배출  install 설치하다
offshore 앞바다에서, 해안에서 떨어진  sporadic 간헐적인  rarely 거의 ~ 않는
correspond with ~와 일치하다, 부합하다  peak 절정

**해설** 풍력 발전이 재생 가능 에너지가 전형적으로 보여주는 장점과 단점을 모두 가지고 있다는 요지의 글이다. ③ 앞에는 풍력 발전의 장점이 제시되고, ③ 뒤에는 단점이 제시되었다. 또한 ③ 뒤에 나열의 시그널 In addition이 제시된 것으로 보아, 앞에도 다른 단점이 제시되었음을 알 수 있다. 따라서 풍력 발전의 첫 번째 단점을 제시하는 주어진 문장이 들어가기에 가장 적절한 곳은 ③이다.

03 ③

## 실전문제

**04** 다음 빈칸에 들어갈 말로 가장 적절한 것을 고르시오.

The source of this economic paralysis are somewhat different in the two countries. In Japan, a combination of highly constraining social patterns, a consensus-based decision making and an ossified political process have suppressed new ideas and made the country resistant to change. In the U.S., there is no shortage of fresh thinking, debate and outrage — the paralysis is caused by _____ of consensus on how problems should be tackled. In a rich nation like the U.S., it's easy to be fooled into thinking there's always more time for problems to get solved. Such tendency has been in Japan, too. The Japanese think they are so wealthy enough that they don't suffer too much from the prolonged period of low growth.

\* ossified : 보수적인, 경화된

① a lack
② a variety
③ a number
④ a neutrality

## 실전 해설

**04**

> Two 개념: ① Japan 합의에 기초한 결정
> ② U.S 합의가 부족 → 차이점 설명
>
> The source of this economic paralysis are somewhat different in the two countries. In Japan, a combination of highly constraining social patterns, a consensus-based decision making and an ossified political process have suppressed new ideas and made the country resistant to change. In the U.S., there is no shortage of fresh thinking, debate and outrage — the paralysis is caused by _____ of consensus on how problems should be tackled. In a rich nation like the U.S., it's easy to be fooled into thinking there's always more time for problems to get solved. Such tendency has been in Japan, too. The Japanese think they are so wealthy enough that they don't suffer too much from the prolonged period of low growth.
>
> * ossified : 보수적인, 경화된

**해석** 이러한 경제 마비의 근원은 두 나라에 있어서 다소 다르다. 일본에서는 매우 제한적인 사회적인 패턴을 가진 조합이고, 합의에 근거를 둔 의사결정과 보수적인 정치적 절차들로 인해서 새로운 아이디어를 억압해왔고 그 결과로 국가가 변화에 약화되었다. 미국에서는, 참신한 생각, 토론 그리고 분노 같은 것에 부족함이란 없기 때문에, (경제) 마비의 원인은 어떻게 문제를 해결해야 하는지에 대한 합의의 부족으로 나타난다. 미국과 같이 부유한 나라에서는, 문제를 해결할 시간이 얼마든지 있다고 생각하는 오류를 범하기 쉽다. 그러한 경향은 일본에서도 존재해 왔다. 일본인들은 충분히 너무 부유해서 장기적으로 낮은 성장에서도 그렇게 고통받지 않았다고 생각한다.

① 부족
② 다양성
③ 많은
④ 중립

**어휘** source 근원, 원천, 원인  paralysis 마비, 파행  combination 조합, 결합
constrain 제한하다, 억제하다  consensus 합의, 일치  decision making 의사 결정
ossified 보수적인, 경화된  suppress 진압하다, 억압하다  resistant 저항하는, 반대하는
shortage 부족, 결핍  debate 토론, 논쟁  outrage 폭동, 격노, 분노
tackle a problem 문제를 다루다, 해결하다  fooled 속기 쉬운 *fool 속이다, 놀리다
tendency 경향  prolonged 오래 계속되는, 장기적인  lack 부족, 결핍  a variety of 다양한
a number of 많은  neutrality 중립

**해설** two 개념을 이용해야 한다. 일본은 합의에 근거를 둔 의사결정이 이루어진다고 했으므로 미국은 이와 반대되는 내용이 빈칸에 들어가야 하므로 빈칸에 들어가기에 가장 적절한 것은 ① '부족'이다.

**정답**
04 ①

## 실전문제

**05** 다음 빈칸에 들어갈 말로 가장 적절한 것을 고르시오.

> Trees and vegetation cool the air by providing shade and through the evaporation of water from leaves. First of all, shade reduces the amount of solar radiation transmitted to underlying surfaces, keeping them cool. Shaded walls may be 5°C to 20°C cooler than the peak temperatures of unshaded surfaces. These cooler walls decrease the quantity of heat transmitted to buildings, thus lowering air conditioning cooling costs. As you know, cooler surfaces lessen the heat island effect by reducing heat transfer to the surrounding air. Another way trees and vegetation cool the air is by absorbing water through their roots and _____.
> This process uses heat from the air to convert water contained in the vegetation into water vapor.

① with cooler surfaces lessening the heat island effect
② with shades reducing the amount of solar radiation
③ using shaded walls made under the vegetation
④ evaporating it through leaf pores

## 실전 해설

**05**

Trees and vegetation cool the air by providing shade and through the evaporation of water from leaves. First of all, shade reduces the amount of solar radiation
↳ 나열의 공간 개념: ① shade ② evaporation → absorbing water
　　　　　　　　　　　　　　　　　　　　　　　　　　→ water vapor

transmitted to underlying surfaces, keeping them cool. Shaded walls may be 5°C to 20°C cooler than the peak temperatures of unshaded surfaces. These cooler walls decrease the quantity of heat transmitted to buildings, thus lowering air conditioning cooling costs. As you know, cooler surfaces lessen the heat island effect by reducing heat transfer to the surrounding air. Another way trees and vegetation cool the air is by absorbing water through their roots and _____. This process uses heat from the air to convert water contained in the vegetation into water vapor.

**해석** 나무와 초목은 그늘을 제공하고 잎으로부터 물이 증발되는 과정을 통해서 공기를 시원하게 해준다. 무엇보다도 우선, 그늘은 아래쪽 표면에 도달하는 태양의 복사(열)의 양을 줄여주어 그곳을 시원하게 유지시켜 준다. 그늘에 가려진 벽의 온도는 그늘이 지지 않은 노면의 최대 온도보다 섭씨 5도에서 20도 정도 더 시원할 수 있다. 이렇게 벽이 더 시원해지게 되면 건물에 전달되는 열의 양이 줄어들게 되며, 그 결과 냉방 비용이 줄어들게 된다. 표면의 온도가 더 낮아지게 되면 주변에 있는 공기로 전달되는 열이 줄어들게 되어 열섬 효과 또한 완화된다. 나무와 초목이 공기를 시원하게 만들어주는 또 다른 한 가지 방식은 뿌리를 통해 물을 흡수함으로써 <u>그것을 잎에 있는 기공을 통해 증발시키는 것</u>에 의한 것이다. 이러한 과정에서 초목이 지니고 있는 물을 수증기로 변화시키기 위해 공기 중에 있는 열을 사용하게 된다.

① 열섬효과를 줄이는 시원한 표면에
② 복사열의 양을 줄이는 그늘에
③ 초목 아래 만들어진 그늘에 가려진 벽을 이용하는 것에
④ 그것을 잎에 있는 기공을 통해 증발시키는 것에

**어휘** vegetation 초목, 식물　provide 제공하다　shade 그늘, 응달　evaporation 증발
leaf 나뭇잎(leaves 나뭇잎들)　reduce 줄이다, 감소시키다　solar radiation 태양 복사(열)
transmit 전송하다, 보내다　shaded wall 그늘이 가려진 벽　peak 절정　unshaded 그늘이 없는
surface 표면　decrease 감소하다　quantity 양　lower 낮추다　lessen 줄이다, 낮추다
heat island 열섬　effect 효과　surrounding 에워싸는, 둘러싸는　absorb 흡수하다
pore 구멍　convert 바꾸다　contain 포함하다　vapor 증기　*water vapor 수증기

**해설** 주어진 지문은 나무와 초목의 시원해지는 효과를 2가지 관점(그늘과 증발)에서 나열하는 내용의 글이고 빈칸은 2번째 효과(증발)에 관한 내용이여야 하므로 빈칸에 들어가기에 가장 적절한 것은 ④ '그것을 잎에 있는 기공을 통해 증발시키는 것에'이다.

**정답**
05 ④

## 실전문제

**06** 다음 글의 흐름으로 보아 주어진 문장이 들어가기에 가장 적절한 곳은?

> For example, conventional television is integrated as it contains images, sound and text, but it is not interactive or based on digital code.

New media can be defined by four characteristics simultaneously: they are media at the turn of the 20th and 21st centuries which are both integrated and interactive and use digital code and hypertext as technical means. It follows that their most common alternative names are multimedia, interactive media and digital media. ( ① ) By using this definition, it is easy to identify media as old or new. ( ② ) The plain old telephone was interactive, but not integrated as it only transmitted speech and sounds and it did not work with digital code. ( ③ ) In contrast, the new medium of interactive television adds interactivity and digital code. ( ④ ) Moreover, the new generations of mobile or fixed telephone are fully digitalized and integrated as they add text, pictures or video and they are connected to the Internet. Even if new media look like complications, their definition may be rather straightforward.

## 실전 해설

**06**

> ↳ old 개념    ↳ 첫 번째 나열을 알리는 시그널
> For example, conventional television is integrated as it contains images, sound and text, but it is not interactive or based on digital code.

New media can be defined by four characteristics simultaneously: they are media at the turn of the 20th and 21st centuries which are both integrated and interactive and use digital code and hypertext as technical means. It follows that their most common alternative names are multimedia, interactive media and digital media. ( ① ) By using this definition, it is easy to identify media as old or new. ( ② ) The plain old telephone was interactive, but not integrated as it only transmitted speech and sounds and it did not work with digital code. ( ③ ) In contrast, the new medium of interactive television adds interactivity and digital code. ( ④ ) Moreover, the new generations of mobile or fixed telephone are fully digitalized and integrated as they add text, pictures or video and they are connected to the Internet. Even if new media look like complications, their definition may be rather straightforward.

**해석** 새로운 매체란 네 가지 특징 모두에 의해 동시에 정의될 수 있는 것으로 말할 수 있다. 그것들은 통합적이고 쌍방향이며 기술적 수단으로 디지털 코드와 하이퍼텍스트를 사용하는 20세기와 21세기 전환기의 매체이다. 그렇기에 그것들의 가장 일반적인 다른 이름이 다중 매체, 쌍방향 매체, 디지털 매체라는 이야기가 된다. 이 정의를 사용하면 매체가 구식인지 신식인지를 구별하는 것이 쉽다. 예를 들어, 전통적인 텔레비전은 그것이 이미지, 소리, 글을 포함하고 있기 때문에, 통합적이지만, 쌍방향이 아니며 디지털 코드에 기반을 두고 있지도 않다. 평범한 구식 전화는 쌍방향이었지만, 그것은 오로지 말과 소리만 전송하기 때문에 통합적이지 않았으며, 디지털 코드로 작동하지 않았다. 대조적으로, 쌍방향의 텔레비전이라는 새로운 매체는 쌍방향성과 디지털 코드를 더한다. 게다가, 새로운 세대의 이동식 또는 고정식 전화는 글, 그림 또는 영상을 추가하고 인터넷과 연결되기 때문에 완전히 디지털화되고 통합적이다. 비록 새로운 미디어는 복잡해보이지만 의외로 그 정의는 단순할 수 있다.

**어휘** define 정의를 내리다 *definition 정의 characteristic(s) 특징, 특성 simultaneously 동시에 integrated 통합적인, 통합된 interactive 쌍방향의, 상호 작용하는 hypertext 하이퍼텍스트(문장 중의 어구나 그것에 붙은 표제, 표제를 모은 목차 등이 서로 연결된 문자 데이터 파일) means 수단, 방법 alternative ① 대안의 ② 양자택일의 definition 정의 identify ① 확인하다 ② 동일시하다 contain 포함하다 conventional 전통적인, 관습적인 based on ~에 기초하는, 기반을 두는 plain 평범한, 보통의 transmit 전송하다, 송신하다 work ① 작동하다 ② 효과가 있다 interactivity 쌍방향성 generation 세대 fixed 고정된 even if 비록 ~일지라도 complication 복잡함 straightforward 단순한

**해설** 주어진 문장은 old media의 첫 번째 예를 제시하고 있으므로 ② 뒤에 있는 plain old telephone 앞에 위치해야 한다. 따라서 주어진 문장이 들어가기에 가장 적절한 곳은 ②이다.

**정답**
06 ②

## 실전문제

**07** 다음 빈칸에 들어갈 말로 가장 적절한 것을 고르시오.

Most important among behavioral differences between bees and wasps is that bees are pollen eaters. Wasps, in contrast, are meat eaters. While both visit flowers for nectar (the "energy drink" of the insect world), bees also visit flowers in order to collect pollen for their young. On the contrary, wasps pursue other insects and drag them back to the nest for their offspring to devour. Besides this ___(A)___ difference, another one shows up between them. To aid in the gathering of pollen, bees are usually hairy (pollen sticks to hair), and many species look like cotton candy with wings. Searching around in flowers is messy business, and a few minutes rummaging among floral parts leaves a bee coated in hundreds of tiny grains of pollen. Using her many legs, the bee grooms herself, wiping all the pollen to the back of her body, where she stuffs it into the spaces between special stiff hairs on the legs or belly. Quite the opposite of the ___(B)___ bee, wasps look like Olympic swimmers, with no hair, skinny-waisted, and with long thin legs.

|     | (A) | (B) |
| --- | --- | --- |
| ① | sensory | fatty |
| ② | sensory | defensive |
| ③ | dietary | furry |
| ④ | dietary | imbalanced |

## 실전 해설

**07**

> Two 개념: ① bees ② wasps → 차이점 설명

Most important among behavioral **differences between bees and wasps** is that **bees** are pollen eaters. **Wasps**, **in contrast**, are meat eaters. While both visit flowers for nectar (the "energy drink" of the insect world), **bees** also visit flowers in order to collect pollen for their young. **On the contrary**, **wasps** pursue other insects and drag them back to the nest for their offspring to devour. Besides this ____(A)____ difference, **another** one shows up between them. To aid in the gathering of pollen, **bees** are usually hairy (pollen sticks to hair), and many species look like cotton candy with wings. Searching around in flowers is messy business, and a few minutes rummaging among floral parts leaves a bee coated in hundreds of tiny grains of pollen. Using her many legs, the **bee** grooms herself, wiping all the pollen to the back of her body, where she stuffs it into the spaces between special stiff hairs on the legs or belly. **Quite the opposite** of the ____(B)____ **bee**, **wasps** look like Olympic swimmers, with no hair, skinny-waisted, and with long thin legs.

**해석** 꿀벌과 말벌의 행동 차이 중에서 가장 중요한 것은 꿀벌이 꽃가루를 먹는다는 점이다. 그와 대조적으로 말벌은 고기를 먹는다. 둘 다 꿀(곤충계의 '에너지 음료')을 구하러 꽃을 찾지만, 꿀벌은 또한 자기 새끼들에게 줄 꽃가루를 모으기 위해 꽃을 찾는다. 그와는 반대로 말벌은 다른 곤충을 쫓아가서 자기 새끼들이 게걸스럽게 먹도록 집으로 끌고 돌아간다. 이런 먹이의 차이 하나로 매우 다른 행동 방식들이 생겼다. 꽃가루 채집을 돕기 위해 꿀벌은 보통 털이 많아서(꽃가루가 털에 들러붙는다), 날개 달린 솜사탕처럼 보이는 (꿀벌의) 종도 많다. 꽃들 속에서 뒤지고 다니는 것은 지저분하게 만드는 일인데, 꽃 부위에서 몇 분 동안 샅샅이 뒤지고 나면 꿀벌의 표면은 수백 개의 미세한 꽃가루 알갱이로 덮인다. 꿀벌은 자신의 많은 다리를 이용하여 자신을 깔끔하게 다듬으면서 모든 꽃가루를 자기 몸의 뒤 쪽으로 쓸어 가는데, 거기에서 그 꽃가루를 다리나 배에 난 뻣뻣한 특수한 털들 사이의 공간에 채워 넣는다. 털로 덮인 꿀벌과는 정반대인 말벌은 털이 전혀 없고 잘록한 허리에 길고 가느다란 다리를 한 올림픽 수영선수처럼 보인다.

① 감각의 - 지방이 많은 ② 감각의 - 끈적거리는 ③ 먹이의 - 털로 덮인 ④ 먹이의 - 끈적거리는

**어휘** **behavioral** 행동의 **wasp** 말벌 **pollen** 꽃가루 **in contrast** 대조적으로 **nectar** (꽃의) 꿀 **young** 새끼(들), 젊은이들 **on the contrary** 반대로, 이에 반해서 **pursue** 추적하다, 뒤쫓다 **offspring** 후손, 자손 **insect** 곤충 **drag** 질질 끌다 **devour** 게걸스럽게 먹다 **result in** ~을 초래하다, 야기하다 **bearing** 행동 방식, 몸가짐, 거동 **aid in** ~에 도움이 되다 **gathering** 수집, 모음 **species** 종(種), 종류 **hairy** 털이 많은 **stick to** ~에 집착하다, 달라붙다 **cotton candy** 솜사탕 **wing** 날개 **search** 찾다 **messy** 지저분하게 만드는, 지저분한 **rummage** 샅샅이 뒤지다 **floral** 꽃의 **coat** (~의) 표면을 덮다, 웃옷을 입히다 **grain** 알갱이, 곡물 **groom** 털을 고르다, 깔끔하게 다듬다 **wipe** ① 쓸다, 쓸어내다 ② 닦다, 닦아내다 *wipe A to B A를 B쪽으로 쓸어내다 **stuff** 채워 넣다 **stiff** 뻣뻣한 **belly** 배 **opposite** 반대, 반대의 **skinny** ① 잘록한, (폭이) 좁은 ② 말라빠진 *skinny-waisted 잘록한 허리의 **thin** 가느다란, 살이 많지 않은

**해설** (A) 새끼들을 위해 꿀벌이 꽃가루를 모으고 말벌이 다른 곤충을 끌어가는 것은 음식 섭취와 관련된 차이이므로 빈칸에는 '먹이의[음식의]'라는 뜻인 dietary가 적절하다.
(B) 꿀벌은 꽃가루를 먹이로 하므로 꽃가루를 채집하기 위해 몸에 털이 많다는 내용으로 보아, 빈칸에는 '털로 덮인'의 의미인 furry가 가장 적절하다.

**정답**
07 ③

## 실전문제

**08** 주어진 글 다음에 이어질 글의 순서로 가장 적절한 것은?

There are some interesting researches related with IGF-1 levels. A study reported in the medical journal *Lancet*, based upon the work of researchers at Brigham Women's Hospital and Harvard Medical School, offers a telling information about the relationship between IGF-1 level and breast cancer.

(A) In pre-menopausal women, on the other hand, the highest IGF-1 group had seven times more risk of breast cancer. There is substantial indirect evidence of a relation between IGF-1 and risk of breast cancer, the authors concluded.

(B) Another research has shown that the consumption of both whole and nonfat milk raises IGF-1 levels in adults; in adolescent females, as little as a pint of milk a day can boost IGF-1 levels by 10 percent. It takes about three glasses(one and a half pints) of nonfat milk a day to achieve the same result in adult women.

(C) The authors in the study estimated that the post-menopausal women with the highest levels of IGF-1 in their blood had three times the risk of breast cancer than the women with the lowest IGF-1 levels.

① (A) - (C) - (B)
② (B) - (A) - (C)
③ (C) - (A) - (B)
④ (C) - (B) - (A)

## 실전 해설

**08**

　　　　　　　　나열의 시작점
There are some interesting researches related with IGF-1 levels. A study reported in the medical journal *Lancet*, based upon the work of researchers at Brigham Women's Hospital and Harvard Medical School, offers a telling information about the relationship between IGF-1 level and breast cancer.

　　　　　　　　　　반대/대조의 시그널
　　　　　　　pre-menopausal과 post-menopausal의 차이점 설명
(A) In pre-menopausal women, on the other hand, the highest IGF-1 group had seven times more risk of breast cancer. There is substantial indirect evidence of a relation between IGF-1 and risk of breast cancer, the authors concluded.
　　　두 번째 나열
(B) Another research has shown that the consumption of both whole and nonfat milk raises IGF-1 levels in adults; in adolescent females, as little as a pint of milk a day can boost IGF-1 levels by 10 percent. It takes about three glasses(one and a half pints) of nonfat milk a day to achieve the same result in adult women.
(C) The authors in the study estimated that the post-menopausal women with the highest levels of IGF-1 in their blood had three times the risk of breast cancer than the women with the lowest IGF-1 levels.

**해석** IGF-1 수준과 관련된 몇몇 흥미로운 연구가 있다. Brigham Women's Hospital 및 Harvard Medical School의 연구자들의 연구에 기초를 둔 <Lancet>이라는 의학 잡지에 보도된 한 연구는 IGF-1의 수준과 유방암 사이의 관계에 대한 효과적인 정보를 제공한다.
(C) 그 연구에서 저자들은 가장 높은 IGF-1 수준을 지닌 폐경기 이후의 여성들이 가장 낮은 IGF-1 수준을 지닌 여성들보다 유방암에 걸릴 위험이 3배나 높았다고 추정했다.
(A) 반면에, 폐경기 이전 여성들에게서, 가장 높은 IGF-1 수준을 지닌 집단은 유방암에 걸릴 더 큰 위험을 7배나 지녔다. IGF-1과 유방암 사이의 관계를 보여주는 실질적인 간접 증거가 존재한다고, 저자들은 결론을 내렸다.
(B) 다른 연구는 전유 및 탈지방 우유 모두를 섭취하는 것이 성인들에게 있어서 IGF-1 수준을 높인다고 하는 것과, 청춘기 여성들에게서, 하루에 1파인트에 그치는 양마저 10%나 IGF-1 수준을 높일 수 있다는 것을 보여주었다. 성인 여성들에게 있어서 동일한 결과를 낳는 데는 탈지방 우유를 하루에 세잔(1과 2분의 1 파인트)이 든다.

**어휘** related with ~와 관련된　IGF-1 인슐린유사 성장인자(Insulin like growth factor 1)
based upon ~에 기초하여　telling 효과적인　breast cancer 유방암
pre-menopausal 폐경기 이전의　*menopause 폐경　*post-menopausal 폐경기 이후의
substantial 상당한, 꽤 많은　indirect 간접적인　evidence 증거　consumption 섭취, 소비
whole milk 전유(全乳)　nonfat milk 탈지방 우유　adolescent 청소년의
pint (무게단위) 파인트　estimate 추정하다

**해설** (A)에 있는 on the other hand를 기준으로 (A)에는 pre-menopausal women이 있고 (C)에 post-menopausal women이 있으므로 (A) 앞에는 (C)가 와야 하고, 나열의 공간개념상 Another가 있는 (B)가 (A) 다음에 이어져야 하므로 주어진 글 다음 이어질 글의 순서는 ③ (C)-(A)-(B)가 된다.

**정답**
08 ③

## 실전문제

**09** 다음 빈칸에 들어갈 말로 가장 적절한 것을 고르시오.

> For a variety of reasons, wildlife officials often redistribute wildlife from one part of an area to another. First, some wildlife plants may be transplanted because they damage grains. Second, some species can be relocated because competitors are too many in one area. A few animals are also situated because their original habitat has not enough supplies of natural food. Another practical reason of redistribution is to move a particular species from a place where population is overabundant to a place in which _____.

① it is poor
② food is short
③ rivals are too many
④ it can damage crops

## 실전 해설

**09**

> ↱ 나열의 시작점
> 
> For a variety of reasons, wildlife officials often redistribute wildlife from one part of an area to another. First, some wildlife plants may be transplanted because they damage grains. Second, some species can be relocated because competitors are too many in one area. A few animals are also situated because their original habitat has not enough supplies of natural food. Another practical reason of redistribution is to move a particular species from a place where population is overabundant to a place in which _____.

※ 나열의 전개 방식
종을 이주시키는 이유
① 곡물을 망침
② 경쟁자가 많아서
③ 먹이공급이 안 돼서
④ 개체수가 많음

**해석** 다양한 이유 때문에, 야생동물보호 공무원들은 종종 야생동물을 한 지역에서 다른 지역으로 재배분시킨다. 우선, 몇몇 야생식물들은 이주가 되는데 그 이유는 그들이 곡물을 망치기 때문이다. 두 번째로 몇몇 종들은 경쟁자들이 너무 많기 때문에 재배치시킬 수도 있다. 몇몇 야생동물들은 원래의 서식지가 천연먹이의 풍부한 공급이 없기 때문에 이주될 수도 있다. 또 다른 실질적인 이유는 한 지역에 너무 개체수가 너무 많은 한 지역의 특정한 종을 <u>개체수가 빈약한</u> 지역으로 옮기는 것이다.

① 개체수가 빈약한
② 음식이 부족한
③ 경쟁자가 너무 많은
④ 개체수가 곡물을 망치는

**어휘** a variety of 다양한  official 공무원, 관리  redistribute 다시 배분하다(이주시키다)
practical 실질적인  transplant ① 이식하다 ② 이주하다  grain 곡물(= crop)  species 종
competition 경쟁  severe 치열한  situate 위치시키다, 두다, 놓다(= locate)  habitat 서식지
lavish ① 사치스러운 ② 풍부한, 풍요로운  practical 실질적인, 실용적인
overabundant 과잉의, 과다한  poor 빈약한  short 부족한

**해설** 나열의 공간 개념을 이용해야 한다. 주어진 지문은 야생 동물의 이주의 원인들을 나열하고 있다. Another 다음 종들의 개체수가 너무 많으므로 개체수가 적은 곳으로 이주해야 한다는 내용이 빈칸에 들어와야 한다. ②, ③, ④는 이미 앞에 있는 이유들에 대한 내용이므로 정답이 될 수 없다. 따라서 정답은 ①이 된다.

정답
09 ①

## 실전문제

**10** 주어진 글 다음에 이어질 글의 순서로 가장 적절한 것은?

It would be hard to find anything more controversial than the subject of cloning. People find it either totally terrific or totally menacing.

(A) But for most people, the cloning of humans is different. The idea of duplicating human beings the same way we make copies of book pages on a copy machine is appalling.

(B) Further, it could be useful in increasing the world's food supply by the cloning of animals. Bigger and healthier animals could be produced.

(C) Cloning holds the promise of cures for what are now incurable diseases, sight for the blind, hearing for the deaf, new organs to replace old worn-out ones.

① (A) − (C) − (B)
② (B) − (A) − (C)
③ (C) − (A) − (B)
④ (C) − (B) − (A)

## 실전 해설

**10**

It would be hard to find anything more controversial than the subject of cloning. People find it either totally terrific or totally menacing.
↳ Two 개념 : ① 복제의 장점 ② 복제의 단점

(A) But for most people, the cloning of humans is different. The idea of duplicating human beings the same way we make copies of book pages on a copy machine is appalling.
(B) Further, it could be useful in increasing the world's food supply by the cloning of animals. Bigger and healthier animals could be produced.
(C) Cloning holds the promise of cures for what are now incurable diseases, sight for the blind, hearing for the deaf, new organs to replace old worn-out ones.

※ 단락의 전개 방식
(C) 복제의 장점
(B) Further, 복제의 두 번째 장점
(A) But 복제의 단점

**해석** 생물 복제라는 주제보다 더 논란이 많은 것을 찾기란 힘들 것이다. 사람들은 그것이 정말 굉장한 것이거나 아니면 완전히 위협적인 것이라고 생각한다.
(C) 생물 복제는, 현재는 치료가 불가능한 질병인 것에 대해서는 치유를, 앞을 못 보는 사람들에게는 시력을, 귀가 먹은 사람들에게는 청력을, 오래 되어 못 쓰게 된 장기를 대체할 새로운 장기를 약속하는 것이다.
(B) 게다가 그것은 동물들을 복제함으로써 세계 식량 공급 증가에 유용할 수 있다. 더 크고 더 건강한 동물들이 생산될 수 있는 것이다.
(A) 그러나 대다수의 사람들에게 인간 복제는 다른 문제이다. 우리가 복사기에서 책 페이지들을 복사하는 것과 같은 방식으로 인간을 복제한다는 생각은 끔찍하다.

**어휘** controversial 논란이 많은  cloning (생물) 복제  terrific 뛰어난, 멋진, 굉장한
menacing 위협적인  duplicate 복사하다, 복제하다  appalling 끔찍한, 오싹한
incurable 치료 불가능한  deaf 귀가 먹은

**해설** Two 개념을 이용해야 한다. 제시문에 ⊕개념(terrific)과 ⊖개념(menacing)을 제시했고, (A)에 But 다음 ⊖개념(appalling)이 있고, (B), (C)는 모두 ⊕개념이므로 (A)가 제일 마지막에 위치해야 한다. 또한 B에 Further(나열의 signal)가 있으므로 (B)는 (C) 다음에 위치해야 한다. 따라서 글의 순서로 가장 적절한 것은 ④ (C) - (B) - (A)이다.

**정답**
10 ④

## 실전문제

**11** 다음 빈칸에 들어갈 말로 가장 적절한 것을 고르시오.

> The primary aims of government should be three: security, justice, and conservation. These are things of the utmost importance to human happiness, and they are things that only government can bring about. At the same time, no one of them is absolute; each may, in some circumstances, have to be sacrificed in some degree for the sake of a greater degree of some other good. I shall say something about each in turn. Most of all the administration is especially in charge of _____.

① protection of life and property
② preservation of cultural remains
③ stage prior to economic development
④ society existing justice and common sense

## 실전 해설

**11**

The primary aims of government should be three: **security**, **justice**, and **conservation**. **These** are things of the utmost importance to human happiness, and **they** are things that only government can bring about. At the same time, no one of **them** is absolute; each may, in some circumstances, have to be sacrificed in some degree for the sake of a greater degree of some other good. **I shall say something about each in turn.** Most of all the administration is especially in charge of _____.

**해석** 정부의 우선적인 목적은 세 개여야 한다. 이는 안전, 정의, 보존이다. 이것들은 인간의 행복에 있어서 가장 중요한 것이며, 오직 정부만이 해낼 수 있는 것이다. 이와 동시에 그것들 중 그 어떤 것도 절대적인 것은 아니다. 이 세 가지는 각각 어떤 상황 안에서 보다 큰 다른 이익을 위해 어느 정도 희생되어야 한다. 나는 차례대로 각각에 대해 이야기하고자 한다. 무엇보다도 우선 정부는 특히 <u>생명과 재산의 보호</u>를 책임진다.

① 생명과 재산의 보호
② 문화 유물의 보존
③ 경제 개발 전 단계
④ 정의와 상식이 존재하는 사회

**어휘** primary 우선적인, 주요한  security 안정, 안전  justice 정의
conservation 보존 *conserve 보호하다  utmost 가장 중요한  government 정부
bring about 야기하다, 초래하다  absolute 절대적인  circumstance 환경, 상황
sacrifice 희생하다  for the sake of ~을 위하여  in turn 차례로, 순서대로
most of all 무엇보다도, 우선  administration 정부  be in charge of ~을 책임지다
protection 보호  property 재산  preservation 보존  remains 유물, 유적  prior to ~ 이전에
common sense 상식

**해설** 나열의 공간 개념을 이용해야 한다. 도입부에서 세 가지 '안전, 정의, 보존'을 제시하고 있고 빈칸 바로 앞 문장에서 각각을 순서대로 설명하겠다고 했으므로 빈칸에는 '안전'에 대한 설명이 있어야 한다. 따라서 빈칸에 들어가기에 가장 적절한 것은 ① '생명과 재산의 보호'이다.

**정답**
11 ①

## 풀이 해법

### 5. 원인(cause)·결과(effect)의 전개 방식

**원인(Cause) → 결과(Effect)의 Signal words**

- thus 그래서, 그러므로 [= therefore, hence, thereby, and(so), so that]
- cause 야기시키다 (= give rise to, lead to, result in, bring about)
- as a result (= consequently) 그 결과로서 (결과적으로)
- the cause (reason) of ~의 원인 (이유)
- this is why 그래서 ~하다
- help / make / contribute to / provoke 돕다 / 만들다 / 기여하다 / 유발하다

**결과(Effect) ← 원인(Cause)의 Signal words**

- as ~ 때문에 (= since, because)
- due to ~ 때문에 (= owing to, on account of, because of)
- the result (effect, consequence) of ~의 결과
- this is because 왜냐하면 ~ 때문에
- follow / be made by 따르다 / ~로 만들어지다
- come from / result from ~로부터 오다 / ~로부터 기인하다

## 연습문제

**EX 1** Read the following pairs of words and phrases. In each pair, which comes first in time? Which causes what? Draw an arrow from the cause to the effect in each pair. And write down the cause and effect under each pair of words.

```
                         EXAMPLE
         heavy snow  ———→  car accident
         cause              effect
```

1. heart problems          obesity

2. diabetes                to change blood sugar

3. coughs                  cold and flu

4. improperly stored food  food poisoning

5. slow infant development poor nutrition

6. skin cancer             too much exposure to the sun

7. viruses                 infectious diseases

8. heart attack            diet high in fat

9. lung cancer             cigarette smoking

10. skiing                 broken leg

## 연습해설

```
                          EXAMPLE
    heavy snow(폭설)  ──────→  car accident(자동차 사고)
    cause                      effect
```

1. heart problems (심장병) ←────── obesity (비만)
   effect                          cause

2. diabetes (당뇨병) ←────── to change blood sugar (혈당변화)
   effect                   cause

3. coughs (기침) ←────── cold and flu (감기 독감)
   effect               cause

4. improperly stored food ──────→ food poisoning
   (잘못된 음식 보관)                 (식중독)
   cause                            effect

5. slow infant development ←────── poor nutrition
   (더딘 유아 성장)                    (열악한 영양)
   effect                           cause

6. skin cancer ←────── too much exposure to the sun
   (피부암)                (태양의 과다 노출)
   effect                 cause

7. viruses (바이러스) ──────→ infectious diseases (전염병)
   cause                    effect

8. heart attack (심장 마비) ←────── diet high in fat (고지방 음식)
   effect                          cause

9. lung cancer (폐암) ←────── cigarette smoking (흡연)
   effect                     cause

10. skiing (스키타기) ──────→ broken leg (부러진 다리)
    cause                    effect

**어휘**
obesity 비만
diabetes 당뇨병
cough 기침
cold 감기
flu 독감
improperly 적절하지 않은, 잘못된
store 저장하다
poisoning 중독
infant 유아
nutrition 영양
exposure 노출

## 연습문제

**EX 2** Read the following sentences. And then underline the signal words and write down the cause and effect in each sentence.

> EXAMPLE
> Shoes with high heels can <u>result in</u> foot problem.
> Cause <u>shoes with high heels</u>     Effect <u>Foot problems</u>

1. Too much alcohol can make you thirsty.
   Cause _____     Effect _____

2. Many car accidents happen because of the flat tire.
   Cause _____     Effect _____

3. Bad food and not enough sleep are two reasons for bad health.
   Cause _____     Effect _____

4. Doctors tell us that exercise can help good health.
   Cause _____     Effect _____

5. To remain awake is produced by much coffee.
   Cause _____     Effect _____

6. Many fires in homes are due to careless smokers.
   Cause _____     Effect _____

7. Heart disease is sometimes the result of eating to much.
   Cause _____     Effect _____

8. Bright sunlight can generate your eyes to hurt.
   Cause _____     Effect _____

9. High insurance costs result from car accidents.
   Cause _____     Effect _____

10. Serious stress can contribute to mental illness.
    Cause _____     Effect _____

## 연습해설

1. Too much alcohol <u>can make</u> you thirsty.
   Cause : too much alcohol ⟶ Effect : thirsty
   Signal : can make
   [해석] 너무 많은 음주가 당신을 갈증나게 할 수 있다.

2. Many car accidents happen <u>because of</u> the flat tire.
   Cause : flat tire ⟶ Effect : many car accidents
   Signal : because of
   많은 자동차 사고가 펑크 난 타이어 때문에 발생한다.

3. Bad food and not enough sleep are <u>two reasons for</u> bad health.
   Cause : bad food and not enough sleep ⟶ Effect : bad health
   Signal : two reasons for
   [해석] 나쁜 음식과 충분하지 않은 수면이 건강악화의 두 가지 이유이다.

4. Doctors tell us that exercise <u>can help</u> good health.
   Cause : exercise ⟶ Effect : good health
   Signal : can help
   [해석] 의사들은 우리에게 운동이 좋은 건강에 도움이 될 수 있다고 말한다.

5. To remain awake <u>is produced by</u> much coffee.
   Cause : much coffe ⟶ Effect : to remain awake
   Signal : is produced by
   [해석] 너무 많은 커피로 인해 깨어있게 한다.

6. Many fires in homes <u>are due to</u> careless smokers.
   Cause : careless smokers ⟶ Effect : many fires in homes
   Signal : are due to
   [해석] 가정에서의 많은 화재는 부주의한 흡연자들 때문이다.

7. Heart disease is sometimes <u>the result of</u> eating too much.
   Cause : eating too much ⟶ Effect : heart disease
   Signal : the result of
   [해석] 심장질환은 가끔 과식의 결과이다.

8. Bright sunlight <u>can generate</u> your eyes to hurt.
   Cause : bright sunlight ⟶ Effect : your eyes to hurt
   Signal : can generate
   [해석] 밝은 햇빛이 당신의 눈을 아프게 할 수 있다.

9. High insurance costs <u>result from</u> car accidents.
   Cause : car accidents ⟶ Effect : high insurance
   Signal : result from
   [해석] 높은 보험료는 자동차 사고에 기인한다.

10. Serious stress <u>can contribute to</u> mental illness.
    Cause : serious stress ⟶ Effect : mental illness
    Signal : can contribute to
    [해석] 심각한 스트레스가 정신질환에 기여할 수 있다.

**어휘** flat tire 펑크난 타이어
awake 깨어있는
due to ~ 때문에
careless 부주의한
disease 질병
bright 밝은
generate 유발하다, 야기하다
insurance 보험
contribute to ~에 기여하다
illness 질병

## 실전문제

**01** 다음 글의 흐름상 어색한 문장은?

In response to the industry's crisis, the CEOs of the industry carried out a large-scale restructuring.

In the mid to late 1990s, Brazil was one of Latin America's fastest growing economies and "was the darling of the international investment community." In particular, the country's middle class was experiencing significant work-related opportunities to improve its standard of living. ( ① ) However, the effects of late-1990 economic "meltdowns" in Russia and Asia were crippling the Brazilian industries. ( ② ) For example, their economic turmoil resulted in a decline in sales of 27.5 percent from 1997 to 1998 for Brazil's automobile industry alone. ( ③ ) In 1998, as a result, employers eliminated over 580,000 jobs. ( ④ ) The fortunes of the middle class became bleak as job losses found them unable to cope with the demands of financial purchases they made during the "good times."

## 실전 해설

**01**

> In response to the industry's crisis, the CEOs of the industry carried out a large-scale restructuring. → 원인

> In the mid to late 1990s, Brazil was one of Latin America's fastest growing economies and "was the darling of the international investment community." In particular, the country's middle class was experiencing significant work-related opportunities to improve its standard of living. ( ① ) However, the effects of late-1990 economic "meltdowns" in Russia and Asia were crippling the Brazilian industries. ( ② ) For example, their economic turmoil resulted in a decline in sales of 27.5 percent from 1997 to 1998 for Brazil's automobile industry alone. ( ③ ) In 1998, as a result [인과관계의 시그널], employers eliminated over 580,000 jobs [결과]. ( ④ ) The fortunes of the middle class became bleak as job losses found them unable to cope with the demands of financial purchases they made during the "good times."

**해석** 1990년대 중엽에서 말 사이에 브라질은 라틴아메리카에서 가장 빠른 성장을 하는 국가 중 하나였고 국제 투자처 가운데 가장 선호되는 곳이었다. 특히 이 나라의 중산층은 생활수준 향상을 위해 중요한 일과 관련 기회를 경험하고 있었다. 그러나 러시아와 아시아의 1990년 말 경제 붕괴가 브라질 경제에 큰 타격을 주었다. 예를 들어 그들의 경제 혼란은 1997년에서 1998년 사이 브라질 자동차 산업에서만 27.5%의 판매 감소라는 결과를 초래했다. 업계 위기 사태에 대한 대응으로 그 업계의 최고 경영자들은 대규모 구조조정을 단행했다. 그 결과로 1998년 기업들은 58만개의 일자리를 없앴다. 실직으로 인해 호황기에 행한 금융 관련 상품 매입요건에 대처할 수 없게 되어 중산층의 자산은 암울한 상태에 빠졌다.

**어휘** economy (경제주체로서의) 국가  mid to late 중엽에서 말 사이에
darling 특히 사랑받는 사람, 총아  investment 투자  in particular 특히
significant ① 상당한 ② 중요한  opportunity 기회  standard of living 생활수준
meltdown ① 붕괴 ② 녹이다  cripple 심각한 손상을 주다, 불구로 만들다  turmoil 혼란
result in ~을 초래하다, 야기하다  decline 감소(하다)  in response to ~에 대응하여
crisis 위기  carry out 수행하다, 실행하다  large-scale 대규모의  restructuring 구조조정
eliminate 제거하다, 없애다  fortune 운, 미래; 재산  bleak 암울한, 절망적인
cope with 대처하다, 처리하다  financial 재정적인

**해설** 인과관계의 논리가 필요하다. ③에 as a result를 기준으로 인과관계[대규모의 구조조정 단행(원인) → 58만개의 일자리 제거(결과)]를 나타내므로 주어진 문장이 들어가기에 가장 적절한 곳은 ③이다.

**정답**
01 ③

## 실전문제

**02** 다음 글을 읽고, 빈칸에 가장 적절한 것을 고르시오.

> Onions, like other plants, are made up of cells. The cells are divided into two sections separated by a thin layer. One section contains a substance which helps chemical processes occur in your body. The other section contains molecules that contain sulfur. When you cut an onion, the contents on each section mix and cause a chemical reaction. This reaction produces molecules which make your eyes water. To prevent crying when you cut an onion, you can _____ for a few minutes before you cut it. That's because chilly temperatures slow down the reaction between the stimulant substance and the sulfur compounds, so fewer of the burning molecules will reach your eyes.

① put it in the freezer
② rub your eyes gently
③ soak it in salty water
④ wash it in warm water

## 실전 해설

**02**

Onions, like other plants, are made up of cells. The cells are divided into two sections separated by a thin layer. One section contains a substance which helps chemical processes occur in your body. The other section contains molecules that contain sulfur. When you cut an onion, the contents on each section mix and cause a chemical reaction. This reaction produces molecules which make your eyes water. To prevent crying when you cut an onion, you can _____ for a few minutes before you cut it. That's because chilly temperatures slow down the reaction between the stimulant substance and the sulfur compounds, so fewer of the burning molecules will reach your eyes.

**해석** 다른 식물들과 마찬가지로 양파는 여러 세포들로 구성된다. 그 세포들은 얇은 막(layer)에 의해서 분리되는 두 부분으로 나뉜다. 한 부분에는 몸에서 화학적 과정이 일어나는 것을 돕는 물질을 포함한다. 또 한 부분에는 황을 포함하는 분자를 포함한다. 양파를 자를 때 각 부분에 들어있는 내용물들이 (서로) 섞여서 화학 반응을 일으킨다. 이러한 반응은 눈에서 눈물을(water) 나게 하는 분자들을 생성한다. 양파를 자를 때 눈물이 나는 것을 막기 위해서는 그것을 자르기 전에 몇 분 동안 냉장고 속에 둘 수 있다. 그 이유는 차가운 온도가 자극적인 물질과 황을 함유한 혼합물 사이의 반응을 늦추기 때문이고 그래서 눈에 도달하는 자극적인(burning) 분자를 더 적게 한다.

① 냉장고 속에 둘
② 눈을 부드럽게 문지를
③ 소금물에 그것을 담글
④ 따뜻한 물에 그것을 씻을

**어휘** be made up of ~로 구성되다  divide 나누다, 쪼개다  separate 분리시키다  thin 얇은  layer 층
sulfur 유황, 황  reaction 반응  molecule 분자  water (눈물이) 나게 하다  chilly 차가운
slow down 늦추다  stimulant 자극적인  substance 물질
compound ① 혼합물, 복합체 ② 혼합[합성]하다  reach ~에 이르다, 다다르다
freezer 냉장고  soak 담그다, 적시다

**해설** 빈칸 다음 원인과 결과의 시그널 That's because를 이용해야 한다. That's because 다음 차가운 온도가 눈물이 나는 반응을 늦출 수 있다(원인)고 했으므로 양파를 차갑게 해야 한다(결과)가 필요하다. 따라서 빈칸에 들어가기에 가장 적절한 것은 ① '냉장고 속에 둘'이다.

**정답**
02 ①

## 실전문제

**03** 다음 빈칸에 들어갈 말로 가장 적절한 것은?

> Medieval people did not distinguish between entertainment which people expect to pay for and general merriment that anyone could take part in at festive times. They regarded both as 'play', as opposed to work, and they called entertainers 'players.' The Church taught that idleness was a sin, that players were idle and that it was idleness to watch them. Even so, the closing of theaters in Roman times had not taken away people's appetite for comedy, tricks and tunes. The most lasting effect had been to _____, so that they had to wander in search of audience.

① let the players take part in the festivals
② employ entertainers for festivals
③ supply players with new ethics
④ deprive players of a workplace

## 실전 해설

**03**

Medieval people did not distinguish between entertainment which people expect to pay for and general merriment that anyone could take part in at festive times. They regarded both as 'play', as opposed to work, and they called entertainers 'players.' The Church taught that idleness was a sin, that players were idle and that it was idleness to watch them. Even so, the closing of theaters in Roman times had not taken away people's appetite for comedy, tricks and tunes. The most lasting effect had been to ＿＿＿＿＿＿＿＿＿＿＿＿＿＿＿＿＿＿ (원인), so that they had to wander in search of audience. → 결과

**해석** 중세 사람들은 돈을 내기를 기대하는 오락과 누구든 축제 때 참여할 수 있는 일반적 유희를 구분하지 않았다. 그들은 이 둘을 노동과는 반대로 '놀이'로 간주했고 예능인을 '노는 사람(놀이꾼)'이라고 불렀다. 교회는 게으름은 죄악이라고 가르쳤고 노는 사람은 게으른 것이며 이들을 지켜보는 것도 게으른 것이라고 가르쳤다. 그럼에도 불구하고 로마 시대의 극장 폐쇄가 희극, 묘기 그리고 음악에 대한 사람들의 욕구를 빼앗아 가지는 못했다. 가장 오래 지속된 효과는 <u>놀이꾼들에게서 일터를 빼앗은 것</u>이며 따라서 이들은 청중을 찾아서 떠돌아다녀야만 했다.
① 놀이꾼들이 축제에 참여하도록 허용하는 것
② 축제에 예능인을 고용하는 것
③ 놀이꾼들에게 새로운 윤리를 제공하는 것
④ 놀이꾼들에게서 일터를 빼앗은 것

**어휘** medieval 중세의  distinguish between A and B A와 B를 구별하다  entertainment 오락  general 일반적인  merriment 즐거움, 기쁨, 유희 *merry 즐거운  take part in ~에 참가하다  regard A as B A를 B로 간주하다  as opposed to ~와는 반대로  idleness 게으름 *idle 게으른  sin 죄, 원죄, 죄악  closing 폐쇄  take away 빼앗다, 가져가버리다  appetite 식욕; 욕구, 욕망  tune 멜로디, 노래  lasting 계속적인, 지속되는 *last 지속[계속]되다  wander 헤매다, 돌아다니다  in search of ~을 찾아서  supply A with B A에게 B를 제공하다  ethics 윤리; 윤리학  deprive A of B A에게서 B를 빼앗다

**해설** 인과 관계의 논리를 이용해야 한다. 빈칸 바로 뒤에 so that(그래서)이 있으므로 빈칸에는 so that 다음 내용의 원인이 있어야 한다. so that 다음 내용이 '청중을 찾아 다녀야 했다'이므로 그 원인에 해당되는 내용이 빈칸에 필요하다. 따라서 빈칸에 들어가기에 가장 적절한 것은 ④ '놀이꾼들에게서 일터를 빼앗은 것'이다.

**정답**
03 ④

## 실전문제

**04** 다음 빈칸에 들어갈 말로 가장 적절한 것을 고르시오.

There are two kinds of different tragic heroes in the history of world. The one is tragic heroes in Shakespeare's plays who have free will. They possess their own defects of character that bring their downfalls. Macbeth is ambitious but weak; Othello is jealous; Hamlet cannot make up his mind — but all three might have made themselves into better human beings. Nothing outside themselves prevents them from taking the right path as opposed to the wrong, or tragic path. On the other hand, for the heroes in Greek tragedies where fate embodied in the oracles prevails, there is no free will. The gods control a man's destiny, and one cannot fight the gods. Regardless of their strength or wisdom, the heroes cannot control their own future. That is why the heroes in Greek tragedies can be compared to _____.

\* oracle : (고대 그리스에서) 신탁

① free will
② fish in the net
③ escaping from oracles
④ those who resist the fate

## 실전 해설

**04**

There are two kinds of different tragic heroes in the history of world. The one is tragic heroes in Shakespeare's plays who have free will. They possess their own defects of character that bring their downfalls. Macbeth is ambitious but weak; Othello is jealous; Hamlet cannot make up his mind — but all three might have made themselves into better human beings. Nothing outside themselves prevents them from taking the right path as opposed to the wrong, or tragic path. On the other hand, for the heroes in Greek tragedies where fate embodied in the oracles prevails, there is no free will. The gods control a man's destiny, and one cannot fight the gods. Regardless of their strength or wisdom, the heroes cannot control their own future. That is why the heroes in Greek tragedies can be compared to _____.

\* oracle : (고대 그리스에서) 신탁

**해석** 세계 역사상 두 종류의 비극적 영웅들이 있다. 그 하나는 자유의지가 있는 셰익스피어 연극의 비극적 주인공들이다. 그들은 그들을 파멸로 이끄는 자신들만의 인물의 결함을 소유하고 있다. 맥베드는 의욕적이지만 약하다. 오델로는 질투심이 있고, 햄릿은 결단력이 부족했다. 하지만 이 셋 모두 그들 스스로를 더 나은 인간으로 만들어 냈다. 그들 자신 이외의 그 어떤 것도 그들이 악이나 비극적인 길로부터 반대편 길을 선택하는 것을 막아낼 수 없다. 반면에 그리스 신화의 비극을 보면 신탁을 통해서 구체화된 운명이 우세할 뿐 자유의지는 없다. 신이 인간의 운명을 조정하고 (인간은) 어느 누구도 신과 싸울 수 없다. 그들의 힘이나 지혜와 상관없이 영웅들은 그들 자신들의 미래를 지배할 수 없다. 그것이 그리스 신화(비극)의 영웅들이 <u>그물에 걸린 물고기</u>에 비유되는 이유이다.
① 자유 의지
② 그물에 걸린 물고기
③ 신탁으로부터 벗어나기
④ 운명에 저항하는 사람들

**어휘** tragic 비극적인  will 의지  possess 소유하다  defect 결함  character 주인공, 인물
downfall 붕괴, 몰락  ambitious 야심에 찬  weak 약한  jealous 질투어린
make up one's mind 결정[결심]하다  as opposed to ~와 반대로  path 길  fate 운명
embody 구체화하다, 구현하다  regardless of ~와 관계없이  strength 힘  wisdom 지혜
compare A to B A를 B에 비유하다  conform 순응하다, 따르다

**해설** two 개념을 이용해야 한다. 주어진 지문은 본문 중간쯤의 On the other hand를 기준으로 위에는 자유의지가 있는 셰익스피어의 주인공들의 이야기와 아래에는 자유 의지가 없는 그리스 비극의 주인공들의 차이점을 기술하고 있다. 따라서 빈칸에 들어가기에 가장 적절한 것은 ② '그물에 걸린 물고기'이다.

**정답**
04 ②

## 기출문제

**01** 주어진 글 다음에 이어질 글의 순서로 가장 적절한 것은? 2025. 국가직 9급

The idea that society should allocate economic rewards and positions of responsibility according to merit is appealing for several reasons.

(A) An economic system that rewards effort, initiative, and talent is likely to be more productive than one that pays everyone the same, regardless of contribution, or that hands out desirable social positions based on favoritism.
(B) Rewarding people strictly on their merits also has the virtue of fairness; it does not discriminate on any basis other than achievement.
(C) Two of these reasons are generalized versions of the case for merit in hiring — efficiency and fairness.

① (A) - (C) - (B)
② (B) - (C) - (A)
③ (C) - (A) - (B)
④ (C) - (B) - (A)

## 기출 분석

**01**

The idea that society should allocate economic rewards and positions of responsibility according to merit is appealing for several reasons.

(A) An economic system that rewards effort, initiative, and talent is likely to be more productive than one that pays everyone the same, regardless of contribution, or that hands out desirable social positions based on favoritism.

(B) Rewarding people strictly on their merits **also** has the virtue of fairness; it does not discriminate on any basis other than achievement.  ↑ 두 번째 나열

↑ 나열의 시작점
(C) **Two of these** reasons are generalized versions of the case for merit in hiring — efficiency and fairness.

- **해석** 사회가 경제적 보상과 책임의 지위를 능력에 따라 배분해야 한다는 생각은 여러 가지 이유에서 매력적이다.
  (C) 이러한 이유 중 두 가지는 채용에 있어서 능력을 중시해야 한다는 주장을 일반화한 것으로, 바로 효율성과 공정성이다.
  (A) 노력, 주도성, 재능을 보상하는 경제 체제는 개인의 기여 여부와 관계없이 모두에게 동일한 보수를 지급하거나, 연줄에 따라 원하는 사회적 지위를 배분하는 경제 시스템보다 더 생산성이 더 높을 가능성이 크다.
  (B) 사람들에게 엄격하게 능력에 따라 보상하는 것은 또한 공정성의 미덕도 있는데, 이는 성취 이외의 어떤 기준으로도 차별하지 않는다는 것이다.

- **어휘** allocate 분배하다, 할당하다  reward 보상하다  position 지위, 직책
  according to ~에 따라, ~에 따르면  merit ① 능력 ② 이점, 장점  appealing 매력적인
  effort 노력, 수고  initiative 진취성, 주도적 행동  be likely to ~할 가능성이 있다
  productive 생산적인  regardless of ~에 관계없이  contribution 기여, 공헌
  hand out 나눠주다, 배포하다  desirable 바람직한  based on ~에 근거하여
  favoritism 편애, 편파, 특혜  strictly 엄격하게  virtue 미덕, 덕목  fairness 공정성
  discriminate 차별하다  basis 기준, 근거  other than ~이외에는, ~을 제외하고는
  achievement 업적, 성취, 달성  generalize 일반화하다, 보편화하다  hire 고용하다
  efficiency 효율성, 능률

- **해설** (C)의 these reasons는 주어진 문장의 reasons를 가리키므로 주어진 문장 다음 (C)가 위치해야 한다. (C)의 Two of these reasons는 efficiency와 fairness이고 (A)는 efficiency(효율성)를 설명하고 (B)에 나열의 시그널 also(두 번째 나열)가 있고 fairness(공정성)에 대한 설명이므로 (A) - (B) 순서가 되어야 한다. 따라서 주어진 글 다음 이어질 글의 순서로 가장 적절한 것은 ③ '(C) - (A) - (B)'이다.

01 ③

## 기출문제

**02** 주어진 글 다음에 이어질 글의 순서로 적절한 것은? 2024. 지방직 9급

> Computer assisted language learning (CALL) is both exciting and frustrating as a field of research and practice.

(A) Yet the technology changes so rapidly that CALL knowledge and skills must be constantly renewed to stay apace of the field.
(B) It is exciting because it is complex, dynamic and quickly changing — and it is frustrating for the same reasons.
(C) Technology adds dimensions to the domain of language learning, requiring new knowledge and skills for those who wish to apply it into their professional practice.

① (A) − (C) − (B)
② (B) − (A) − (C)
③ (B) − (C) − (A)
④ (C) − (B) − (A)

## 기출 분석

**02**

> Two 개념: ① CALL의 좌절(⊖) ② CALL의 흥미로운 점(⊕)
> Computer assisted language learning (CALL) is both exciting and frustrating as a field of research and practice.

(A) Yet the technology changes so rapidly that CALL knowledge and skills must be constantly renewed to stay apace of the field. (⊖)
(B) It is exciting because it is complex, dynamic and quickly changing — and it is frustrating for the same reasons. (둘 다 설명)
(C) Technology adds dimensions to the domain of language learning, requiring new knowledge and skills for those who wish to apply it into their professional practice. (⊕)

※ 단락의 전개 방식
(B) 둘 다(⊕/⊖) 설명
(C) ⊕ 설명
(A) Yet ⊖ 설명

**해석** 컴퓨터 보조 언어 학습(CALL)은 연구와 실습의 한 분야로서 흥미롭기도 하고 좌절감을 주기도 한다.
(B) 그것은 복잡하고 역동적이며 빠르게 변화하기 때문에 흥미로우며 같은 이유로 좌절감을 준다.
(C) 기술은 언어 학습 영역에 차원들을 더해 주어 그것을 자신들의 전문적인 실습에 적용하고자 하는 사람들에게 새로운 지식과 기술을 요구한다.
(A) 그러나 기술은 너무 빠르게 변화해서 CALL 지식과 기술은 그 분야의 빠른 속도에 (보조를) 맞추기 위해 지속적으로 갱신되어야 한다.

**어휘** assist 돕다  frustrating 좌절시키다  field 분야  practice 실행, 실습  rapidly 빠르게, 신속하게  constantly 지속적으로, 계속해서  renew 갱신하다  stay apace 빠른 속도에 (보조를) 맞추다  *apace 빠른 속도로, 빨리  complex 복잡한  dynamic 역동적인  dimension 차원  require 요구하다  those who ~하는 사람들  apply 적용하다  professional 전문적인

**해설** two 개념을 이용해야 한다. 주어진 글은 컴퓨터 보조 언어 학습(CALL)이 흥미(exciting)와 좌절감(frustrating)을 동시에 준다는 내용이고 (B)에서 그 두 가지를 다시 한 번 더 설명하고 있으므로 주어진 문장 다음에는 (B)가 위치해야 한다. (C)에서 컴퓨터 보조 언어 학습(CALL)의 흥미로운 점(requiring new knowledge and skills)을 설명하고 (A)에서 반대/대조의 연결어 yet을 이용해서 좌절감(must be constantly renewed)이 이어져야 하므로 (B) 다음 (C)와 (A)의 순으로 이어지는 것이 가장 적절하다. 따라서 주어진 글 다음에 이어질 글의 순서로 가장 적절한 것은 ③ (B) — (C) — (A)이다.

02 ③

## 기출문제

**03** 주어진 문장이 들어갈 위치로 적절한 것은? 2024. 지방직 9급

> But she quickly popped her head out again.

The little mermaid swam right up to the small window of the cabin, and every time a wave lifted her up, she could see a crowd of well-dressed people through the clear glass. Among them was a young prince, the handsomest person there, with large dark eyes. ( ① ) It was his birthday, and that's why there was so much excitement. ( ② ) When the young prince came out on the deck, where the sailors were dancing, more than a hundred rockets went up into the sky and broke into a glitter, making the sky as bright as day. ( ③ ) The little mermaid was so startled that she dove down under the water. ( ④ ) And look! It was just as if all the stars up in heaven were falling down on her. Never had she seen such fireworks.

## 기출 분석

**03**

But she quickly popped her head out again.

The little mermaid swam right up to the small window of the cabin, and every time a wave lifted her up, she could see a crowd of well-dressed people through the clear glass. Among them was a young prince, the handsomest person there, with large dark eyes. ( ① ) It was his birthday, and that's why there was so much excitement. ( ② ) When the young prince came out on the deck, where the sailors were dancing, more than a hundred rockets went up into the sky and broke into a glitter, making the sky as bright as day. ( ③ ) The little mermaid was so startled that she dove down under the water. ( ④ ) And look! It was just as if all the stars up in heaven were falling down on her. Never had she seen such fireworks.

**해석** 인어공주는 선실의 작은 창문 바로 앞까지 수영을 했고 파도가 그녀를 들어 올릴 때마다, 그녀는 투명한 유리를 통해 (옷을) 잘 차려입은 한 무리의 사람들을 볼 수 있었다. 그들 중에는 크고 짙은 눈을 가진 그곳에서 가장 잘생긴 젊은 왕자가 있었다. 그날은 그의 생일이었고 그래서 그곳에서는 아주 많은 신남이 있었다. 그 젊은 왕자가 선원들이 춤을 추고 있는 갑판으로 나왔을 때 100개가 넘는 폭죽이 하늘로 올라갔다가 부서져 반짝이며 하늘을 낮처럼 밝게 만들었다. 인어공주는 너무 놀라서 물속으로 들어갔다. 그러나 그녀는 빠르게 다시 머리를 밖으로 내밀었다. 그리고 보라! 마치 하늘에 있는 모든 별들이 그녀에게 쏟아지는 것 같았다. 그녀는 그러한 불꽃놀이를 한 번도 본 적이 없었다.

**어휘** pop A out A를 밖으로 내밀다 *pop 튀어 나오다, (불쑥) 나타나다  little mermaid 인어공주  right up to 바로 ~앞까지  cabin 선실  every time S + V ~할 때마다  wave 파도  lift up 위로 들어 올리다  a crowd of 한 무리의 사람들 *crowd 군중  deck 갑판  sailor 선원  well-dressed (옷을) 잘 차려입은  clear 깨끗한, 투명한  prince 왕자  dive down 잠수하다  rocket 폭죽  glitter ① 반짝이다 ② 반짝이는 빛  startle 놀라게 하다  firework 불꽃놀이, 폭죽  heaven 하늘, 천국

**해설** 시간 순서 전개 방식을 이용해야 한다. 주어진 지문은 인어공주가 선실을 들여다보다가 폭죽이 터지고 그로 인해 놀라서 다시 물 안으로 들어간 후 다시 고개를 물 밖으로 내미는 시간 순서 전개 방식을 따르고 있다. 따라서 주어진 문장이 들어갈 위치로 가장 적절한 것은 ④이다.

**정답**
03 ④

## 기출문제

**04** 밑줄 친 부분에 들어갈 말로 적절한 것을 고르시오. *2024. 지방직 9급*

> Javelin Research noticed that not all Millennials are currently in the same stage of life. While all Millennials were born around the turn of the century, some of them are still in early adulthood, wrestling with new careers and settling down. On the other hand, the older Millennials have a home and are building a family. You can imagine how having a child might change your interests and priorities, so for marketing purposes, it's useful to split this generation into Gen Y.1 and Gen Y.2. Not only are the two groups culturally different, but they're in vastly different phases of their financial life. The younger group is financial beginners, just starting to show their buying power. The latter group has a credit history, may have their first mortgage and is raising young children. The _____ in priorities and needs between Gen Y.1 and Gen Y.2 is vast.

① contrast
② reduction
③ repetition
④ ability

## 기출 분석

**04**

Javelin Research noticed that not all Millennials are currently in the same stage of life. While all Millennials were born around the turn of the century, some of them are still in early adulthood, wrestling with new careers and settling down. On the other hand, the older Millennials have a home and are building a family. You can imagine how having a child might change your interests and priorities, so for marketing purposes, it's useful to split this generation into Gen Y.1 and Gen Y.2. Not only are the two groups culturally different, but they're in vastly different phases of their financial life. The younger group is financial beginners, just starting to show their buying power. The latter group has a credit history, may have their first mortgage and is raising young children. The _____ in priorities and needs between Gen Y.1 and Gen Y.2 is vast.

**해석** Javelin Research는 모든 밀레니얼 세대가 현재 같은 삶의 단계에 있는 것은 아니라는 것을 알아차렸다. 모든 밀레니얼 세대가 세기의 전환기에 태어났지만, 그중 일부는 아직 초기 성인 단계에서 새로운 직업과 씨름하며 자리를 잡아가고 있다. 반면에, 나이가 더 많은 밀레니얼 세대는 집이 있고 가정을 만들어가고 있다. 당신은 아이를 낳는 것이 당신의 관심사와 우선순위가 어떻게 달라질지 상상할 수 있고 그래서 마케팅 목적을 위해 이 세대를 Y.1 세대와 Y.2 세대로 나누는 것이 유용하다. 두 집단은 문화적으로 다를 뿐만 아니라 재정적으로 아주 다른 삶의 단계에 있다. 더 어린 집단은 재정 초보자들로서 이제 막 구매력을 발휘하기 시작한다. 후자 집단은 신용기록이 있고 첫 주택담보대출을 받았을 수도 있으며, 어린 자녀들을 키우고 있다. Y.1 세대와 Y.2 세대 간 우선순위와 필요의 <u>차이</u>는 아주 크다.

① 차이
② 감소
③ 반복
④ 능력

**어휘** notice 알아차리다  Millennial ①천년의 ②1980년대에서 1990년도에 태어난 사람들  currently 현재
stage 단계  turn 전환기  adulthood 성인기, 성년기  wrestle 씨름하다, 레슬링하다
career 직업, 경력  settle down 정착하다  on the other hand 반면에  priority 우선순위
split 나누다, 쪼개다  generation 세대  culturally 문화적으로  vastly 거대하게, 아주, 매우
phase ①단계 ②상, 모습  financial 재정상의, 재정적인  the latter 후자(의)
mortgage ①담보대출 ②저당 잡히다  vast 거대한  reduction 감소  repetition 반복

**해설** two 개념을 이용해야 한다. 주어진 지문은 Y.1 세대와 Y.2 세대 간의 차이점을 설명하고 있으므로 빈칸에 들어갈 말로 적절한 것은 ① '차이'이다.

**정답**
04 ①

## 기출문제

**05** 밑줄에 들어갈 말로 적절한 것을 고르시오. 2024. 지방직 9급

> Cost pressures in liberalized markets have different effects on existing and future hydropower schemes. Because of the cost structure, existing hydropower plants will always be able to earn a profit. Because the planning and construction of future hydropower schemes is not a short-term process, it is not a popular investment, in spite of low electricity generation costs. Most private investors would prefer to finance _____, leading to the paradoxical situation that although an existing hydropower plant seems to be a cash cow, nobody wants to invest in a new one. Where public shareholders/owners (states, cities, municipalities) are involved, the situation looks very different because they can see the importance of the security of supply and also appreciate long-term investments.

① more short-term technologies
② all high technology industries
③ the promotion of the public interest
④ the enhancement of electricity supply

## 기출 분석

**05**

Two 개념: ① 기존의 수력발전 ② 미래의 수력발전 → 차이점 설명

Cost pressures in liberalized markets have different effects on existing and future hydropower schemes. Because of the cost structure, existing hydropower plants will always be able to earn a profit. Because the planning and construction of future hydropower schemes is not a short-term process, it is not a popular investment, in spite of low electricity generation costs. Most private investors would prefer to finance _____, leading to the paradoxical situation that although an existing hydropower plant seems to be a cash cow, nobody wants to invest in a new one. Where public shareholders/owners (states, cities, municipalities) are involved, the situation looks very different because they can see the importance of the security of supply and also appreciate long-term investments.

**해석** 자유화된 시장에서의 비용 압력은 기존 및 미래의 수력발전 계획에 서로 다른 영향을 준다. 비용 구조 때문에 기존의 수력발전소는 항상 수익을 낼 수 있을 것이다. 미래 수력발전 계획에 대한 계획과 건설 계획은 단기간의 과정이 아니기 때문에 낮은 전력 생성 비용에도 불구하고 대중적인 투자는 아니다. 대부분의 민간 투자자들은 <u>더 단기간의 기술</u>에 자금을 대는 것을 선호하는데 이는 기존 수력발전소가 캐시 카우처럼 보이는 데도 불구하고 아무도 새로운 곳에 투자하지 않으려는 역설적인 상황을 초래한다. 공공 주주/소유주(주, 시, 지자체)가 참여하는 경우 그들은 공급 안정성의 중요성을 인식하고 장기적인 투자의 진가를 인정하기 때문에 상황은 매우 다르게 보인다.
① 더 단기간의 기술
② 모든 첨단 기술 산업
③ 공공 이익의 증진
④ 전력 공급의 강화

**어휘** pressure 압박  liberalized 자유화된  have effects on ~에 영향을 주다  existing 기존의  hydropower 수력발전  scheme 계획  structure 구조  existing 기존의  plant 발전소, 공장  earn 벌다, 얻다  profit 수익  construction 건설  short-term 단기간의  process 과정  popular 대중적인  investment 투자  in spite of ~에도 불구하고  electricity 전기, 전력  generation ① 세대 ② 발생, 생성  private ① 사적인 ② 민간의, 민영의  investor 투자자  *invest 투자하다  prefer 선호하다  finance ① 재원, 자금 ② 자금을 대다  lead to ~을 초래하다, 야기하다  paradoxical 역설적인  situation 상황  cash cow 캐시 카우, 고수익 사업[상품]  public 공적인, 공공의  shareholder 주주  municipality 지방 자치제, 지자체  involve ① 포함하다 ② 관계시키다 ③ 참여시키다  security 안전, 안정성  supply 공급(하다)  appreciate 진가를 인정하다, 중요시하다  promotion 증진, 향상  interest ① 흥미, 관심 ② 이익, 이자  enhancement 강화, 향상

**해설** two 개념(기존 vs. 미래)을 이용해야 한다. 기존의 수력발전은 수익을 낼 수 있고, 단기과정인데 반해 미래 수력 발전은 단기과정이 아니고 인기 있는 투자도 아니므로 문맥상 투자자들이 투자할 곳은 기존 수력발전이어야 한다. 선택지에 기존 수력발전을 설명하는 short-term(단기) technologies가 있으므로 빈칸에 들어가기에 가장 적절한 것은 ① '더 단기간의 기술'이다. 참고로 빈칸 다음 민간 투자자들(private investors)과는 달리 공공 주주들/소유주들(public shareholders/owners)은 공급 안정성(security of supply)과 장기적인 투자(long-term investments)를 중요하게 여긴다고 했고 선택지 ③ public interest와 ④ electricity supply는 모두 미래의 기술과 관련된 내용이므로 정답이 될 수 없다.

05 ①

## 기출문제

**06** 다음 글의 흐름상 가장 어색한 문장은? 2022. 국가직 9급

> Beliefs about maintaining ties with those who have died vary from culture to culture. For example, maintaining ties with the deceased is accepted and sustained in the religious rituals of Japan. Yet among the Hopi Indians of Arizona, the deceased are forgotten as quickly as possible and life goes on as usual. ___(A)___, the Hopi funeral ritual concludes with a break-off between mortals and spirits. The diversity of grieving is nowhere clearer than in two Muslim societies—one in Egypt, the other in Bali. Among Muslims in Egypt, the bereaved are encouraged to dwell at length on their grief, surrounded by others who relate to similarly tragic accounts and express their sorrow. ___(B)___, in Bali, bereaved Muslims are encouraged to laugh and be joyful rather than be sad.

|     | (A)      | (B)          |
|-----|----------|--------------|
| ①   | However  | Similarly    |
| ②   | In fact  | By contrast  |
| ③   | Therefore| For example  |
| ④   | Likewise | Consequently |

## 기출 분석

**06**

Beliefs about maintaining ties with those who have died vary from culture to culture. For example, maintaining ties with the deceased is accepted and sustained in the religious rituals of Japan. Yet among the Hopi Indians of Arizona, the deceased are forgotten as quickly as possible and life goes on as usual. ___(A)___, the Hopi funeral ritual concludes with a break-off between mortals and spirits. The diversity of grieving is nowhere clearer than in two Muslim societies—one in Egypt, the other in Bali. Among Muslims in Egypt, the bereaved are encouraged to dwell at length on their grief, surrounded by others who relate to similarly tragic accounts and express their sorrow. ___(B)___, in Bali, bereaved Muslims are encouraged to laugh and be joyful rather than be sad.

**[해석]** 사망한 사람들과 유대를 유지하는 것에 관한 믿음은 문화마다 다르다. 예를 들어 일본의 종교 의식에서는 고인과 유대를 유지하는 것이 받아들여지고 지속된다. 하지만 애리조나의 Hopi 인디언들 사이에서 망자는 가능한 한 빨리 잊히고 삶은 늘 그렇듯이 지속된다. 사실상, Hopi족의 장례의식은 인간과 영혼 사이의 단절로 결론이 난다. 슬퍼하기의 다양성은 이집트와 발리 즉, 두 이슬람교 사회에서 가장 분명하다. 이집트의 이슬람교도 사이에서 유족들은 마찬가지로 비극적인 이야기와 자신들의 슬픔을 표현하는 사람들에게 둘러싸여 그들의 슬픔을 충분히 심사숙고하도록 권장된다. 이와는 반대로, 발리에서는 이슬람교 유족들이 슬퍼하기보다는 웃고 기뻐하도록 권장된다.

**[어휘]** belief 믿음  maintain 유지하다  tie 유대  deceased 사망한, 작고한  sustain 지속시키다
religious 종교적인  ritual (종교적) 의식  go on 계속되다, 계속하다
as usual 늘 그렇듯이, 여느 때처럼  funeral 장례식  break-off 단절, 중단
mortal ① 영원히 살 수 없는, 언젠가는 반드시 죽는 ② 사람, 인간  diversity 다양성
grieve 비통해하다, 슬프게 하다 *grief 비통, 슬픔  bereave 사별하다, 여의다
dwell on 심사숙고하다  at length 상세하게, 충분히  surround 에워싸다, 둘러싸다
tragic 비극적인  account 설명, 이야기  sorrow 슬픔  similarly 마찬가지로(= likewise)
therefore 그러므로, 그래서  consequently 결과적으로

**[해설]** (A) 앞에 Hopi 인디언들은 고인을 가능한 한 빨리 잊는다는 내용이 있고 (A) 뒤에는 Hopi족의 장례의식이 인간과 영혼사이의 단절이라는 내용이 있으므로 (A)에는 논리의 방향이 같은 연결사 In fact가 필요하다. (B)는 two개념(반대/대조의 공간 개념)을 이용해야 한다. (B) 앞에 두 이슬람 문화의 차이점을 제시하고 있으므로(Egypt→슬픔을 표현/Bali→웃고 기뻐함) (B)에는 By contrast가 있어야 한다. 따라서 정답은 ②이다.

**정답**
06 ②

## 기출문제

**07** 다음 글의 제목으로 가장 적절한 것은? 2022. 국가직 9급

Do people from different cultures view the world differently? A psychologist presented realistic animated scenes of fish and other underwater objects to Japanese and American students and asked them to report what they had seen. Americans and Japanese made about an equal number of references to the focal fish, but the Japanese made more than 60 percent more references to background elements, including the water, rocks, bubbles, and inert plants and animals. In addition, whereas Japanese and American participants made about equal numbers of references to movement involving active animals, the Japanese participants made almost twice as many references to relationships involving inert, background objects. Perhaps most tellingly, the very first sentence from the Japanese participants was likely to be one referring to the environment, whereas the first sentence from Americans was three times as likely to be one referring to the focal fish.

① Language Barrier Between Japanese and Americans
② Associations of Objects and Backgrounds in the Brain
③ Cultural Differences in Perception
④ Superiority of Detail-oriented People

## 기출 분석

**07**

> Two 개념: ① 일본인 ② 미국인 → 사물을 보는 시각의 차이점
>
> Do people from different cultures view the world differently? A psychologist presented realistic animated scenes of fish and other underwater objects to Japanese and American students and asked them to report what they had seen. Americans and Japanese made about an equal number of references to the focal fish, but the Japanese made more than 60 percent more references to background elements, including the water, rocks, bubbles, and inert plants and animals. In addition, whereas Japanese and American participants made about equal numbers of references to movement involving active animals, the Japanese participants made almost twice as many references to relationships involving inert, background objects. Perhaps most tellingly, the very first sentence from the Japanese participants was likely to be one referring to the environment, whereas the first sentence from Americans was three times as likely to be one referring to the focal fish.

**해석** 다른 문화의 사람들은 세상을 달리 볼까? 한 심리학자는 일본과 미국 학생들에게 물고기와 다른 수중 물체의 사실적인 애니메이션 장면을 보여 주었고 그들이 본 것을 보고하도록 요청했다. 미국인들과 일본인들은 이 초점 대상인 물고기를 거의 같은 수로 언급했지만, 일본인들은 물, 바위, 거품, 그리고 비활성식물과 동물들을 포함한 배경 요소들에 대해 60% 이상 언급했다. 게다가, 일본과 미국의 참가자가 대략 같은 수의 활동적인 동물을 포함한 움직임을 언급했던 반면, 일본 참가자는 비활성 배경 물체와 관련된 관계에 대해서는 거의 2배 가까이 더 언급을 했다. 아마도 가장 확실한 것은 일본인 참가자의 첫 번째 문장은 환경을 언급하는 문장이었을 것이고 반면에, 미국인의 첫 번째 문장은 초점 대상인 물고기를 언급하는 문장이었을 것인데 그 가능성은 3배 더 높았다.

① 일본인과 미국인 사이의 언어 장벽
② 뇌 안의 물체와 배경의 연관성
③ 인식의 문화적 차이
④ 세부지향적인 사람들의 우월성

**어휘** present 보여주다, 제공하다  realistic 사실적인  animated ① 생생한, 살아있는 ② 만화영화로 된  scene 장면  reference ① 언급 ② 참고  focal 중심의, 초점의  inert 무기력한, 비활성의  participant 참가자  tellingly 확실하게, 강력하게  barrier 장벽, 장애물  association 연관성, 관련  perception 인식  superiority 우월성  A-oriented A지향적인

**해설** 단락의 도입부에 반대/대조를 나타내는 시그널 different(서로 다른 소재에 대한 차이점)를 이용해야 한다. 주어진 지문은 똑같은 사물을 보는 두 문화 사람들(미국인 vs. 일본인)의 차이점을 소개하는 내용의 글이므로 이 글의 제목으로 가장 적절한 것은 ③ '인식의 문화적 차이'이다.

**정답**
07 ③

## 기출문제

**08** 다음 글의 흐름상 가장 어색한 문장은? 2021. 국가직 9급

The term burnout refers to a "wearing out" from the pressures of work. Burnout is a chronic condition that results as daily work stressors take their toll on employees. ① The most widely adopted conceptualization of burnout has been developed by Maslach and her colleagues in their studies of human service workers. Maslach sees burnout as consisting of three interrelated dimensions. The first dimension — emotional exhaustion — is really the core of the burnout phenomenon. ② Workers suffer from emotional exhaustion when they feel fatigued, frustrated, used up, or unable to face another day on the job. The second dimension of burnout is a lack of personal accomplishment. ③ This aspect of the burnout phenomenon refers to workers who see themselves as failures, incapable of effectively accomplishing job requirements. ④ Emotional labor workers enter their occupation highly motivated although they are physically exhausted. The third dimension of burnout is depersonalization. This dimension is relevant only to workers who must communicate interpersonally with others (e.g. clients, patients, students) as part of the job.

## 기출 분석

**08**

The term burnout refers to a "wearing out" from the pressures of work. Burnout is a chronic condition that results as daily work stressors take their toll on employees. ① The most widely adopted conceptualization of burnout has been developed by Maslach and her colleagues in their studies of human service workers. Maslach sees burnout as consisting of three interrelated dimensions. The first dimension — emotional exhaustion — is really the core of the burnout phenomenon. ② Workers suffer from emotional exhaustion when they feel fatigued, frustrated, used up, or unable to face another day on the job. The second dimension of burnout is a lack of personal accomplishment. ③ This aspect of the burnout phenomenon refers to workers who see themselves as failures, incapable of effectively accomplishing job requirements. ④ Emotional labor workers enter their occupation highly motivated although they are physically exhausted. The third dimension of burnout is depersonalization. This dimension is relevant only to workers who must communicate interpersonally with others (e.g. clients, patients, students) as part of the job.

※ 나열의 시작점
※ 첫 번째 나열의 개념이 이 자리에 다시 나올 수 없다.

**해석** 번아웃은 일의 압박으로부터 "기진맥진"을 일컫는 용어이다. 번아웃은 일상적인 업무스트레스 요인의 결과물이 직원들에게 큰 해를 입히는 만성질환이다. 가장 널리 채택된 번아웃의 개념화는 Maslach와 그녀의 동료들이 사람을 대하는 근로자들에 대한 연구에서 개발되었다. Maslach는 번아웃을 세 가지 서로 관련된 관점으로 구성되어 있다고 여긴다. 첫 번째 관점인 감정적 피로감이 진정으로 번아웃 현상의 핵심이다. 근로자들이 피로감, 좌절감 그리고 몹시 지쳤다고 느끼거나 직장에서 또 다른 하루에 직면할 수 없을 때 감정적 피로로부터 고통을 받는다. 번아웃의 두 번째 관점은 개인적 성취의 부족이다. 번아웃 현상의 이러한 관점은 자기 스스로 업무 요구 사항을 효과적으로 달성할 수 없는 실패자로 여기는 근로자들을 일컫는다. (비록 감정 노동자들이 육체적으로는 피곤하다 하더라도 상당히 동기 부여된 상태로 자신들의 일을 시작한다.) 번아웃의 세 번째 관점은 비인격화이다. 이 관점은 단지 업무상 다른 사람들(예를 들어 고객, 환자, 학생)과 관계를 맺어야 하는 노동자들에 해당된다.

**어휘** refer to ① ~을 참고하다 ② ~을 언급하다, ~라고 일컫다  wear out 닳아빠지다, 기진맥진하다
stressor 스트레스 요인  chronic condition 만성질환
take a toll on ~에게 해를 입히다, ~에게 피해를 주다  adopt 채택하다
conceptualization 개념화  colleague 동료  see A as B A를 B로 여기다, 간주하다
consist of ~로 구성되다  interrelated 상호 관련된  dimension ① 차원 ② 관점
exhaustion 피로, 탈진  fatigued 피로한, 지친  frustrated 좌절된  used up 몹시 지친
phenomenon 현상  failure 실패  incapable 할 수 없는  highly 아주, 매우, 상당히
requirement 요구 사항  motivated 동기 부여된, 의욕을 가진  depersonalization 비인격화
interpersonally 대인관계에서

**해설** 주어진 지문은 번아웃의 ⊖ 관점 세 가지를 나열하는 내용의 글이다. 따라서 ④ '비록 감정 노동자들이 육체적으로는 피곤하다 하더라도 상당히 동기 부여된 상태로 자신들의 일을 시작한다'는 내용의 ⊕ 관점은 글의 흐름상 어색하다. 따라서 정답은 ④이다.

**정답** 08 ④

## 기출문제

**09** 주어진 문장이 들어갈 위치로 가장 적절한 것은? 2021. 지방직 9급

> And working offers more than financial security.

Why do workaholics enjoy their jobs so much? Mostly because working offers some important advantages. ( ① ) It provides people with paychecks—a way to earn a living. ( ② ) It provides people with self-confidence; they have a feeling of satisfaction when they've produced a challenging piece of work and are able to say, "I made that". ( ③ ) Psychologists claim that work also gives people an identity; they work so that they can get a sense of self and individualism. ( ④ ) In addition, most jobs provide people with a socially acceptable way to meet others. It could be said that working is a positive addiction; maybe workaholics are compulsive about their work, but their addiction seems to be a safe—even an advantageous—one.

## 기출 분석

**09**

> And working offers more than financial security.

Why do workaholics enjoy their jobs so much? Mostly because working offers some important advantages. ( ① ) It provides people with paychecks — a way to earn a living. ( ② ) It provides people with self-confidence; they have a feeling of satisfaction when they've produced a challenging piece of work and are able to say, "I made that". ( ③ ) Psychologists claim that work also gives people an identity; they work so that they can get a sense of self and individualism. ( ④ ) In addition, most jobs provide people with a socially acceptable way to meet others. It could be said that working is a positive addiction; maybe workaholics are compulsive about their work, but their addiction seems to be a safe — even an advantageous — one.

※ 단락의 전개 방식
일이 주는 이점
① 돈을 제공
② 자신감 생성
③ 정체성 제공
④ 사교성 제시

- **해석** 왜 일 중독자들은 그들의 일을 그렇게나 즐기는 것인가? 주로 일하는 것이 그들에게 몇 가지 중요한 이점들을 제공하기 때문이다. 그것은 사람들에게 생계를 유지할 수 있는 방법인 봉급을 지급한다. 그리고 일은 재정적인 안정 그 이상을 제공한다. 그것은 사람들에게 자신감을 생성한다. 그래서 그들이 도전할 만한 한 가지 일을 끝내고 "내가 해냈어"라고 말할 때, 그들은 만족감을 느낀다. 심리학자들은 일은 또한 사람에게 정체성을 준다고 주장한다. 그래서 그들은 자아와 개성을 느낄 수 있도록 일을 한다. 게다가, 대부분의 직업은 사람들에게 사회적으로 용인된 타인을 만날 수 있는 방법을 제공한다. 사람들은 일이 긍정적인 중독이라고 말한다. 아마도 일 중독자들은 그들의 일에 대해 강박적일 수 있지만, 그 중독은 안전하고 심지어 이로워 보인다.

- **어휘** financial 재정적인, 재정상의  security 안전, 안보  workaholic 일 중독자
  provide A with B A에게 B를 제공하다  paycheck 봉급  self-confidence 자신감
  challenging 도전적인  psychologist 심리학자  claim 주장하다  identity 정체성  self 자아
  individualism 개성  addiction 중독  compulsive 강박적인, 충동적인  advantageous 이로운

- **해설** 이 글은 일이 주는 몇 가지 장점을 나열하고 있다. 따라서 나열의 공간개념을 이용해야 한다. ① 다음 문장에 일이 주는 첫 번째 장점인 봉급 지급이 언급되어 있고 ② 다음 문장에 두 번째 장점인 자신감과 관련된 내용이 나열되므로 주어진 문장이 들어갈 위치로 가장 적절한 것은 ②이다.

09 ②

## 기출문제

**10** 주어진 문장이 들어갈 위치로 가장 적절한 것은? 2019. 지방직 9급

> The same thinking can be applied to any number of goals, like improving performance at work.

The happy brain tends to focus on the short term. ( ① ) That being the case, it's a good idea to consider what short-term goals we can accomplish that will eventually lead to accomplishing long-term goals. ( ② ) For instance, if you want to lose thirty pounds in six months, what short-term goals can you associate with losing the smaller increments of weight that will get you there? ( ③ ) Maybe it's something as simple as rewarding yourself each week that you lose two pounds. ( ④ ) By breaking the overall goal into smaller, shorter-term parts, we can focus on incremental accomplishments instead of being overwhelmed by the enormity of the goal in our profession.

## 기출 분석

**10**

> 유사의 공간 개념: ① 살 빼기 ② 직장에서 성취 → 유사점 설명
> 
> The same thinking can be applied to any number of goals, like improving performance at work.
>   └ 직장

> The happy brain tends to focus on the short term. ( ① ) That being the case, it's a good idea to consider what short-term goals we can accomplish that will eventually lead to accomplishing long-term goals. ( ② ) For instance, if you want
> ┌→ 살 빼기
> to lose thirty pounds in six months, what short-term goals can you associate with losing the smaller increments of weight that will get you there? ( ③ ) Maybe it's
> ┌→ 살 빼기
> something as simple as rewarding yourself each week that you lose two pounds. ( ④ ) By breaking the overall goal into smaller, shorter-term parts, we can focus on incremental accomplishments instead of being overwhelmed by the enormity of the goal in our profession.
>   └ 직장

**해석** 행복한 뇌는 단기간에 집중하는 경향이 있다. 그게 그렇다면, 장기적인 목표를 이룰 수 있게 해주는 어떤 단기간의 목표를 우리가 달성할 수 있을지 고려해 보는 것은 좋은 생각이다. 예를 들어, 만약 당신이 6개월 안에 30파운드를 빼고 싶다면 당신은 그 목표치에 도달할 수 있도록 조금씩 늘려서 몸무게를 빼는 것과 어떤 단기간의 목표를 결합시킬 수 있을까? 아마도 그렇게 하면 매주 2파운드를 감량할 때마다 당신 스스로에게 보상하는 것만큼 간단한 일이 될 수도 있다. <u>같은 생각이 직장에서의 과업을 향상시키는 것과 같은 어떤 목표들에도 적용될 수 있다.</u> 전체적인 목표를 더 작은 단기간의 부분으로 나눔으로써, 우리는 우리의 직업에서 목표의 거대함에 압도되는 대신 조금씩 늘어나는 성취에 집중할 수 있다.

**어휘** goal 목표  improve 향상시키다  performance 수행, 과업  tend to ⓥ ⓥ하는 경향이 있다
It(That/This) is the case 그게 그렇다  short-term 단기간의  *long-term 장기간의
accomplish 성취하다, 이루다  associate 연합[결합]시키다
increment 증가, (주로 조금씩) 늘어남  *incremental 증가하는, 조금씩 늘어나는
overall 전체적인, 전반적인  instead of ~대신에  overwhelm 압도하다  enormity 거대함
profession 직업

**해설** 유사의 공간 개념(제시문에 유사의 시그널 same이 있다)을 이용해야 한다. ①부터 ③까지는 체중 감량 시 목표설정에 대한 내용이고 ④부터 직장에서의 과업향상목표에 대한 설명이 이어지므로 주어진 제시문(체중감량에 대한 내용이 아니라 직장과 관련된 내용)은 ④에 들어가는 것이 문맥상 가장 자연스럽다.

**정답**
10 ④

## 기출문제

**11** 밑줄 친 (A), (B)에 들어갈 말로 가장 적절한 것은? 2020. 국가직 9급

> Advocates of homeschooling believe that children learn better when they are in a secure, loving environment. Many psychologists see the home as the most natural learning environment, and originally the home was the classroom, long before schools were established. Parents who homeschool argue that they can monitor their children's education and give them the attention that is lacking in a traditional school setting. Students can also pick and choose what to study and when to study, thus enabling them to learn at their own pace. ___(A)___, critics of homeschooling say that children who are not in the classroom miss out on learning important social skills because they have little interaction with their peers. Several studies, though, have shown that the home-educated children appear to do just as well in terms of social and emotional development as other students, having spent more time in the comfort and security of their home, with guidance from parents who care about their welfare. ___(B)___, many critics of homeschooling have raised concerns about the ability of parents to teach their kids effectively.

|   | (A) | (B) |
|---|---|---|
| ① | Therefore | Nevertheless |
| ② | In contrast | In spite of this |
| ③ | Therefore | Contrary to that |
| ④ | In contrast | Furthermore |

## 기출 분석

**11**

> Two 개념: ① homeschooling 지지자 ② homeschooling 비판자 → 차이점 설명
>
> Advocates of homeschooling believe that children learn better when they are in a secure, loving environment. Many psychologists see the home as the most natural learning environment, and originally the home was the classroom, long before schools were established. Parents who homeschool argue that they can monitor their children's education and give them the attention that is lacking in a traditional school setting. Students can also pick and choose what to study and when to study, thus enabling them to learn at their own pace. ___(A)___, critics of homeschooling say that children who are not in the classroom miss out on learning important social skills because they have little interaction with their peers. Several studies, though, have shown that the home-educated children appear to do just as well in terms of social and emotional development as other students, having spent more time in the comfort and security of their home, with guidance from parents
> ↳ ⊕ 개념
> who care about their welfare. ___(B)___, many critics of homeschooling have raised concerns about the ability of parents to teach their kids effectively.
> ↳ ⊖ 개념

**해석** 홈스쿨링 지지자들은 아이들이 안전하고 사랑스러운 환경에 있을 때 더 잘 배운다고 믿는다. 많은 심리학자들은 집을 가장 자연스러운 학습 환경으로 간주하고, 원래 집은 학교가 만들어지기 훨씬 전부터 교실이었다. 홈스쿨링을 하는 학부모들은 자녀의 교육을 관찰할 수 있고 전통적인 학교 환경에서는 부족한 관심을 (자녀들에게) 줄 수 있다고 주장한다. 학생들은 또한 무엇을 공부할지, 언제 공부할지를 선택할 수 있기 때문에 그들 자신만의 속도로 학습할 수 있다. 이와는 대조적으로, 홈스쿨링에 대한 비평가들은 학교에서 공부를 하지 않는 아이들은 또래와의 상호작용이 거의 없기 때문에 중요한 사회적 기술을 배우지 못한다고 말한다. 하지만, 몇몇 연구들은 홈스쿨링을 하는 아이들도 다른 학생들만큼 사회적이고 정서적인 발달이 잘되는 것 같고, 그들의 복지에 신경을 쓰는 부모들의 지도와 함께 가정의 편안함과 안전 속에서 더 많은 시간을 보낸다는 것을 보여주었다. 그럼에도 불구하고, 홈스쿨링에 대한 많은 비평가들이 아이들을 효과적으로 가르칠 수 있는 부모의 능력에 대한 우려를 제기해 왔다.

**어휘** advocate 옹호자  secure 안전한  *security 안전  psychologist 심리학자
establish 설립하다, 세우다  critic 비평가  interaction 상호 작용  peer 또래
appear to ⓥ ⓥ인 것 같다  in terms of ~의 관점에서  comfort 편안함  welfare 복지
concern ① 걱정 ② 관심  effectively 효과적으로  therefore 그래서, 그러므로
nevertheless 그럼에도 불구하고  contrary to ~와는 반대로  furthermore 더욱이, 게다가

**해설** Two 개념(홈스쿨링 지지자 vs. 홈스쿨링 비판자)을 이용해야 한다. (A) 앞에는 홈스쿨링 지지자들의 ⊕ 개념이 있고 (A) 뒤에는 홈스쿨링을 비판하는 비평가들의 ⊖ 입장이 설명되고 있으므로 (A)에는 반대/대조의 연결사가 필요하다. (B) 앞에는 홈스쿨링의 ⊕ 개념이 있고 (B) 뒤에는 홈스쿨링의 ⊖ 개념이 있으므로 역시 반대/대조의 연결어가 필요하다. 따라서 정답은 ②가 된다.

**정답**
11 ②

## 기출문제

**12** 밑줄 친 (A), (B)에 들어갈 말로 가장 적절한 것은? 2020. 지방직 9급

Assertive behavior involves standing up for your rights and expressing your thoughts and feelings in a direct, appropriate way that does not violate the rights of others. It is a matter of getting the other person to understand your view point. People who exhibit assertive behavior skills are able to handle conflict situations with ease and assurance while maintaining good interpersonal relations. _____(A)_____, aggressive behavior involves expressing your thoughts and feelings and defending your rights in a way that openly violates the rights of others. Those exhibiting aggressive behavior seem to believe that the rights of others must be subservient to theirs. _____(B)_____, they have a difficult time maintaining good interpersonal relations. They are likely to interrupt, talk fast, ignore others, and use sarcasm or other forms of verbal abuse to maintain control.

|     | (A) | (B) |
| --- | --- | --- |
| ① | In contrast | Thus |
| ② | Similarly | Moreover |
| ③ | However | On one hand |
| ④ | Accordingly | On the other hand |

## 기출 분석

※ Two 개념
① Assertive 행동
② Aggressive 행동
→ 차이점 설명

**12**

Assertive behavior involves standing up for your rights and expressing your thoughts and feelings in a direct, appropriate way that does not violate the rights of others. It is a matter of getting the other person to understand your view point. People who exhibit assertive behavior skills are able to handle conflict situations with ease and assurance while maintaining good interpersonal relations. _____(A)_____, aggressive behavior involves expressing your thoughts and feelings and defending your rights in a way that openly violates the rights of others. Those exhibiting aggressive behavior seem to believe that the rights of others must be subservient to theirs. _____(B)_____, they have a difficult time maintaining good interpersonal relations. They are likely to interrupt, talk fast, ignore others, and use sarcasm or other forms of verbal abuse to maintain control.

- **해석** 단호한 행동은 타인의 권리를 침해하지 않는 직접적이고 적절한 방식으로 당신의 권리를 옹호하고 당신의 생각과 감정을 나타내는 것을 포함한다. 그것은 타인이 당신의 관점을 이해하도록 하는 문제이다. 단호한 행동기술을 보여주는 사람들은 좋은 대인관계를 유지하면서 갈등 상황을 쉽고 분명하게 처리할 수 있다. 이와는 대조적으로 공격적 행동은 타인의 권리를 공공연히 침해하는 방식으로 당신의 권리를 방어하고 생각과 감정을 표현하는 것을 포함한다. 공격적 행동을 보이는 사람들은 타인의 권리는 자신들의 권리에 종속되어야만 한다고 믿는 것처럼 보인다. 따라서, 그들은 좋은 대인관계를 유지하는 데 어려움을 겪는다. 그들은 통제를 유지하기 위해 방해하고 빨리 말하며, 타인을 무시하고, 비꼬거나 다른 형태의 폭언을 사용하기 쉽다.

- **어휘** assertive 단호한  stand up for 옹호하다  right 권리  express 나타내다, 표현하다
  appropriate 적절한, 적당한  violate 침해하다, 위반하다  view point 관점
  exhibit 전시하다, 보여주다  handle 처리하다, 다루다  conflict 갈등  situation 상황
  with ease 쉽게  assurance 확신, 분명함  maintain 유지하다
  interpersonal relationship 대인관계  aggressive 공격적인  involve 포함하다
  openly 공공연히  subservient 종속되는  be likely to ⓥ ⓥ하기 쉽다, ⓥ할 가능성이 있다
  interrupt 방해하다, 가로막다  sarcasm 비꼼, 빈정댐  verbal 말로 하는, 구두의
  abuse ① 학대 ② 남용  *verbal abuse 폭언

- **해설** 주어진 지문은 단호한 행동의 긍정적 측면과 공격적 행동의 부정적 관점을 비교(two개념)하는 내용의 글이므로 (A)에는 반대/대조의 연결사가 있어야 하고 (B)의 앞뒤 내용은 인과관계(타인의 권리가 당신의 권리에 종속된다고 여기는 것: 원인 → 좋은 대인관계를 유지하기 어렵다: 결과)를 나타내므로 (B)에는 인과관계의 연결사가 Thus가 필요하다. 따라서 정답은 ①이다.

**정답**
12 ①

## 기출문제

**13** 다음 빈칸 (A), (B)에 들어갈 말로 가장 적절한 것은? 2019. 국가직 9급

> Visionaries are the first people in their industry segment to see the potential of new technologies. Fundamentally, they see themselves as smarter than their opposite numbers in competitive companies — and, quite often, they are. Indeed, it is their ability to see things first that they want to leverage into a competitive advantage. That advantage can only come about if no one else has discovered it. They do not expect, _____(A)_____, to be buying a well-tested product with an extensive list of industry references. Indeed, if such a reference base exists, it may actually turn them off, indicating that for this technology, at any rate, they are already too late. Pragmatists, _____(B)_____, deeply value the experience of their colleagues in other companies. When they buy, they expect extensive references, and they want a good number to come from companies in their own industry segment.

|  | (A) | (B) |
|---|---|---|
| ① | therefore | on the other hand |
| ② | however | in addition |
| ③ | nonetheless | at the same time |
| ④ | furthermore | in conclusion |

## 기출 분석

**13**

Visionaries are the first people in their industry segment to see the potential of new technologies. Fundamentally, they see themselves as smarter than their opposite numbers in competitive companies — and, quite often, they are. Indeed, it is their ability to see things first that they want to leverage into a competitive advantage. That advantage can only come about if no one else has discovered it. They do not expect, ____(A)____, to be buying a well-tested product with an extensive list of industry references. Indeed, if such a reference base exists, it may actually turn them off, indicating that for this technology, at any rate, they are already too late. Pragmatists, ____(B)____, deeply value the experience of their colleagues in other companies. When they buy, they expect extensive references, and they want a good number to come from companies in their own industry segment.

**해석** 선지자들은 그들의 업종 부문에서 새로운 기술에 대한 가능성을 보는 최초의 사람들이다. 근본적으로 선지자들은 그들 자신을 경쟁 회사에 있는 경쟁자들보다 더 똑똑하다고 보고 그리고 꽤 자주 그들은 정말 똑똑하다. 실제로 그들의 능력은 경쟁 우위로 활용하고 싶은 것들을 처음으로 보는 것이다. 그러한 장점은 오직 아무도 그것을 발견하지 못했을 때만 발생할 수 있다. <u>그래서</u>, 그들은 광범위한 업계의 참고 자료 목록을 가지고 있는 충분히 조사된 제품을 사기를 기대하지 않는다. 실제로 만약 그런 참고 자료가 존재한다면 이는 그들의 흥미를 잃게 만드는 것이고 그들이 이 기술에 관해 어쨌든 이미 너무 늦었다는 것을 시인하게 되는 것이다. <u>반면에</u>, 실용주의자들은 다른 회사들에 있는 그들 동료들의 경험을 매우 가치 있게 평가한다. 그들이 구매를 할 때 그들은 광범위한 참고 자료를 기대하고 그들 자신의 업종 부문에 있는 회사들로부터 더 많은 참고 자료가 나오기를 원한다.

**어휘** visionary 선지자, 선각자  segment 부분, 영역  potential 잠재력  opposite 반대의  competitive 경쟁하는  leverage into (지렛대로) 활용하다  *leverage 지렛대  well-tested 잘 검증된  extensive 광범위한  reference 참고 자료  exist 존재하다  turn somebody off ~의 흥미를 잃게 하다  indicate 나타내다, 보여주다  at any rate 어쨌든  pragmatist 실용주의자  colleague 동료  a good number 많이

**해설** 빈칸 앞 문장에서 '그러한 장점이란 그것을 아무도 발견한 사람이 없을 때에 발생하는 것'이라고 하였고, (A) 뒤에서 '그러한 이유로 선지자들은 광범위한 기업의 참조 자료가 있는 이미 잘 검증된 제품들은 구입하지 않는다'고 하였으므로 (A)에는 인과관계의 연결사가 필요하다. (B)는 Two개념을 이용해야 한다. (B) 앞에는 선지자들의 관점이고 (B) 뒤에는 실용주의자들의 관점으로 서로 상반된 개념이 설명되고 있으므로 (B)에는 반대/대조의 연결사가 필요하다. 따라서 정답은 ①이 된다.

**정답**
13 ①

## 기출문제

**14** 다음 빈칸에 들어갈 말로 가장 적절한 것은? 2018. 지방직 9급

> Does terrorism ever work? 9/11 was an enormous tactical success for al Qaeda, partly because it involved attacks that took place in the media capital of the world and the actual capital of the United States, _____(A)_____ ensuring the widest possible coverage of the event. If terrorism is a form of theater where you want a lot of people watching, no event in human history was likely ever seen by a larger global audience than the 9/11 attacks. At the time, there was much discussion about how 9/11 was like the attack on Pearl Harbor. They were indeed similar since they were both surprise attacks that drew America into significant wars. But they were also similar in another sense. Pearl Harbor was a great tactical success for Imperial Japan, but it led to a great strategic failure : Within four years of Pearl Harbor the Japanese empire lay in ruins, utterly defeated. _____(B)_____, 9/11 was a great tactical success for al Qaeda, but it also turned out to be a great strategic failure for Osama bin Laden.

|     | (A) | (B) |
| --- | --- | --- |
| ① | thereby | Similarly |
| ② | while | Therefore |
| ③ | while | Fortunately |
| ④ | thereby | On the contrary |

## 기출 분석

**14.**

Does terrorism ever work? 9/11 was an enormous tactical success for al Qaeda, partly because it involved attacks that took place in the media capital of the world and the actual capital of the United States, ____(A)____ ensuring the widest possible coverage of the event. If terrorism is a form of theater where you want a lot of people watching, no event in human history was likely ever seen by a larger global audience than the 9/11 attacks. At the time, there was much discussion about how 9/11 was like the attack on Pearl Harbor. They were indeed similar since they were both surprise attacks that drew America into significant wars. But they were also similar in another sense. Pearl Harbor was a great tactical success for Imperial Japan, but it led to a great strategic failure: Within four years of Pearl Harbor the Japanese empire lay in ruins, utterly defeated. ____(B)____, 9/11 was a great tactical success for al Qaeda, but it also turned out to be a great strategic failure for Osama bin Laden.

**해석** 테러리즘은 효과가 있을까? 9/11 공격은 알카에다에게는 거대한 전술적 성공을 거두었다. 부분적인 이유는 이것이 세계의 언론의 중심지이며 미국의 실질적인 수도에서 일어난 공격을 수반했고, 그로 인해서 이 사건의 가능한 한 가장 폭넓은 보도를 확실하게 할 수 있었기 때문이다. 테러리즘이 많은 사람들이 보고 싶어하는 극장의 한 형태라면 인류의 역사에서 9/11 공격보다 더 많은 전 세계 시청자들에 의해 시청된 사건은 없을 것이다. 그 당시 9/11 공격이 진주만 공격과 어떻게 같은 것인지에 대해 많은 토론이 있었다. 그것들 모두 미국을 중요한 전쟁으로 끌어들인 기습 공격이었기 때문에 그것들은 실제로 유사했다. 그러나 그것들은 또한 다른 의미에서 비슷했다. 진주만 공격은 제국주의 일본의 전술적인 성공이었다. 그러나 그 공격은 전략적인 실패로 이어졌다. 즉, 다시 말해서 진주만 공격 이후 4년 만에 일본 제국은 폐허가 되었으며, 완전히 패배했다. 마찬가지로 9/11 공격은 알카에다의 전술적인 성공이었다. 그러나 이 역시 오사마 빈 라덴에게 전략적인 큰 실패로 판명됐다.

**어휘** enormous 거대한  tactical 전술적인  partly 부분적으로  take place 일어나다, 발생하다
capital 수도, 자본, 대문자  ensure 확실하게(분명하게)하다  coverage 보도
Pearl Harbor 진주만  attack 공격  *surprise attack 기습 공격  significant 중요한
imperial 제국의  strategic 전략적인  *strategy 전략  empire 제국  in ruins 폐허[엉망]가 된
utterly 완전히  defeat 물리치다, 패배시키다  turn out to ⓥ ⓥ라고 판명되다
thereby 그로 인해서  on the contrary 거꾸로, 반대로

**해설** (A) 앞 부분은 원인에 해당하고 뒷부분은 결과에 해당한다. 따라서 인과관계의 signal인 thereby가 들어가는 것이 적절하다.
(B) 앞에 진주만 공격에 대한 개념과 (B) 뒤에 9/11 공격에 대한 개념이 있으므로(서로 다른 소재에 대한 공통점) (B)에는 유사의 signal인 Similarly가 들어가야 한다. 따라서 정답은 ①이 된다.

14 ①

## 기출문제

**15** 다음 글의 제목으로 가장 적절한 것을 고르시오. 2016. 지방직 9급

> Few words are tainted by so much subtle nonsense and confusion as *profit*. To my liberal friends the word connotes the proceeds of fundamentally unrespectable and unworthy behaviors: minimally, greed and selfishness; maximally, the royal screwing of millions of helpless victims. *Profit* is the incentive for the most unworthy performance. To my conservative friends, it is a term of highest endearment, connoting efficiency and good sense. To them, *profit* is the ultimate incentive for worthy performance. Both connotations have some small merit, of course, because profit may result from both greedy, selfish activities and from sensible, efficient ones. But overgeneralizations from either bias do not help us in the least in understanding the relationship between profit and human competence.

① Relationship Between Profit and Political Parties
② Who Benefits from Profit
③ Why Making Profit Is Undesirable
④ Polarized Perceptions of Profit

## 기출 분석

※ Two 개념
① liberal friends
② conservative friends
→ Profit에 대한 차이점 설명

**15**

Few words are tainted by so much subtle nonsense and confusion as *profit*. To my liberal friends the word connotes the proceeds of fundamentally unrespectable and unworthy behaviors : minimally, greed and selfishness; maximally, the royal screwing of millions of helpless victims. *Profit* is the incentive for the most unworthy performance. To my conservative friends, it is a term of highest endearment, connoting efficiency and good sense. To them, *profit* is the ultimate incentive for worthy performance. Both connotations have some small merit, of course, because profit may result from both greedy, selfish activities and from sensible, efficient ones. But overgeneralizations from either bias do not help us in the least in understanding the relationship between profit and human competence.

**해석** 이윤이라는 단어만큼 미묘한 논리 부재와 혼란으로 오점을 남긴 단어는 거의 없다. 나의 자유분방한 친구들에게 그 단어는 기본적으로 존경받을 수도 없고 어울리지도 않는 행동의 결과로 나온 수익이라는 의미를 지닌다. 최소한으로 표현하자면 탐욕과 이기심이며 최대한으로 표현하자면 수백만의 무기력한 피해자들을 왕처럼 착취한다는 것이다. 이익은 가장 무가치한 행위에 대한 동기이다. 나의 보수적인 친구들에게 이 단어는 최고의 애정을 담은 표현이며 효율성과 좋은 의미를 지니는 말이다. 그들에게 이윤이란 가치 있는 활동을 위한 궁극적 자극을 의미한다. 이윤이 탐욕적이고 이기적인 활동의 결과이면서 합리적이고 효율적인 활동의 결과이기도 하기 때문에 두 가지 함의는 물론 어느 정도 약간이라도 가치가 있다. 하지만 어느 한쪽의 편견에서 지나치게 일반화하는 것은 이윤과 능력의 관계를 이해하는 데 있어 아무런 도움도 되지 않는다.
① 이윤과 정당 간의 관계
② 누가 이윤으로부터 혜택을 얻나
③ 왜 이윤을 내는 것은 바람직하지 않나
④ 이윤에 대한 양극의 인식

**어휘** taint 더럽히다, 오점을 남기다　subtle ① 미묘한 ② 감지하기 힘든　confusion 혼란, 혼동
liberal 자유로운, 개방적인　connote (함축적으로) 의미하다　*connotation (함축적) 의미
proceeds 수입, 수익　fundamentally 기본적으로　unrespectable 존경받을 수 없는
unworthy ① 자격이 없는 ② 어울리지 않는　minimally 최소한으로(↔ maximally 최대한으로)
greed 탐욕　*greedy 탐욕스러운　selfishness 이기, 이기적임　royal screwing 몹시 가혹한 배반
helpless 무기력한　victim 희생자[물]　incentive 인센티브; 동기, 자극　conservative 보수적인
endearment 애정을 담은 말　efficiency 효율성　*efficient 효율적인　ultimate 궁극적인
sensible 분별 있는　overgeneralization 과잉 일반화　bias 편견　competence 능력
political party 정당　undesirable 바람직하지 않은　polarized 양극화된　perception 인식

**해설** 이 글은 첫 번째 문장에서 언급한 것처럼 profit(이 글의 중심소재)에 대한 두 가지의 confusion(작가의 견해)을 설명하고 있으므로 이 글의 제목으로 적절한 것은 ④ '이윤에 대한 양극의 인식'이다. ④에 polarize가 어려운 단어였지만 ①, ②, ③이 모두 오답이기 때문에 정답을 구하는 데 있어서는 별 어려움이 없었다.

**정답**
15 ④

## 기출문제

**16** 다음 글의 ㉠, ㉡에 들어갈 가장 적절한 것은? 2015. 국가직 9급

> The chimpanzee—who puts two sticks together in order to get at a banana because no one of the two is long enough to do the job—uses intelligence. So do we all when we go about our business, "figuring out" how to do things. Intelligence, in this sense, is taking things for granted as they are, making combinations which have the purpose of facilitating their manipulation; intelligence is thought in the service of biological survival. Reason, ____㉠____, aims at understanding; it tries to find out what is beneath the surface, to recognize the kernel, the essence of the reality which surrounds us. Reason is not without a function, but its function is not to further physical as much as mental and spiritual existence. ____㉡____, often in individual and social life, reason is required in order to predict (considering that prediction often depends on recognition of forces which operate underneath the surface), and prediction sometimes is necessary even for physical survival.

|   | ㉠ | ㉡ |
|---|---|---|
| ① | for example | Therefore |
| ② | in the same way | Likewise |
| ③ | consequently | As a result |
| ④ | on the other hand | However |

## 기출 분석

**16**

The chimpanzee—who puts two sticks together in order to get at a banana because no one of the two is long enough to do the job—uses intelligence. So do we all when we go about our business, "figuring out" how to do things. Intelligence, in this sense, is taking things for granted as they are, making combinations which have the purpose of facilitating their manipulation; intelligence is thought in the service of biological survival. Reason, ㉠_____, aims at understanding; it tries to find out what is beneath the surface, to recognize the kernel, the essence of the reality which surrounds us. Reason is not without a function, but its function is not to further physical as much as mental and spiritual existence. ㉡_____, often in individual and social life, reason is required in order to predict (considering that prediction often depends on recognition of forces which operate underneath the surface), and prediction sometimes is necessary even for physical survival.

- **해석** 막대기 하나만 가지고는 바나나에 닿기에 충분히 길지 않아서 두 개의 막대기를 이어 붙인 침팬지는 지능을 사용한다. 우리도 일하는 방식들을 '터득해' 가면서 할 일들을 할 때 우리 또한 지능을 사용한다. 지능이란, 이러한 의미에서 볼 때, 사물들을 있는 그대로 받아들이고, 조합의 조작을 촉진하려는 목적을 가진 조합들을 만들어 내는 것을 의미한다; 지능은 생물학적 생존을 위해 생각된다. 반면에 이성은 이해하는 데 목적이 있다; 이성은 표면 밑에 무엇이 있는지 알아내고, 우리를 둘러싼 현실의 핵심 알맹이, 즉 정수를 인식하려 한다. 이성은 기능이 있지만 그 기능은 정신적이고 영적인 존재만큼 육체적 존재를 신장시키는 것은 아니다. 그러나 종종 개인과 사회의 삶에서 이성은 예측하기 위해 필요한데(예측이 표면 아래에서 작동하는 힘들을 인식하는 것에 기반하고 있는 것을 고려한다면) 종종 이 예측들은 육체적 생존을 위해서도 필수이다.

- **어휘** put together 하나로 합치다  stick 막대기  get at ~에 닿다  intelligence 지능
  go about one's business 자기 할 일을 하다  take ~ for granted ~을 당연하게 받아들이다
  combination 조합  purpose 목적  facilitate 용이하게 하다, 촉진하다  manipulation 조작
  in the service of ~을 위해서  biological 생물학적인  aim at ~을 목표로 하다
  essence 본질, 핵심  beneath ~의 밑에  surface 표면  kernel 핵심, 알맹이
  further 신장시키다  spiritual 영적인, 정신적인

- **해설** 단락의 도입부에 two 개념(intelligence와 reason)이 있으므로 ㉠에는 반대/대조의 연결사가 필요하고, ㉡에는 앞에 not to further physical(육체적인 것이 아니다)이 있고 뒤에 necessary for physical survival(육체적 생존에 필수적인)이 있으므로 역시 반대/대조의 연결사가 필요하다. 따라서 정답은 ④가 된다.

16 ④

MEMO

김세현 영어 전혀 다른 개념 독해

PART

05

일관성

# PART 05 일관성

English Reading

### 출제 유형

1. 주어진 문장이 들어갈 위치로 가장 적절한 것은?
2. 주어진 글 다음에 이어질 글의 순서로 가장 적절한 것은?

### 풀이 해법

올바른 독해법 + Pattern and Signal 이용
1. 시간 순서(Time Order)의 Signal 이용

### 연습문제

**EX 1** 주어진 문장이 들어갈 위치로 가장 적절한 것은?

Four years later, in 1429, those same voices told her to help the king of France fight the British, who were trying to take control of France in the Hundred Years War.

Joan of Arc, the national heroine and patron saint of France, was born in 1412 to a family of poor peasants. ( ① ) In 1425, at the age of thirteen, Joan claimed to hear voices that she believed belonged to the early Christian saints. ( ② ) When the king believed her story and gave her troops to command, Joan put on a suit of armor and led her soldiers to victory. ( ③ ) Yet when Joan was captured by the British in 1430 and tried for heresy and for wearing masculine dress, the French king refused to help her, allowing her to be condemned to death. ( ④ ) On May 30, 1431, Joan was burned at the stake, still swearing loyalty to the king of France.

## 연습해설

### EX 1

Four years later, in 1429, those same voices told her to help the king of France fight the British, who were trying to take control of France in the Hundred Years War.

Joan of Arc, the national heroine and patron saint of France, was born in 1412 to a family of poor peasants. ( ① ) In 1425, at the age of thirteen, Joan claimed to hear voices that she believed belonged to the early Christian saints. ( ② ) When the king believed her story and gave her troops to command, Joan put on a suit of armor and led her soldiers to victory. ( ③ ) Yet when Joan was captured by the British in 1430 and tried for heresy and for wearing masculine dress, the French king refused to help her, allowing her to be condemned to death. ( ④ ) On May 30, 1431, Joan was burned at the stake, still swearing loyalty to the king of France.

- **해석** 프랑스의 국가적 여걸이자 수호성인인 잔 다르크는 1412년에 가난한 농부의 가정에서 태어났다. 1425년 13세에 잔 다르크는 초기 기독교 성인들의 목소리라고 믿었던 소리가 들린다고 주장했다. 4년 후 1429년에 그 동일한 목소리가 프랑스의 왕이 영국과 싸우는 것을 도와주라고 그녀에게 말했는데, 당시 영국은 백년 전쟁에서 프랑스를 지배하려고 하고 있었다. 왕이 그녀의 이야기를 믿고 지휘할 군대를 그녀에게 주었을 때, 잔 다르크는 갑옷과 투구를 착용하고 병사들을 승리로 이끌었다. 하지만 1430년에 잔 다르크가 영국군에게 붙잡혀서 이단적인 행동과 남자의 옷을 입은 것에 대해 재판을 받게 되었을 때, 프랑스의 왕은 그녀를 돕는 것을 거절하여 사형 선고를 받게 했다. 1431년 5월 30일에 잔 다르크는 기둥에 묶여 화형을 당하였는데, 여전히 프랑스의 왕에 대한 충성을 맹세하면서 숨을 거두었다.
- **어휘** heroine (여자) 영웅  patron saint 수호성인(守護聖人)  peasant 농부  claim 주장하다  troop 군대  command 명령하다  put on (옷을) 입다  armor 갑옷  capture 사로잡다  heresy 이단  masculine 남성의  condemn to 형을 선고하다  stake 말뚝, 화형대  swear 맹세하다  loyalty 충성
- **해설** 시간 순서 전개 방식과 지시형용사를 이용해야 한다. 주어진 제시문에 '4년 후 1429년에' 라는 내용이 있고 지시형용사 those가 있으므로 문맥상 주어진 제시문은 ②에 들어가는 것이 가장 적절하다.

01 ②

### 연습문제

**EX 2** 주어진 문장이 들어갈 위치로 가장 적절한 것은?

Nevertheless, building continued, and the seven-story structure was finished between 1360 and 1370.

What caused the Tower of Pisa to lean sideways? The famous bell tower leans because of the unstable soil on which it was built. ( ① ) In 1173 construction started on the 180-foot bell tower, which is located in Pisa, a small town in the Italian province of Tuscany. ( ② ) It began to lean as soon as the first three floors were completed. ( ③ ) Leaning a bit more each year, by the time it was closed for repairs in 1990, the tower tilted 14.5 feet out of line when measured from the top story. ( ④ ) Engineers on the project worked to stabilize the foundation, straightening the tower only slightly to prevent damage. The tower, which was built alongside a church, wouldn't be remarkable if it were not for its slant, but with its characteristic angle, it continues to attract thousands of visitors to Pisa.

## 연습해설

### EX 2

Nevertheless, building continued, and the seven-story structure was finished between 1360 and 1370.

What caused the Tower of Pisa to lean sideways? The famous bell tower leans because of the unstable soil on which it was built. ( ① ) In 1173 construction started on the 180-foot bell tower, which is located in Pisa, a small town in the Italian province of Tuscany. ( ② ) It began to lean as soon as the first three floors were completed. ( ③ ) Leaning a bit more each year, by the time it was closed for repairs in 1990, the tower tilted 14.5 feet out of line when measured from the top story. ( ④ ) Engineers on the project worked to stabilize the foundation, straightening the tower only slightly to prevent damage. The tower, which was built alongside a church, wouldn't be remarkable if it were not for its slant, but with its characteristic angle, it continues to attract thousands of visitors to Pisa.

- **해석** 무엇이 피사의 탑을 옆으로 기울게 했을까? 그 유명한 종탑은 그것이 세워진 불안정한 토양 때문에 기운다. 1173년에 이탈리아의 토스카나 지방에 있는 작은 마을인 피사에 위치한, 180파트의 종탑 건설이 시작되었다. 이것은 첫 3층이 완성되자마자 기울어지기 시작했다. <u>그럼에도 불구하고, 건설은 계속되었고, 7층짜리 구조물이 1360년과 1370년 사이에 완성이 되었다.</u> 매년 조금씩 기울어지면서 그것이 1990년에 수리를 하기 위해 폐쇄될 즈음에는 꼭대기 층에서 측정할 때 일직선에서 14.5피트 벗어나 기울어졌다. 프로젝트의 엔지니어들은 그 탑의 손상을 막기 위해서 그 탑을 단지 약간만 바로 세우면서 그 기초를 안정시키기 위해 작업했다. 교회와 나란히 세워졌던 그 탑은 그것의 경사가 없다면 주목받지 못할 것이다. 그러나 그것의 특징적인 각도 때문에 그것은 수천 명의 방문객을 피사로 계속 끌고 있다.

- **어휘** nevertheless 그럼에도 불구하고  story 층  structure 구조(물)  lean 기울다  sideway 옆으로  unstable 불안정한  soil 토양, 흙  construction 건설, 건축  locate 위치시키다  province 지역  Tuscany 토스카나  as soon as ~하자마자  by the time ~할 때쯤, ~할 때까지  repair 수리(하다), 고치다  tilt 기울다  stabilize 안정시키다  foundation 토대, 기초  straighten 똑바르게 하다  slightly 조금씩, 약간  remarkable 두드러진, 눈에 띄는  if it were not for ~이 없다면  characteristic 특색을 이루는, 특징짓는  angle 각  attract 매혹시키다, 유혹하다

- **해설** 시간 순서 전개 방식을 이용해야 한다. 주어진 문장에 between 1360 and 1370이 있으므로 시간 순서상 주어진 문장은 ②와 ③에 들어가야 한다. 또한 ② 뒤에 처음 3층이 완성되자마자 건물이 기울기 시작했다고 했고 ③ 뒤에 그 탑이 1990년 수리를 위해 폐쇄되었다는 내용이 있으므로 문맥상 주어진 문장은 ③에 들어가는 것이 가장 적절하다.

정답
02 ③

### 연습문제

**EX 3** 주어진 글 다음에 이어질 글의 순서로 가장 적절한 것은?

Powerful ChatGPT capable of translating conversations from one language into another have been developed since the beginning of the 21st century.

(A) After that, another part of AI program analyzes the awkward jumble of words and meanings and produces an intelligible sentence based on the rules of Korean syntax and the machine's data of what the original English sentence meant.

(B) To interpret a conversation from English into Korean, AI first analyzes an English sentence, determining its spoken structure and identifying the subject, verb, objects, and modifiers. Next, the words are shifted by an English-Korean dictionary.

(C) The AI-produced translation is polished by a learned data previously and a number of AI-based chatbot editors, at the end of the process. ChatGPT will help you have real-time conversations, find inspiration and be more productive.

① (A) − (C) − (B)
② (B) − (A) − (C)
③ (C) − (A) − (B)
④ (C) − (B) − (A)

### EX 3

Powerful ChatGPT capable of translating conversations from one language into another have been developed since the beginning of the 21st century.

(A) After that, another part of AI program analyzes the awkward jumble of words and meanings and produces an intelligible sentence based on the rules of Korean syntax and the machine's data of what the original English sentence meant.

(B) To interpret a conversation from English into Korean, AI first analyzes an English sentence, determining its spoken structure and identifying the subject, verb, objects, and modifiers. Next, the words are shifted by an English-Korean dictionary.

(C) The AI-produced translation is polished by a learned data previously and a number of AI-based chatbot editors, at the end of the process. ChatGPT will help you have real-time conversations, find inspiration and be more productive.

**해석** 대화를 한 언어에서 다른 언어로 번역할 수 있는 고성능 챗지피티가 21세기 초부터 개발되었다.
(B) 대화를 영어에서 한국어로 표현하기 위해 AI는 먼저 영어 문장을 분석하고, 영어의 대화체 구조를 결정하고 또한 주어, 동사, 목적어 그리고 수식어를 확인한다. 그다음 영어문장이 AI 챗봇에 의해 한국어로 변환된다.
(A) 그런 다음 AI 프로그램의 다른 부분에서 뒤죽박죽 섞인 어색한 단어들과 의미들을 분석해서 한국어 통사론의 규칙과 AI 데이터가 이해한 영어 원문이 의미하는 것을 기반으로 하여 이해할 수 있는 문장을 만들어 낸다.
(C) 그 과정의 마지막에 AI가 만들어 낸 번역은 이전에 학습된 데이터와 많은 AI기반 챗봇 편집자들에 의해 세련돼진다. 챗지피티는 당신이 실시간 대화를 할 수 있게 해주고 영감을 얻을 수 있게 해주며 더욱 생산적이 될 수 있도록 도와줄 것이다.

**어휘** capable ~할 수 있는, 유능한  translate 번역하다  *translation 변역  analyze 분석하다
awkward 어색한  jumble 뒤죽박죽 섞인 것  intelligible 이해할 수 있는  sentence 문장
syntax 통사론, 구문론  express 표현하다  determine 결정하다  structure 구조  identify 확인하다
subject 주어  verb 동사  object 목적어  modifier 수식어  shift 이동하다, 변환시키다
polish 광을 내다, 세련돼지다  previously 이전에  a number of 많은  editor 편집자  real-time 실시간
inspiration 영감  productive 생산적인

**해설** 시간 순서 전개 방식을 이용해야 한다. (B)의 first부터 시간 순서가 시작되어야 하고 (C)의 at the end of the process가 있으므로 (C)가 제일 마지막에 위치해야 한다. 따라서 주어진 글 다음 이어질 글의 순서로 가장 적절한 것은 ② (B)-(A)-(C)이다.

03 ②

## 풀이 해법

2. 반대/대조(Contrast)의 Signal 이용

### 연습문제

**EX 1** 다음 글의 흐름으로 보아, 주어진 문장이 들어가기에 가장 적절한 곳은?

However, without dust there would be less rainfall and sunsets would be less beautiful.

Most of us who have ever cleaned a house would be much happier were it not for dust. ( ① ) Rain is formed when water molecules in the air collect around particles of dust. ( ② ) Thus water vapor could be much less likely to turn to rain but for the dust particles. ( ③ ) The water vapor and dust particles also serve to refract the rays of the sun. ( ④ ) At sunrise and sunset, when the sun is below the horizon, the dust and water vapor molecules refract the longer red wavelengths of light, so we can see them for more time than any of the other wavelengths. The more dust particles in the air, the more colorful the sunrise or sunset.

## 연습해설

### EX 1

┌ However를 기준으로 뒤에 ⊖개념이 있으므로 앞에는 ⊕개념이 있어야 한다.　　　　　　　⊖개념 ┐
However, without dust there would be less rainfall and sunsets would be less beautiful.

　　　　　　　　　　　　　　　　　　　　　　　　　┌ ⊕개념
Most of us who have ever cleaned a house would be much happier were it not for dust. ( ① ) Rain is formed when water molecules in the air collect around particles of dust. ( ② ) Thus water vapor could be much less likely to turn to rain but for the dust particles. ( ③ ) The water vapor and dust particles also serve to refract the rays of the sun. ( ④ ) At sunrise and sunset, when the sun is below the horizon, the dust and water vapor molecules refract the longer red wavelengths of light, so we can see them for more time than any of the other wavelengths. The more dust particles in the air, the more colorful the sunrise or sunset.

**해석** 집을 청소해 본 대다수는 만약에 먼지가 더 적으면 훨씬 더 행복해 할 수도 있다. <u>하지만, 먼지가 없다면 강수량도 적을 것이고 일몰도 아름답지 않을 것이다.</u> 비는 공기 중의 물 분자가 먼지 분자 주위에 모여들 때 형성된다. 따라서 수증기는 먼지 입자가 없다면 비로 바뀔 가능성이 거의 없을 수 있다. 수증기와 먼지 입자는 또한 태양의 광선을 굴절시키는 역할을 한다. 태양이 수평선 아래에 있을 때인 일출과 일몰 때, 먼지와 수증기 분자는 더 길고 붉은 빛의 파장을 굴절시켜서 우리는 어떤 다른 파장보다 더 오랜 시간동안 그것들을 볼 수 있게 된다. 공기 중에 먼지 입자가 많으면 많을수록, 일출과 일몰은 더욱 더 색감이 풍부해진다.

**어휘** were it not for ~이 없다면(=without, but for)　dust 먼지　precipitation 강수량
sunset 일몰　molecule 분자　collect 모이다　molecule 분자　particle 입자　vapor 증기
serve to ⓥ ⓥ하는 역할을 하다　refract 굴절시키다　horizon 수평선, 지평선　wavelength 파장

**해설** 주어진 문장 다음 ⊖개념이 있으므로 However를 기준으로 앞 문장에는 ⊕개념이 있어야 한다. 본문에서 ⊕개념은 본문 첫 번째 문장이므로 주어진 문장이 들어가기에 가장 적절한 곳은 ①이다.

01 ①

## 풀이 해법

**3. 인과 관계(Cause and effect)의 Signal 이용**

### 연습문제

**EX 1** 주어진 문장이 들어갈 위치로 가장 적절한 것은?

Consequently, many researchers are working on a way to make stem cells to grow completely new organs.

Scientists are working on many other human organs and tissues. For example, they have successfully generated, or grown, a piece of liver. This is an exciting achievement since people cannot live without a liver. ( ① ) In other laboratories, scientists have created a human jawbone and a lung. ( ② ) While these scientific breakthroughs are very promising, they are also limited. ( ③ ) Scientists cannot use cells for a new organ from a very diseased or damaged organ. ( ④ ) Stem cells are very simple cells in the body that can develop into any kind of complex cells, such as skin cells or blood cells and even heart and liver cells. In other words, stem cells can grow into all different kinds of cells.

## 연습해설

### EX 1

Consequently, many researchers are working on a way to make stem cells to grow completely new organs.

Scientists are working on many other human organs and tissues. For example, they have successfully generated, or grown, a piece of liver. This is an exciting achievement since people cannot live without a liver. ( ① ) In other laboratories, scientists have created a human jawbone and a lung. ( ② ) While these scientific breakthroughs are very promising, they are also limited. ( ③ ) Scientists cannot use cells for a new organ from a very diseased or damaged organ. ( ④ ) Stem cells are very simple cells in the body that can develop into any kind of complex cells, such as skin cells or blood cells and even heart and liver cells. In other words, stem cells can grow into all different kinds of cells.

**해석** 과학자들은 많은 다른 사람의 장기와 조직에 대해 노력을 들이고 있다. 예를 들어, 그들은 성공적으로 간 조각을 만들어 내거나 기르고 있다. 이는 흥미로운 성과인데 그 이유는 사람은 간 없이는 살 수 없기 때문이다. 다른 실험실에서 과학자들은 인간의 턱뼈와 폐를 만들었다. 이러한 과학적 발전은 매우 유망하지만, 그것들은 또한 제한적이다. 과학자들은 심하게 병을 앓았거나 손상된 장기로는 새로운 장기에 사용할 수 없다. <u>결과적으로 많은 연구자들은 완전히 새로운 장기를 기르기 위해 줄기세포를 만드는 방법에 노력을 들이고 있다.</u> 줄기세포는 피부 세포나 혈액세포, 심지어 심장과 간세포와 같은 어떤 종류의 복잡한 세포로도 발전할 수 있는 신체의 매우 단순한 세포이다. 다시 말해서, 줄기 세포는 모든 다른 종류의 세포로 자랄 수 있다.

**어휘** work on ~에 노력을 들이다, 착수하다  organ 장기  tissue 조직  generate 만들어내다, 발생시키다
grow ① 성장하다, 자라다 ② 재배하다, 기르다  liver 간  laboratory 실험실  jawbone 턱 뼈
lung 폐, 허파  breakthrough ① 돌파구 ② (획기적) 발견 ③ (큰) 발전, 약진
promising 유망한, 촉망되는  diseased 질병에 걸린, 병을 앓고 있는  stem cell 줄기세포
complex 복잡한  specifically ① 분명히, 명확하게 ② 특히, 특별히  additionally 게다가, 더욱이
consequently 결과적으로  accordingly 따라서

**해설** 주어진 문장에 있는 인과관계의 시그널 Consequently를 이용해야 한다. Consequently 다음에는 무언가의 결과에 대한 내용이 있어야 하고 주어진 문장은 '연구자들은 완전히 새로운 장기를 기르기 위해 줄기세포를 만드는 방법에 노력을 들이고 있다' 설명하고 있으므로 이에 대한 원인은 ③ 뒤의 '과학자들은 심하게 병을 앓았거나 손상된 장기로는 새로운 장기에 사용할 수 없다'는 내용이므로 이 결과에 해당하는 주어진 문장이 들어가기에 가장 적절한 곳은 ④이다.

01 ④

## 풀이 해법

**4. 예시의 Signal(for example, for instance) 이용**

**1) 큰 흐름의 예시**

예가 하나, 둘, 셋 나열될 때 첫 번째 예를 들면서 for example[instance]가 나온다.

### 연습문제

**EX 1** 주어진 문장이 들어갈 위치로 가장 적절한 것은?

In India, for instance, some coins have square sides.

When we think of money, we usually think of coins or bills. ( ① ) In the modern world, almost every country uses coins and paper money to exchange for other objects of value. ( ② ) The sizes and shapes of coins are different in several countries, and the size and color of paper money also vary. ( ③ ) In Japan, coins have holes in the center. ( ④ ) Finally, in the United States, all paper money is the same size and the same color; only the printing on the bills is different.

# 연습해설

### EX 1

In India, for instance, some coins have square sides.

When we think of money, we usually think of coins or bills. ( ① ) In the modern world, almost every country uses coins and paper money to exchange for other objects of value. ( ② ) The sizes and shapes of coins are different in several countries, and the size and color of paper money also vary. ( ③ ) In Japan, coins have holes in the center. ( ④ ) Finally, in the United States, all paper money is the same size and the same color; only the printing on the bills is different.

**해석** 우리가 돈을 떠올릴 때, 우리는 보통 동전과 지폐를 떠올린다. 현대 사회에서, 거의 모든 나라는 다른 가치를 지닌 물건들과 교환을 하려고 동전과 지폐를 사용한다. 동전의 크기와 모양은 여러 나라에서 다르고 지폐의 크기와 색깔 역시 다양하다. <u>예를 들어, 인도에서는 몇 개의 동전은 사각형이다.</u> 일본에서는 동전 중앙에 구멍이 있다. 마지막으로, 미국에서는 모든 지폐는 같은 크기이며 색도 같다, 하지만 지폐에 인쇄되는 것이 다르다.

**어휘** bill ① 지폐 ② 법안  exchange 교환하다  modern 근대의, 현대의  vary 다양하다, 다르다
square ① 정사각형 ② 광장  hole 구멍  printing 인쇄(물)

**해설** 주어진 지문은 동전의 크기와 모양이 나라마다 다르다는 내용의 글이고 그 차이점을 나열의 시그널을 이용해서 열거하고 있다. 주어진 문장은 예로서 나열하고 있고 그 첫 번째 예를 들면서 for instance가 나와야 하므로 주어진 문장이 들어가기에 가장 적절한 곳은 ③이다.

정답
01 ③

### 풀이 해법

2) 작은 흐름의 예시

예가 하나, 둘, 셋 나열되지 않고 단지 한 문장에 대한 구체적인 예가 제시될 때 사용된다.

### 연습문제

**EX 1** 주어진 문장이 들어갈 위치로 가장 적절한 것은?

For example, residents in Florida become ill from the cold, as they do not have heating in their homes.

A cold winter causes several problems in Florida. First of all, very cold weather can give rise to orange trees to die. ( ① ) In fact, oranges are pretty vulnerable to chilly weather. ( ② ) Very cold weather can also cause ailments. ( ③ ) Cold weather can bring about fewer tourists, too. ( ④ ) There are many hotels and vacation places in Florida, so these places are in trouble if there are fewer tourists.

## 연습해설

### EX 1

For example, residents in Florida become ill from the cold, as they do not have heating in their homes.

A cold winter causes several problems in Florida. First of all, very cold weather can give rise to orange trees to die. ( ① ) In fact, oranges are pretty vulnerable to chilly weather. ( ② ) Very cold weather can also cause ailments. ( ③ ) Cold weather can bring about fewer tourists, too. ( ④ ) There are many hotels and vacation places in Florida, so these places are in trouble if there are fewer tourists.

**해석** 추운 겨울은 플로리다에 몇 가지 문제점을 야기한다. 우선, 추운 날씨로 인해 오렌지 나무가 죽는다. 사실, 오렌지는 추운 날씨에 몹시 취약하다. 매우 추운 날씨는 또한 질병을 초래한다. 예를 들어, 플로리다의 거주자들은 집에 난방 기구를 갖고 있지 않기 때문에 감기로부터 아플 수 있다. 추운 날씨는 또한 관광객의 수를 감소시킨다. 많은 호텔과 휴양지가 플로리다에 있고, 그래서 이 지역들은 관광객이 감소하면 어려움에 빠진다.

**어휘** resident 거주자, 거주민  cold ① 추운 ② 감기  heating 난방
give rise to 야기하다, 초래하다(= cause, bring about)  pretty ① 예쁜 ② 아주, 매우
vulnerable 취약한, 공격받기 쉬운  ailment 질병  tourist 관광객

**해설** 예시의(크다 > 작다)논리가 필요하다. 주어진 문장은 질병에 대한 구체적 예로 감기를 제시하고 있으므로 문맥상 주어진 문장은 ③에 들어가는 것이 가장 적절하다.

01 ③

## 풀이 해법

**5. 지시어 이용**

**1) 지시형용사 이용**

지시형용사 : this(these) + ⓝ / that(those) + ⓝ / such + ⓝ

위의 지시형용사 다음에 나오는 ⓝ는 반드시 바로 앞 문장에 있어야 한다.

### 연습문제

**EX 1** 주어진 글 다음에 이어질 글의 순서로 가장 적절한 것은?

Neuroscientists and those in middle age or beyond know that brains alter and slow as we grow older. Processing speed, which is a measure of how rapidly our brains can absorb, assess and respond to new information, seems to be particularly hard hit. Most people who are older than about 40 perform worse on tests of processing speed than those who are younger, with the effects accelerating as the decades pass.

(A) In young brains, these messages whip from neuron to neuron with boggling speed. But in older people, brain scans show, the white matter can be skimpier and less efficient. Messages stutter and slow.

(B) Scientists suspect that this decline of processing speed is due in large part to a continuous fraying of our brain's white matter, which is its wiring.

(C) White matter consists of specialized cells and their offshoots that pass messages between neurons and from one part of the brain to another.

\* boggling 놀랄만한, 아연케 하는 \*\* white matter 백질
\*\*\* offshoot 분파, 줄기

① (A) − (C) − (B)
② (B) − (C) − (A)
③ (C) − (A) − (B)
④ (C) − (B) − (A)

## 연습해설

### EX 1

Neuroscientists and those in middle age or beyond know that brains alter and slow as we grow older. Processing speed, which is a measure of how rapidly our brains can absorb, assess and respond to new information, seems to be particularly hard hit. Most people who are older than about 40 perform worse on tests of processing speed than those who are younger, with the effects accelerating as the decades pass.

(A) In young brains, these messages whip from neuron to neuron with boggling speed. But in older people, brain scans show, the white matter can be skimpier and less efficient. Messages stutter and slow.
(B) Scientists suspect that this decline of processing speed is due in large part to a continuous fraying of our brain's white matter, which is its wiring.
(C) White matter consists of specialized cells and their offshoots that pass messages between neurons and from one part of the brain to another.

\*white matt\* boggling 놀랄만한, 아연케 하는 \*\* white matter 백질
\*\*\* offshoot 분파, 줄기

**해석** 신경과 전문의들이나 중년 또는 그 이상의 사람들은 우리가 나이가 들면서 뇌가 변하고 둔화된다는 것을 안다. 얼마나 빠르게 우리의 뇌가 새로운 정보를 흡수하고 평가하고 그리고 반응하는지에 척도가 되는 처리 과정이 특히 큰 타격을 입는 것 같다. 40살 이상의 사람들 대부분은 젊은이들보다 처리 속도에 대한 테스트 결과가 더 나빠지는데 이는 수십 년이 지나면서 더 가속화된다.
(B) 과학자들은 이러한 감소가 대체로 우리의 뇌에 있는 배선 장치 역할을 하는 백질(white matter)이 닳아 없어지기 때문이라고 의심한다.
(C) 백질은 특별한 세포와 그 세포 줄기들로 구성되어 있는데 이것들이 뉴런 사이에 그리고 뇌의 한 부분에서 다른 부분으로 메시지를 전달한다.
(A) 젊은 뇌에서는 이 메시지가 놀랄만한 속도로 뉴런 사이에서 채찍질한다(빠르게 전달된다). 하지만, 그런 나이든 뇌에서는 백질이 더 많이 노출되고 그래서 뇌 스캔의 효율성이 더 떨어짐을 보여준다. 메시지는 더듬거리지고 둔화된다.

**어휘** neuroscientist 신경과 전문의, 신경학자 alter 변하다, 바꾸다 processing ① 처리 ② 가공 measure ① 재다, 측정하다 ② 척도, 기준 ③ 대책, 조치 rapidly 빠르게, 신속하게 absorb 흡수하다 assess 평가하다 respond to ~에 반응하다 hard hit 큰 타격을 입은, 심각한 영향을 받은 accelerate 가속화하다 skimpy 노출이 심한 in large 대체로 efficient 효율적인 stutter ① 말을 더듬다 ② 더디다 suspect 의심하다 due to ~때문에 whip ① 채찍 ② 채찍질하다 concomitant 수반되는 fraying 닳아 해어짐 wiring 배선, 배선장치 neuron 뉴런, 운동신경세포

**해설** 지시형용사(this, that, such)를 이용해서 문제를 해결할 수 있어야 한다. (B)의 this decline은 주어진 제시문의 마지막 부분 처리 속도(processing speed)의 악화를 의미하므로 주어진 제시문 다음에는 (B)가 위치해야 하고 (A)의 these messages는 (C)의 messages를 지칭하므로 주어진 글 다음 이어질 글의 순서로 가장 적절한 것은 ② (B)-(C)-(A)이다.

**정답**
01 ②

### 풀이 해법

**2) 지시(인칭)대명사 이용**

지시(인칭)대명사 : this(these) / that(those) / it(they) / he, she, one(s) ...
위의 지시(인칭)대명사 바로 앞 문장에는 반드시 가리키는 명사가 있어야 한다.

### 연습문제

**EX 1** 주어진 문장이 들어갈 위치로 가장 적절한 것은?

They see that "A" happened before "B", so they mistakenly assume that "A" caused "B". This is an error known in logic as a post hoc fallacy.

Even worse than reaching a conclusion with just a little evidence is the fallacy of reaching a conclusion without any evidence at all. ( ① ) Sometimes people mistake a separate event for a cause-and-effect relationship. ( ② ) For example, suppose you see a man in a black jacket hurry into a bank; you notice he is nervously carrying his briefcase, and a few moments later you hear a siren. ( ③ ) You therefore leap to the conclusion that the man in the black jacket has robbed the bank. ( ④ ) However, such a leap tends to land far from the truth of the matter as you have absolutely no evidence — only a suspicion based on coincidence. This is a post hoc fallacy.

## 연습해설

### EX 1

> They see that "A" happened before "B", so they mistakenly assume that "A" caused "B". This is an error known in logic as a post hoc fallacy.

> Even worse than reaching a conclusion with just a little evidence is the fallacy of reaching a conclusion without any evidence at all. ( ① ) Sometimes people mistake a separate event for a cause-and-effect relationship. ( ② ) For example, suppose you see a man in a black jacket hurry into a bank; you notice he is nervously carrying his briefcase, and a few moments later you hear a siren. ( ③ ) You therefore leap to the conclusion that the man in the black jacket has robbed the bank. ( ④ ) However, such a leap tends to land far from the truth of the matter as you have absolutely no evidence — only a suspicion based on coincidence. This is a post hoc fallacy.

**해석** 단지 약간의 증거만을 가지고 결론에 도달하는 것보다 훨씬 더 나쁜 것은 전혀 어떤 증거도 없이 결론에 이르는 오류이다. 때때로 사람들은 분리된 사건을 인과 관계로 오해한다. 그들은 A가 B보다 먼저 일어난 것을 보고, A가 B의 원인이었다는 잘못된 추정을 한다. 이것은 논리학에서 인과 관계의 오류라고 알려진 오류이다. 예를 들어, 당신은 검은 옷옷을 입은 사람이 은행으로 급히 들어가는 것을 본다고 추정해 보자. 즉, 당신은 그가 그의 가방을 초조하게 가지고 가는 것을 주시하고, 몇 분 있다가 사이렌 소리를 듣는다. 따라서 당신은 그 불길한 검은 옷옷을 입은 사람이 은행에서 강도질을 했다고 속단한다. 그러나 그러한 비약은 그 문제의 진실과 거리가 먼 경향이 있다. 왜냐하면 당신은 단지 우연의 일치에 기초한 의심만 있을 뿐 증거가 전혀 없기 때문이다. 이것이 인과 설정의 오류이다.

**어휘** mistakenly 잘못하여, 실수로  assume 추정하다, 생각하다  logic 논리
post hoc fallacy 인과관계의 오류  *fallacy 오류  reach ~에 이르다, 다다르다  conclusion 결론
evidence 증거  separate 분리된  relationship 관계  suppose 추정하다, 생각하다
nervously 초조하게  briefcase (서류용) 가방  rob 강탈하다, 빼앗다  *rob A of B A에게서 B를 빼앗다
leap 건너뛰다; 건너뜀, 도약  tend to ⓥ ⓥ하려는 경향이 있다  land 착륙하다, 도달하다
absolutely 절대적으로, 분명히  suspicion 의심  coincidence 우연의 일치

**해설** 주어진 문장의 They는 문맥상 ①에 있는 people을 대신하므로 주어진 문장은 ②에 들어가는 것이 가장 적절하다.

01 ②

## 풀이 해법

**3) 정관사 이용**

정관사: the + ⓝ

a + ⓝ 다음에 위의 정관사 the + ⓝ가 나온다(이때 명사는 동일 명사이다).

참고) 반드시 a + ⓝ가 the + ⓝ 바로 앞 문장에 나오는 것은 아니다.

## 연습문제

**EX 1** 주어진 글 다음에 이어질 글의 순서로 가장 적절한 것은?

Our understanding of media differences helps clarify the interaction between the type of skill or knowledge being measured and the medium in which it is being assessed.

(A) The written test does a good job of measuring explicit knowledge, but to assess the Cubs' hands-on knowledge, the actual test would be a much fairer and more accurate measure of their understanding.

(B) Their ability to intercept a baseball at the precise place where it falls to earth would clearly demonstrate that they understand things like velocity and trajectory. But were we to give the ballplayers a paper-and-pencil test on the principles of physics, they probably would not score as well.

(C) For example, consider what the members of the Chicago Cubs could demonstrate about their knowledge of physics if they were given a practical "test" in the ball park.

① (A) - (C) - (B)
② (B) - (C) - (A)
③ (C) - (A) - (B)
④ (C) - (B) - (A)

### 연습해설

**EX 1**

Our understanding of media differences helps clarify the interaction between the type of skill or knowledge being measured and the medium in which it is being assessed.

(A) The written test does a good job of measuring explicit knowledge, but to assess the Cubs' hands-on knowledge, the actual test would be a much fairer and more accurate measure of their understanding.

(B) Their ability to intercept a baseball at the precise place where it falls to earth would clearly demonstrate that they understand things like velocity and trajectory. But were we to give the ballplayers a paper-and-pencil test on the principles of physics, they probably would not score as well.

(C) For example, consider what the members of the Chicago Cubs could demonstrate about their knowledge of physics if they were given a practical "test" in the ball park.

**해석** 우리가 매체들의 차이를 이해하고 있으면 측정되고 있는 기술이나 지식의 종류와 그 기술이나 지식이 평가되고 있는 매체 사이의 상호 작용을 분명하게 하는 데 도움이 된다.
(C) 예를 들면, 만약에 시카고 컵스(미국의 프로 야구팀)의 선수들이 야구 경기장에서 실제로 하는 '시험'을 치르게 되면 물리학 지식에 관해서 그들이 무엇을 보여 줄 수 있을지를 생각해 보아라.
(B) 공이 땅으로 떨어지는 정확한 위치에서 공을 가로챌 수 있는 그들의 능력은 속도나 궤적과 같은 것들을 그들이 이해하고 있음을 명확히 보여 줄 것이다. 하지만 만약에 우리가 야구 선수들에게 물리학 법칙에 관해 필기시험을 치르게 한다면 그들은 아마도 그만큼(실제로 하는 시험을 치렀을 때만큼) 좋은 점수를 받지는 못할 것이다.
(A) 필기시험은 명시적 지식을 측정하는 일은 잘해내지만, 컵스 선수들의 실질적으로 해내는 지식을 평가하기 위해서는 실제 테스트가 그들의 이해력을 훨씬 더 올바르고 더 정확하게 측정할 것이다.

**어휘** clarify 분명하게 하다  interaction 상호 작용  measure 재다, 측정하다  medium 매체, 매개체  assess 평가하다  explicit 명백한  hands-on 실제로 해보는[조작해 보는]  ballplayer 프로 야구 선수  principle 원리, 원칙  physics 물리학  demonstrate 보여주다, 증명하다  ball park 야구장  intercept 가로채다, 도중에서 빼앗다  precise 정확한  velocity 속도  trajectory 궤도, 궤적

**해설** 지시대명사와 부정관사 → 정관사를 이용해야 한다. (B)에 a paper-and-pencil test 뒤에는 (A)의 The written test가 있어야 하고 (C)에 a practical test 뒤에는 (A)의 the actual test가 있어야 한다. 또한 (B)의 Their는 (C)에 있는 시카고 컵스의 선수들(members)을 지칭하므로 (C) 다음 (B)가 이어져야 한다. 따라서 글의 순서로 가장 적절한 것은 ④ (C) − (B) − (A)이다.

01 ④

### 풀이 해법

**6. 공간적 순서(Spatial Order) 이용**
1) 나열의 Signal을 이용한 공간 개념
   ① 같은 내용의 것들은 하나의 공간으로 묶는다.
   ② 나열의 Signal을 이용하여 공간을 분할시킨다. (나열의 Signal은 생략가능하다.)

### 연습문제

**EX 1** 주어진 문장이 들어갈 위치로 가장 적절한 것은?

They were also a way to show that their owners were affluent or powerful.

Gardens today are beautiful places to go and relax, but have had many purposes over the years. In the past they were planted to honor the gods, or used in religious ceremonies such as funerals and weddings. ( ① ) Certain trees were also sacred in their own culture; especially, yew trees were important for Celts, as were fig trees in Egypt. ( ② ) The ancient Greeks planted oaks for their Gods, and many cultures believed gardens were holy. ( ③ ) Ancient rulers created huge gardens to display their wealth, in the same way that large palaces were symbols of prosperity. ( ④ ) In Roman times the garden became an extension of the house, representing the owner's status in society, rather than a holy place.

## 연습해설

### EX 1

They were also a way to show that their owners were affluent or powerful.

Gardens today are beautiful places to go and relax, but have had many purposes over the years. In the past they were planted to honor the gods, or used in religious ceremonies such as funerals and weddings. ( ① ) Certain trees were also sacred in their own culture; especially, yew trees were important for Celts, as were fig trees in Egypt. ( ② ) The ancient Greeks planted oaks for their Gods, and many cultures believed gardens were holy. ( ③ ) Ancient rulers created huge gardens to display their wealth, in the same way that large palaces were symbols of prosperity. ( ④ ) In Roman times the garden became an extension of the house, representing the owner's status in society, rather than a holy place.

- 해석  오늘날 정원은 가서 쉬는 아름다운 장소지만 수년간 많은 목적으로 사용되어 왔다. 과거에 정원은 신을 기리기 위해 조성되거나 장례식과 결혼식과 같은 종교적인 의식에 사용되었다. 어떤 나무들은 또한 몇몇 문화에서 신성시 되었는데 이집트에서 무화과가 그랬듯이 켈트족에게 특히 주목(朱木)은 중요했다. 고대 그리스인들은 신을 위해 작은 숲을 조성했고 그들 자신의 문화에서 정원을 신성시 했다. <u>그것들(정원)은 또한 그 소유주가 부유하거나 권력이 많음을 보여주기 위한 방법이었다.</u> 고대 지배자들은 큰 성이 부의 상징인 것처럼 자신들의 부를 과시하기 위해 거대한 정원을 만들었다. 로마시대에 정원은 집의 연장이 되었고 성스러운 장소라기보다는 소유주의 사회적 지위를 나타냈다.

- 어휘  purpose 목적  over the years 수년 동안  honor 존경하다  religious 종교의, 종교적인
funeral 장례식  certain ① (명사 앞에서) 어떤, 특정한 ② (동사 뒤에서) 확실한, 분명한  sacred 신성한
especially 특히  yew tree 주목(朱木)  fig tree 무화과나무  oak 참나무  holy 신성한
affluent 부유한  ruler 지배자  huge 거대한  wealth 부(富)  palace 궁전, 사원
prosperity 번성[번영], 번창  extension 연장, 확장  represent ① 보여주다, 암시하다 ② 대표하다
status 지위  rather than ~라기 보다는

- 해설  나열의 공간 개념을 이용해야 한다. ②까지는 정원이 신을 기리기 위한 목적으로 사용되었음을 설명하고 있고 ③부터는 정원의 또 다른 목적인 지배자의 부유함과 권력에 관한 내용이 이어지므로 also가 있는 주어진 문장은 ③에 들어가는 것이 가장 적절하다.

01 ③

## 풀이 해법

2) 반대/대조의 공간 개념(two 개념)
두 개의 상반된 내용이 하나의 단락을 이룬다.

## 연습문제

**EX 1** 주어진 문장이 들어갈 위치로 가장 적절한 것은?

At a classical concert, conversely, the better the performance, the more still the audience will be.

Consider the differences in the behavior of rock and classical music audiences. At a rock concert, the audience will yell, whistle, sing along, and stamp their feet. ( ① ) They may even stand during the entire performance. ( ② ) The better the music, the more active they'll be. ( ③ ) Members of the audience are so highly disciplined that they keep themselves from even clearing their throats. ( ④ ) No matter what effect the powerful music has on their intellects and feelings, they will sit motionlessly, too.

## 연습해설

### EX 1

At a classical concert, conversely, the better the performance, the more still the audience will be.

Consider the differences in the behavior of rock and classical music audiences. At a rock concert, the audience will yell, whistle, sing along, and stamp their feet. ( ① ) They may even stand during the entire performance. ( ② ) The better the music, the more active they'll be. ( ③ ) Members of the audience are so highly disciplined that they keep themselves from even clearing their throats. ( ④ ) No matter what effect the powerful music has on their intellects and feelings, they will sit motionlessly, too.

**해석** 록 음악과 고전음악 청중들 간의 행동의 차이를 생각해보자. 록 콘서트에서 청중들은 소리를 지르고, 휘파람을 불며, 노래를 따라 부르고, 발을 굴러댈 것이다. 심지어 공연 내내 서있기도 한다. 음악이 좋으면 좋을수록, 그들은 더 적극적이 된다. <u>이와는 반대로, 고전음악의 콘서트에서는 더 좋은 공연일수록, 청중들은 더 고요해진다.</u> 그 청중들은 너무나 훈련이 잘 되어 있어서 헛기침마저도 삼간다. 강렬한 음악이 그들의 지성이나 감정에 어떠한 영향을 미쳐도 그들은 또한 움직임 없이 앉아만 있을 것이다.

**어휘** yell 소리 지르다  whistle 휘파람을 불다  sing along 함께 노래하다  stamp one's feet 발을 구르다
conversely 이와는 반대로  still ①고요한, 조용한 ②정지된  disciplined 훈련받은
keep A from ~ing A가 ~하는 것을 막다[못하게 하다]
clear one's throat 헛기침을 하다, (헛기침을 해서) 목을 가다듬다

**해설** two 개념을 이용해야 한다. ①과 ②에서 록 음악을 듣는 청중에 관한 설명을 하고 있는데 ③에는 청중들이 헛기침마저도 삼간다고 했으므로 ③에서 논리의 공백이 생겼고 또한 ③부터 고전음악 청중들의 설명이 이어지므로 주어진 문장이 들어가기에 가장 적절한 곳은 ③이다.

01 ③

### 풀이 해법

**3) 유사의 공간 개념**
서로 다른 소재에 대한 공통점이 하나의 단락을 이룰 때 하나의 소재에서 다른 소재로 전환되는(A에서 B로 넘어가는) 지점에서 유사의 Signal이 나온다.

### 연습문제

**EX 1** 주어진 글 다음에 이어질 글의 순서로 가장 적절한 것은?

People who don't get enough sleep may lack energy, feel depressed or irritable, have trouble remembering everyday things, and get sick more often than people who get enough sleep.

(A) Poor sleep also leads to accidents. More than 200,000 auto accidents happen each year because drivers fall asleep at the wheel. The 1989 Exxon Valdez oil spill was at least partially caused by the actions of a tired tanker operator.

(B) They seem to age faster and they may have problems concentrating at work or school. Some scientists believe a lack of sleep may be partially responsible for such health problems as high blood pressure, heart problems, and even obesity.

(C) Likewise, too much sleep can be as harmful as too little. Recent studies have shown that adults who get 7 to 8 hours of sleep a night live longer and are less likely to get heart disease than those who sleep less or more.

① (A) − (B) − (C)
② (B) − (A) − (C)
③ (B) − (C) − (A)
④ (C) − (B) − (A)

## 연습해설

### EX 1

People who don't get enough sleep may lack energy, feel depressed or irritable, have trouble remembering everyday things, and get sick more often than people who get enough sleep.

(A) Poor sleep also leads to accidents. More than 200,000 auto accidents happen each year because drivers fall asleep at the wheel. The 1989 Exxon Valdez oil spill was at least partially caused by the actions of a tired tanker operator.

(B) They seem to age faster and they may have problems concentrating at work or school. Some scientists believe a lack of sleep may be partially responsible for such health problems as high blood pressure, heart problems, and even obesity.

(C) Likewise, too much sleep can be as harmful as too little. Recent studies have shown that adults who get 7 to 8 hours of sleep a night live longer and are less likely to get heart disease than those who sleep less or more.

**해석** 잠을 충분히 자지 못한 사람들은 잠을 충분히 자는 사람들보다 활기가 부족하고, 풀이 죽어 있거나 화를 잘 내고, 일상의 일을 기억하는 데 어려움을 느끼고, 쉽게 병이 난다.
(B) 그들은 더 빨리 노화되고 직장이나 학교에서 집중하는 데 곤란을 겪는 것으로 보인다. 어떤 과학자들은 잠의 부족이 고혈압, 심장 질환, 심지어는 비만과 같은 건강 질환을 일으키는 데 어느 정도 원인을 제공한다고 확신한다.
(A) 잠의 부족은 사고를 일으키기도 한다. 매년 20여만 건 이상의 자동차 사고가 운전자가 운전 중에 잠이 들기 때문에 발생한다. 1989년의 엑손 발데즈호 석유 누출 사건은 적어도 부분적으로는 피곤한 유조차 조작자의 행동에 원인이 있었다.
(C) 마찬가지로, 잠을 너무 많이 자는 것은 너무 안 자는 것만큼 해롭다. 최근의 연구는 하룻밤에 7시간에서 8시간 수면을 취하는 성인이 그보다 더 많이 자거나 덜 자는 사람들보다 더 오래 살고 심장 질환에 걸릴 가능성도 더 적다는 사실을 보여준다.

**어휘** depressed 우울한  irritable 화내는, 짜증내는  have trouble ~ing ~하는 데 어려움을 겪다  at the wheel 운전 중에  spill ① 쏟다 ② 유출  partially 부분적으로  obesity 비만

**해설** (B)의 They는 주어진 문장의 People을 대신하고 (B), (A) 모두 잠을 너무 적게 자는 사람의 문제점을 제시하고 있고 (C)의 Likewise를 기준으로 잠을 많이 자는 사람들도 문제가 있다는 내용이 이어져야 하므로 주어진 문장 다음 이어질 글의 순서로 가장 적절한 것은 ② (B) - (A) - (C)이다.

정답
01 ②

## 실전문제

**01** 주어진 글 다음에 이어질 글의 순서로 가장 적절한 것은?

Tucson is a city in the desert. Its population has grown rapidly over the last twenty years, putting stress on one vital resource: water.

(A) A quick review of water use indicated landscaping consumed too much water, accounting for over half the total water used by the city. The one policy encouraged residents to weed out trees and bushes and replace them with rocks, sand, and other non-living landscape.

(B) For the last decade a strong water conservation ethic has developed, and city leaders took some extraordinary steps to encourage conservation when they created landscaping policies.

(C) This helped reinforce the so-called xeriscape philosophy (landscaping that uses little water). The policies were expressed as landscape ordinances. Additional encouragement included recommendations via public service announcements and consumer publications.

*xeriscape : 내건성 조경

① (A) – (B) – (C)
② (B) – (A) – (C)
③ (C) – (A) – (B)
④ (C) – (B) – (A)

## 실전 해설

**01**

Tucson is a city in the desert. Its population has grown rapidly over the last twenty years, putting stress on one vital resource: water.

(A) A quick review of water use indicated landscaping consumed too much water, accounting for over half the total water used by the city. The one policy encouraged residents to weed out trees and bushes and replace them with rocks, sand, and other non-living landscape.

(B) For the last decade a strong water conservation ethic has developed, and city leaders took some extraordinary steps to encourage conservation when they created landscaping policies.

(C) This helped reinforce the so-called xeriscape philosophy (landscaping that uses little water). The policies were expressed as landscape ordinances. Additional encouragement included recommendations via public service announcements and consumer publications.

\* xeriscape : 내건성 조경

**해석**  Tucson은 사막에 있는 도시이다. 그곳의 인구는 지난 20년 동안 급속히 증가해 왔는데, 그로 인해 한 가지 필수적인 자원인 물에 무리가 갔다.
(B) 지난 10년간 강력한 물 보존 윤리가 생겨났으며, 도시의 지도자들은 조경 정책을 만들어 내면서 (수자원) 보존을 장려하기 위한 몇 가지 특별한 조치들을 취했다.
(A) 짧은 시간 동안 물 사용을 검토해 본 결과 조경이 너무 많은 물을 소모하며, (그에 사용하는) 물의 양은 그 도시가 사용하는 전체 물의 절반이 넘는 양에 해당한다는 것이 드러났다. 그 하나의 정책은 주민들에게 나무와 관목을 제거하고 그것들을 바위, 모래, 다른 무생물 경관으로 대체하도록 권장했다.
(C) 이것은 이른바 내건성 조경 철학(물을 거의 사용하지 않는 조경)을 강화하는 데 도움이 되었다. 그러한 정책은 조경 관련 조례로 표현되었다. 추가적인 장려책에는 공익 광고와 소비자를 위한 출판물을 통한 권고가 포함되었다.

**어휘**  stress ① 스트레스, 부담 ② 강조(하다)   vital 필수적인   resource 자원
account for ① 차지하다 ② 설명하다   resident 거주자   weed out 뽑다, 제거하다
conservation 보존, 보호   ethic 윤리   extraordinary 보기 드문, 비범한
landscape ① 경치, 풍경 ② 조경   public service announcement 공익광고
ordinance 조례, 법령   via ~을 경유해서, ~을 통하여   publication 출판

**해설**  (B)에 나열의 시그널 some이 있고 (A)에 첫 번째 나열을 알리는 시그널 one, 그리고 (C)에 additional이 있으므로 나열의 전개방식상 주어진 문장 다음 이어질 글의 순서로 가장 적절한 것은 ② (B) - (A) - (C)가 된다.

01 ②

## 실전문제

**02** 주어진 문장이 들어갈 위치로 가장 적절한 것은?

> But let us say that the ranger who painted the sign meant to say just the opposite.

An ambiguous term is one which has more than a single meaning and whose context does not clearly indicate which meaning is intended. For instance, a sign posted at a fork in a trail which reads "Bear To The Right" can be understood in two ways. ( ① ) The more probable meaning is that it is instructing hikers to take the right trail, not the left. ( ② ) He was trying to warn hikers against taking the right trail because there is a bear in the area through which it passes. ( ③ ) The ranger's language was therefore careless, and open to misinterpretation which could have serious consequences. ( ④ ) The only way to avoid ambiguity is to spell things out as explicitly as possible: "Keep left. Do not use trail to the right. Bears in the area."

## 실전 해설

02
> But let us say that the ranger who painted the sign meant to say just the opposite.

An ambiguous term is one which has more than a single meaning and whose context does not clearly indicate which meaning is intended. For instance, a sign posted at a fork in a trail which reads "Bear To The Right" can be understood in two ways. ( ① ) The more probable meaning is that it is instructing hikers to take the right trail, not the left. ( ② ) He was trying to warn hikers against taking the right trail because there is a bear in the area through which it passes. ( ③ ) The ranger's language was therefore careless, and open to misinterpretation which could have serious consequences. ( ④ ) The only way to avoid ambiguity is to spell things out as explicitly as possible: "Keep left. Do not use trail to the right. Bears in the area."

↳ 지시대명사 He가 가리키는 명사가 바로 앞 문장에 있어야 한다.

**해석** 모호한 용어는 하나 이상의 의미를 가지고 있으며 그 용어의 맥락이 어떤 의미가 의도되었는지를 정확하게 보여주지 않는 것을 의미한다. 예를 들어, 등산로의 갈림길에 게시된 "오른쪽에 곰(오른쪽으로 가시오)"이라는 표지판은 두 가지 방식으로 오해받을 수 있다. 더 개연성 있는 의미는 그것이 그는 등산가들에게 왼쪽이 아닌 오른쪽 길을 선택하라고 지시하는 것이다. <u>하지만 그 표지판을 그린 관리인은 정반대의 뜻을 의도했다.</u> 그는 등산가들에게 오른쪽 길은 그곳을 통과하는 곰이 있으니까 그쪽을 이용하지 말 것을 경고하려고 했었다. 관리인의 언어는 따라서 부주의했고 심각한 결과를 가져올 수 있는 오해의 소지가 있었다. 모호함을 피할 수 있는 유일한 방법은 그것들을 가능한 한 명확하게 설명하는 것이다. "좌측통행하세요. 오른쪽 길을 사용하지 마세요. 이 지역에 곰이 나옵니다."

**어휘** ranger 관리원, 경비원  the opposite (정)반대  ambiguous 애매모호한  context 맥락, 전후사정
indicate 나타내다, 보여주다  trail ①길 ②자국  intend 의도하다
fork ①포크 ②(도로의) 분기점[갈래], 갈림길  read ~라고 쓰여 있다
bear to the right 오른쪽으로 돌다  instruct 지시하다  warn 경고하다
misinterpretation 오해, 오역  ambiguity 애매모호함  spell out ~을 자세히 설명하다
explicitly 명확하게

**해설** 지시대명사를 이용해야 한다. ②의 He는 주어진 문장의 ranger를 대신하므로 주어진 문장은 ②에 들어가는 것이 가장 적절하다.

02 ②

## 실전문제

**03** 주어진 글 다음에 이어질 글의 순서로 가장 적절한 것은?

There's a direct similarity to pop music in the classical song, more commonly called an "art song," which does not focus on the development of melodic material.

(A) But the pop song will rarely be sung and played exactly as written; the singer is inclined to embellish that vocal line to give it a "styling," just as the accompanist will fill out the piano part to make it more interesting and personal. The performers might change the original tempo and mood completely.

(B) Both the pop song and the art song tend to follow tried-and-true structural patterns. And both will be published in the same way — with a vocal part and a basic piano one written out underneath.

(C) You won't find such change of approach by the performers of songs by Franz Schubert or Richard Strauss. These will be performed note for note because both the vocal and piano parts have been painstakingly written down by the composer with an ear for how each relates to the other.

\* embellish : 꾸미다   \*\* tried-and-true : 유효성이 증명된

① (B) - (A) - (C)
② (B) - (C) - (A)
③ (C) - (A) - (B)
④ (C) - (B) - (A)

## 실전 해설

**03**

There's a direct similarity to pop music in the classical song, more commonly called an "art song," which does not focus on the development of melodic material.

▶ pop과 classic의 유사점

┌ 차이점 설명
(A) But the pop song will rarely be sung and played exactly as written; the singer is inclined to embellish that vocal line to give it a "styling," just as the accompanist will fill out the piano part to make it more interesting and personal. The performers might change the original tempo and mood completely.

┌ pop과 classic의 유사점
(B) Both the pop song and the art song tend to follow tried-and-true structural patterns. And both will be published in the same way — with a vocal part and a basic piano one written out underneath.

┌ 지시형용사 such 다음 명사(extremes)는 반드시 앞 문장에 있어야 한다.
(C) You won't find such extremes of approach by the performers of songs by Franz Schubert or Richard Strauss. These will be performed note for note because both the vocal and piano parts have been painstakingly written down by the composer with an ear for how each relates to the other.

\* embellish : 꾸미다  \*\* tried-and-true : 유효성이 증명된

**해석** 더 일반적으로는 '예술가곡'이라 불리는 고전 성악에는 대중음악과 직접적인 유사점이 있는 음악이 있는데, 그것은 멜로디 내용의 전개에 초점을 맞추지 않는다.
(B) 대중음악과 예술가곡 둘 다 유효성이 입증된 구조적 패턴을 따르는 경향이 있다. 그리고 둘 다 같은 방식으로, 즉 노래 파트와 그 아래쪽에 기본적인 피아노 파트가 세세하게 적힌 상태로 출판되기 마련이다.
(A) 그러나 대중음악이 작곡된 대로 정확히 노래가 불리거나 연주되는 경우는 드물 것이다. 반주자가 피아노 파트를 채워 넣어 그것을 더 흥미롭고 개인적인 특성을 갖게 하는 것과 마찬가지로, 가수도 노래 파트를 꾸며서 그것에 '모양내기'를 제공하는 경향이 있다. 공연자가 본래의 박자와 분위기를 완전히 바꿀 수도 있을 것이다.
(C) Franz Schubert나 Richard Strauss가 작곡한 노래의 연주자에게서는 그러한 접근법의 변화를 찾지 못할 것이다. 이런 곡은 음표 하나하나가 정확히 연주되기 마련인데, 그 이유는 작곡가가 노래 파트와 피아노 파트가 각자서로에게 어떻게 관련을 맺는지를 이해하는 귀를 가지고 작곡가가 두 파트를 고심하여 작곡했기 때문이다.

**어휘** direct 직접적인  melodic material 멜로디의 내용  rarely 거의 ~ 않는  exactly 정확하게  be inclined to ⓥ ⓥ하는 경향이 있다  embellish 꾸미다, 장식하다  vocal line 가수  accompanist 반주자  tempo 박자, 속도  mood 분위기  tried-and-true 유효성이 증명된  underneath 그 아래로  note 음표  painstakingly 고심하여

**해설** 대중음악과 예술가곡이라는 두 부류의 음악에 관해 언급한 주어진 글 다음에, 이들 둘의 일반적 특징과 공통점에 관해 설명하는 (B)가 이어지고 (A)의 But을 기준으로 둘의 차이점을 설명하는 내용이 이어지므로 (B) 다음에는 (A)가 위치해야 한다. 또한 (C)의 such change는 (A)의 변화를 설명하고 있으므로 (C)는 글의 흐름상 제일 마지막에 위치해야 한다. 따라서 주어진 글 다음 이어질 글의 순서로 가장 적절한 것은 ① (B) - (A) - (C)이다.

**정답**
03 ①

## 실전문제

**04** 주어진 문장이 들어갈 위치로 가장 적절한 것은?

> Unless there exists a close friendship, both the North and South American stand about two to three feet away from the other person.

North Americans do not maintain eye contact during a conversation; however, South Americans do. A person from North America usually meets the other person's eyes for a few seconds, looks away, and then back again but a South American looks directly into the other person's eyes and considers it impolite not to do so. ( ① ) Another difference is the contrast in using hand movements while speaking. ( ② ) While the South American uses many gestures, the North American, uses them only occasionally. ( ③ ) The North and South American, though, have more in common regarding the distance each maintains from the person he or she is talking with. ( ④ )

## 실전 해설

**04**

> North와 South의 유사점
> 
> Unless there exists a close friendship, both the North and South American stand about two to three feet away from the other person.

North와 South의 차이점

North Americans do not maintain eye contact during a conversation; however, South Americans do. A person from North America usually meets the other

North와 South의 차이점

person's eyes for a few seconds, looks away, and then back again but a South American looks directly into the other person's eyes and considers it impolite not

또 다른 차이점 나열

to do so. ( ① ) Another difference is the contrast in using hand movements while

North와 South의 차이점

speaking. ( ② ) While the South American uses many gestures, the North American, uses them only occasionally. ( ③ ) The North and South American,

North와 South의 유사점

though, have more in common regarding the distance each maintains from the person he or she is talking with. ( ④ )

- **해석** 북미 사람들은 대화 중에 시선을 마주치는 것을 유지하지 않지만 남미 사람들은 그렇게 한다(시선을 마주친다). 북미 출신의 사람은 대개 상대방의 눈을 몇 초 동안 마주치고 시선을 돌리고 그리고 나서 다시 돌아온다. 어떤 남미 사람은 상대방의 눈을 똑바로 쳐다보며 그렇게 하지 않는 것을 무례하다고 여긴다. 또 다른 차이점은 이야기 동안 손동작을 사용할 때의 차이다. 남미 사람은 많은 제스처를 사용한다. 하지만 북미 사람은 가끔씩만 사용한다. 하지만 북미 사람과 남미 사람은 각각 자신이 얘기하고 있는 사람과 유지하는 거리에 대해서는 더 많은 공통점을 가진다. 친밀한 우정이 존재하지 않으면 북미 사람과 남미 사람 둘 다 상대방으로부터 2에서 3피트 떨어져 서 있다.

- **어휘** contrast 차이, 대조  hand movement 손동작  maintain 유지하다
  eye contact 시선을 마주치는 것  look away 시선을 돌리다  directly 똑바로  impolite 무례한
  occasionally 가끔  have ~ in common ~을 공통으로 가지다  regarding ~에 관하여
  distance 거리  close 친밀한  away from ~에서 떨어져  figure out 알아내다

- **해설** 주어진 지문은 북미와 남미 사람들의 차이점과 공통점을 동시에 설명하는 글이다. 주어진 제시문은 북미와 남미사람들의 공통점을 설명하고 있고 ③부터 반대/대조의 연결어 though를 이용해서 북미와 남미사람들의 공통점을 설명하고 있다. 또한 ③에 대한 보충부연 설명이 주어진 문장에 있으므로 주어진 문장이 들어가기에 가장 적절한 곳은 ④이다.

**정답**
04 ④

## 실전문제

**05** 다음 주어진 문장이 들어가기에 가장 적절한 곳은?

> The Watergate break-in initially gave Nixon's team a tactical sucess, but it ended up triggering a massive political scandal that forced the president to resign, as we know.

In 2018, the Cambridge Analytica collected data from millions of Facebook users without their agreement. The data was used to influence voter behavior in the 2020 U.S. presidential election, giving the campaign a powerful success. ( ① ) The operation was conducted quietly and efficiently, going undetected for years. ( ② ) But once it was revealed, the strong, negative criticism took place swiftly and severely. ( ③ ) Public trust in Facebook plummeted, executives were summoned before Congress. ( ④ ) In the same way, the Cambridge Analytica scandal began with a seemingly successful tactic, but it ultimately resulted in far-reaching downfalls for both politics and tech companies.

## 실전 해설

**05**

> The Watergate break-in initially gave Nixon's team a tactical sucess, but it ended up triggering a massive political scandal that forced the president to resign, as we know.

> In 2018, the Cambridge Analytica collected data from millions of Facebook users without their agreement. The data was used to influence voter behavior in the 2020 U.S. presidential election, giving the campaign a powerful success. ( ① ) The operation was conducted quietly and efficiently, going undetected for years. ( ② ) But once it was revealed, the strong, negative criticism took place swiftly and severely. ( ③ ) Public trust in Facebook plummeted, executives were summoned before Congress. ( ④ ) In the same way, the Cambridge Analytica scandal began with a seemingly successful tactic, but it ultimately resulted in far-reaching downfalls for both politics and tech companies.

- **해석** 2018년에 <케임브리지 애널리티카>가 수천만 명의 페이스북 사용자들의 동의 없이 데이터를 수집한 사실이 드러났다. 이 데이터는 2020년 미국 대선에서 유권자의 행동에 영향을 주기 위해 사용되었고, 선거 캠페인에 강력한 성공을 제공한 것으로 알려졌다. 이 작업은 수년간 조용하고 효율적으로 진행되어 들키지 않았다. 그러나 이 사실이 밝혀지자, 강하고 부정적인 비판이 빠르고 거세게 일어났다. 대중의 페이스북에 대한 신뢰는 급격히 떨어졌고, 경영진은 의회 청문회에 소환되었다. 우리도 아는 것처럼 워터게이트 침입 사건은 처음에는 닉슨 측에 전술적인 성공을 안겨주었지만, 결국 대통령이 사임하게 된 대규모 정치 스캔들로 이어졌다. 이와 마찬가지로, 케임브리지 애널리티카 스캔들도 처음에는 성공적인 전술처럼 보였지만, 결국 정치권과 기술 기업 모두에 광범위한 몰락을 초래하게 되었다.

- **어휘** break-in 침입  initially 처음에는  tactical 전술적인  end up 결국 ~하게 되다  trigger 유발하다  massive 대규모의  resign 사임하다  collect 모으다, 수집하다  operation 작전  conduct 수행하다  undetected 들키지 않은  reveal 드러내다  criticism 비판  take place 발생하다, 일어나다  swiftly 빠르게, 신속하게  severe 심각한  plummet 급락하다  executive 경영진, 간부  summon 소환하다  Congress 의회  seemingly 겉보기에는  tactic 전술  ultimately 궁극적으로  far-reaching 광범위한  downfall 몰락

- **해설** 유사의 시그널 In the same way를 이용해야 한다. ④에 In the same way를 기준으로 서로 다른 소재(Watergate break-in vs. Cambridge Analytica scandal)에 대한 공통점(전술적 성공 하지만 궁극적 몰락)을 설명하고 있으므로 주어진 제시문은 ④에 들어가는 것이 가장 적절하다.

**정답**
05 ④

## 06 주어진 글 다음에 이어질 글의 순서로 가장 적절한 것은?

The fruit ripening process brings about the softening of cell walls, sweetening and the production of chemicals that give colour and flavour. The process is induced by the production of a plant hormone called ethylene.

(A) If ripening could be slowed down by interfering with ethylene production or with the processes that respond to ethylene, fruit could be left on the plant until it was ripe and full of flavour but would still be in good condition when it arrived at the supermarket shelf.

(B) In some countries they are then sprayed with ethylene before sale to the consumer to induce ripening. However, fruit picked before it is ripe has less flavour than fruit picked ripe from the plant. Biotechnologists therefore saw an opportunity in delaying the ripening and softening process in fruit.

(C) The problem for growers and retailers is that ripening is followed sometimes quite rapidly by deterioration and decay and the product becomes worthless. Tomatoes and other fruits are, therefore, usually picked and transported when they are unripe.

① (A) − (C) − (B)
② (B) − (C) − (A)
③ (C) − (A) − (B)
④ (C) − (B) − (A)

## 실전 해설

**06**

The fruit ripening process brings about the softening of cell walls, sweetening and the production of chemicals that give colour and flavour. The process is induced by the production of a plant hormone called ethylene.

(A) If ripening could be slowed down by interfering with ethylene production or with the processes that respond to ethylene, fruit could be left on the plant until it was ripe and full of flavour but would still be in good condition when it arrived at the supermarket shelf. → 시간 순서상 마지막

(B) In some countries they are then sprayed with ethylene before sale to the consumer to induce ripening. However, fruit picked before it is ripe has less flavour than fruit picked ripe from the plant. Biotechnologists therefore saw an opportunity in delaying the ripening and softening process in fruit.
  지시대명사 they가 가리키는 명사가 반드시 바로 앞 문장에 있어야 한다.
  시간 순서상 시작점

(C) The problem for growers and retailers is that ripening is followed sometimes quite rapidly by deterioration and decay and the product becomes worthless. Tomatoes and other fruits are, therefore, usually picked and transported when they are unripe.
  시간 순서상 중간점

**해석** 과일 숙성 과정은 세포벽의 연화와 감미, 색깔과 맛을 주는 화학물질의 생산이라는 결과를 가져온다. 이 과정은 에틸렌이라고 불리는 식물 호르몬의 생산에 의해서 유도된다.
(C) 재배업자와 소매업자에게 문제는 숙성 이후에 때로는 아주 빠르게 품질 저하와 부패가 뒤따라서 제품이 가치 없게 된다는 것이다. 그러므로 토마토와 다른 과일은 일반적으로 익지 않았을 때 수확되어 운송된다.
(B) 일부 국가에서는 그런 다음 숙성을 유도하기 위해 소비자에게 판매하기 전에 에틸렌을 그것들에 살포한다. 그러나 익기 전에 수확된 과일은 식물에서 익은 상태로 수확된 과일보다 맛이 덜하다. 따라서 생명공학자들은 과일의 숙성 및 연화 과정을 지연하는 데 있어서 기회를 엿보았다.
(A) 에틸렌 생산을 방해하거나 에틸렌에 반응하는 과정을 방해함으로써 숙성을 늦출 수 있다면, 과일은 익어서 맛이 가득 찰 때까지 식물에 붙어 있을 수 있지만, 슈퍼마켓 선반에 도착했을 때에도 여전히 좋은 상태를 유지할 것이다.

**어휘** ripening 숙성 *ripen 익다, 숙성하다  bring about 초래하다, 야기하다
softening 연화 *soften 부드럽게 하다, 부드러워지다  sweeten 달게 하다  chemical 화학 물질
flavour(= flavor) 맛, 풍미  retailer 소매상  rapidly 빠르게, 신속하게
deterioration (품질) 저하  decay 부패(하다)  worthless 가치가 없는  transport 운송하다
unripe 익지 않은  spray 살포하다, 뿌리다  induce 유도하다  biotechnologist 생명공학자
delay 연기하다, 미루다  interfere with ~을 방해하다  shelf 선반

**해설** 시간 순서 전개 방식과 대명사를 이용해야 한다. (B)의 They는 (C) 마지막 문장의 Tomatoes와 other fruits를 대신하므로 (B) 앞에는 (C)가 위치해야 하고 시간 순서상 (C)의 운송이 먼저 되고 그 다음 (A)의 도착이 이루어져야 하므로 (A)는 제일 마지막에 위치해야 한다. 따라서 주어진 문장 다음 이어질 글의 순서로 가장 적절한 것은 ④ (C) - (B) - (A)이다.

**정답**
06 ④

## 07 주어진 문장이 들어갈 위치로 가장 적절한 것은?

> In contrast, the "entertainment" story is designed to help us forget about our problems — to take us on vacation.

The "art" story, what we call literature, is meant to illuminate life as we actually experience it. For that reason, it tends to focus on the human experience, emphasizing character and emotion. ( ① ) That is, the entertainment story serves as a thrilling or scary escape, rather than revealing an honest or true reflection of life. ( ② ) It therefore tends to focus on situation and plot and deemphasizes the messy and confusing aspects of experience. ( ③ ) That your creative writing teacher keeps encouraging you toward art and away from entertainment doesn't imply a value judgment. ( ④ ) Nobody is saying that art is good and entertainment is bad. The two are simply different; they meet different needs, and there should be room for both.

## 실전 해설

**07**

> Two 개념: ① art story ② entertainment → 차이점 설명
>
> In contrast, the "entertainment" story is designed to help us forget about our problems — to take us on vacation.

The "art" story, what we call literature, is meant to illuminate life as we actually experience it. For that reason, it tends to focus on the human experience, emphasizing character and emotion. ( ① ) That is, the entertainment story serves as a thrilling or scary escape, rather than revealing an honest or true reflection of life. ( ② ) It therefore tends to focus on situation and plot and deemphasizes the messy and confusing aspects of experience. ( ③ ) That your creative writing teacher keeps encouraging you toward art and away from entertainment doesn't imply a value judgment. ( ④ ) Nobody is saying that art is good and entertainment is bad. The two are simply different; they meet different needs, and there should be room for both.

**해석** 우리가 '문학'이라고 부르는 '예술' 이야기는 우리가 실제로 경험하는 바의 삶을 조명하기 위한 것이다. 그런 이유 때문에 그것은 인간의 경험에 초점을 맞추는 경향이 있으며, 성격과 감정을 강조한다. 이와는 대조적으로, '오락' 이야기는 우리들이 골칫거리들을 잊어버리도록 도우려고, 즉 우리에게 휴가를 주려고 설계되었다. 즉, 다시 말해서 오락 이야기는 삶에 대한 솔직하거나 진솔한 반영을 드러내는 것이 아니라 아주 신나거나 무서운 탈출구 역할을 한다. 그러므로 그것은 상황과 플롯에 초점을 맞추는 경향이 있으며 경험의 어수선하고 혼란스러운 측면들은 경시한다. 여러분의 문예 창작 선생님이 예술을 가까이하고 오락을 멀리하도록 계속 권하는 것이 어떤 가치 판단을 의미하지는 않는다. 그 누구도 예술은 좋고 오락은 나쁘다는 식으로 말하고 있지 않다. 이 둘은 그저 다를 뿐인데, 그들은 서로 다른 요구들을 충족시키고, 그래서 둘 다를 위한 여지가 있어야 한다.

**어휘** entertainment 오락, 접대  literature 문학  illuminate ① 조명하다, ② (이해하기 쉽게) 밝히다
emphasize 강조하다  character 성격, 특징, 등장인물  emotion 감정, 정서
thrilling 아주 신나는, 흥분되는  scary 무서운  escape 도피, 탈출
reveal 드러내다  reflection ① 반영 ② 심사숙고  plot ① 플롯, 구성 ② 음모
deemphasize 덜 강조하다, 중요성을 깎아내리다  messy 엉망인, 지저분한
confusing 혼란스러운  aspect 측면, 양상  imply 의미하다, 시사하다, 암시하다
meet 충족[만족]시키다

**해설** 반대/대조의 공간 개념을 이용해야 한다. 도입부에 "art" story가 언급되어 있고 ① 뒤에서부터 entertainment에 대한 설명이 나오므로 주어진 문장이 들어가기에 가장 적절한 곳은 ①이다.

**정답**
07 ①

## 실전문제

**08** 주어진 글 다음에 이어질 글의 순서로 가장 적절한 것은?

The first commercially successful steam engine was built in England in 1712, but it was very slow. Then, an inventor named James Watt came up with crucial innovations.

(A) Rather, they could be located where fuel was readily available and where workers already lived. Also, factories could be built closer to roads and ports from which raw materials and finished products could be easily shipped.

(B) His engine was faster and more efficient at driving machinery. By 1800 about 500 of Watt's steam engines were chugging and hissing in mines and factories throughout Britain.

(C) The widespread use of steam engines began when inventors put them to use in the textile mills. Using steam power instead of water power meant that factories no longer had to be built near ready supplies of water.

① (B) − (A) − (C)
② (B) − (C) − (A)
③ (C) − (A) − (B)
④ (C) − (B) − (A)

## 실전 해설

**08**

The first commercially successful steam engine was built in England in 1712, but it was very slow. Then, an inventor named James Watt came up with crucial innovations.

> Rather 앞에는 부정어가 있어야 한다.

(A) Rather, they could be located where fuel was readily available and where workers already lived. Also, factories could be built closer to roads and ports from which raw materials and finished products could be easily shipped.

> 지시대명사 His 앞에는 His를 가리키는 명사가 있어야 한다.

(B) His engine was faster and more efficient at driving machinery. By 1800 about 500 of Watt's steam engines were chugging and hissing in mines and factories throughout Britain.

(C) The widespread use of steam engines began when inventors put them to use in the textile mills. Using steam power instead of water power meant that factories no longer had to be built near ready supplies of water.
↳ 부정어

**해석** 사업적으로 최초의 성공한 증기 엔진은 1712년 영국에서 만들어졌지만 그것은 속도가 아주 느렸다. 그리고 나서 James Watt라는 이름의 발명가가 결정적인 혁신을 생각해냈다.

(B) 그의 엔진은 더 빠르고 구동 기계로는 더욱 효과적이었다. 1800년경에 500개의 증기 엔진이 영국 전역에 걸쳐 탄광이나 공장으로 칙칙폭폭 소리를 내며 달리기 시작했다.

(C) 증기 엔진 사용의 확산은 발명가들이 직물 공장에서 증기 엔진을 설치하면서 시작되었다. 수력 대신 증기 엔진을 사용하는 것은 공장이 더 이상 즉시 물을 공급할 수 있는 근처에 세워질 필요가 없다는 것을 의미했다.

(A) 오히려 공장은 연료를 즉시 이용하는 곳에 그리고 노동자들이 이미 살고 있었던 곳에 세워졌다. 또한 공장은 원자재나 완성된 제품을 쉽게 실을 수 있는 도로나 항구 근처에 세워졌다.

**어휘** commercially 상업적으로  crucial 중대한, 결정적인  chug 칙칙 소리를 내다  hiss 쉬익[쉿]하는 소리를 내다  mine 탄광  textile 직물, 옷감  mill ① 방앗간, 제분소 ② 공장  ready ① 준비된 ② 언제든지 ~할 수 있는  readily 손쉽게, 즉시  available 이용 가능한  port 항구  raw material 원자재  ship ① 배 ② 선적하다

**해설** 대명사 His와 Rather를 이용해야 한다. (B)의 His는 주어진 문장의 James Watt을 대신하므로 주어진 문장 다음에는 (B)가 와야 하고 (A)의 Rather 앞에는 부정문이 있어야 하므로 (C) 마지막 문장 no longer 앞에 위치해야 한다. 따라서 주어진 문장 다음 이어질 글의 순서로 가장 적절한 것은 ② (B) - (C) - (A)이다.

**정답**
08 ②

## 실전문제

**09** 주어진 문장이 들어갈 위치로 가장 적절한 것은?

> Another more serious instance includes depicting rotting slums as 'substandard housing'.

The term euphemism derives from a Greek word meaning 'to speak with good words' and involves substituting a more pleasant, less objectionable way of saying something for a blunt or more direct way. Why do people use euphemisms? ( ① ) They do so probably to help smooth out the 'rough edges' of life, to make the unbearable bearable and the offensive inoffensive. ( ② ) However, euphemisms can become dangerous when they are used to create misperceptions of important issues. ( ③ ) For example, a politician may describe that one of his statements was 'somewhat at variance with the truth,' meaning that he lied. ( ④ ) Such a description makes the miserable conditions appear reasonable and the need for action less important.

## 실전 해설

**09**

> 두 번째 나열
> Another more serious instance includes depicting rotting slums as 'substandard housing'.

The term euphemism derives from a Greek word meaning 'to speak with good words' and involves substituting a more pleasant, less objectionable way of saying something for a blunt or more direct way. Why do people use euphemisms? ( ① ) They do so probably to help smooth out the 'rough edges' of life, to make the unbearable bearable and the offensive inoffensive. ( ② ) However, some euphemisms can become dangerous when they are used to create misperceptions of important issues. ( ③ ) For example, a politician may describe that one of his statements was 'somewhat at variance with the truth,' meaning that he lied. ( ④ ) Such a description makes the miserable conditions appear reasonable and the need for action less important.

- **해석** 완곡어법이라는 말은 '좋은 단어들로 말하다'를 의미하는 그리스 단어에서 유래했으며, 무언가를 말하는 더 듣기 좋고 불쾌감이 덜한 방식으로 직설적이거나 보다 직접적인 방식을 대체하는 것과 관련되어 있다. 그들은 아마도 삶의 '거친 가장자리'를 부드럽게 만드는 것을 돕고, 견딜 수 없는 것을 견딜 만하게 하며, 불쾌한 것을 거슬리지 않게 만들기 위해 그렇게 한다. 그러나 몇몇 완곡어법은 중요한 문제점들에 대해 잘못된 인식을 만들도록 사용될 때 위험해질 수 있다. 예를 들어, 어느 정치가가 자신의 말 중 하나가 '약간 진실과 상충 관계'에 있었다고 묘사할 수도 있는데, 이것은 그가 거짓말을 했다는 뜻이다. <u>또 다른 더 심각한 예는 썩어가는 빈민가를 '표준 이하 주거'라고 묘사하는 것을 포함한다.</u> 그러한 묘사는 비참한 상태를 적당해 보이도록 하고 조치의 필요성을 덜 중요하게 만든다.

- **어휘** euphemism 완곡어법   derive from ① ~로부터 유래하다 ② ~로부터 얻다
  substitute A for B B를 A로 대체[대신]하다   objectionable 불쾌한   blunt ① 무딘 ② 직설적인
  smooth ① 매끄러운 ② 매끄럽게 하다   rough ① 거친 ② 어림잡아, 대충   edge 가장자리
  bearable 견딜 수 있는(≠ unbearable 견딜 수 없는) *bear ① 참다, 견디다 ② 지탱[유지]하다
  ③ 낳다 ④ 곰   offensive ① 불쾌한, 화나게 하는 ② 공격적인(≠ defensive)   politician 정치가
  describe 묘사하다 (= depict) *depiction 묘사   statement 진술   somewhat 다소, 약간
  at variance with ~와 상충하는[모순되는]   instance 사례   rotting 썩어가는
  substandard 기준[표준] 이하인

- **해설** 나열의 공간 개념을 이용해야 한다. ② 뒤에 나열의 시그널 some이 있고 바로 이어 첫 번째 시그널 For example이 있고 그 다음 문장에 주어진 문장의 another(두 번째 나열)가 나오는 것이 적절하므로 주어진 문장이 들어가기에 가장 적절한 곳은 ④이다.

09 ④

## 실전문제

**10** 주어진 문장이 들어갈 위치로 가장 적절한 것은?

Even so, it is not the money in itself that is valuable, but the fact that it can merely potentially yield more positive experiences.

Money — beyond the bare minimum necessary for food and shelter — is nothing more than a means to an end. And yet, so often we confuse means with ends, and sacrifice happiness (end) for money (means). It is easy to do this when material wealth is elevated to the position of the ultimate end, as it so often is in our society. This is not to say that the accumulation and production of material wealth is in itself wrong. ( ① ) Material prosperity can help individuals, as well as society, attain higher levels of happiness. ( ② ) Financial security can liberate us from work we do not find meaningful and from having to worry about the next paycheck. ( ③ ) Moreover, the desire to make money can challenge and inspire us. ( ④ ) Material wealth in and of itself does not necessarily generate meaning or lead to emotional wealth.

## 실전 해설

**10**

반대/대조의 시그널 / 개념

Even so, it is not the money in itself that is valuable, but the fact that it can merely potentially yield more positive experiences.

Money — beyond the bare minimum necessary for food and shelter — is nothing more than a means to an end. And yet, so often we confuse means with ends, and sacrifice happiness (end) for money (means). It is easy to do this when material wealth is elevated to the position of the ultimate end, as it so often is in our society. This is not to say that the accumulation and production of material wealth is in itself wrong. ( ① ) Material prosperity can help individuals, as well as society, attain higher levels of happiness. ( ② ) Financial security can liberate us from work we do not find meaningful and from having to worry about the next paycheck. ( ③ ) Moreover, the desire to make money can challenge and inspire us. ( ④ ) Material wealth in and of itself does not necessarily generate meaning or lead to emotional wealth.

**해석** 음식과 안식처에 필요한 기본적인 최소한의 범위를 벗어나는 돈은 목적에 대한 수단에 불과하다. 하지만 아주 흔히 우리는 수단을 목적과 혼동하여 돈(수단)을 위해서 행복(목적)을 희생한다. 우리 사회에서 아주 흔히 그렇듯이, 물질적 부유함이 궁극적인 목적의 위치로 높여질 때에 이렇게 하기 쉽다. 이것은 물질적 부의 축적과 생산이 그 자체로서 잘못된 것이라고 말하는 것이 아니다. 물질적 풍요는 사회뿐만 아니라 개인이 더 높은 수준의 행복을 얻을 수 있도록 도와줄 수 있다. 재정적 안정은 우리가 의미 있다고 생각하지 않는 일로부터 그리고 다음번 월급에 대해서 걱정해야 하는 것으로부터 우리를 해방시켜 줄 수 있다. 더욱이, 돈을 벌고자 하는 욕구는 우리에게 도전 정신을 심어 주고 영감을 줄 수 있다. <u>그럼에도 불구하고, 가치가 있는 것은 돈 '그 자체로서'가 아니라 그것이 단지 잠재적으로 더 긍정적인 경험만을 만들 뿐이라는 사실이다.</u> 물질적 부유함이 본질적으로 그리고 그 자체로서 의미를 만들어 내거나 감정적인 풍요로움을 반드시 가져오는 것은 아니다.

**어휘** even so 그럼에도 불구하고  in itself 그 자체로, 본질적으로
yield 생산하다, 만들어내다; 양보하다; 항복[굴복]하다  bare 벌거벗은; 가장 기본적인
shelter 안식처, 거처  nothing more than ~에 지나지 않는, ~에 불과  means 수단
end 목적  confuse A with B A를 B와 혼동하다  sacrifice 희생하다  wealth 부(富)
elevate 들어 올리다  ultimate 궁극적인  accumulation 축적, 쌓음  prosperity 번성, 번영
attain 얻다, 획득하다  financial 재정의, 재정상의  liberate 자유롭게 하다
paycheck 월급, 급여  moreover 더욱이, 게다가  inspire 영감을 주다
not necessarily 반드시 ~할 것은 아니다  generate 만들어내다, 생성하다

**해설** ①부터 ③까지 돈의 긍정적인 내용을 언급하다 ④에 명시적 시그널 없이 부정적인 내용이 나오므로 ④에서 논리의 공백이 생겼다. 주어진 문장에 반대/대조를 나타내는 시그널 Even so가 있고 돈에 대한 부정적 내용이 이어지므로 주어진 문장이 들어가기에 가장 적절한 곳은 ④이다.

정답
10 ④

## 실전문제

**11** 주어진 글 다음에 이어질 글의 순서로 가장 적절한 것은?

A critical insight of modern biology is that our family history extends to all other living things. Unlocking this relationship means comparing different species with one another in a very precise way. An order to life is revealed in the features creatures have: closely related ones share more features with each other than do those more distantly related.

(A) The reason is the fish, like people, have backbones, skulls, and appendages, all of which are lacking in flies. We can follow this logic to add species after species and find the family tree that relates people, fish, and flies to the millions of other species on the planet.

(B) Until somebody finds that the fly is hairy with breasts, we would consider flies distant relatives to cows and people. Add a fish to this comparison, and we discover that fish are more closely related to cows and people than they are to flies.

(C) A cow shares more organs and genes with people than it does with a fly: hair, warm-bloodedness, and mammary glands are shared by mammals and absent in insects.

\* order : 계통 \*\* appendage : (몸체의 다리·꼬리 등을 가리키는) 부속지(肢)
\*\*\* mammary gland : 젖샘

① (A) - (C) - (B)
② (B) - (A) - (C)
③ (C) - (A) - (B)
④ (C) - (B) - (A)

## 실전 해설

**11**

A critical insight of modem biology is that our family history extends to all other living things. Unlocking this relationship means comparing different species with one another in a very precise way. An order to life is revealed in the features creatures have: closely related ones share more features with each other than do those more distantly related.

(A) The reason is the fish, like people, have backbones, skulls, and appendages, all of which are lacking in flies. We can follow this logic to add species after species and find the family tree that relates people, fish, and flies to the millions of other species on the planet.
  *(the fish 앞에 a fish가 있어야 한다.)*

(B) Until somebody finds that the fly is hairy with breasts, we would consider flies distant relatives to cows and people. Add a fish to this comparison, and we discover that fish are more closely related to cows and people than they are to flies.
  *(the fly 앞에 a fly가 있어야 한다. / a fish 뒤에 the fish가 있어야 한다.)*

(C) A cow shares more organs and genes with people than it does with a fly: hair, warm-bloodedness, and mammary glands are shared by mammals and absent in insects.
  *(a fly 뒤에 the fly가 있어야 한다.)*

\* order : 계통  \*\* appendage : (몸체의 다리·꼬리 등을 가리키는) 부속지(肢)
\*\*\* mammary gland : 젖샘

**해석** 현대 생물학의 대단히 중요한 통찰력은 우리의 가계사가 다른 모든 생물들에게까지 확장된다는 것이다. 이 관계를 밝히는 것은 매우 정확한 방식으로 다양한 종을 서로서로 비교하는 것을 의미한다. 생물의 계통은 생물들이 지니고 있는 특징에서 드러나는데, 밀접하게 관련된 것들은 관련이 더 먼 것들이 그런 것보다 서로서로 더 많은 특징을 공유한다.

(C) 소는 파리와 그런 것보다 사람과 더 많은 기관과 유전자를 공유하는데, 털, 온혈, 젖샘은 포유동물에 의해 공유되지만, 곤충에게는 없다.

(B) 누군가 그 파리가 가슴이 있고 털이 많은 파리라는 것을 알아낼 때까지 우리는 파리를 소와 사람의 먼 친척으로 간주할 것이다. 이 비교에 물고기를 추가해보라. 그러면 우리는 물고기가 파리보다 소와 사람에게 더 가깝게 관련된다는 것을 알게 된다.

(A) 그 이유는 물고기는 사람처럼 척추와 두개골과 부속지를 가지고 있는데 그 모든 것들이 파리에는 없다. 우리는 이 논리를 따라 종을 잇달아 보태어 사람, 물고기, 파리를 지구의 수백만의 다른 종과 관련지어 주는 가계도를 찾아낼 수 있다.

**어휘** critical ① (대단히) 중요한 ② 비판적인  insight 통찰력  biology 생물학  extend 확장하다, 확장되다  unlock 밝히다, 자물쇠를 열다  relationship 관계  compare A with B A와 B를 비교하다  species 종(들)  precise 정확한, 정밀한  reveal 드러내다, 밝히다  feature 특징  insect 곤충  backbone 척추, 등뼈  skull 두개골  logic 논리  family tree 가계도  planet 지구, 행성  hairy 털이 많은  breast 가슴, 젖  relative 친척  organ (생물의) 기관, 장기  gene 유전자  warm-bloodedness 온혈  mammal 포유류  absent 없는, 부재의

**해설** 부정관사 → 정관사를 이용해야 한다. (C)의 a fly 다음 (A)의 the fly가 위치해야 하고 (B)의 a fish 다음 (A)의 the fish가 위치해야 하므로 주어진 문장 다음 이어질 글의 순서로 가장 적절한 것은 ④ (C) − (B) − (A)이다.

**정답**
11 ④

## 실전문제

**12** 주어진 문장이 들어갈 위치로 가장 적절한 것은?

> They quickly pick out a whole series of items of the same type, making a handful of, say, small screws.

People make extensive use of searching images. One unexpected context is sorting. Suppose you have a bag of small hardware — screws, nails, and so on — and you decide to organize them into little jars. You dump the stuff out on a table and begin separating the items into coherent groups. ( ① ) It is possible to do this by randomly picking up individual objects, one by one, identifying each one, and then moving it to the appropriate jar. ( ② ) But what most people do is very different. ( ③ ) They put them in the jar and then go back and do the same for a different kind of item. ( ④ ) So the sorting sequence is nonrandom, producing runs of items of a single type. It is a faster, more efficient technique, and much of the increased efficiency is due to the use of searching images.

## 실전 해설

**12**

> They가 가리키는 명사가 반드시 바로 앞 문장에 있어야 한다.
>
> They quickly pick out a whole series of items of the same type, making a handful of, say, small screws.

People make extensive use of searching images. One unexpected context is sorting. Suppose you have a bag of small hardware — screws, nails, and so on — and you decide to organize them into little jars. You dump the stuff out on a table and begin separating the items into coherent groups. ( ① ) It is possible to do this by randomly picking up individual objects, one by one, identifying each one, and then moving it to the appropriate jar. ( ② ) But what most people do is very different. ( ③ ) They put them in the jar and then go back and do the same for a different kind of item. ( ④ ) So the sorting sequence is nonrandom, producing runs of items of a single type. It is a faster, more efficient technique, and much of the increased efficiency is due to the use of searching images.

↑ them을 가리키는 명사가 반드시 바로 앞 문장에 있어야 한다.

**해석** 사람들은 탐색상을 폭넓게 활용한다. 한 가지 예상 밖의 상황은 분류하기이다. 여러분이 작은 철물, 즉 나사, 못, 기타 등등이 들어 있는 가방을 가지고 있고 그것들을 작은 단지 안에 정리해 넣기로 한다고 가정해 보라. 여러분은 그 물건들을 탁자 위에 쏟아 놓고 그 물품들을 일관성 있는 집단으로(같은 형태로) 분리하기 시작한다. 개별적인 물건들을 하나씩 무작위로 집어, 각각을 식별하고, 그러고 나서 그것을 적절한 단지로 옮김으로써 이 일을 할 수 있다. 그러나 대부분 사람이 하는 바는 매우 다르다. 그들은 재빨리 같은 형태를 한 일련의 모든 물품을 골라내는데, 이를테면 작은 나사를 한 움큼 쥔다. 그들은 그것들을 단지에 넣고, 그러고 나서 되돌아가 다른 물품에 대해 똑같이 한다. 그래서 분류 순서는 무작위가 아니고, 단 한 가지 형태로 된 물품을 연속적으로 만들어 낸다. 그것은 더 빠르고, 더 효율적인 기법인데, 향상된 효율성의 많은 부분은 탐색상의 활용에 기인한다.

**어휘** extensive 폭넓은  searching image 탐색상(探索像: 찾고자 하는 대상의 이미지)  sort 분류하다  hardware 철물  separate 분리하다  coherent 일관성 있는  identify 식별하다  appropriate 적절한  sequence 순서, 차례  efficient 효율적인

**해설** 주어진 문장에 있는 They는 문맥상 ②에 있는 most people를 대신하므로 주어진 문장이 들어가기에 가장 적절한 것은 ③이다.

**정답**
12 ③

## 실전문제

**13** 주어진 글 다음에 이어질 글의 순서로 가장 적절한 것은?

It takes time to develop and launch products. Consequently, many companies know 6-12 months ahead of time that they will be launching a new product.

(A) This marketing technique is called demand creation. It involves creating a buzz about a new potentially revolutionary nutrient or training technique through publishing articles and/or books that stimulate the reader's interest. Once this is done, a new product is launched.

(B) Over a series of issues, you begin to see more articles discussing this new nutrient and potential to enhance training and/or performance. Then, after 4-6 months, a new product is coincidentally launched that contains the ingredient that has been discussed in previous issues. Books and supplement reviews have also been used as vehicles to promote the sale of fitness and nutrition products.

(C) In order to create interest in the product, companies will often launch pre-market advertising campaigns. In the nutrition industry, articles are often written discussing a new nutrient under investigation.

① (B) - (A) - (C)
② (B) - (C) - (A)
③ (C) - (A) - (B)
④ (C) - (B) - (A)

## 실전 해설

**13**

It takes time to develop and launch products. Consequently, many companies know 6-12 months ahead of time that they will be launching a new product.

(A) [지시형용사 This 다음 명사(technique)는 반드시 바로 앞 문장에 있어야 한다.] This marketing technique is called demand creation. It involves creating a buzz about a new potentially revolutionary nutrient or training technique through publishing articles and/or books that stimulate the reader's interest. Once this is done, a new product is launched.

(B) [지시형용사 this 다음 명사(nutrient)는 반드시 앞 문장에 있어야 한다.] Over a series of issues, you begin to see more articles discussing this new nutrient and potential to enhance training and/or performance. Then, after 4-6 months, a new product is coincidentally launched that contains the ingredient that has been discussed in previous issues. Books and supplement reviews have also been used as vehicles to promote the sale of fitness and nutrition products.

(C) In order to create interest in the product, companies will often launch pre-market advertising campaigns. In the nutrition industry, articles are often written discussing a new nutrient under investigation.

**해석** 제품을 개발하고 출시하는 것은 시간이 걸린다. 결과적으로, 많은 회사들은 자신들이 신제품을 출시할 것을 6~12개월 먼저 안다.
(C) 그 제품에 대한 관심을 창출하기 위해 회사들은 흔히 출시 전 광고 캠페인에 착수하곤 한다. 영양제 업계에서는 연구 중인 새로운 영양분에 대해 논의하는 기사가 흔히 작성된다.
(B) 일련의 간행물에 걸쳐 이 새로운 영양분과 훈련 그리고/또는 경기력을 향상시킬 수 있는 잠재력에 대해 논의하는 더 많은 기사를 보기 시작한다. 그런 다음 4~6개월 후에, 이전의 간행물에서 논의되었던 성분을 함유한 신제품이 우연의 일치처럼 출시된다. 책과 보충제 논평 기사도 건강 및 영양 제품의 판매를 촉진하기 위한 도구로 이용되어 왔다.
(A) 이런 마케팅 기술을 수요 창출이라고 부른다. 그것은 독자의 관심을 자극하는 기사 그리고/또는 책의 출간을 통해, 어쩌면 혁명적일 수도 있는 새로운 영양분이나 훈련 기법에 관한 소문을 만들어내는 것을 포함한다. 일단 이것이 이루어지고 나면 신제품이 출시된다.

**어휘** launch (제품을) 출시하다 buzz 소문, 풍문 potentially 어쩌면 (~일지도 모를) revolutionary 혁명적인 article 글, 기사 stimulate 자극하다 enhance 향상하다 coincidentally 우연의 일치로 contain 함유하다 ingredient 성분 supplement 영양보충제 review 논평 기사 vehicle 도구, 수단, 매체 nutrition 영양(제) under investigation 연구 중인

**해설** (A)의 This marketing technique은 (B)의 마케팅 기법을 가리키므로 (A) 앞에는 (B)가 위치해야 하고 (C) 마지막 문장에 있는 a new nutrient는 (B)의 this new nutrient로 이어져야 하므로 주어진 문장 다음 이어질 글의 순서로 가장 적절한 것은 ④ (C) - (B) - (A)이다.

정답
13 ④

## 실전문제

**14** 주어진 문장이 들어갈 위치로 가장 적절한 것은?

> They also rated how generally extroverted those fake extroverts appeared, based on their recorded voices and body language.

Some years ago, a psychologist named Richard Lippa called a group of introverts to his lab and asked them to act like extroverts while pretending to teach a math class. ( ① ) Then he and his team, with video cameras in hand, measured the length of their strides, the amount of eye contact they made with their "students," the percentage of time they spent talking, and the volume of their speech. ( ② ) Then Lippa did the same thing with actual extroverts and compared the results. ( ③ ) He found that although the latter group came across as more extroverted, some of the fake extroverts were surprisingly convincing. ( ④ ) It seems that most of us know how to fake to some extent. Whether or not we're aware that the length of our strides and the amount of time we spend talking and smiling mark us as introverts and extroverts, we know it unconsciously.

## 실전 해설

**14**

> They가 가리키는 명사가 반드시 바로 앞 문장에 있어야 한다.
>
> **They** also rated how generally extroverted those fake extroverts appeared, based on their recorded voices and body language.

Some years ago, a psychologist named Richard Lippa called a group of introverts to his lab and asked them to act like extroverts while pretending to teach a math class. ( ① ) Then he and his team, with video cameras in hand, measured the length of their strides, the amount of eye contact they made with their "students," the percentage of time they spent talking, and the volume of their speech. ( ② ) Then Lippa did the same thing with actual extroverts and compared the results. ( ③ ) He found that although the latter group came across as more extroverted, some of the fake extroverts were surprisingly convincing. ( ④ ) It seems that most of us know how to fake to some extent. Whether or not we're aware that the length of our strides and the amount of time we spend talking and smiling mark us as introverts and extroverts, we know it unconsciously.

**해석** 수년 전, Richard Lippa라는 이름의 심리학자가 내성적인 사람들 한 집단을 그의 실험실에 불러 놓고, (그들에게) 수학 수업을 가르치는 체하면서 그들에게 외향적인 사람들처럼 행동할 것을 요청했다. 그리고 나서 그와 그의 팀은 손에 비디오 카메라를 들고 그들의 보폭, 그들이 '학생들'과 시선을 마주치는 양, 이야기하는 데 사용하는 시간의 비율, 그리고 학생들의 연설의 음량을 측정했다. 그들은 또한 실험 대상자들의 녹화된 목소리와 몸짓 언어에 근거하여 그들이 전체적으로 얼마나 외향적인 것처럼 보이는지도 평가했다. 그 다음 Lippa는 실제 외향적인 사람들과도 똑같은 실험을 하여 그 결과를 비교했다. 비록 후자 집단이 더 외향적인 인상을 주기는 했지만, 가짜로 외향적인 사람들의 일부는 놀랍게도 진짜 외향적인 사람처럼 그럴듯해 보인다는 것을 그는 발견했다. 우리 대부분은 어느 정도까지는 속이는 방법을 알고 있는 것처럼 보인다. 우리의 보폭과 우리가 이야기하고 미소를 짓는 데 보내는 시간의 양이 우리를 내성적인 사람과 외향적인 사람으로 특징짓는다는 것을 우리가 인지하고 있든지 아니든지 간에, 우리는 그것을 무의식적으로 알고 있다.

**어휘** introvert 내성적인 사람  extrovert 외향적인 사람  pretend to ⓥ ⓥ인 체하다
measure ① 재다, 측정하다 ② 대책, 조치  length 길이  stride 한 걸음(의 폭)
extroverted 외향적인  come across as ~라는 인상을 주다
convincing 그럴듯해 보이는, 설득력 있는  fake 가짜의; 속이다

**해설** 지시대명사를 이용해야 한다. 주어진 문장에 있는 They는 문맥상 ①에 있는 he and his team을 지칭하므로 주어진 문장이 들어가기에 가장 적절한 곳은 ②이다.

**14** ②

## 실전문제

**15** 주어진 글 다음에 이어질 글의 순서로 가장 적절한 것은?

> Fingerprint analysis is a fundamentally subjective process; when identifying distorted prints, investigators must choose which features to highlight, and even highly trained experts can be swayed by outside information.

(A) He proposes that fingerprint evidence be presented in probabilistic terms and that examiners should be free to talk about probable or possible matches.

(B) And yet, the subjective nature of this process is rarely highlighted during court cases and is badly understood by most jurors. Christophe Champod, a professor at the University of Lausanne in Switzerland, thinks the language of certainty that investigators are forced to use hides the element of subjective judgment from the court.

(C) In a criminal case, for example, an examiner could testify that there was a 95 percent chance of a match if the defender left the mark but a one-in-a-billion chance of a match if someone else left it. "Once certainty is quantified," says Champod, "it becomes clear."

① (A) – (C) – (B)
② (B) – (A) – (C)
③ (B) – (C) – (A)
④ (C) – (A) – (B)

## 실전 해설

**15**

Fingerprint analysis is a fundamentally subjective process; when identifying distorted prints, investigators must choose which features to highlight, and even highly trained experts can be swayed by outside information.

> 지시대명사 He가 가리키는 명사가 반드시 바로 앞 문장에 있어야 한다.

(A) He proposes that fingerprint evidence be presented in probabilistic terms and that examiners should be free to talk about probable or possible matches.

(B) And yet, the subjective nature of this process is rarely highlighted during court cases and is badly understood by most jurors. Christophe Champod, a professor at the University of Lausanne in Switzerland, thinks the language of certainty that investigators are forced to use hides the element of subjective judgment from the court.

(C) In a criminal case, for example, an examiner could testify that there was a 95
> For example을 기준으로 크다 > 작다 논리가 적용되어야 한다.

percent chance of a match if the defender left the mark but a one-in-a-billion chance of a match if someone else left it. "Once certainty is quantified," says Champod, "it becomes clear."

**해석** 지문 분석은 근본적으로 주관적인 과정으로서, 일그러뜨려진 지문을 식별할 때 조사관들은 어떤 특성을 강조해야 할지 선택해야 하고, 고도로 훈련된 전문가들조차도 외부의 정보에 흔들릴 수 있다.
(B) 하지만 이 과정의 주관적 속성은 법정 소송 사건이 진행되는 동안에 좀처럼 강조되지 않고, 대부분의 배심원들에 의해 잘못 이해된다. 스위스 Lausanne 대학교의 교수인 Christophe Champod는 조사관들이 사용하도록 강요받는 확신의 언어가 주관적 판단이라는 요소를 법정에서 숨긴다고 생각한다.
(A) 그는 지문 증거가 확률적인 관점에서 제시되고 조사관은 거의 확실하거나 가능성 있는 일치에 관하여 자유롭게 이야기할 것을 제안한다.
(C) 예를 들어서, 형사 사건에서 조사관은 만일 피고가 자국을 남겼다면 95%의 일치가능성이 있지만, 그 밖의 누군가 남겼다면 10억분의 1의 일치가능성이 있다고 증언할 수도 있을 것이다. "일단 확실성이 양으로 표시되고 나면, 명백해진다."라고 Champod는 말한다.

**어휘** fingerprint 지문  analysis 분석  fundamentally 근본적으로  subjective 주관적인
distort 일그러뜨리다, 왜곡하다  investigator 조사관  feature 특성, 특징  highlight 강조하다
expert 전문가  sway 흔들다, 동요하다  rarely 좀처럼 (거의) ~하지 않는
court case 법정 소송 사건  juror 배심원  element 요소, 성분, 원소  terms 관점, 표현
criminal case 형사 사건  certainty 확실함, 확신  hide 감추다, 숨기다
present 주다, 제시하다, 보여주다  probabilistic 확률적인  probable 가능성 있는, 있음직한
testify 증언하다, 증명하다  defender 피고  quantify 양으로 표시하다, 수량화하다

**해설** 주어진 문장에 '어떤 특성을 강조해야 할지 선택해야' 한다는 내용이 있고 (B)에 And yet을 기준으로 '좀처럼 강조되지 않는다'는 설명이 있으므로 주어진 문장 다음에는 (B)가 이어져야 하고 (A)에 있는 He는 문맥상 (B)에 있는 Christophe Champod를 가리키므로 (B) 다음에는 (A)가 위치해야 한다. 또한 (A)에 examiners가 있고, (C)에는 for example 다음 an examiner가 있으므로 크다/작다 논리상 (A) 다음에는 (C)가 위치해야 한다. 따라서 주어진 문장 다음 이어질 글의 순서로 가장 적절한 것은 ② (B) - (A) - (C)이다.

**정답**
15 ②

## 실전문제

**16** 주어진 문장이 들어갈 위치로 가장 적절한 것은?

> There are also clinical cases that show the flip side of this coin.

Humans can tell lies with their faces. Although some are specifically trained to detect lies from facial expressions, the average person is often misled into believing false and manipulated facial emotions. One reason for this is that we are "two-faced." By this I mean that we have two different neural systems that manipulate our facial muscles. One neural system is under voluntary control and the other works under involuntary control. ( ① ) There are reported cases of individuals who have damaged the neural system that controls voluntary expressions. ( ② ) They still have facial expressions, but are incapable of producing deceitful ones. ( ③ ) The emotion that you see is the emotion they are feeling, since they have lost the needed voluntary control to produce false facial expressions. ( ④ ) These people have injured the system that controls their involuntary expressions, so that the only changes in their demeanor you will see are actually willed expressions.

\* demeanor : 태도, 표정

## 실전 해설

**16**

There are also clinical cases that show the flip side of this coin.

Humans can tell lies with their faces. Although some are specifically trained to detect lies from facial expressions, the average person is often misled into believing false and manipulated facial emotions. One reason for this is that we are "two-faced." By this I mean that we have two different neural systems that manipulate our facial muscles. One neural system is under voluntary control and the other works under involuntary control. ( ① ) There are reported cases of individuals who have damaged the neural system that controls voluntary expressions. ( ② ) They still have facial expressions, but are incapable of producing deceitful ones. ( ③ ) The emotion that you see is the emotion they are feeling, since they have lost the needed voluntary control to produce false facial expressions. ( ④ ) These people have injured the system that controls their involuntary expressions, so that the only changes in their demeanor you will see are actually willed expressions.

→ 논리의 공백을 이용해야 한다.

* demeanor : 태도, 표정

- **해석** 사람은 얼굴로 거짓말을 할 수 있다. 비록 어떤 사람들은 얼굴 표정으로부터 거짓말을 탐지하도록 특별히 훈련되어 있지만, 보통 사람은 흔히 거짓되고 조작된 얼굴에 나타난 감정을 믿도록 현혹된다. 이것의 한 가지 이유는 우리가 '두 얼굴이기' 때문이다. 이 말로써 내가 의미하는 것은 얼굴 근육을 조종하는 두 가지 서로 다른 신경 체계가 우리에게 있다는 것이다. 하나의 신경 체계는 자발적인 통제 하에 있고 다른 하나는 비자발적인 통제 하에서 작동한다. 자발적인 표현을 통제하는 신경 체계가 손상된 사람들의 보고된 사례들이 있다. 그들은 여전히 얼굴 표정은 가지고 있지만, 속이는 얼굴 표정을 지을 수는 없다. 그들은 거짓의 얼굴 표정을 짓기 위해 필요한 자발적인 통제를 잃었으므로, 여러분이 보는 감정은 그들이 느끼고 있는 감정이다. <u>그 동전의 반대쪽 면을 보여 주는 임상 사례도 있다.</u> 이 사람들은 자신의 비자발적 표현을 통제하는 시스템을 다쳤으며, 그래서 여러분이 보는 그들의 유일한 표정의 변화는 실제로 자발적인 표정일 것이다.

- **어휘** clinical case 임상 사례  flip side 다른 면[이면], 뒷면  tell lies 거짓말하다  specifically 특별히  detect 감지하다  facial 얼굴의  expression ① 표현 ② 표정  mislead 현혹하다, 오도하다  manipulate 다루다, 조작하다  neural 신경의  voluntary 자발적인  *involuntary 비자발적인  be incapable of ~할 수 없다  deceitful 속이는  willed 자발적인, 자신의 의지로 결정된

- **해설** 자발적인 얼굴 표현을 통제하는 신경 체계가 손상되어 비자발적인 얼굴 표현만 할 수 있는 사람의 사례에 대해 이야기하다가 그 반대의 경우(자발적 표정)로 넘어가는 내용이 ④에 있으므로 '그 동전의 반대쪽 면을 보여 주는 임상 사례도 있다.'라는 내용의 주어진 문장이 들어가기에 가장 적절한 곳은 ④이다.

**정답**
16 ④

## 기출문제

**01** 주어진 글 다음에 이어질 글의 순서로 가장 적절한 것은? 2025. 지방직 9급

Usually toddlers picking things up from the ground means trouble.

(A) The family reported the find to the Israel Antiquities Authority, which determined it is a beetle-shaped seal from the Middle Bronze Age.
(B) But as 3-year-old Ziv Nitzan of Israel brushed away the sand on what seemed to be a rock, she revealed a nearly 4,000-year-old Egyptian artifact.
(C) Ziv was awarded a certificate for good citizenship, and the Heritage Minister of Israel said the seal "connects us to a grand story," and that "even children can be a part of discovering history."

① (A) - (C) - (B)
② (B) - (A) - (C)
③ (B) - (C) - (A)
④ (C) - (B) - (A)

## 기출 분석

**01**

Usually toddlers picking things up from the ground means trouble.

(A) The family reported the find to the Israel Antiquities Authority, which determined it is a beetle-shaped seal from the Middle Bronze Age.
(B) But as 3-year-old Ziv Nitzan of Israel brushed away the sand on what seemed to be a rock, she revealed a nearly 4,000-year-old Egyptian artifact.
(C) Ziv was awarded a certificate for good citizenship, and the Heritage Minister of Israel said the seal "connects us to a grand story," and that "even children can be a part of discovering history."

**해석** 보통 아기가 땅에서 무언가를 줍는 일은 골칫거리를 의미한다.
(B) 그러나 이스라엘의 세 살배기 Ziv Nitzan은 돌처럼 보이던 것의 모래를 털어내다 거의 4,000년 된 이집트 유물을 발견했다.
(A) 그 가족은 이 발견물을 이스라엘 유물청에 신고했고, 그곳은 그것이 청동기 시대 중기의 딱정벌레 모양을 한 인장임을 알아냈다.
(C) Ziv는 모범 시민 상장을 받았으며, 이스라엘 문화유산부 장관은 그 인장이 "우리를 위대한 이야기와 연결해 준다"며 "아이들도 역사를 발견하는 데 일원이 될 수 있다"라고 말했다.

**어휘** toddler 유아, 아장아장 걷는 아이  pick up 집다, 줍다  report 신고하다  find 발견물  authority 당국  determine 판단하다, 확인하다  beetle 딱정벌레  shaped ~ 모양의  seal 인장, 도장  bronze age 청동기 시대  brush away 털어내다  reveal 드러내다, 밝혀내다  nearly 거의  artifact 유물  award 수여하다  certificate 증서, 상장  minister 장관  grand 웅장한, 위대한  discover 발견하다

**해설** (B)의 But을 기준으로 주어진 문장과의 비교대상(toddlers vs. 3-year-old Ziv Nitzan)에 대한 차이점(toddlers → 골칫거리 vs. 3-year-old Ziv Nitzan → 고대 이집트 유물을 발견)을 설명하고 있으므로 주어진 글 다음에는 (B)가 위치해야 하고 a + 명사(a beetle-shaped seal) 다음 the + 명사(the seal)가 이어져야 하므로 (A) 다음 (C)가 이어져야 한다. 따라서 주어진 글 다음 이어질 글의 순서로 가장 적절한 것은 ② '(B) – (A) – (C)'이다.

01 ②

## 기출문제

**02** 주어진 문장이 들어갈 위치로 가장 적절한 것은? 2025. 지방직 9급

> However, according to Mike Tipton, a professor at University of Portsmouth, this is far from the quickest way of lowering your body temperature.

There are plenty of simple, scientifically supported techniques that will help you handle the heat. ( ① ) If you're feeling the heat and somebody offers you a fan, it's likely that you'll try and cool your face first. ( ② ) Certainly, all that breeze on your face will stimulate cold receptors there, which will give you a very powerful sensation of comfort. But actually, it's not going to extract the heat from your body. Instead, a better cooling strategy is to immerse your hands in cold water for 15 to 20 minutes. ( ③ ) Your hands have a high surface area to mass area — they have lots of blood flowing in them when you're hot. ( ④ ) If your core temperature is hot, your body will send blood to the extremities in order to lose heat.

## 기출 분석

**02**

> However, according to Mike Tipton, a professor at University of Portsmouth, this is far from the quickest way of lowering your body temperature.

There are plenty of simple, scientifically supported techniques that will help you handle the heat. ( ① ) If you're feeling the heat and somebody offers you a fan, it's likely that you'll try and cool your face first. ( ② ) Certainly, all that breeze on your face will stimulate cold receptors there, which will give you a very powerful sensation of comfort. But actually, it's not going to extract the heat from your body. Instead, a better cooling strategy is to immerse your hands in cold water for 15 to 20 minutes. ( ③ ) Your hands have a high surface area to mass area — they have lots of blood flowing in them when you're hot. ( ④ ) If your core temperature is hot, your body will send blood to the extremities in order to lose heat.

**해석** 더위를 다루는 데 도움이 될, 간단하면서도 과학적으로 입증된 방법들이 많이 있다. 당신이 더위를 느끼고 있는데 누군가가 선풍기를 건네준다면, 당신은 아마 먼저 얼굴을 식히려 할 것이다. <u>하지만 Portsmouth 대학의 교수인 Mike Tipton에 따르면, 이것은 당신의 체온을 낮추는 가장 빠른 방법과는 거리가 멀다.</u> 확실히 당신의 얼굴에 닿는 그러한 모든 바람은 그곳의 냉감 수용체를 자극해서 당신에게 매우 강력한 편안함의 느낌을 줄 것이다. 하지만 실제로 그것은 당신의 신체에서 열을 빼내지는 못할 것이다. 대신, 더 효과적인 냉각 방법은 손을 차가운 물에 15~20분 동안 담그는 것이다. 당신의 손은 질량 대비 넓은 표면적을 갖고 있어, 당신이 더울 때 그 속에서 많은 혈액이 흐른다. 만약 당신의 심부 체온이 높다면, 열을 방출하기 위해 신체는 혈액을 말단 부위로 보낼 것이다.

**어휘** lower 낮추다  temperature 온도  support 입증하다, 지지하다  handle 다루다, 처리하다  fan 부채  likely ~할 가능성이 있는  cool 식히다  certainly 확실히  breeze 산들바람, 미풍  stimulate 자극하다  receptor 수용체  sensation 느낌  comfort 편안함, 쾌적함  extract 빼내다  strategy 전략  immerse 담그다  surface 표면  area 면적  mass 질량  core 중심부  extremity 끝, 말단, 사지, 수족

**해설** 지시대명사 this를 이용해야 한다. 주어진 문장의 this는 ① 뒤의 선풍기로 얼굴을 식히는 것이고 ② 뒤의 that breeze(바람)를 지칭하므로 주어진 문장이 들어가기에 가장 적절한 곳은 ②이다.

**정답**
02 ②

## 기출문제

**03** 주어진 글 다음에 이어질 글의 순서로 적절한 것은? 2024. 국가직 9급

> Interest in movie and sports stars goes beyond their performances on the screen and in the arena.

(A) The doings of skilled baseball, football, and basketball players out of uniform similarly attract public attention.

(B) Newspaper columns, specialized magazines, television programs, and Web sites record the personal lives of celebrated Hollywood actors, sometimes accurately.

(C) Both industries actively promote such attention, which expands audiences and thus increases revenues. But a fundamental difference divides them: What sports stars do for a living is authentic in a way that what movie stars do is not.

① (A) − (C) − (B)
② (B) − (A) − (C)
③ (B) − (C) − (A)
④ (C) − (A) − (B)

## 기출 분석

**03**

Interest in movie and sports stars goes beyond their performances on the screen and in the arena. → 유사의 공간 개념: ① movie ② sports → 유사점 설명

(A) The doings of skilled baseball, football, and basketball players out of uniform similarly attract public attention.
  └ 유사의 시그널

(B) Newspaper columns, specialized magazines, television programs, and Web sites record the personal lives of celebrated Hollywood actors, sometimes accurately.
  ┌ 유사의 시그널       ┌ such 다음 명사(attention)가 바로 앞 문장에 있어야 한다.

(C) Both industries actively promote such attention, which expands audiences and thus increases revenues. But a fundamental difference divides them: What sports stars do for a living is authentic in a way that what movie stars do is not.

**해석** 영화 스타와 스포츠 스타에 대한 관심은 극장과 경기장에서 그들이 행하는 것들을 뛰어 넘는다.
(B) 신문 칼럼, 전문 잡지, 텔레비전 프로그램 그리고 웹 사이트는 유명 할리우드 배우의 사생활을 때로는 정확하게 기록한다.
(A) 마찬가지로 유니폼을 입지 않은 노련한 야구, 축구, 농구 선수의 행동도 대중의 관심을 끈다.
(C) 두 업계 모두 그러한 관심을 능동적으로 장려하는데, 이는 관객을 늘리고 그래서 수익을 증가시킨다. 하지만 그들을 나누는 근본적인 차이가 있다. 즉, 그것은 스포츠 스타가 생계를 유지하기 위해 하는 일이 영화 스타가 하는 일과는 다르게 진정성이 있다는 점이다.

**어휘** go beyond 뛰어 넘다  performance 성과, 실적  arena 경기장  doing 행동
skilled 노련한, 숙련된  attract 매혹시키다  attention 관심, 주의  column 칼럼
specialized 전문화된  record 기록하다  celebrated 유명한  accurately 정확하게
industry 업계  actively 능동적으로, 적극적으로  promote 장려하다  expand 확장하다, 늘리다
revenue 수익  fundamental 근본적인  divide 나누다, 구분하다  do for a living 생계를 유지하다
authentic 진짜인, 진정한

**해설** two 개념(movie stars vs. sports stars)과 지시형용사(such)를 이용해야 한다. 주어진 글에서 영화 스타와 스포츠 스타 둘을 모두 설명하고 있고 (B)에서 영화 스타들의 설명을 하고 (A)의 similarly(서로 다른 소재에 대한 공통점 설명)를 이용하여 스포츠 스타에 대한 설명을 이어나가는 것이 글의 흐름상 자연스럽다. 또한 (C)의 such attention 바로 앞에는 attention이 있어야 하므로 (C) 바로 앞에는 (A)가 위치해야 한다. 따라서 주어진 글 다음 이어질 글의 순서로 가장 적절한 것은 ② (B) - (A) - (C)이다.

정답
03 ②

## 기출문제

**04** 주어진 문장이 들어갈 위치로 적절한 것은? 2024. 국가직 9급

Tribal oral history and archaeological evidence suggest that sometime between 1500 and 1700 a mudslide destroyed part of the village, covering several longhouses and sealing in their contents.

From the village of Ozette on the westernmost point of Washington's Olympic Peninsula, members of the Makah tribe hunted whales. ( ① ) They smoked their catch on racks and in smokehouses and traded with neighboring groups from around the Puget Sound and nearby Vancouver Island. ( ② ) Ozette was one of five main villages inhabited by the Makah, an Indigenous people who have been based in the region for millennia. ( ③ ) Thousands of artifacts that would not otherwise have survived, including baskets, clothing, sleeping mats, and whaling tools, were preserved under the mud. ( ④ ) In 1970, a storm caused coastal erosion that revealed the remains of these longhouses and artifacts.

## 기출 분석

**04**

Tribal oral history and archaeological evidence suggest that sometime between 1500 and 1700 a mudslide destroyed part of the village, covering several longhouses and sealing in their contents.

From the village of Ozette on the westernmost point of Washington's Olympic Peninsula, members of the Makah tribe hunted whales. ( ① ) They smoked their catch on racks and in smokehouses and traded with neighboring groups from around the Puget Sound and nearby Vancouver Island. ( ② ) Ozette was one of five main villages inhabited by the Makah, an Indigenous people who have been based in the region for millennia. ( ③ ) Thousands of artifacts that would not otherwise have survived, including baskets, clothing, sleeping mats, and whaling tools, were preserved under the mud. ( ④ ) In 1970, a storm caused coastal erosion that revealed the remains of these longhouses and artifacts.

**해석** 워싱턴주의 올림픽반도 가장 서쪽 지점에 있는 Ozette 마을에서 Makah족의 구성원들은 고래를 사냥했다. 그들은 포획물을 선반 위나 훈제실에서 훈제했고 Puget Sound만 주변 및 Vancouver섬 근처에 있는 인근 부족들과 거래했다. Ozette는 그 지역에 수천 년간 터를 잡고 살아온 토착민인 Makah족이 거주하던 다섯 개의 주요 마을 중 하나였다. 부족의 구전 역사와 고고학적 증거는 1500년에서 1700년 사이 어느 때에 진흙 사태가 마을 일부를 파괴하면서, 여러 채의 전통 가옥들을 덮어 그 안에 들어있는 내용물들이 빠져나가지 못하게 했다는 것을 보여준다. 그러지 않았다면(내용물들이 빠져나갔다면) 살아남지 못했을, 바구니, 의복, 수면 매트, 고래잡이 도구를 포함한 수천 개의 물건들이 진흙 아래에 보존되어 있었다. 1970년, 한 폭풍으로 인해 해안 침식이 일어났고, 그것이 이 전통 가옥들과 인공물들의 유물들을 드러냈다.

**어휘** tribal 부족의  oral 말로 하는, 구전의  archaeological 고고학인  evidence 증거  mudslide 진흙 사태  destroy 파괴하다  longhouse 전통가옥  seal in ~을 빠져 나가지 못하게 하다  content 내용(물)  westernmost 가장 서쪽에 있는  peninsula 반도  tribe 부족  hunt 사냥하다  whale 고래  smoke (고기나 생선을) 훈제하다  catch 포획물  rack 선반, 받침대  smokehouse 훈제실  trade 거래하다  neighboring 인근의, 이웃의  nearby 근처에  inhabit 거주하다  indigenous 토착의, 고유의  be based in ~에 터를 잡다  region 지역, 영역  millennia(millennium의 복수형) 수천 년  *millennium 천년  otherwise 그렇지 않으면  survive 살아남다, 생존하다  whaling 고래잡이  preserve 보존하다  mud 진흙  coastal 해안의  erosion 침식  reveal 드러내다, 밝히다  remains 유물, 유적  artifact 인공물

**해설** 논리의 공백을 찾는 문제이다. ②에 'Ozette는 수천 년간 터를 잡고 살아온 원주민인 Makah족이 거주하던 다섯 개의 주요 마을 중 하나였다'는 설명을 한 다음 '수천 개의 유물이 진흙 아래에 보존되어 있었다'는 ③의 내용은 글의 흐름상 매우 어색하다. 바로 이 부분에서 논리의 공백이 생겼기 때문에 주어진 문장이 들어가기에 가장 적절한 곳은 ③이다.

04 ③

## 기출문제

**05** 주어진 글 다음에 이어질 글의 순서로 적절한 것은? 2024. 지방직 9급

> Computer assisted language learning (CALL) is both exciting and frustrating as a field of research and practice.

> (A) Yet the technology changes so rapidly that CALL knowledge and skills must be constantly renewed to stay apace of the field.
> (B) It is exciting because it is complex, dynamic and quickly changing — and it is frustrating for the same reasons.
> (C) Technology adds dimensions to the domain of language learning, requiring new knowledge and skills for those who wish to apply it into their professional practice.

① (A) − (C) − (B)
② (B) − (A) − (C)
③ (B) − (C) − (A)
④ (C) − (B) − (A)

## 기출 분석

**05**

┌ Two 개념: ① CALL의 좌절(⊖) ② CALL의 흥미로운 점(⊕)
Computer assisted language learning (CALL) is both exciting and frustrating as a field of research and practice.

(A) Yet the technology changes so rapidly that CALL knowledge and skills must be constantly renewed to stay apace of the field. (⊖)
(B) It is exciting because it is complex, dynamic and quickly changing — and it is frustrating for the same reasons. (둘 다 설명)
(C) Technology adds dimensions to the domain of language learning, requiring new knowledge and skills for those who wish to apply it into their professional practice. (⊕)

※ 단락의 전개 방식
 (B) 둘 다(⊕/⊖) 설명
 (C) ⊕ 설명
 (A) Yet ⊖ 설명

**해석** 컴퓨터 보조 언어 학습(CALL)은 연구와 실습의 한 분야로서 흥미롭기도 하고 좌절감을 주기도 한다.
 (B) 그것은 복잡하고 역동적이며 빠르게 변화하기 때문에 흥미로우며 같은 이유로 좌절감을 준다.
 (C) 기술은 언어 학습 영역에 차원들을 더해 주어 그것을 자신들의 전문적인 실습에 적용하고자 하는 사람들에게 새로운 지식과 기술을 요구한다.
 (A) 그러나 기술은 너무 빠르게 변화해서 CALL 지식과 기술은 그 분야의 빠른 속도에 (보조를) 맞추기 위해 지속적으로 갱신되어야 한다.

**어휘** assist 돕다  frustrating 좌절시키다  field 분야  practice 실행, 실습
 rapidly 빠르게, 신속하게  constantly 지속적으로, 계속해서  renew 갱신하다
 stay apace 빠른 속도에 (보조를) 맞추다  *apace 빠른 속도로, 빨리
 complex 복잡한  dynamic 역동적인  dimension 차원  require 요구하다
 those who ~하는 사람들  apply 적용하다  professional 전문적인

**해설** two 개념을 이용해야 한다. 주어진 글은 컴퓨터 보조 언어 학습(CALL)이 흥미(exciting)와 좌절감(frustrating)을 동시에 준다는 내용이고 (B)에서 그 두 가지를 다시 한 번 더 설명하고 있으므로 주어진 문장 다음에는 (B)가 위치해야 한다. (C)에서 컴퓨터 보조 언어 학습(CALL)의 흥미로운 점(requiring new knowledge and skills)을 설명하고 (A)에서 반대/대조의 연결어 yet을 이용해서 좌절감(must be constantly renewed)이 이어져야 하므로 (B) 다음 (C)와 (A)가 이어지는 것이 글의 순서로 가장 적절하다. 따라서 주어진 글 다음에 이어질 글의 순서로 가장 적절한 것은 ③ (B) - (C) - (A)이다.

**정답**
05 ③

## 기출문제

**06** 주어진 문장이 들어갈 위치로 적절한 것은? 2024. 지방직 9급

But she quickly popped her head out again.

The little mermaid swam right up to the small window of the cabin, and every time a wave lifted her up, she could see a crowd of well-dressed people through the clear glass. Among them was a young prince, the handsomest person there, with large dark eyes. ( ① ) It was his birthday, and that's why there was so much excitement. ( ② ) When the young prince came out on the deck, where the sailors were dancing, more than a hundred rockets went up into the sky and broke into a glitter, making the sky as bright as day. ( ③ ) The little mermaid was so startled that she dove down under the water. ( ④ ) And look! It was just as if all the stars up in heaven were falling down on her. Never had she seen such fireworks.

## 기출 분석

**06**

> But she quickly popped her head out again.

The little mermaid swam right up to the small window of the cabin, and every time a wave lifted her up, she could see a crowd of well-dressed people through the clear glass. Among them was a young prince, the handsomest person there, with large dark eyes. ( ① ) It was his birthday, and that's why there was so much excitement. ( ② ) When the young prince came out on the deck, where the sailors were dancing, more than a hundred rockets went up into the sky and broke into a glitter, making the sky as bright as day. ( ③ ) The little mermaid was so startled that she dove down under the water. ( ④ ) And look! It was just as if all the stars up in heaven were falling down on her. Never had she seen such fireworks.

- **해석** 인어공주는 선실의 작은 창문 바로 앞까지 수영을 했고 파도가 그녀를 들어 올릴 때마다, 그녀는 투명한 유리를 통해 (옷을) 잘 차려입은 한 무리의 사람들을 볼 수 있었다. 그들 중에는 크고 짙은 눈을 가진 그곳에서 가장 잘생긴 젊은 왕자가 있었다. 그날은 그의 생일이었고 그래서 그곳에서는 아주 많은 신남이 있었다. 그 젊은 왕자가 선원들이 춤을 추고 있는 갑판으로 나왔을 때 100개가 넘는 폭죽이 하늘로 올라갔다가 부서져 반짝이며 하늘을 낮처럼 밝게 만들었다. 인어공주는 너무 놀라서 물속으로 들어갔다. 그러나 그녀는 빠르게 다시 머리를 밖으로 내밀었다. 그리고 보라! 마치 하늘에 있는 모든 별들이 그녀에게 쏟아지는 것 같았다. 그녀는 그러한 불꽃놀이를 한 번도 본 적이 없었다.

- **어휘** pop A out A를 밖으로 내밀다 *pop 튀어 나오다, (불쑥) 나타나다  little mermaid 인어공주  right up to ~ 바로 ~앞까지  cabin 선실  every time S + V ~할 때마다  wave 파도  lift up 위로 들어 올리다  a crowd of 한 무리의 사람들 *crowd 군중  well-dressed (옷을) 잘 차려입은  clear 깨끗한, 투명한  prince 왕자  deck 갑판  sailor 선원  rocket 폭죽  glitter ① 반짝이다 ② 반짝이는 빛  startle 놀라게 하다  dive down 잠수하다  heaven 하늘, 천국  firework 불꽃놀이, 폭죽

- **해설** 시간 순서 전개 방식을 이용해야 한다. 주어진 지문은 인어공주가 선실을 들여다보다가 폭죽이 터지고 그로 인해 놀라서 다시 물 안으로 들어간 후 다시 고개를 물 밖으로 내미는 시간 순서 전개 방식을 따르고 있다. 따라서 주어진 문장이 들어갈 위치로 가장 적절한 것은 ④이다.

06 ④

## 기출문제

**07** 주어진 문장이 들어갈 위치로 알맞은 것은? 2023. 국가직 9급

> They installed video cameras at places known for illegal crossings, and put live video feeds from the cameras on a Web site.

Immigration reform is a political minefield. ( ① ) About the only aspect of immigration policy that commands broad political support is the resolve to secure the U.S. border with Mexico to limit the flow of illegal immigrants. ( ② ) Texas sheriffs recently developed a novel use of the Internet to help them keep watch on the border. ( ③ ) Citizens who want to help monitor the border can go online and serve as "virtual Texas deputies." ( ④ ) If they see anyone trying to cross the border, they send a report to the sheriff's office, which follows up, sometimes with the help of the U.S. Border Patrol.

## 기출 분석

**07**

> They가 가리키는 명사가 반드시 바로 앞 문장에 있어야 한다.
>
> **They** installed video cameras at places known for illegal crossings, and put live video feeds from the cameras on a Web site.

Immigration reform is a political minefield. ( ① ) About the only aspect of immigration policy that commands broad political support is the resolve to secure the U.S. border with Mexico to limit the flow of illegal immigrants. ( ② ) Texas sheriffs recently developed a novel use of the Internet to help them keep watch on the border. ( ③ ) Citizens who want to help monitor the border can go online and serve as "virtual Texas deputies." ( ④ ) If they see anyone trying to cross the border, they send a report to the sheriff's office, which follows up, sometimes with the help of the U.S. Border Patrol.

**해석** 이민 개혁은 정치적 지뢰밭이다. 광범위한 정치적 지지를 받는 이민 정책의 거의 유일한 측면은 불법 이민자의 흐름을 제한하기 위해 멕시코와의 미국 국경을 안전하게 지키겠다는 결의이다. 텍사스 보안관들은 최근에 국경을 감시하는 것을 돕기 위해 새로운 인터넷 사용법을 개발했다. 그들은 불법 횡단을 하는 것으로 알려진 장소에 비디오 카메라를 설치했고, 카메라의 실시간 비디오 자료를 웹사이트에 올렸다. 국경을 감시하는 것을 돕고 싶어 하는 시민들은 온라인에 접속해 '가상의 텍사스 보안관 보' 역할을 할 수 있다. 만약 국경을 넘으려 하는 사람을 발견하면 그들은 보안관 사무실로 보고서를 보내고 후속 조치가 이루어지는데 이때 미국 국경 순찰대의 도움을 받기도 한다.

**어휘** install 설치하다  illegal 불법적인  crossing 횡단  live video feeds 실시간 비디오 자료  immigration reform 이민 개혁  minefield 지뢰밭  aspect 측면, 관점  policy 정책  command support 지지를 받다  resolve ① 결의하다, 다짐하다 ② 결의, 다짐 ③ 해결하다  secure 안전하게 하다, 확보하다  border 국경  flow 흐름, 유입  immigrants 이민자  keep watch on ~을 감시하다  sheriff 보안관  novel 새로운  deputy 보, 대리  follow up 후속 조치를 하다  U.S. Border Patrol 미국 국경 순찰대

**해설** 주어진 문장의 They는 ② 뒤의 Texas sheriffs를 가리키므로 주어진 문장이 들어가기에 가장 적절한 곳은 ③이다.

**정답**
07 ③

## 기출문제

**08** 주어진 글 다음에 이어질 글의 순서로 가장 적절한 것은? 2023. 국가직 9급

All civilizations rely on government administration. Perhaps no civilization better exemplifies this than ancient Rome.

(A) To rule that large area, the Romans, based in what is now central Italy, needed an effective system of government administration.
(B) Actually, the word "civilization" itself comes from the Latin word civis, meaning "citizen."
(C) Latin was the language of ancient Rome, whose territory stretched from the Mediterranean basin all the way to parts of Great Britain in the north and the Black Sea to the east.

① (A) - (B) - (C)
② (B) - (A) - (C)
③ (B) - (C) - (A)
④ (C) - (A) - (B)

### 기출 분석

**08**

All civilizations rely on government administration. Perhaps no civilization better exemplifies this than ancient Rome.

(A) To rule that large area, the Romans, based in what is now central Italy, needed an effective system of government administration.
(B) Actually, the word "civilization" itself comes from the Latin word civis, meaning "citizen."
(C) Latin was the language of ancient Rome, whose territory stretched from the Mediterranean basin all the way to parts of Great Britain in the north and the Black Sea to the east.

> 지시형용사 that 다음 명사(large areas)가 반드시 바로 앞 문장에 있어야 한다.

**해석** 모든 문명은 정부 행정에 의존한다. 아마도 고대 로마보다 이에 대한 전형적인 예가 되는 문명은 없을 것이다.
(B) 실제로, '문명'이라는 단어 자체는 '시민'을 의미하는 라틴어 'civis'에서 왔다.
(C) 라틴어는 고대 로마의 언어였는데 고대 로마의 영토는 지중해 유역에서부터 북쪽의 영국 일부와 동쪽의 흑해에 이르는 모든 길로 펼쳐져 있었다.
(A) 현재 이탈리아의 중부에 기반을 두었던 로마인들이 그토록 넓은 지역을 통치하기 위해선 효과적인 정부 행정 시스템이 필요했다.

**어휘** civilization 문명  rely on ~에 의존하다  administration 행정
exemplify 전형적인 예가 되다, 예를 들다  ancient 고대의  rule 지배하다
effective 효과적인  actually 실제로  Latin 라틴어  citizen 시민  territory 영토
stretch 펼치다, 뻗어있다  Mediterranean 지중해  basin ① 유역 ② 큰 그릇, 대야
Great Britain 영국  Black Sea 흑해

**해설** 문명에 대한 기본 개념을 제시한 주어진 글 다음 그 문명에 대한 자세한 용어설명이 나오는 (B)가 이어져야 하고 (A)의 that large area(그 거대한 영토)는 (C)의 territory stretched from the Mediterranean basin all the way to parts of Great Britain in the north and the Black Sea to the east를 지칭하므로 주어진 문장 다음 이어질 글의 순서로 가장 적절한 것은 ③ (B) - (C) - (A)이다.

정답
08 ③

김세현 영어 전혀 다른 개념 독해

PART

# 06

# 빈칸 완성

# PART 06 빈칸 완성

### 출제 유형

다음 빈칸에 들어갈 말로 가장 적절한 것을 고르시오.

### 풀이 해법

1. Clues that Signal Main Idea

### 연습문제

**EX 1** 밑줄 친 부분에 들어갈 말로 가장 적절한 것을 고르시오.

The success of the human species is due to _____ in part. An elephant is bigger, a tiger stronger, but man very resistant. A fish swims better, a kangaroo can jump farther; but a kangaroo cannot swim like a man can, nor can a fish live on land. A tiger can digest more meat, but starves when surrounded by bananas. A cow can eat spinach, but not fish. Man adapts his diet: he is omnivorous. And he can climb, jump, run and swim — less well than specialists — but no specialist can do all that man can.

① physical flexibility
② physical strength
③ social adaptability
④ social character

## 연습해설

### EX 1

The success of the human species is due to _____ in part. An elephant is bigger, a tiger stronger, but man very resistant. A fish swims better, a kangaroo can jump farther; but a kangaroo cannot swim like a man can, nor can a fish live on land. A tiger can digest more meat, but starves when surrounded by bananas. A cow can eat spinach, but not fish. Man adapts his diet: he is omnivorous. And he can climb, jump, run and swim — less well than specialists — but no specialist can do all that man can.

**해석** 인간 종의 성공은 부분적으로 신체적 유연성 때문이다. 코끼리는 크고 호랑이는 힘이 세지만 인간은 매우 저항적이다. 물고기는 더 잘 수영하고 캥거루는 더 멀리 뛸 수 있지만 캥거루는 인간만큼 수영을 할 수 없고 또한 물고기는 육지에서 살 수 없다. 호랑이는 더 많은 고기를 소화시킬 수 있지만 바나나에 둘러 싸여 있으면 굶어 죽는다. 소는 시금치를 먹을 수 있지만 물고기는 먹을 수 없다. 인간은 자신의 식성을 적응시킨다. 즉, 인간은 잡식성이다. 인간은 전문가보다 못하지만 오를 수도 있고 점프하거나 뛰고 수영할 수 있다. 하지만 어떤 전문가도 인간만큼 다 할 수는 없다.

① 신체적 유연성
② 신체적 힘
③ 사회적 적응
④ 사회적 특성

**어휘** due to ~때문에  resistant 저항하는  starve 굶주리다  surround 에워 싸다, 둘러싸다
spinach 시금치  adapt 적응하다[시키다]  omnivorous 잡식성의  flexibility 유연성
strength 힘  character ① 특성 ② 주인공

**해설** 빈칸 완성은 항상 이 글이 무엇에 관한 글(Main Idea)인가를 떠올려야 한다. 주어진 지문은 인간의 성공이 신체적 유연성 때문이라는 내용의 글이므로 빈칸에 들어갈 말로 가장 적절한 것은 ① '신체적 유연성'이다.

**정답**
01 ①

## 풀이 해법

2. Clues that Signal Patterns

### 연습문제

**EX 1** 밑줄 친 부분에 들어갈 말로 가장 적절한 것을 고르시오.

On the surface, effective listening might seem to require little more than an acute sense of hearing. But, in fact, there's a big difference between hearing and listening. Hearing occurs when sound waves travel through the air, enter your ears, and are transmitted by the auditory nerve to your brain. As long as neither your brain nor your ears are impaired, hearing is involuntary. It occurs spontaneously with little conscious effort. Listening, in contrast, _____ that includes attending to, understanding, and evaluating the words or sounds you hear.

① is a willing act
② is a sharp sense of hearing
③ doesn't have to be voluntary
④ needs an involuntary behavior

## 연습해설

### EX 1

On the surface, effective listening might seem to require little more than an acute sense of hearing. But, in fact, there's a big difference between hearing and listening. Hearing occurs when sound waves travel through the air, enter your ears, and are transmitted by the auditory nerve to your brain. As long as neither your brain nor your ears are impaired, hearing is involuntary. It occurs spontaneously with little conscious effort. Listening, in contrast, _____ that includes attending to, understanding, and evaluating the words or sounds you hear.

**해석** 겉보기에는, 효과적인 경청은 예리한 청각에 지나지 않는 것 같다. 하지만, 사실, 청취와 경청에는 큰 차이가 있다. 청취는, 음파가 공기를 통과하여 귀에 들어가 청각신경에 의해 뇌에 전달될 때, 발생한다. 당신의 뇌와 귀 모두가 손상되지 않는 한, 청취는 비자발적이다. 그것은 거의 의식적인 노력을 하지 않아도 자발적으로 발생한다. 반면에 경청은, 당신이 듣는 단어나 소리에 대해 주의를 기울이고, 이해하고, 평가를 하는 행동을 포함하는 <u>자발적인 행위이다</u>.
① 자발적인 행위이다
② 날카로운 청각이다
③ 자발적일 필요가 없다
④ 비자발적인 행동을 필요로 한다

**어휘** on the surface 표면적으로  effective 효과적인  little more than ~에 지나지 않는, ~에 불과한  acute ① 예리한 ② 급성의  sense 감각  transmit 전송하다  auditory 청각의  impaired 손상당한, 상처 입은  involuntary 비자발적인  spontaneously 저절로, 비자발적으로  evaluate 평가하다

**해설** two 개념(반대/대조의 공간 개념)을 이용해서 정답을 구할 수 있어야 한다. 도입부에 hearing(청취)와 listening(경청)은 다르다고 했고 그다음 순서대로 hearing을 설명하고 있다. 이때 hearing은 involuntary 하다고 했으므로 이와 반대되는 listening은 voluntary(자발적인)이어야 한다. 따라서 빈칸에 들어갈 말로 가장 적절한 것은 ① '자발적인 행위이다'이다.

정답
01 ①

### 연습문제

**EX 2** 밑줄 친 부분에 들어갈 말로 가장 적절한 것을 고르시오.

Trees and vegetation cool the air by providing shade and through the evaporation of water from leaves. First of all, shade reduces the amount of solar radiation transmitted to underlying surfaces, keeping them cool. Shaded walls may be 5°C to 20°C cooler than the peak temperatures of unshaded surfaces. These cooler surfaces decrease the quantity of heat transmitted to buildings, thus lowering air conditioning cooling costs. As you know, _____ lessen the heat island effect by reducing heat transfer to the surrounding air. Another way trees and vegetation cool the air is by absorbing water through their roots and evaporating it through leaf pores. This process uses heat from the air to convert water contained in the vegetation into water vapor.

① leaves evaporating water
② evaporation and shade
③ unshaded surfaces
④ cooler walls

## 연습해설

### EX 2

Trees and vegetation cool the air by providing shade and through the evaporation of water from leaves. First of all, shade reduces the amount of solar radiation transmitted to underlying surfaces, keeping them cool. Shaded walls may be 5°C to 20°C cooler than the peak temperatures of unshaded surfaces. These cooler surfaces decrease the quantity of heat transmitted to buildings, thus lowering air conditioning cooling costs. As you know, _____ lessen the heat island effect by reducing heat transfer to the surrounding air. Another way trees and vegetation cool the air is by absorbing water through their roots and evaporating it through leaf pores. This process uses heat from the air to convert water contained in the vegetation into water vapor.

**해석** 나무와 초목은 그늘을 제공하고 잎으로부터 물이 증발되는 과정을 통해서 공기를 시원하게 해준다. 무엇보다도 우선, 그늘은 아래쪽 표면에 도달하는 태양의 복사(열)양을 줄여주어 그곳을 시원하게 유지시켜 준다. 그늘에 가려진 벽의 온도는 그늘이 지지 않은 노면의 최대 온도보다 섭씨 5도에서 20도 정도 더 시원할 수 있다. 이렇게 표면이 더 시원해지게 되면 건물에 전달되는 열의 양이 줄어들게 되며, 그 결과 냉방 비용이 줄어들게 된다. 여러분들도 다 아는 것처럼 <u>더 시원한 벽은</u> 주변에 있는 공기로 전달되는 열이 줄어들게 되어 열섬 효과 또한 완화된다. 나무와 초목이 공기를 시원하게 만들어주는 또 다른 한 가지 방식은 뿌리를 통해 물을 흡수하여 그것을 잎에 있는 기공을 통해 증발시키는 것에 의한 것이다. 이러한 과정에서 초목이 지니고 있는 물을 수증기로 변화시키기 위해 공기 중에 있는 열을 사용하게 된다.

① 물을 증발하는 나뭇잎들은
② 증발과 응답은
③ 그늘이 없는 표면은
④ 더 시원한 벽은

**어휘** vegetation 초목, 식물  provide 제공하다  shade 그늘, 응달  evaporation 증발
leaf 나뭇잎(leaves 나뭇잎들)  reduce 줄이다, 감소시키다  solar radiation 태양 복사(열)
transmit 전송하다, 보내다  shaded wall 그늘이 가려진 벽  peak 절정  unshaded 그늘이 없는
surface 표면  decrease 감소하다  quantity 양  lower 낮추다  lessen 줄이다, 낮추다
heat island 열섬  effect 효과  surrounding 에워싸는, 둘러싸는  absorb 흡수하다  pore 구멍
convert 바꾸다  contain 포함하다  vapor 증기  *water vapor 수증기

**해설** 주어진 지문은 나무와 초목의 시원해지는 효과를 2가지 관점(그늘과 증발)에서 나열하는 내용의 글이고 빈칸은 첫 번째 효과(그늘)에 관한 내용이어야 하므로 빈칸에 들어가기에 가장 적절한 것은 ④ '더 시원한 벽은'이다.

**정답**
02 ④

## 풀이 해법

3. Clues that Signal Likeness

### 연습문제

**EX 1** 밑줄 친 부분에 들어갈 말로 가장 적절한 것을 고르시오.

> Electrical resistance (measured in ohms) refers to how easily an electrical current passes through some material. Some substances, such as many metals, are low in resistance, so electrical currents pass easily through them. In contrast, materials such as glass and rubber are high in resistance and thus are poor electrical conductors. The actual resistance of any given material when it is placed in an electrical circuit depends upon its physical properties, e.g. diameter and length in the case of wire. The resistance of an electric wire decreases as the diameter of the wire increases. That is, all other things equal, a wire of small diameter is _____ than one of larger diameter. In addition, the resistance of any material increases as its length increases: a 2-foot length of wire is twice as resistant as a 1-foot length of the same wire.

① more resistant
② less resistant
③ decreasing
④ increasing

## 연습해설

### EX 1

Electrical resistance (measured in ohms) refers to how easily an electrical current passes through some material. Some substances, such as many metals, are low in resistance, so electrical currents pass easily through them. In contrast, materials such as glass and rubber are high in resistance and thus are poor electrical conductors. The actual resistance of any given material when it is placed in an electrical circuit depends upon its physical properties, e.g. diameter and length in the case of wire. The resistance of an electric wire decreases as the diameter of the wire increases. That is, all other things equal, a wire of small diameter is _____ than one of larger diameter. In addition, the resistance of any material increases as its length increases: a 2-foot length of wire is twice as resistant as a 1-foot length of the same wire.

- **해석** (옴으로 측정되는) 전기 저항은 전류가 어떤 물질을 얼마나 쉽게 통과하는가와 관련이 있다. 여러 가지 금속과 같은 일부 물질들은 저항이 낮고, 그래서 전류가 그것들을 쉽게 통과한다. 이와는 대조적으로 유리와 고무 같은 물질들은 저항이 높으며, 따라서 전기의 전도가 잘 되지 않는다. 어느 한 물질이 전기 회로에 놓였을 때 그것의 실제 저항은 예를 들어, 전선의 경우에는 직경과 길이와 같은 물리적 특성에 좌우된다. 전선의 저항은 전선의 직경이 증가함에 따라 감소한다. 즉, 다른 모든 것들이 동일하다면, 작은 직경의 전선이 더 큰 직경의 전선보다 저항이 더 크다. 게다가 어떤 물질의 저항은 그것의 길이가 증가함에 따라 증가하는데, 2피트 길이의 전선은 동일한 1피트 길이의 전선보다 저항이 두 배 더 크다.
  ① 저항이 더 큰
  ② 저항이 더 적은
  ③ 감소하는
  ④ 증가하는

- **어휘** electrical resistance 전기 저항 *resistance 저항  ohm 옴(전기 저항의 단위; 기호.Ω)
  refer to ~와 관련이 있다, ~을 나타내다  electrical current 전류  substance 물질
  conductor 전도체  circuit 회로  property 특성, 속성  diameter 직경, 지름  length 길이

- **해설** 빈칸 앞에 **That is**를 기준으로 논리의 방향이 같아야 한다. **That is** 바로 앞 문장에 '전선의 지름이 증가하면 저항은 감소한다고 했으므로 빈칸에는 이와 논리의 방향이 같은 내용이 있어야 한다. 따라서 빈칸에 들어가기에 가장 적절한 것은 ① '저항이 더 큰'이다.

**정답**
01 ①

## 풀이 해법

4. Clues that Signal Differences

**연습문제**

**EX 1** 다음 빈칸에 들어갈 말로 가장 적절한 것을 고르시오.

One of the most traditional side effects of smoking cessation is weight gain. Studies say that although weight gain does not apply to everyone who stops smoking, it occurs to many people, resulting in them gaining about 10 pounds on average. But researchers are skeptical about weight gain caused by smoking cessation in the long run. Smoking makes people become insulin-resistant. When people are resistant to insulin, their blood becomes high in glucose. This is what causes them to have some disease related to insulin-sensitivity. When one quits smoking, the insulin-sensitivity improves, which allows the person to have a higher metabolic rate. This means that, unlike conventional beliefs that people gain weight when they quit smoking, they eventually _____ as the body gets more active metabolically.

① lose weight
② restart smoking
③ forget about smoking
④ make smoking cessation easy

## 연습해설

### EX 1

One of the most traditional side effects of smoking cessation is weight gain. Studies say that although weight gain does not apply to everyone who stops smoking, it occurs to many people, resulting in them gaining about 10 pounds on average. But researchers are skeptical about weight gain caused by smoking cessation in the long run. Smoking makes people become insulin-resistant. When people are resistant to insulin, their blood becomes high in glucose. This is what causes them to have some disease related to insulin-sensitivity. When one quits smoking, the insulin-sensitivity improves, which allows the person to have a higher metabolic rate. This means that, unlike conventional beliefs that people gain weight when they quit smoking, they eventually _____ as the body gets more active metabolically.

**해석** 가장 전통적인 금연의 부작용 중 하나는 체중 증가이다. 연구에 의하면 체중 증가가 담배를 끊는 사람 모두에게 적용되지 않지만, 많은 사람들에게 나타나 평균 약 10파운드의 체중 증가로 이어진다고 한다. 그러나 어떤 학자들은 결국 금연으로 인한 체중 증가에 대해 회의적이다. 흡연은 사람들이 인슐린에 내성을 갖게 만든다. 사람들이 인슐린에 대해 내성을 갖게 되면, 그 사람들의 피는 포도당의 수치가 높아진다. 이것은 그들로 하여금 인슐린 민감성과 관련된 어떤 질병에 걸리게 한다. 사람이 담배를 끊을 때, 인슐린 민감성이 증진되어, 그 사람으로 하여금 신진 대사율이 더 높아지게 한다. 이것은 사람들이 담배를 끊을 때 체중이 늘어난다는 전통적 믿음과 달리, 신체가 신진 대사에 있어 더 활발해지기 때문에 이들은 결국 <u>체중이 줄어들 것이다</u>.

① 체중이 줄어든다
② 흡연을 다시 시작하다
③ 흡연에 대해 잊어버리다
④ 금연을 쉽게 해 준다

**어휘** side effect 부작용  cessation 중지  weight gain 체중 증가  result in 초래하다, 야기하다  skeptical 회의적인  in the long run 결국  insulin-resistant 인슐린 내성  *resistant 저항하는  metabolic rate 대사율  *metabolic 신진대사의  *metabolism 신진대사  sensitivity 민감성  glucose 포도당  conventional 전통적인

**해설** Unlike를 기준으로 반대/대조의 논리가 필요하다. 기존의 믿음은 '금연을 하면 살이 찐다'고 했으므로 빈칸에는 이와 반대되는 내용이 있어야 한다. 따라서 빈칸에 들어가기에 가장 적절한 것은 ① '체중이 줄어들 것이다'이다.

01 ①

## 5. Clues that Signal Cause and Effect

**EX 1** 다음 빈칸에 들어갈 말로 가장 적절한 것을 고르시오.

Climate change, deforestation, widespread pollution and the sixth mass extinction of biodiversity all define living in our world today — an era that has come to be known as "the Anthropocene". These crises are underpinned by production and consumption which greatly exceeds global ecological limits, but blame is far from evenly shared. The world's 42 wealthiest people own as much as the poorest 3.7 billion, and they generate far greater environmental impacts. Some have therefore proposed using the term "Capitalocene" to describe this era of ecological devastation and growing inequality. That's because _____ reflects capitalism's logic.

① the better world that is still within our reach
② the accumulation of wealth in fewer pockets
③ a burning desire for a better future
④ an effective response to capitalism

## 연습해설

### EX 1

Climate change, deforestation, widespread pollution and the sixth mass extinction of biodiversity all define living in our world today — an era that has come to be known as "the Anthropocene". These crises are underpinned by production and consumption which greatly exceeds global ecological limits, but blame is far from evenly shared. The world's 42 wealthiest people own as much as the poorest 3.7 billion, and they generate far greater environmental impacts. Some have therefore proposed using the term "Capitalocene" to describe this era of ecological devastation and growing inequality. That's because _____ reflects capitalism's logic.

**해석** 기후 변화, 삼림파괴, 널리 퍼져 있는 오염과 여섯 번째 생물다양성의 대량멸종 모두 "인류세"라고 알려지게 된 시대의 오늘날 우리 세계에 사는 것을 정의한다. 이러한 위기들은 지구 생태계의 한계를 훨씬 초과하는 생산과 소비에 의해 확증되지만, 결코 책임은 균등하게 분배되지 않고 있다. 세계에서 가장 부유한 사람들 42명은 37억의 가장 빈곤한 사람들이 가진 것만큼 소유하고 있고, 그들은 환경에 훨씬 큰 영향을 준다. 그래서 몇몇 사람들은 생태계 파괴와 성장 불균형적인 이 시기를 묘사하기 위해 "자본세"라는 용어를 사용할 것을 제안했다. 그것(자본세를 사용할 것을 제안)은 <u>더 소수의 주머니 속으로 부가 축적되는 자본주의 논리를 반영</u>하기 때문이다.

① 여전히 우리가 다다를 수 있는 더 좋은 세상
② 더 소수의 주머니 속으로 부가 축적
③ 기후변화에 대한 효과적인 대응
④ 더욱 실행 가능한 미래를 향한 타오르는 갈망

**어휘** deforestation 삼림파괴 widespread 널리 퍼져있는 mass 대량의 extinction 멸종 biodiversity 생물다양성 era 시대, 시기 Anthropocene 인류세 crises crisis의 복수형 *crisis 위기 underpin ① 뒷받침하다 ② 확증하다 comsumption 소비 exceed 초과하다, 능가하다 ecological 생태학적인 blame ① 비난 ② 책임 far from 결코 ~않는 evenly 균등하게, 균일하게 wealthy 부유한 *wealth 부 generate 만들어내다, 발생시키다 term 용어 Capitalocene 자본세 devastation 파괴 inequality 불균형 reflect 반영하다 capitalism 자본주의 logic 논리 highly 아주, 매우 accumulation 축적 response 반응 viable 실행 가능한

**해설** 빈칸을 기준으로 인과관계를 이용해야 한다. 부익부 빈익빈에 따라 소수만이 부를 축적하게 된다는 내용(원인)이 빈칸 앞에 있으므로 그 결과에 해당되는 내용이 결과로 이어져야 하므로 빈칸에 들어가기에 가장 적절한 것은 ② '더 소수의 주머니 속으로 부가 축적'이다.

01 ②

## 풀이 해법

**6. Clues that Signal Inference(Most Likely Answer)**

### 연습문제

**EX 1** 다음 빈칸에 들어갈 말로 가장 적절한 것을 고르시오.

For the most part, we like things that are familiar to us. To prove the point to yourself, try a little experiment. Get the negative of an old photograph that shows a front view of your face and have it developed into a pair of pictures—one that shows you as you actually look and one that shows a reverse image so that the right and left sides of your face are interchanged. Now decide which version of your face you like better and ask a good friend to make the choice, too. If you are like most people, you should notice something odd: Your friend will prefer the true print, but you will prefer the reverse image. Why? Because you both will be responding favorably to the more familiar face—your friend to _____ and you to the reversed one you find in the mirror every day.

① his own true face
② other people's faces
③ the one the world sees
④ the negative of his own face

## 연습해설

### EX 1

For the most part, we like things that are familiar to us. To prove the point to yourself, try a little experiment. Get the negative of an old photograph that shows a front view of your face and have it developed into a pair of pictures—one that shows you as you actually look and one that shows a reverse image so that the right and left sides of your face are interchanged. Now decide which version of your face you like better and ask a good friend to make the choice, too. If you are like most people, you should notice something odd: Your friend will prefer the true print, but you will prefer the reverse image. Why? Because you both will be responding favorably to the more familiar face—your friend to _____ and you to the reversed one you find in the mirror every day.

**해석** 대체로 우리들은 우리들에게 친숙한 것들을 좋아한다. 그 점을 스스로 입증하기 위해 간단한 실험을 해 보라. 당신의 얼굴을 정면으로 보여 주는 옛날 사진의 원판을 가지고 두 개의 사진, 즉 실제 모습을 그대로 보여 주는 사진과 얼굴의 좌우가 서로 바뀐 반대된 이미지를 보여 주는 사진으로 현상하라. 이제 어떠한 형의 얼굴이 더 마음에 드는지 결정하고, 친한 친구에게도 선택을 해보라고 요청하라. 대부분의 사람들과 비슷하다면 당신은 이상한 점을 주목하게 될 것인데, 그것은 당신의 친구는 원래 모습을 담은 것을 더 좋아할 것이지만 당신은 반대된 이미지를 더 좋아하게 될 것이라는 점이다. 왜 그럴까? 당신과 친구 둘 다 더 친숙한 얼굴, 즉 당신의 친구는 세상 사람들이 바라보는 얼굴, 그리고 당신은 매일 거울 속에서 발견하는 반대된 모습에 호의적으로 반응할 것이기 때문이다.
① 그 자신의 진짜 얼굴
② 다른 사람들의 얼굴
③ 세상 사람들이 바라보는 얼굴
④ 그 자신의 (사진)원판

**어휘** familiar 친숙한  develop (사진을) 현상하다  a pair of 한 쌍의  actually 실제로
reverse ① 뒤바꾸다, 뒤집다 ② 뒤바뀐, 뒤집힌  interchange 교환[교체]하다  odd 이상한, 낯선
prefer 선호하다  respond to ~에 반응하다  favorably 우호적으로  mirror ① 거울 ② 반영하다

**해설** 단락의 도입부에 two 개념을 이용해야 한다. 이 글은 당신은 reverse image가 좋고 당신의 친구는 원래 당신 모습을 좋아한다는 내용의 글이다. 빈칸의 위치는 당신의 친구와 관련된 내용이므로 빈칸에는 당신의 실제 모습의 선택지가 있어야 한다. 따라서 정답은 ③ '사람들이 바라보는 얼굴'이다.

01 ③

## 실전문제

**01** 다음 빈칸에 들어갈 말로 가장 적절한 것을 고르시오.

People seem to be more motivated by the thought of losing something than by the thought of gaining something of equal value. According to some researchers, college students experienced much stronger emotions when asked to imagine losses as opposed to gains in their romantic relationships or in their grade point averages. Especially, under conditions of risk and uncertainty, the threat of potential loss plays a critical role in human decision-making. In this vein, physicians' advice to smokers, describing the number of years to be gained if they do quit, might be somewhat _____ as compared with advice describing the number of years of life to be lost if they do not quit.

① abnormal
② effective
③ immeasurable
④ inefficient

## 실전 해설

**01**

> Main Idea : 얻는 것보다 잃는 것에 더 동기부여가 된다.

People seem to be more motivated by the thought of losing something than by the thought of gaining something of equal value. According to some researchers, college students experienced much stronger emotions when asked to imagine losses as opposed to gains in their romantic relationships or in their grade point averages. Especially, under conditions of risk and uncertainty, the threat of potential loss plays a critical role in human decision-making. In this vein, physicians' advice to smokers, describing the number of years to be gained if they do quit, might be somewhat _____ as compared with advice describing the number of years of life to be lost if they do not quit.

**해석** 사람들은 같은 가치를 가진 뭔가를 획득한다는 생각보다는 뭔가를 잃을 것이라는 생각에 의해 동기를 더 받는 것처럼 보인다. 몇몇 연구가들에 따르면, 대학생들은 그들의 낭만적 관계가 좋아지는 것을 상상하거나 평균 평점이 좋아지는 것을 상상할 때보다 그것들을 상실하는 것을 상상할 때 훨씬 더 격한 감정을 경험하였다고 한다. 특히, 위험과 불확실성이라는 조건하에서 잠재적 상실의 위협이 인간의 의사결정에 중요한 역할을 한다. 이러한 맥락에서 보면, 내과 의사들이 흡연자들에게 하는 담배를 딱 끊으면 수명이 길어진다는 내용의 충고는 끊지 않으면 짧아질 수명을 언급하는 충고와 비교해볼 때 다소 <u>비효율적일지도</u> 모를 일이다.
① 비정상적인
② 효과적인
③ 측정할 수 없는
④ 비효율적인

**어휘** motivate 동기를 부여하다  gain 얻다, 획득하다  as opposed to ~와는 대조적으로
especially 특히  uncertainty 불확실  potential 잠재적인  critical 중대한
decision-making 의사 결정  in this vein 이런 맥락에서  as compared with ~와 비교하여

**해설** 주어진 지문은 얻는 것보다 잃는 것에 대해 사람들은 더 강력한 동기부여가 되기 때문에 얻는 것을 강조할 때는 효과가 덜하다는 글이므로 정답은 ④번이 된다.

정답
01 ④

## 실전문제

**02** 다음 빈칸에 들어갈 말로 가장 적절한 것을 고르시오.

It has been argued — especially in the modernist period when an authoritative, public style for biography was being reacted against — that all biography is a form of autobiography. Even biographers who resist the notion that the story they are telling has anything to do with them, and put themselves in the narrative as little as possible, have to admit that their choice of subject has been made for writers' intervention, and so there is little such thing as an entirely _____ treatment. We write from a certain position, constructed by our history, nationality, race, gender, class, education, beliefs. More specifically, there is likely to be some shared experience between the writer and the subject. A drama writer might well write the life of an actor, a musicologist of a composer. It would be hard, if not impossible, for them to write a life of a mountaineer or a gardener, a chemist or an architect, with no experience — or at least no understanding at all — of those professions.

① subjective
② personal
③ exclusive
④ objective

## 실전 해설

**02**

It has been argued — especially in the modernist period when an authoritative, public style for biography was being reacted against — that all biography is a form of autobiography. Even biographers who resist the notion that the story they are telling has anything to do with them, and put themselves in the narrative as little as possible, have to admit that their choice of subject has been made for writers' intervention, and so there is little such thing as an entirely _____ treatment. We write from a certain position, constructed by our history, nationality, race, gender, class, education, beliefs. More specifically, there is likely to be some shared experience between the writer and the subject. A drama writer might well write the life of an actor, a musicologist of a composer. It would be hard, if not impossible, for them to write a life of a mountaineer or a gardener, a chemist or an architect, with no experience — or at least no understanding at all — of those professions.

**해석** 특히 전기에 대한 권위적이고 공적인 문체에 대한 반대가 일어나고 있던 모더니즘 시대에는 모든 전기가 자서전의 한 형태라고 주장되어 왔다. 자신들이 말하고 있는 이야기가 자신들과 조금이라도 관련이 있다는 견해에 반대하고, 이야기에 가능한 한 적게 개입하는 전기 작가들조차도 대상 인물 선택에 작가의 개입이 만들어지고 그래서 완전히 <u>객관적인</u> 표현법과 같은 것은 거의 없다는 것을 인정해야 한다. 우리는 우리의 역사, 국적, 인종, 성별, 계층, 교육, 신념에 의해 구축된 특정한 입장에서 서술한다. 더 구체적으로 말하자면, 작가와 대상 인물 간의 어떤 공유된 경험이 있을 가능성이 있다. 아마도 드라마 작가는 배우의 삶을, 음악학 연구가는 작곡가의 삶을 서술할 것이다. 그들이 산악가나 정원사, 화학자나 건축가라는 직종에 대한 경험이 없거나 하다못해 전혀 알지 못한 채 그들의 삶을 서술하기는 불가능하지는 않지만 어려울 것이다.

① 주관적인
② 개인적인
③ 배타적인
④ 객관적인

**어휘** argue 주장하다  especially 특히  modernist period 모더니즘 시대
authoritative 권위적인  biography 전기  react against ~에 대해 반대하다
autobiography 자서전  resist 저항하다, 반대하다  notion 견해, 개념
have anything to do with ~와 조금이라도 관계가 있다
put oneself in ~에 개입하다  narrative 이야기  admit 인정하다
subject ① 대상, 피실험자 ② 주제  treatment ① 표현법 ② 처리  certain 어떤
cunstruct 건설하다, 구조하다  nationality 국적, 국민성  race 인종
drama critic 연극 평론가  might well ⓥ 아마도 ⓥ할 것이다
musicologist 음악학 연구가  composer 작곡가  chemist 화학자
architect 건축가  at laeast 적어도  profession 직업, 직종

**해설** 인과관계의 시그널 and so(대상 인물 선택에 작가의 개입 : 원인 → 완전히 객관적인 표현법과 같은 것은 거의 없다 : 결과)를 이용해야 한다. 단 부정어 little이 있으므로 작가의 개입과는 반대되는 내용이 있어야 한다. 따라서 빈칸에 들어가기에 가장 적절한 것은 ④ '객관적인'이다.

**정답**
02 ④

## 실전문제

**03** 다음 빈칸에 들어갈 말로 가장 적절한 것을 고르시오.

The interesting results of experiments with capuchin monkeys were reported. According to the experiments, capuchin monkeys seemed to abhor the state of _____. They were divided into two groups and placed in adjoining compartments with visual and vocal contact. The animals were given a token that they could immediately exchange it for some food by returning it to the experimenter. In the controlled experiment, both specimens received a cucumber slice for each token exchanged, and around 5 percent of them failed to exchange their tokens for food. In one experiment, the first group received a grape as a compensation, while the second was given the usual cucumber. That these animals prefer grapes to cucumbers had apparently been established by previous research. Strikingly, the second group's refusal rate for food rose to more than 50 percent. In another experiment, the first group received a grape with no need to pick up a token and exchange it for food. The refusal rate in the second group rose to more than 80 percent under this treatment.

\* capuchin monkey : 꼬리 감는 원숭이

① trick
② treatment
③ indifference
④ discrimination

## 실전 해설

**03**

　　　　　　　　　　　　　　　　　　　: 집중해야 할 정보

The interesting results of experiments with capuchin monkeys were reported.
　　　　　　　　　　　　　　Main Idea : 꼬리 감는 원숭이는 차별을 싫어한다.
According to the experiments, capuchin monkeys seemed to abhor the state of _____. They were divided into two groups and placed in adjoining compartments with visual and vocal contact. The animals were given a token that they could immediately exchange it for some food by returning it to the experimenter. In the controlled experiment, both specimens received a cucumber slice for each token exchanged, and around 5 percent of them failed to exchange their tokens for food. In one experiment, the first group received a grape as a compensation, while the second was given the usual cucumber. That these animals prefer grapes to cucumbers had apparently been established by previous research. Strikingly, the second group's refusal rate for food rose to more than 50 percent. In another experiment, the first group received a grape with no need to pick up a token and exchange it for food. The refusal rate in the second group rose to more than 80 percent under this treatment.

\* capuchin monkey : 꼬리 감는 원숭이

**해석** 꼬리 감는 원숭이에 관한 흥미로운 실험 결과가 보고되었다. 실험에 따르면 꼬리 감는 원숭이는 차별의 상태를 혐오하는 것 같았다. 그들은 두 그룹으로 나뉘어서 시각적이고 음성적인 접촉이 되는 인접한 칸에 배치되었다. 이 동물에게 실험자에게 되돌려 주면 즉시 그것을 음식으로 교환할 수 있는 토큰이 주어졌다. 통제 실험에서 두 표본은 교환된 각각의 토큰에 대해 오이 조각을 받았고 대략 5퍼센트가 토큰을 음식으로 교환하지 않았다. 한 실험에서 첫 번째 그룹은 보상으로 포도를 받은 반면, 두 번째 그룹은 보통 오이가 주어졌다. 이 동물은 오이보다 포도를 선호한다는 것이 이전의 조사에서 명백히 확인된바 있었다. 놀랍게도, 두 번째 그룹의 음식에 대한 거절 비율은 50퍼센트 이상까지 올라갔다. 또 다른 실험에서 첫 번째 그룹은 토큰을 집어 들어 그것을 음식으로 교환할 필요 없이 포도를 받았다. 이런 대접을 받은 두 번째 그룹의 거절 비율은 80퍼센트 이상까지 올라갔다.

① 속임수
② 대접
③ 무관심
④ 차별

**어휘** state 상태  divide 나누다  place 두다, 놓다  abhor 혐오하다, 증오하다  adjoining 인접한, 가까운  compartment 칸막이 방  token 토큰, 징표  immediately 즉시  exchange 교환하다  experimenter 실험가, 실험자  specimen 견본, 표본  cucumber 오이  compensation 보상  apparently 명백히  establish 세우다, 설립하다  previous 이전의  refusal 거부, 거절  rate 비율  pick up 줍다  treatment 취급, 대접  enhance 향상하다  indifference 무관심  discrimination 차별

**해설** 주어진 지문은 꼬리 감는 원숭이들이 차별을 싫어한다는 내용의 글이므로 빈칸에 들어가기에 가장 적절한 것은 ④ '차별'이다.

**정답**
03 ④

## 실전문제

**04** 밑줄 친 부분에 들어갈 말로 가장 적절한 것을 고르시오.

One study showed that a certain word (e.g., boat) seemed more pleasant when presented after related words (e.g., sea, sail). That result occurred because of conceptual fluency, a type of processing fluency related to how easily information comes to our mind. Because "sea" primed the context, the heightened predictability caused the concept of "boat" to enter people's minds more easily, and that ease of processing produced a pleasant feeling that became assigned to the word "boat." Marketers can take advantage of conceptual fluency and enhance the effectiveness of their advertisements by strategically _____.
For example, an experiment showed that consumers found a ketchup ad more favorable when the ad was presented after an ad for mayonnaise. The mayonnaise ad primed consumers' schema for condiments, and when the ad for ketchup was presented afterward, the idea of ketchup came to their minds more easily. As a result of that heightened conceptual fluency, consumers developed a more positive attitude toward the ketchup advertisement.

① expressing their genuine concern for consumers
② exposing consumers to related scientific data
③ arranging their ads in predictive contexts
④ providing a full image of their products

## 실전 해설

**04**

One study showed that a certain word (e.g., boat) seemed more pleasant when presented after related words (e.g., sea, sail). That result occurred because of conceptual fluency, a type of processing fluency related to how easily information comes to our mind. Because "sea" primed the context, the heightened predictability caused the concept of "boat" to enter people's minds more easily, and that ease of processing produced a pleasant feeling that became assigned to the word "boat." Marketers can take advantage of conceptual fluency and enhance the effectiveness of their advertisements by strategically _____.

[Likeness(논리의 방향이 같다) 이용]   [빈칸에 대한 구체적인 예가 다음 문장에 있다.]

For example, an experiment showed that consumers found a ketchup ad more favorable when the ad was presented after an ad for mayonnaise. The mayonnaise ad primed consumers' schema for condiments, and when the ad for ketchup was presented afterward, the idea of ketchup came to their minds more easily. As a result of that heightened conceptual fluency, consumers developed a more positive attitude toward the ketchup advertisement.

**해석** 한 연구는 특정 단어(예를 들면, 배)가 관련 단어(예를 들면, 바다, 항해하다)이후에 제시되었을 때 더욱 호감이 느껴지는 것 같다는 점을 보여 주었다. 그 결과는 정보가 얼마나 쉽게 우리 머릿속에 떠오르는가와 관련된 일종의 가공 유창성의 유형인 개념적 유창성 때문에 발생했다. '바다'가 맥락을 준비시켰기 때문에 고조된 예측가능성이 '배'의 개념이 사람들의 머릿속에 좀 더 쉽게 들어올 수 있도록 야기했고, 그 처리의 용이함이 '배'라는 단어에 부여되는 호감을 만들어냈다. 전략적으로 마케터들은 예상케 하는 맥락들 속에 자신들의 광고들을 배치함으로써 개념적 유창성을 이용하여 자신들의 광고의 효과를 강화할 수 있다. 예를 들어, 한 실험은 소비자들이 케첩 광고가 마요네즈 광고 후에 제시되었을 때 그 케첩 광고를 더 호의적이라고 느꼈다는 것을 보여 주었다. 마요네즈 광고는 소비자들의 양념에 대한 스키마를 준비시켰고, 케첩 광고가 그 뒤에 제시되면 케첩에 대한 개념이 그들의 머릿속에 더 쉽게 떠올랐다. 그러한 고조된 개념적 유창성의 결과로 소비자들은 그 케첩 광고에 대해 더 긍정적인 태도를 형성했다.

① 소비자들에게 진심어린 배려를 표현함으로써
② 관련된 과학적 데이터에 소비자들을 노출시킴으로써
③ 예상케 하는 맥락들 속에 자신들의 광고들을 배치함으로써
④ 자신들의 상품에 대한 전체 이미지를 제공함으로써

**어휘** certain 어떤  pleasant 기쁜, 기분 좋은  present 제공하다, 보여주다
conceptual 개념적인  fluency 유창함, 유창성  process ① 과정, 절차 ② 가공하다
prime ① 최고의, 으뜸의 ② 주된, 주요한 ③ 준비시키다  context 맥락, 문맥  heightened 고조된
predictability 예측가능성  *predictive 예측 가능한  concept 개념  assign 부여하다, 할당하다
take advantage of ~을 이용하다, 활용하다  enhance 강화시키다  effectiveness 효율성
strategically 전략적으로  favorable 우호적인
schema 개요, 윤곽, 스키마(정보를 통합하고 조직화하는 인지적 개념 또는 틀)
condiment 양념  attitude 마음가짐, 태도

**해설** 빈칸 바로 다음에 나오는 for example(likeness → 논리의 방향이 같다) 을 이용해야 한다. for example 다음 케첩 광고가 마요네즈 광고 후에 제시되었을 때 그 케첩 광고가 더 호의적이라는 내용이 있으므로 빈칸에 들어가기에 가장 적절한 것은 ③ '예상케 하는 맥락들 속에 자신들의 광고들을 배치함으로써'이다.

**정답**
04 ③

## 실전문제

**05** 다음 빈칸에 들어갈 말로 가장 적절한 것을 고르시오.

In their collaborative work, Karen Reivich and Andrew Shatter discuss the notion of tunnel vision, which is about focusing on a small part of reality while essentially ignoring the rest. For example, if there are twenty students attending my lecture and one of them is asleep, focusing my attention exclusively on the sleeping student to the exclusion of all the other students in the class is tunnel vision. Conversely, if nineteen of them are asleep and only one is listening to what I have to say, concluding that my lecture was a success because one student was intellectually engaged is also a form of tunnel vision. Whether leading to a positive or a negative focus, tunnel vision is about _____. Generally, perfectionists engage in negative tunnel vision: they dismiss the good in their lives while giving center stage to the bad.

① poor eyesight
② denial of intimacy
③ skeptical attitudes
④ detachment from reality

## 실전 해설

**05**

In their collaborative work, Karen Reivich and Andrew Shatter discuss the notion of tunnel vision, which is about focusing on a small part of reality while essentially ignoring the rest ← 집중해야 할 정보. For example, if there are twenty students attending my lecture and one of them is asleep, focusing my attention exclusively on the sleeping student to the exclusion of all the other students in the class is tunnel vision. Conversely, if nineteen of them are asleep and only one is listening to what I have to say, concluding that my lecture was a success because one student was intellectually engaged is also a form of tunnel vision. Whether leading to a positive or a negative focus, tunnel vision is about _____. Generally, perfectionists engage in negative tunnel vision: they dismiss the good in their lives while giving center stage to the bad.

← Main Idea : 터널 시야는 현실로부터의 분리에 관한 것이다.

- **해석** 그들의 협동 작업에서, Karen Reivich와 Andrew Shatter는 터널 시야의 개념에 관해 논의하는데, 터널 시야란 현실의 작은 부분에 초점을 맞추는 반면에 (현실의) 나머지는 본질적으로 무시하는 것에 관한 것이다. 예를 들어, 내 강의를 수강하는 학생이 20명인데 그 중 한 명이 잠을 자고 있다면, 수업을 듣고 있는 모든 다른 학생들을 배제하고서 오로지 잠자는 그 학생에게만 내 주의력을 쏟는 것이 터널 시야이다. 반대로, 19명이 잠자고 있는데 한 학생만이 내가 말해야 하는 것을 듣고 있다면, 한 학생이 지적으로 열심히 참여하고 있으니까 내 수업은 성공이라고 결론을 내리는 것 또한 터널 시야이다. 긍정적인 주목으로 이어지든 부정적인 주목으로 이어지든 간에 터널 시야는 현실로부터의 분리에 관한 것이다. 일반적으로 완벽주의자들이 부정적인 터널 시야에 관여하는데, 그들은 삶에서 좋은 것은 묵살하고 반면에 나쁜 것을 중심 무대에 올려놓는다.
  ① 나쁜 시력
  ② 친밀감의 거부
  ③ 회의적 태도
  ④ 현실로부터의 분리

- **어휘** collaborative 협력의, 협동의  notion 개념  vision 시야  ignore 무시하다  lecture 강의, 강연  exclusively 독점적으로, 배타적으로  exclusion 제외  intellectually 지적으로  engage 참여하다  lead to 초래하다, 야기하다  perfectionist 완벽주의자  dismiss 무시하다  denial 거부, 거절  intimacy 친근함, 긴밀함  skeptical 회의적인  detachment 분리  reality 현실

- **해설** 주어진 지문은 중심소재인 터널 시야에 관하여 작가는 현실과 분리된 개념이라고 주장하고 있으므로 빈칸에 들어갈 말로 가장 적절한 것은 ④ '현실로부터의 분리'이다.

05 ④

06 다음 빈칸에 들어갈 말로 가장 적절한 것을 고르시오.

Take a moment to cast your mind back over the past week or so, and think about something you regret. Was it something you did or something you failed to do? It seems that _____.
As an example, consider Mary and Laura, who invest their money in companies A and B. Mary invests in company A and considers switching to company B but she decides not to. Laura invests in company B and considers switching to company A and she decides to do so. They both find out that they would have been better off by $1,000 if they had taken different actions. Who do you think feels more regret? Most people judge that Laura will regret her action more than Mary will regret her inaction.

① unplanned actions always give rise to regrets
② people regret their failures rather than successes to act
③ people regret their actions more than their failures to act
④ people regret most when their relationship with others are compromised

## 실전 해설

**06**

Take a moment to cast your mind back over the past week or so, and think about something you regret. Was it something you did or something you failed to do? It seems that _____. As an example, consider

> Two 개념: ① Mary(행함) ② Laura(행하지 않음) → 차이점 설명(Laura가 더 많이 후회함)

Mary and Laura, who invest their money in companies A and B. Mary invests in company A and considers switching to company B but she decides not to. Laura invests in company B and considers switching to company A and she decides to do so. They both find out that they would have been better off by $1,000 if they had taken different actions. Who do you think feels more regret? Most people judge that Laura will regret her action more than Mary will regret her inaction.

**해석** 잠깐 시간을 내어 지난 주 정도에 있었던 일을 상기해 보고, 당신이 후회하는 것에 대해 생각해보라. 그것은 당신이 행한 일이었는가, 아니면 행하지 못한 일이었는가? 사람들은 행하지 못한 것보다 행한 것을 더 후회하는 것 같다. 한 예로, 돈을 A회사와 B회사에 투자한 Mary와 Laura가 있다고 생각해보자. Mary는 A회사에 투자를 하고, B회사로 옮겨 투자를 할 생각을 하지만 그렇게 하지 않기로 결정한다. Laura는 B회사에 투자를 하고, A회사로 옮겨 투자를 할 생각을 하고 그렇게 하기로 결정한다. 그 두 사람은 다른 조치를 취했더라면 1,000달러만큼 더 벌 수 있었을 것이라는 사실을 알게 된다. 당신은 누가 더 후회를 느낄 것이라고 생각하는가? Mary가 행하지 못한 일을 후회하는 것보다 Laura가 행한 일을 더 후회할 것이라고 대부분의 사람들은 판단한다.
① 계획하지 않은 행동은 늘 후회를 초래한다
② 사람들은 행한 것보다 행하지 못한 것에 더 후회한다
③ 사람들은 행하지 못한 것보다 행한 것을 더 후회한다
④ 사람들은 타인과의 관계가 악화될 때 가장 후회한다

**어휘** cast 던지다  over ① ~동안에 ② ~보다 더 ③ ~에 관하여 ④ ~위에
compromise ① 타협하다 ② 손상[악화]시키다  invest A in B A를 B에 투자하다
switch 바꾸다  regret 후회하다  judge 판단하다  give rise to 야기시키다, 초래하다
profitable 이로운, 이득이 되는  take action 행동을 하다[취하다]

**해설** 주어진 지문은 하지 않았던 것보다 한 것에 더 많이 후회한다는 내용의 글이므로 빈칸에 들어가기에 가장 적절한 것은 ③ '사람들은 행하지 못한 것보다 행한 것을 더 후회한다'이다. 참고로 이 지문은 two 개념을 이용해야 한다.

06 ③

## 실전문제

**07** 다음 빈칸에 들어갈 말로 가장 적절한 것을 고르시오.

People eat out for many and varied reasons and the traditional role of the housewife as food provider has changed to that of additional earner. But the fact that restaurants are busiest on weekends rather than during the working week suggests other less practical reasons. Diners expect to derive pleasure from eating in the public sphere; not only for the satisfaction of appetite but for social and psychological enjoyment. In the restaurant eating is transformed into an entertaining experience. Relieved of the chores of preparing a meal and in a different environment where one chooses what to eat and is waited upon, diners are free to enjoy, converse and interact, so that even a simple family outing to a McDonald's can _____.

① strip off psychological satisfaction
② reflect the current market trend
③ be another duty to carry out
④ provide a sense of occasion

## 실전 해설

**07**

▨ : 집중해야 할 정보

People eat out for many and varied reasons and the traditional role of the housewife as food provider has changed to that of additional earner. But the fact that restaurants are busiest on weekends rather than during the working week suggests other less practical reasons. Diners expect to derive pleasure from eating in the public sphere; not only for the satisfaction of appetite but for social and psychological enjoyment. In the restaurant eating is transformed into an entertaining experience. Relieved of the chores of preparing a meal and in a different environment where one chooses what to eat and is waited upon, diners are free to enjoy, converse and interact, so that even a simple family outing to a McDonald's can _____.

↳ Main Idea : 식당에서 밥을 먹는 이유는 맛 그 자체도 있지만 심리적 만족감도 얻을 수 있기 때문이다.

**해석** 사람들은 많은 다양한 이유 때문에 외식을 하고 가정주부의 음식을 준비하는 전통적 역할도 추가적인 돈 버는 사람의 역할로 바뀌고 있다. 하지만 주중보다 주말에 레스토랑이 더 바쁘다는 사실은 다른 덜 실질적인 이유를 암시한다. 외식하는 사람들(diners)은 식당(public sphere)에서 밥을 먹음으로써 즐거움을 얻는데 이는 식욕에 대한 만족뿐 아니라 사교적이고 심리적인 기쁨도 역시 얻을 수 있다는 것이다. 식당에서의 식사가 즐거운 경험으로 바뀐다는 것이다. 음식을 준비해야 하는 여러 가지 일들에서 벗어나서 무엇을 먹을까 선택하고 그것을 기다리는 다른 환경에서 외식하는 사람들은 즐기고 대화하고 교류하면서 자유를 만끽한다. 그래서 아주 단순한 맥도날드 식당으로 가는 가족 소풍[외식]조차도 <u>행사의 느낌을 제공한다</u>.
① 심리적 만족감을 없앤다
② 현재의 시장 경향을 반영한다
③ 수행해야 할 또 다른 의무이다
④ 행사의 느낌을 제공한다

**어휘** eat out 외식하다  varied 다양한(=various)  traditional 전통적인  additional 추가적인
earner (수입을) 벌어들이는 사람  diner 식사하는 사람  *dining room 식당  *dine 식사하다
derive ① 얻다, 획득하다 ② 유래하다  *derive A from B A를 B로부터 얻다
*derive from ~에 유래하다  sphere ①(공)구 ②영역  appetite 식욕
transform 바꾸다, 변신하다  entertain ① 즐겁게 하다 ② 접대[대접]하다
relieve A of B A를 B에게서 덜어주다[완화시켜주다]  chore 허드렛일  converse 대화하다
interact 상호작용하다  outing 소풍  strip off 없애다, 제거하다  *strip 벗다, 벗기다
current 현재의  duty 의무, 임무  carry out 수행[실행]하다  occasion ① 행사 ② 기회, 경우, 때

**해설** 주어진 지문은 외식이 단지 맛만을 위한 것이 아니라 심리적으로 이벤트의 느낌을 준다는 내용의 글이므로 빈칸에 들어가기에 가장 적절한 것은 ④ '행사의 느낌을 제공한다'이다.

**정답**
07 ④

## 실전문제

**08** 밑줄 친 (A), (B)에 들어갈 말로 가장 적절한 것은?

> The number-one variable that led to high rate of retention(students staying in school) and contributed to a stable learning environment was the relationship between the adult faculty and the students. As a high school principal, I would pass this lesson to many young teachers biweekly in a month every year by urging them to ___(A)___ one common belief: trying to become just another friend to their students. The truth is that most students had already had enough peers. What they didn't have were enough ___(B)___ in their lives.

|   | (A) | (B) |
|---|-----|-----|
| ① | evade | friends |
| ② | evade | grown-ups |
| ③ | keep | friends |
| ④ | keep | grown-ups |

## 실전 해설

**08**

The number-one variable that led to high rate of retention(students staying in school) and contributed to a stable learning environment was the relationship between the adult faculty and the students. As a high school principal, I would pass this lesson to many young teachers biweekly in a month every year by urging them to __(A)__ one common belief: trying to become just another friend to their students. The truth is that most students had already had enough peers. What they didn't have were enough __(B)__ in their lives.

↳ Main Idea : 아이들은 이미 충분한 친구가 있으므로 그들에게 필요한 것은 어른이다.

**해석** 높은 잔류(학교에 학생들이 머무르는) 비율을 이끌고 안정된 학습 환경에 기여하는 첫 번째 변수는 학생들과 성인 교직자들과의 관계였다. 나는 고등학교 교장으로서 젊은 선생님들에게 한 달에 격주로 매년 한 가지 보편적 믿음 즉, 학생들에게 단지 또 다른 친구가 되려고 노력하는 것을 피하라는 교훈을 전해 주었다. 대부분의 학생들은 이미 충분한 또래들을 갖고 있다는 것이 사실이다. 학생들에게 없는 것은 그들의 삶에 필요한 어른들이었다.

**어휘** variable 변수  retention 보유, 유지, 잔류  contribute to ~에 기여하다  stable 꾸준한, 안정된  faculty 교직원  pass on 건네주다, 전해주다  biweekly 격주로  urge 촉구하다  evade 회피하다, 피하다  peers 또래  grown-up 성인, 어른

**해설** 이 글은 학생들에게 필요한 것은 어른들이므로 더 이상 학생들의 친구가 되지 말고 학생들을 올바른 길로 이끌 수 있는 어른들이 되어야 한다는 내용이다. 따라서 (A)에는 학생들에게 친구가 되는 것을 피하라는(evade) 내용이 나와야 하고 (B)에는 어른들(grown-ups)이 와야 한다.

**정답**
08 ②

## 실전문제

**09** 다음 빈칸에 들어갈 말로 가장 적절한 것을 고르시오.

Common observations of people's behavior, both at work and in everyday life, suggest that most individuals possess both favorable and unfavorable characteristics. Yet research evidence indicates that interviewers frequently perceive people in simple 'black and white' terms. Candidates tend to be judged as all good or all bad. For example, if a candidate has a single outstanding characteristic, interviewers typically tend to minimize or ignore any weakness she or he has in other areas. This goes the same way for a candidate who has an extremely outstanding detriment, e.g. a stutter, which would block out all the candidate's favorable attributes in the interviewer's eyes. Therefore, in order to ensure success in an interview, you must _____.

① get rid of your born dialects
② say your weaknesses honestly
③ emphasize your good characteristics
④ prepare for the interview well in advance

## 실전 해설

**09**

Common observations of people's behavior, both at work and in everyday life, suggest that most individuals possess both favorable and unfavorable characteristics. Yet research evidence indicates that interviewers frequently perceive people in simple 'black and white' terms. Candidates tend to be judged as all good or all bad. For example, if a candidate has a single outstanding good characteristic, interviewers typically tend to minimize or ignore any weakness she or she has in other areas. This goes the same way for a candidate who has an extremely outstanding detriment, e.g. a stutter, which would block out all the candidate's favorable attributes in the interviewer's eyes. Therefore, in order to ensure success in an interview, you must _____.

↳ 유사의 시그널 이용

↳ Main Idea : 약점은 감추고 장점을 부각하라.

**해석** 직장에서나 일상생활에서 사람들의 행동을 관찰해 보면 대부분의 사람들이 좋은 특성과 좋지 않은 특성을 동시에 지니고 있다는 것을 보여준다. 그러나 연구에서 나온 증거는 면접하는 사람들이 자주 단순히 '흑이냐 백이냐'의 관점에서 사람을 본다는 것을 보여준다. 지원자들은 전적으로 좋든지, 아니면 전적으로 나쁘든지 판단이 된다. 가령, 지원자가 하나의 뛰어난 좋은 특징을 가지고 있다면, 면접하는 사람들은 보통 지원자가 다른 분야에서 가지고 있는 모든 약점을 최소화하거나 무시하는 경향이 있다. 이것은 가령 말을 더듬은 것 같은 두드러지는 결점을 가진 지원자에게도 해당이 되는데, 이러한 점은 후보자가 가진 좋은 특성을 면접하는 사람의 눈에 띄지 않게 할 것이다. 그러므로 인터뷰에서 확실하게 성공하기 위해서, <u>자신이 가진 좋은 특성을 강조해야 한다.</u>
① 타고난 사투리를 없애야 한다
② 약점을 솔직하게 말해야 한다
③ 자신이 가진 좋은 특성을 강조해야 한다
④ 인터뷰를 미리 잘 준비해야 한다

**어휘** observation 관찰  suggest ① 제안하다 ② 암시하다  possess 소유하다
favorable 우호적인, 유리한  characteristic 특징, 특성  evidence 증거
indicate ① 암시하다 ② 보여주다  frequently 빈번히  perceive 인식하다
term ① 용어 ② 기간  candidate 지원자  tend to ⓥ ⓥ하려는 경향이 있다
single 한 개의  outstanding 두드러진, 눈에 띄는  typically 전형적으로
minimize 최소화하다  ignore 무시하다  weakness 약점  areas ① 영역 ② 분야(=field)
detriment 결함, 결점  e.g.(=for example)  stutter 말 더듬기
block out 막다, 차단하다  attribute 특성 *attribute(=ascribe) A to B A를 B 탓으로 돌리다
in order to ~하기 위해서  ensure 확실하게 하다  get rid of 제거하다, 없애다
dialect 방언, 사투리  emphasize 강조하다  in advance 미리, 앞서서

**해설** 주어진 지문은 면접을 할 때 지원자가 약점을 최소화하고 자신의 장점을 부각하라는 내용의 글이므로 빈칸에 들어가기에 가장 적절한 것은 ③ '자신이 가진 좋은 특성을 강조해야 한다'이다.

09 ③

## 실전문제

**10** 다음 빈칸에 들어갈 말로 가장 적절한 것은?

> The Hawthorne experiment was conducted in the late 1920s and early 1930s. The management of Western Electric's Hawthorne plant, located near Chicago, wanted to find out if environmental factors such as lightning, could affect workers' productvity and morale. A team of social scientists experimented with a small group of employees who were set apart from their coworkers. The environmental conditions of this group's work area were controlled, and the subjects themselves were closely observed. To the great surprise of the researchers, the productivity of these workers increased irrespective of any change in their environmental conditions. The rate of work increased even when the change (such as sharp decrease in the level of light in the workplace) seemed unlikely to have such an effect. It was concluded that the presence of the observers had caused the workers in the experimental group to feel special. As a result, the employees came to know and trust one another, and they developed a strong belief in the importance of their job. The researchers believed that _____.

① productivity in electric plants tends to be low
② workers' attitudes are more important than their outer conditions
③ the rate of work increased in the plant depends on environmental conditions
④ even those Hawthorne workers who were not in the experiment improved their productivity

## 실전 해설

**10**

: 집중해야 할 정보

The Hawthorne experiment was conducted in the late 1920s and early 1930s. The management of Western Electric's Hawthorne plant, located near Chicago, wanted to find out if environmental factors such as lightning, could affect workers' productvity and morale. A team of social scientists experimented with a small group of employees who were set apart from their coworkers. The environmental conditions of this group's work area were controlled, and the subjects themselves were closely observed. To the great surprise of the researchers, the productivity of these workers increased irrespective of any change in their environmental conditions. The rate of work increased even when the change (such as sharp decrease in the level of light in the workplace) seemed unlikely to have such an effect. It was concluded that the presence of the observers had caused the workers in the experimental group to feel special. As a result, the employees came to know and trust one another, and they developed a strong belief in the importance of their job. The researchers believed that _____.

↳ Main Idea : 생산성 증가는 환경적 요인이 아니라 근로자의 태도에 달려있다.

**해석** 1920년대 후반 그리고 1930년대 초반에 Hawthorne의 실험이 행해졌다. Chicago 인근에 있는 Western Electric의 Hawthorne 공장의 경영진은 조명과 같은 환경적 요인이 근로자의 생산성과 사기에 영향을 주는지 알고 싶었다. 사회 과학자들은 근로자들을 동료들과 분리시켜 실험을 했다. 이 근로자들의 작업장은 통제되었고 피실험자들(근로자들)은 가까이에서 관찰되었다. 연구자들은 이 근로자들에게 환경변화가 있었음에도 불구하고 생산성이 증가하는 것에 크게 놀랐다. 작업장의 조명이 크게 어두워졌는데도 작업량이 증가한 것은 이러한 환경적 요인이 영향을 주지 않는 것 같다. 결론은 관찰자들의 존재가 실험 집단의 근로자들로 하여금 (스스로를) 특별하다고 느끼게 했던 것이다. 결과적으로 근로자들은 서로를 알게 되었고 신뢰하게 되었으며 그들의 일의 중요성에 대한 강한 믿음이 생겨나게 된 것이다. 연구가들은 그들의 외적 조건보다 근로자의 태도가 더 중요하다고 믿었다.
① 전기 공장의 생산성은 낮아지는 경향이 있다
② 그들의 외적 조건보다 근로자의 태도가 더 중요하다
③ 공장에서 증가된 작업량은 환경적 조건에 달려있다
④ 실험에 참가하지 않았던 Hawthorne 노동자들조차도 그들의 생산성을 증가시켰다

**어휘** conduct 실행하다  productivity 생산성  morale 사기  set apart 분리하다, 떼어놓다  irrespective of ~와 관계없이  presence 존재  come to ⓥ ⓥ하게끔 되다  tend to ⓥ ⓥ하는 경향이 있다

**해설** 주어진 지문은 생산성을 증가시키는 원인이 환경적 요인이 아니라 근로자들의 태도에 달려 있다는 내용의 글이므로 빈칸에 들어가기에 가장 적절한 것은 ② '그들의 외적 조건보다 근로자의 태도가 더 중요하다'이다.

10 ②

## 실전문제

**11** 밑줄 친 부분에 들어갈 말로 가장 적절한 것은?

> Mathematics definitely influenced Renaissance art. Renaissance art was different from the art in the Middle Ages in many ways. Prior to the Renaissance, objects in paintings were flat and symbolic rather than real in appearance. Artists during the Renaissance reformed painting. They kept objects in paintings from being represented _____. Mathematics was used to portray the essential form of objects in perspective, as they appeared to the human eye. Renaissance artists achieved perspective using geometry, which led to a naturalistic, precise, three-dimensional representation of the real world. The application of mathematics to art, particularly in paintings, was one of the primary characteristics of Renaissance art.

① in detail
② in abstraction
③ with accuracy
④ with reality

## 실전 해설

**11**

Two 개념: ① Renaissance ② Middle Ages → 차이점 설명

Mathematics definitely influenced Renaissance art. Renaissance art was different from the art in the Middle Ages in many ways. Prior to the Renaissance, objects in paintings were flat and symbolic rather than real in appearance. Artists during the Renaissance reformed painting. They kept objects in paintings from being represented _____. Mathematics was used to portray the essential form of objects in perspective, as they appeared to the human eye. Renaissance artists achieved perspective using geometry, which led to a naturalistic, precise, three-dimensional representation of the real world. The application of mathematics to art, particularly in paintings, was one of the primary characteristics of Renaissance art.

**해석** 수학은 분명히 르네상스 예술에 영향을 주었다. 르네상스 예술은 여러 가지 면에서 중세의 예술과 달랐다. 르네상스 이전에는 그림에 있는 물체들이 외관상 사실적이라기보다는 평평하고 상징적이었다. 르네상스 시대의 예술가들은 그림을 다시 만들었다. 그들은 그림 속의 물체들이 추상적으로 표현되는 것을 막았다. 물체들의 본질적인 형태가 원근법으로, 다시 말해 인간의 눈에 보이는 대로 그리기 위해 수학이 사용되었다. 르네상스 시대의 예술가들은 기하학을 사용하여 원근법을 성취했는데 그것은 실제 세계를 사실적이고 정확하고 3차원적으로 묘사하게 했다. 수학을 예술, 특히 그림에 응용한 것은 르네상스 예술의 주된 특징 중 하나였다.

① 세부적으로
② 추상적으로
③ 정확하게
④ 현실성 있게

**어휘** definitely 명확히  the Middle Ages 중세  prior to ~에 앞서, 먼저
object 물건, 물체  flat 평평한  symbolic 상징적인  in appearance 외견상
represent ① 대표하다, 대신하다 ② 설명하다, 묘사하다  *representation ① 대표, 대신 ② 설명, 묘사
reform 다시 만들다, 개편하다  portray 그리다, 묘사하다  perspective 원근법, 투시 화법
achieve 성취하다, 달성하다  geometry 기하학  result in ~ 결국 ~이 되다
naturalistic 사실적인  precise 정확한, 정밀한  three-dimensional 3차원의
application 응용, 적용  primary 첫째의, 주요한  characteristic 특징

**해설** 르네상스 예술가들은 물체들의 본질적인 형태를 인간의 눈에 보이는 대로 그렸다는 것과 실제 세계를 사실적이고 정확하고 3차원적으로 묘사했다고 했고 빈칸 앞에 '막다'라는 뜻의 keep A from B가 있으므로 빈칸에는 이와 반대되는 내용인 ② '추상적으로'가 가장 적절하다.

11 ②

## 실전문제

**12** 다음 글의 빈칸에 들어갈 말로 가장 적절한 것은?

> Some species of mammals form social groups consisting of many individuals. Within this group, _____.
> Within the group, each pair of individuals will amount to a mutual agreement about which will be "boss" over the other. This agreement is reached during their initial contacts, and determines which individual will back down during future encounters. From then on, when that pair of individuals approaches an item of mutual interest, like food, the higher ranking individual takes the item and the other moves on; battle rarely happens. If each encounter instead resulted in the death of one of the group members, then, pretty soon there would be no members left and the species would be extinct from the earth. When the members of a species do not fight to the death, then, those members are more likely to live long enough to bring forth children.

① some individuals can be leaders through fighting
② the companionship of others is rarely accessible to all
③ duel is often limited by forming a dominance hierarchy
④ an individual's position in the hierarchy is generally based on size

## 실전 해설

**12**

집중해야 할 정보

Some species of mammals form social groups consisting of many individuals.
⎿ Main Idea : 포유류는 상호 합의하에 서열을 정해서 서로 싸움을 줄인다.
Within this group, _____. Within the group, each pair of individuals will amount to a mutual agreement about which will be "boss" over the other. This agreement is reached during their initial contacts, and determines which individual will back down during future encounters. From then on, when that pair of individuals approaches an item of mutual interest, like food, the higher ranking individual takes the item and the other moves on; battle rarely happens. If each encounter instead resulted in the death of one of the group members, then, pretty soon there would be no members left and the species would be extinct from the earth. When the members of a species do not fight to the death, then, those members are more likely to live long enough to bring forth children.

**해석** 몇몇 종의 포유류는 많은 개체로 구성된 사회적 집단을 형성한다. 이 집단 내에서 싸움은 지배 계급을 형성함으로써 흔히 제한된다. 그 집단 내에서 각 쌍의 개체들은 다른 개체에 대해 누가 '우두머리'가 될 것인지에 대한 상호 합의에 이르게 된다. 이 합의는 그들의 최초 만남에서 이뤄지고 어느 개체가 차후의 만남에서 물러설 것인지를 결정한다. 그때부터 그 개체 쌍이 먹이와 같은 공동으로 관심이 있는 대상물에 접근할 때 더 높은 서열의 개체가 그 대상물을 차지하고 다른 개체는 이동해 간다. 그래서 싸움은 좀처럼 발생하지 않는다. 대신에 매번 만날 때마다 그 집단 구성원 중 하나가 죽음을 초래한다면, 그러면 조만간 남겨진 구성원은 사라지게 될 것이고 그 종은 지구에서 멸종될 것이다. 종의 구성원들이 죽을 때까지 싸우지 않으면, 그 구성원들은 새끼들을 가질 만큼 충분히 오래 살 가능성이 더 클 것이다.
① 일부 개체들은 싸움을 통해서 우두머리가 된다
② 다른 동물들과의 친분 관계가 모두에게 이루어지는 경우는 거의 없다
③ 싸움은 지배 계급을 형성함으로써 흔히 제한된다
④ 계급에서의 개체의 지위는 일반적으로 크기를 토대로 한다

**어휘** species 종  mammal 포유류  consist of ~으로 구성되다  mutual 상호의, 공동의  agreement 합의  initial 최초의, 처음의  encounter 만남, 접촉  back down 물러서다, 굴복하다  companionship 친분 관계  dominate 지배하다  *dominance 지배  hierarchy 계급  duel 결투, 싸움

**해설** 주어진 지문은 몇몇 종의 포유류는 많은 개체로 구성된 사회적 집단을 형성하고 각 쌍의 개체들은 누가 우두머리가 될 것인지를 상호 합의해 계급을 만들고 싸움을 줄인다는 내용의 글이다. 따라서 빈칸에 들어갈 말로 가장 적절한 것은 ③ '싸움은 지배 계급을 형성함으로써 흔히 제한된다'이다.

**정답**
12 ③

## 실전문제

**13** 다음 빈칸에 들어갈 말로 가장 적절한 것은?

> Writing is a love-hate relationship. You start out hating everything you're writing, and end up blinded by love for every word you've put on paper, or the other way around. So how can you analyze your own work without bias? There are certain things you can do to gain some perspective. In order to judge your own work objectively, you must get distance. Putting your work away for a while sometimes weeks or months can allow you to come back not so enamored by it. Falling in love with a new piece of material can also help. It gives you a chance to read it almost as if it's someone else's. This is the first, and perhaps most important step, because _____ is the greatest foe for evaluating your own writing.

① unfamiliarity
② ignorance
③ complexity
④ intimacy

## 실전 해설

**13**

Writing is a love-hate relationship. You start out hating everything you're writing, and end up blinded by love for every word you've put on paper, or the other way around. So how can you analyze your own work without bias? There are certain

*Main Idea : 자신의 작품에 대한 객관성을 확보하려면 그 작품에서 멀어져라.*

things you can do to gain some perspective. In order to judge your own work objectively, you must get distance. Putting your work away for a while sometimes weeks or months can allow you to come back not so enamored by it. Falling in love with a new piece of material can also help. It gives you a chance to read it almost as if it's someone else's. This is the first, and perhaps most important step, because _____ is the greatest foe for evaluating your own writing.

↳ 부정어

**해석** 글을 쓴다는 것은 애증 관계이다. 당신은 자신이 쓰는 모든 것을 증오하면서 시작하고, 당신이 종이에 썼던 모든 단어에 대한 사랑에 눈이 멀어 끝을 내거나, 그 반대가 된다. 따라서 어떻게 하면 편견이 없이 당신 자신의 작품을 분석할 수 있는가? 총체적 관점을 얻기 위해서 당신이 할 수 있는 일들이 있다. 당신 자신의 작품을 객관적으로 판단하기 위해서 당신은 거리를 두어야 한다. 잠시 동안, 때로 몇 주나 몇 달을 당신의 작품을 멀리하는 것은 당신으로 하여금 그것에 대해 매혹되지 않은 채로 돌아오도록 할 수 있다. 새로운 작품과 사랑에 빠지는 것도 역시 도움이 된다. 그렇게 하는 것은 거의 다른 사람의 것처럼 그것을 읽을 기회를 당신에게 준다. 이것은 그 무엇보다, 그리고 아마도 가장 중요한 과정일 것이다. 왜냐하면 <u>친밀감</u>은 당신 자신의 글을 평가하는 데 가장 큰 적이기 때문이다.

① 낯섦
② 무시
③ 복잡함
④ 친밀감

**어휘** love-hate 애증  end up 결국 ~하게 되다  the other way around 반대로, 거꾸로
analyze ① 분석하다 ② 검토하다  bias 선입견, 편견(=prejudice)  certain 특정한
perspective ① 관점, 시각 ② 원근감  objectively 객관적으로  for a while 잠시 동안, 얼마간
enamored 사랑에 빠진, 홀딱 반한  evaluate 평가하다, 감정하다
unfamiliarity 낯섦, 익숙지 않음, 잘 모름  complexity 복잡성[함]  intimacy 친숙함, 친밀감

**해설** 주어진 지문은 편견 없이 자기 작품을 분석하기 위해서는 그 작품과 멀어져야 한다는 내용의 글이다. 다만 빈칸 다음 부정어 foe가 있으므로 빈칸에는 작품과 멀어져야 한다는 내용과 반대되는 말이 필요하다. 따라서 빈칸에 들어가기에 가장 적절한 것은 ④ '친밀감'이다.

**정답**
13 ④

## 실전문제

**14** 다음 빈칸에 들어갈 말로 가장 적절한 것을 고르시오.

> Have you ever heard the expression 'a baker's dozen?' If you have, do you know what it means? You may have wondered how the term originated. In England, in the fifteenth century, bakers had very bad reputations. People would go into a bakery and ask for a certain amount of bread and then complain that they didn't get all that they had paid for. So very strict laws were passed, stating exactly how much each kind of bread or other baked good was supposed to weigh the same. To make sure that they wouldn't be accused of cheating and possibly fined, bakers gave an extra loaf with each dozen ordered. That way, the customers could never claim that they didn't get their money's worth. To the present day, we call _____ of anything 'a baker's dozen.'

① eleven
② twelve
③ thirteen
④ fifteen

## 실전 해설

**14**

Have you ever heard the expression 'a baker's dozen?' If you have, do you know what it means? You may have wondered how the term originated. In England, in the fifteenth century, bakers had very bad reputations. People would go into a bakery and ask for a certain amount of bread and then complain that they didn't get all that they had paid for. So very strict laws were passed, stating exactly how much each kind of bread or other baked good was supposed to weigh the same.

Main Idea : 고발당하지 않으려고 빵을 하나씩 더 주었다.

To make sure that they wouldn't be accused of cheating and possibly fined, bakers gave an extra loaf with each dozen ordered. That way, the customers could never claim that they didn't get their money's worth. To the present day, we call _____ of anything 'a baker's dozen.'

**해석** A baker's dozen이라는 표현을 들어본 적이 있는가? 만약 들어본 적이 있다면 그것이 무슨 뜻인지 알고 있는가? 아마 그 뜻이 어디로부터 왔는지 궁금해할지 모른다. 15세기 영국에서는 빵 굽는 사람들에 대한 평판이 아주 좋지 않았다. 사람들은 제과점에 가서 어느 정도의 빵을 주문하고는 그들이 지불한 만큼의 빵을 받지 못한 것에 대해 불평을 하곤 했다. 그래서 각각의 빵과 다른 과자가 가격대비 정확히(the same) 얼마의 무게가 나가야 하는지 표기하는(stating) 아주 엄격한 법안이 통과되었다. 속임수로 인해서 고소당하고 혹시라도 벌금을 부과받지 않도록 하기 위해서 제과점 주인들은 12개 주문에 덤(extra loaf)으로 빵을 더 얹어 주었다. 이러한 방법으로 손님들은 그들이 지불한 돈만큼을 받지 못한 것에 대한 요구를 할 수 없었다. 오늘날 우리는 어떤 것의 13개째 A baker's dozen이라고 부르고 있다.

**어휘** expression 표현  wonder 궁금해하다  term ① 기간 ② 용어  originate ① 유래하다 ② 비롯되다
reputation 평판  ask for 요구[요청]하다  complain 불평하다  strict 엄격한  good 상품
weigh 무게가 나가다  accuse 고발하다  cheat 사기, 속임수  fine 벌금을 내다
extra 여분의, 추가의  loaf (빵) 한 덩어리  dozen 한 다스[열두 개]  customer 고객, 손님
claim ① 주장하다 ② 불평하다  present ① 현재의 ② 선물 ③ 출석한
call A B A를 B라고 부르다

**해설** 사람들의 불평을 듣고 싶지 않아 빵 12개에 하나를 덤으로 더 주었다는 내용의 글이므로 빈칸에 들어가기에 가장 적절한 것은 ③이다.

14 ③

## 실전문제

**15** 다음 빈칸에 들어갈 말로 가장 적절한 것은?

> Set a time frame for the goal. For example, I want to read the next PART within two weeks. Time limits help to maintain focus and momentum. Setting a time limit that is too short may lead to more anxiety or a poor job since you rush to complete the goal. On the contrary, time limits that are too far away may not offer the sense of urgency that helps us to complete goals. By and large, we know that worriers can do one of two things, that is to say, they either _____, or they dive in without thinking. Both these styles are influenced by how worriers react to uncertain situations. If you recognize the first of these traits in yourself, then it might be worth giving yourself more urgent deadlines; if you recognize the second you may need to give yourself more time.

① put things off as long as possible
② try to rush to the aims too quickly
③ are concerned about completing goals
④ set a time limit that is tight for themselves

## 실전 해설

**15**

Set a time frame for the goal. For example, I want to read the next PART within two weeks. Time limits help to maintain focus and momentum. Setting a time limit that is too short may lead to more anxiety or a poor job since you rush to complete the goal. On the contrary, time limits that are too far away may not offer the sense of urgency that helps us to complete goals. By and large, we know that worriers can do one of two things, that is to say, they either _____, or they dive in without thinking. Both these styles are influenced by how worriers react to uncertain situations. If you recognize the first of these traits in yourself, then it might be worth giving yourself more urgent deadlines; if you recognize the second you may need to give yourself more time.

> Two 개념 : ① time limit → short  ② time limit → long  → 차이점 설명

**[해석]** 목표를 위해 쓸 수 있는 시간을 설정하라, 예를 들면, '나는 다음 장을 2주 이내에 읽기를 원한다.' 와 같은 것이다. 시한은 집중과 추진력을 유지하는 데 도움이 된다. 너무 짧은 시한을 설정하는 것은 목표를 완수하기 위해서 급히 서두르게 되므로 더 많은 불안감이나 부실한 일을 초래할 수 있다. 반면에, 너무 멀리 떨어져 있는 시한은 우리가 목표를 완수하도록 도와주는 긴박한 느낌을 주지 않을 수 있다. 대체로, 걱정을 많이 하는 사람들은 이 두 가지 일 중 하나를 할 수 있다는 것을 우리는 안다. 즉, 다시 말해서 그들은 <u>가능한 한 오랫동안 일을 미루거나</u> 아니면 아무 생각 없이 일에 뛰어든다. 이 두 가지 유형은 불확실한 상황에 대해 어떻게 반응하느냐에 의해 영향을 받는다. 당신 자신에게 이 속성들 중 첫 번째 것이 있음을 인식한다면, 자신에게 더 긴박한 마감 기한을 주는 것이 가치가 있을 것이다. 두 번째 것을 인식한다면 자신에게 더 많은 시간을 줄 필요가 있을 것이다.

① 가능한 한 오랫동안 일을 미루거나
② 너무 간단히 목표에 뛰어들려고 하거나
③ 목표를 달성하는 데 걱정하거나
④ 스스로 타이트한 시한을 설정하거나

**[어휘]** momentum 추진력, 가속도   short ① 짧은 ② 부족한   anxiety 걱정, 근심
rush ① (급히) 서두르다 ② (갑자기) 돌진하다   urgency 긴급한, 긴박함 *urgent 긴급한, 긴박한
complete 완성하다   by and large 대체로   dive in ① 뛰어들다 ② 몰두하다
react to ~에 반응하다   uncertain 불확실한   recognize 인식하다, 인정하다   trait 특성
put off 연기하다, 미루다   aim 목표   be concerned about ~에 대해 걱정하다

**[해설]** two 개념(시한을 짧게 잡는 것 vs 시한을 길게 잡는 것)을 이용해야 한다. 빈칸 다음 시한을 짧게 잡는 것에 대한 설명이 있으므로 빈칸에는 시한을 길게 잡는 것에 대한 설명이 있어야 한다. 따라서 빈칸에 들어가기에 가장 적절한 것은 ① '가능한 한 오랫동안 일을 미루거나'가 된다.

**[정답]**
15 ①

## 실전문제

**16** 다음 빈칸에 들어갈 말로 가장 적절한 것은?

There are two opposing types of manager at work. Managers who adopt an autocratic style generally issue orders and expect them to be obeyed without question. The military commander prefers and usually needs the autocratic style on the battle field. Because no one else is consulted, the autocratic style allows for rapid decision making. On the other hand, managers who adopt a democratic style generally ask for input from subordinates before making decisions but retain final decision-making power. For example, the manager of a technical group may ask other group members to interview job applicants, but the manager _____.

① doesn't really do anything at all
② will meet with other subordinates
③ can rely on his followers to support him
④ will autocratically make the hiring decision

## 실전 해설

**16**

There are two opposing types of manager at work. Managers who adopt an autocratic style generally issue orders and expect them to be obeyed without question. The military commander prefers and usually needs the autocratic style on the battle field. Because no one else is consulted, the autocratic style allows for rapid decision making. On the other hand, managers who adopt a democratic style generally ask for input from subordinates before making decisions but retain final decision-making power. For example, the manager of a technical group may ask other group members to interview job applicants, but the manager _____.

**해석** 직장에서 두 개의 서로 다른 유형의 관리자들이 있다. 독재적인 스타일을 채택하는 관리자들은 일반적으로 명령을 하고 그 명령이 의문의 여지없이 복종되기를 기대한다. 군대의 사령관은 전장에서 독재적인 스타일을 선호하며 (전장에서는) 대개 독재적인 스타일이 필요하다. 누구에게도 조언을 구하지 않으므로 독재적인 스타일은 신속한 의사결정을 가능하게 한다. 반면에, 민주적인 스타일을 채택하는 관리자는 일반적으로 결정을 내리기 전에 부하들로부터의 의견 제공을 요청하지만 최종적인 의사결정권은 자신이 보유한다. 예를 들어, 전문적인 집단의 관리자는 다른 구성원들에게 구직자를 인터뷰할 것을 요청하겠지만, 그 관리자는 <u>독단적으로 고용 결정을 하게 될 것이다</u>.

① 전혀 어떤 것도 하지 않는다
② 다른 부하직원들과 함께 만날 것이다
③ 그를 지지하는 사람들에 의존할 수 있다
④ 독단적으로 고용 결정을 하게 될 것이다

**어휘** opposing 반대하는  autocratic 독단적인, 독재의  obey 복종하다
military commander 군 사령관  battlefield 전쟁터  consult 상담하다
rapid 빠른, 신속한  democratic 민주적인  input ① 조언 ② 투입, 입력
subordinate 부하직원  retain 보유[유지]하다  applicant 지원자, 응시자

**해설** 주어진 지문은 두 가지 서로 다른 유형의 관리자에 관한 글이다. 하지만 빈칸의 내용은 빈칸 시작점인 For example(likeness)을 이용해야 한다. For example 앞에 부하직원들에게 자문을 구하지만 선택은 본인이 직접 한다는 내용이 있으므로 정답은 ④ '독단적으로 고용 결정을 하게 될 것이다'가 된다.

**정답**
16 ④

## 실전문제

**17** 밑줄 친 부분에 들어갈 말로 가장 적절한 것을 고르시오.

> Both the frequency and purpose of most regularly scheduled meetings can be significantly changed without any loss of effectiveness. The time it takes for everyone to show up, get settled in, and get rolling is a big drain. Very often a one-hour monthly meeting can be more productive than two forty-five-minute biweekly ones. Any meeting that is held more than once a month should be explored very carefully. Many meetings have parallel or overlapping functions in their purpose or frequency which can easily be folded into one another. The irony of meetings is that the number of subjects to be discussed contracts to accommodate the time available. As a consequence, meetings that are _____ would be far more productive.

① finished early
② held regularly
③ combined together
④ divided with detail

## 실전 해설

**17**

Both the frequency and purpose of most regularly scheduled meetings can be significantly changed without any loss of effectiveness. The time it takes for everyone to show up, get settled in, and get rolling is a big drain. Very often a

↳ Main Idea : 회의는 자주 하는 것보다 한 번에 묶어서 하는 것이 효율적이다.

one-hour monthly meeting can be more productive than two forty-five-minute biweekly ones. Any meeting that is held more than once a month should be explored very carefully. Many meetings have parallel or overlapping functions in their purpose or frequency which can easily be folded into one another. The irony of meetings is that the number of subjects to be discussed contracts to accommodate the time available. As a consequence, meetings that are _____ would be far more productive.

**해석** 대부분의 정기적으로 예정된 회의의 빈도[횟수]와 목적은 효율성을 잃지 않고서도 의미 있게 바뀔 수 있다. 모든 사람들이 나타나서 자리를 잡고 진행되어가기 시작하는 데 걸리는 시간은 커다란 낭비가 된다. 매달 있는 한 시간의 회의는 2주마다 하는 두 번의 45분의 회의보다 아주 종종 더 생산적일 수 있다. 한 달에 한 번 이상 열리는 회의는 (어떤 것이든지) 주의 깊게 살펴져야 한다. 많은 회의들은 쉽게 서로서로 접혀질 수 있는(중복될 수 있는) 목적과 빈도[횟수]에 있어서 유사하거나 겹칠 수 있는 기능을 갖는다. 회의의 아이러니는 토론되는 주제의 숫자가 (토론을 하는 데)이용 가능한 시간을 맞추기 위해서 줄어든다는 것이다. 결과적으로, <u>서로 결합된</u> 회의들이 훨씬 더 생산적일 것이다.

① 일찍 끝난
② 정기적으로 열리는
③ 서로 결합된
④ 세부적으로 쪼개진

**어휘** frequency 빈도, 횟수  purpose 목적(= end)  regularly 규칙적으로
significantly ① 중요하게 ② 의미 있게  effectiveness 효율(성)  show up 나타나다, 등장하다
settle in ① 자리를 잡다 ② 적응하다  productive 생산적인  biweekly 격주마다
parallel ① 평행한 ② 유사한  function 기능(하다)  subject ① 주제 ② 피험자 ③ 대상
contract ① 줄이다, 축소시키다 ② 계약서, 계약하다  accommodate 수용하다, 맞추다
as a consequence 결과적으로  productive 생산적인  regularly 규칙적으로
divide 쪼개다, 나누다  with detail 세부적으로, 상세하게

**해설** 주어진 지문은 회의를 자주 여러 번 하는 것보다는 한 번에 묶어서 하는 것이 효율적이라는 내용의 글이므로 빈칸에 들어가기에 가장 적절한 것은 ③ '서로 결합된'이다.

**17** ③

## 실전문제

**18** 밑줄 친 부분에 들어갈 말로 가장 적절한 것을 고르시오.

> Brain development is a fascinating construction tale. At some times during pregnancy, the fetus's brain makes 250,000 new nerve cells per minute. Babies are born with 100 billion neurons, but only a relatively small number of them are connected. In the first decade of life, a child's brain forms trillions of connections. New research has shown that early childhood experiences do not only create a background for development and learning, but they directly affect the way the brain is wired. In turn, the wiring profoundly affects our feelings, language, and thought. Experiences do not just influence a child's development; they finish the job of coining and molding the brain. In sum, about a forth of the brain grows in the womb but three quarters of the brain also develops outside, in response to environment. That is, _____.
>
> \* fetus : 태아  \*\* womb : 자궁

① experience leads to brain development
② nature and nurture always work together
③ the brain is the sacred temple of the gene
④ the brain has something to do with environment

## 실전 해설

**18**

Brain development is a fascinating construction tale. At some times during pregnancy, the fetus's brain makes 250,000 new nerve cells per minute. Babies are born with 100 billion neurons, but only a relatively small number of them are connected. In the first decade of life, a child's brain forms trillions of connections. New research has shown that early childhood experiences do not only create a background for development and learning, but they directly affect the way the brain is wired. In turn, the wiring profoundly affects our feelings, language, and thought. Experiences do not just influence a child's development; they finish the job of coining and molding the brain. In sum, about a forth of the brain grows in the womb but three quarters of the brain also develops outside, in response to environment. That is, _____.

↳ Likeness(논리의 방향이 같다)

\* fetus : 태아  \*\* womb : 자궁

**해석** 뇌 발달은 (그 과정이) 하나의 흥미진진한 구조 형성의 이야기이다. 임신 기간 중 몇몇 시기에 태아의 뇌는 분당 25만개의 새로운 신경 세포를 만든다. 아기들은 1,000억 개의 뉴런을 가지고 태어나지만, 상대적으로 적은 수의 뉴런만이 서로 연결된다. 삶의 첫 10년 사이에 아이의 뇌는 수조 개의 연결을 형성한다. 새로운 연구에 따르면, 어린 시절 초기의 경험은 발달과 학습을 위한 바탕을 만들어 낼 뿐만 아니라 뇌가 연결되는 방식에 직접적으로 영향을 준다. 차례로 그 연결이 우리의 감정과 언어, 그리고 사고에 깊이 영향을 미친다. 경험들은 아이의 발달에만 영향을 주는 것이 아니라 뇌를 만들고 주조하는 일도 완성한다. 요약해보면, 뇌의 약 4분의 1은 자궁 안에서 성장하지만 뇌의 약 4분의 3은 환경에 반응하면서 자궁 밖에서도 발달한다. 즉, 선천과 후천은 항상 함께 작용한다.
① 경험이 뇌 발달을 초래한다
② 선천과 후천은 항상 함께 작용한다
③ 뇌는 유전자의 신성한 사원이다
④ 뇌는 환경과 약간의 관계가 있다

**어휘** fascinating 매력적인  construction ① 구조 ② 건설 ③ 건축물
collaborate 협력하다, 공동으로 작업하다  pregnancy 임신(기간)  nerve cell 신경 세포
neuron 뉴런, 신경 단위  trillion 1조  background 배경, 바탕
wire ① 전보를 보내다, 연결하다 ② 전선, 철사  in turn 차례로  profoundly 깊이, 심오하게
coin 만들다, 주조하다  mold ① 주조하다, 틀에 넣어 만들다 ② 틀, 주물 ③ 곰팡이
sculpt 조각하다, 형상을 만들다  in response to ~에 반응해서, ~에 답하여
have something to do with ~와 약간 관계가 있다  nurture 양육  sacred 신성한

**해설** 빈칸 앞에 있는 That is를 이용해야 한다(Likeness). 자궁 안에서 그리고 자궁 밖에서 (환경에 반응해서) 뇌는 발달한다고 했으므로 빈칸에 가장 적절한 것은 ② '선천과 후천은 항상 함께 작용한다.'이다.

18 ②

## 실전문제

**19** 다음 빈칸에 들어갈 말로 가장 적절한 것을 고르시오.

> Two very important numbers associated with an atom are the atomic number and the mass number. Chemists tend to memorize these numbers as sports fans memorize baseball stats, but clever chemistry students do not need to resort to memorization when they have the all-important periodic table at their disposal. Here are the basics about atomic numbers and mass numbers. The atomic number is the number of protons in the nucleus of an atom. Atomic numbers identify elements, because the number of protons is what gives an element its unique identity. Changing the number of protons changes the identity of the element. Atomic numbers are listed as a subscript to the left side of an element's chemical symbol. The mass number is the value of merging the number of protons and neutrons in the nucleus of an atom. Thus, subtracting the atomic number from the mass number gives you the number of _____ in the nucleus of an atom.

① atoms
② protons
③ electrons
④ neutrons

## 실전 해설

**19**

Two very important numbers associated with an atom are the atomic number and the mass number. Chemists tend to memorize these numbers as sports fans memorize baseball stats, but clever chemistry students do not need to resort to memorization when they have the all-important periodic table at their disposal. Here are the basics about atomic numbers and mass numbers. The atomic number is the number of protons in the nucleus of an atom. Atomic numbers identify elements, because the number of protons is what gives an element its unique identity. Changing the number of protons changes the identity of the element. Atomic numbers are listed as a subscript to the left side of an element's chemical symbol. The mass number is the value of merging the number of protons and neutrons in the nucleus of an atom. Thus, subtracting the atomic number from the
↳ 인과관계(mass number-atomic number = neutron)
mass number gives you the number of _____ in the nucleus of an atom.

**해석** 원자와 관련이 있는 두 가지 매우 중요한 숫자는 '원자번호'와 '질량 수'이다. 스포츠팬들이 야구의 통계 수치들을 외워두는 것처럼 화학자들은 흔히 이 숫자들을 외워두는 경향이 있지만, 화학을 공부하는 머리가 좋은 학생들은 아주 중요한 주기율표를 그들이 원하는 대로 쓸 수 있을 때에는 암기에 의존할 필요가 없다. 원자 번호와 질량 수에 관한 기본 사항들이 여기에 있다. 원자 번호는 원자핵 속에 있는 양성자의 수이다. 양성자 수는 원소에 독특한 정체성을 부여해주는 것이기 때문에, 원자 번호는 원소와 동일한 것으로 간주된다. 양성자의 수를 변화시키면 원소의 정체성이 달라진다. 원자 번호는 원소의 화학 기호 왼쪽 아래쪽에 표시된다. 질량 수는 원자의 핵 속에 들어 있는 양성자 수와 중성자 수를 합친 것이다. 질량 수에서 원자 번호를 빼면 원자의 핵 속에 들어 있는 중성자의 수를 알 수 있다.
① 원자
② 양성자
③ 전자
④ 중성자

**어휘** associate ① 관계[관련]시키다 ② 연상시키다  atom 원자 *atomic 원자의  mass ① 질량 ② 대중
chemist 화학자  clever 영리한  chemistry 화학  resort to ~에 의지하다
periodic table 주기율표  proton 양성자  nucleus ① 핵 ② 핵심
identify ① 확인[증명]하다 ② 동일시하다(identify A with B)  element ① (구성) 요소 ② 성분
unique 유일무이한, 독특한  identity 정체성  side ① 편 ② 쪽  symbol ① 상징 ② 기호
value (수학) 값  subtract 빼다(↔ add: 더하다)  neutron 중성자  electron 전자

**해설** 인과관계의 시그널 Thus를 이용해야 한다. Thus를 기준으로 인과관계(빈칸 앞에 있는 That is를 이용해야 한다(Likeness). [질량 수 = 양성자(the number of proton = atomic number) + 중성자 : 원인 → 질량 수 - 양성자 = 중성자 : 결과]환경에 반응해서)의 논리상 빈칸에 들어가기에 가장 적절한 것은 ④ '중성자'이다.

**정답**
19 ④

## 실전문제

**20** 다음 빈칸에 들어갈 말로 가장 적절한 것은?

> I would like to compare the shift from analog to digital film-making to the shift from fresco and tempera to oil painting in the early Renaissance. A painter making a fresco has limited time before the paint dries, and once it has dried, no further changes to the image are possible. Similarly, a traditional filmmaker has limited means of modifying images once they are recorded on film. Medieval tempera painting can be compared to the practice of special effects during the analog period of cinema. A painter working with tempera could modify and rework the image, but the process was painstaking and slow. The switch to oils greatly liberated painters by allowing them to quickly create much larger compositions as well as to modify them as long as necessary. Similarly, _____ _____ digital technology redefines what can be done with cinema.

① by equating oil painting with analog film-making
② by allowing a filmmaker to treat a film image as an oil painting
③ with the shift from oil painting styles to fresco ones in making films
④ by integrating fresco painting techniques into the film-making process

## 실전 해설

**20**

I would like to compare the shift from analog to digital film-making to the shift from fresco and tempera to oil painting in the early Renaissance. A painter making a fresco has limited time before the paint dries, and once it has dried, no further changes to the image are possible. Similarly, a traditional filmmaker has limited means of modifying images once they are recorded on film. Medieval tempera painting can be compared to the practice of special effects during the analog period of cinema. A painter working with tempera could modify and rework the image, but the process was painstaking and slow. The switch to oils greatly liberated painters by allowing them to quickly create much larger compositions as

*유사의 공간 개념: ① analog → digital ② fresco, tempera → oil painting*

well as to modify them as long as necessary. Similarly, _____ _____ digital technology redefines what can be done with cinema.

**해석** 나는 아날로그에서 디지털로의 영화 제작 방식의 전환을 초기 르네상스 시대에 프레스코 화법(새로 석회를 바른 벽에 그것이 마르기 전에 그림을 그리는 것)과 템페라 화법(안료에 달걀노른자와 물을 섞어 그린 그림)에서 유화 화법으로의 이동에 비유하고 싶다. 프레스코화를 그리는 화가는 물감이 마르기 전에 한정된 시간을 가지게 되어, 일단 물감이 마르고 나면, 그림에 더 이상의 변화를 주는 것은 가능하지 않다. 마찬가지로, 전통적인 영화 제작자는 일단 영상이 필름에 기록되고 나면 그것을 수정할 수 있는 제한적인 수단을 가진다. 중세의 템페라 화법은 영화를 아날로그 방식으로 제작하던 시기의 특수효과 실행에 비유될 수 있다. 템페라화를 그리는 화가는 그림을 수정하고 다시 그릴 수 있었지만, 그 과정은 고생스럽고 느렸다. 유화로의 전환은 화가들이 필요한 만큼 오랫동안 작품을 수정하는 것뿐만 아니라 빠르게 훨씬 더 큰 작품을 그리는 것을 가능하게 함으로써 그들을 대단히 자유롭게 해주었다. 마찬가지로, <u>영화 제작자가 유화 화법처럼 영화 영상을 다루는 것을 가능하게 함으로써</u>, 디지털 기술은 영화로 할 수 있는 일을 재정립한다.

① 유화 화법을 아날로그 영화 제작 방식과 동일시함으로써
② 영화 제작자가 유화 화법처럼 영화 영상을 다루는 것을 가능하게 함으로써
③ 영화 제작에 있어서 유화 방식에서 프레스코화 방식으로 전환하면서
④ 프레스코 화법을 영화 제작 과정에 통합함으로써

**어휘** compare A to B A를 B에 비유하다   shift 이동, 전환
fresco 프레스코 화법(새로 석회를 바른 벽에 그것이 마르기 전에 그림을 그리는 것)
tempera 템페라 화법(안료에 달걀노른자와 물을 섞어 그림을 그리는 것)   further 더 이상의
means 수단   modify 수정하다, 고치다   medieval 중세의   image 영상, 그림
rework 다시 하다   painstaking 고생스러운, 힘든   liberate 자유롭게 하다
composition ① 작문 ② 작곡 ③ 작품   treat ① 다루다, 취급하다 ② 치료하다
redefine 재정립하다   integrate 통합하다

**해설** 필자는 아날로그 방식의 영화 제작 방식을 프레스코 화법과 템페라 화법에 비유하고 있고, 디지털 방식의 영화 제작 방식을 유화 화법에 비유하고 있다. 유화 화법이 수고로운 작업으로부터 화가들을 자유롭게 해주었던 것처럼, 디지털 기술도 영화 제작자들이 영화로 할 수 있는 일을 재정립하고 있다는 내용이 Similarly 앞뒤로 이어지고 있으므로 빈칸에 들어갈 말로 가장 적절한 것은 ② '영화 제작자가 유화 화법처럼 영화 영상을 다루는 것을 가능하게 함으로써'이다.

**정답**
20 ②

## 실전문제

**21** 다음 글의 빈칸에 들어갈 말로 가장 적절한 것은?

What story could be harsher than that of the *Great Auk*, the large black-and-white seabird that in northern oceans took the place of a penguin? Its tale falls and rises like a Greek tragedy, with island populations savagely destroyed by humans until almost all were gone. However, the very last colony found safety on a special island, one protected from the destruction of humankind by vicious and unpredictable ocean currents. These waters presented no problem to perfectly adapted seagoing birds, but they prevented humans from making any kind of safe landing. After enjoying a few years of comparative safety, disaster of a different kind struck the *Great Auk*. Volcanic activity caused the island refuge to sink completely beneath the waves, and surviving individuals were forced to find shelter elsewhere. The new island home they chose _____ in one terrible way. Humans could access it with comparative ease, and they did! Within just a few years the last of this once-plentiful species was entirely eliminated.

① lacked the benefits of the old
② denied other colonies easy access
③ faced unexpected natural disasters
④ had a similar disadvantage to the last island

## 실전 해설

**21**

: 집중해야 할 정보

What story could be harsher than that of the *Great Auk*, the large black-and-white seabird that in northern oceans took the place of a penguin? Its tale falls and rises like a Greek tragedy, with island populations savagely destroyed by humans until almost all were gone. However, the very last colony found safety on a special island, one protected from the destruction of humankind by vicious and unpredictable ocean currents. These waters presented no problem to perfectly adapted seagoing birds, but they prevented humans from making any kind of safe landing. After enjoying a few years of comparative safety, disaster of a different kind struck the *Great Auk*. Volcanic activity caused the island refuge to sink completely beneath the waves, and surviving individuals were forced to find shelter elsewhere. The new island home they chose _____ in

↳ Main Idea : 화산으로 새들이 다른 곳으로 이동 → 인간에게 피해를 입음.

one terrible way. Humans could access it with comparative ease, and they did! Within just a few years the last of this once-plentiful species was entirely eliminated.

**해석** 어떤 이야기가 북쪽 대양에서 펭귄을 대신했던 흑백의 대형 바닷새인 큰바다쇠 오리의 이야기보다 더 가혹할 수 있을까? 그 새의 이야기는 한 편의 그리스 비극처럼 쇠퇴하고 융성하는데, 섬의 개체군은 거의 모두가 사라질 때까지 인간에 의해 잔혹하게 죽임을 당했다. 하지만 진짜 마지막 집단이 한 특별한 섬, 사납고 예측할 수 없는 해류에 의해 인간의 파괴로부터 보호를 받았던 한 섬에서 안전을 찾아냈다. 이런 바다는 완벽하게 적응하여 바다 여행에 알맞은 새에게는 아무 문제도 일으키지 않았지만, 사람들에게는 어떤 종류의 안전한 상륙도 하지 못하게 했다. 몇 년을 비교적 안전하게 지낸 뒤에 다른 종류의 재난이 큰바다쇠 오리에게 타격을 주었다. 화산 활동은 그 섬의 피난처가 완전히 바닷속에 가라앉게 했고 살아남은 개체들은 어쩔 수 없이 다른 곳으로 피난해야 했다. 그것들이 선택한 새로운 섬 서식지에는 하나의 끔찍한 측면에서 <u>옛것의 이점들이 없었다</u>. 인간들이 비교적 쉽게 그것(그 섬 서식지)에 접근할 수 있었고, 인간들은 실제로 그렇게 했다! 단지 몇 년 이내에 이 한 때 많았던 종의 마지막 개체가 완전히 제거되었다.
① 옛것의 이점들이 없었다
② 다른 집단들에게 쉬운 접근을 허용하지 않았다
③ 예기치 못한 자연 재해에 직면했다
④ 마지막 섬과 비슷한 단점이 있었다.

**어휘** harsh 가혹한  take the place of ~을 대신하다, ~의 뒤를 잇다  tragedy 비극, 참사
population 개체(수), 전체 주민, 인구  destroy 파괴하다  colony ① 집단 ② 거주지 ③ 식민지
vicious 악랄한, 사악한  current 해류, 흐름  present ① (어려움 등을) 일으키다 ② 주다, 제공하다
adapt 적응시키다  seagoing 바다 여행에 알맞은, 항해에 알맞은  landing 상륙, 착륙
disaster 재난, 천재지변  volcanic 화산의  refuge 피난처, 피난
comparative 비교적인, 상대적인  eliminate 제거하다, 없애다

**해설** 주어진 지문은 큰바다쇠 오리의 마지막 집단이 머물렀던 섬은 인간이 안전하게 상륙할 수 없는 장소였지만, 그 섬 전체가 바다 속에 가라앉음으로써 이들은 어쩔 수 없이 다른 섬으로 피신하게 되었는데 그 새로운 섬은 인간이 쉽게 접근할 수 있어서 인간이 큰바다쇠 오리를 완전히 제거해 버렸다는 내용이므로 빈칸에 들어갈 말로 가장 적절한 것은 ① '옛것의 이점들이 없었다'이다.

정답
21 ①

## 실전문제

**22** 다음 빈칸에 들어가 말로 가장 적절한 것은?

> Unlike deviance in other settings, deviance in sports often involves _____ norms and expectations. For example, most North Americans see playing football as a positive activity. Young men are encouraged to 'be all they can be' as football players and to live by slogans such as "There is no 'I' in t-e-a-m." They are encouraged to increase their weight and strength, so that they can play more effectively and contribute to the success of their teams. When young men go too far in their acceptance of expectations to become bigger and stronger, when they are so committed to playing football and improving their skills on the field that they use muscle-building drugs, they become deviant. This type of 'overdoing-it-deviance' is dangerous, but it is grounded in completely different social dynamics from the dynamics that occur in the 'antisocial deviance' enacted by alienated young people who reject commonly accepted rules and expectations.

① a positive deviance of the desire to avoid

② wasted efforts and resources in establishing

③ antisocial deviance to get independent of and free from

④ an unquestioned acceptance of and extreme conformity to

## 실전 해설

**22**

> _____ : 집중해야 할 정보
> Main Idea : 운동을 더 잘하라는 기대에 부응하기 위해 젊은 선수들이 근육강화제를 복용한다.

Unlike deviance in other settings, deviance in sports often involves _____ norms and expectations. For example, most North Americans see playing football as a positive activity. Young men are encouraged to 'be all they can be' as football players and to live by slogans such as "There is no 'I' in t-e-a-m." They are encouraged to increase their weight and strength, so that they can play more effectively and contribute to the success of their teams. When young men go too far in their acceptance of expectations to become bigger and stronger, when they are so committed to playing football and improving their skills on the field that they use muscle-building drugs, they become deviant. This type of 'overdoing-it-deviance' is dangerous, but it is grounded in completely different social dynamics from the dynamics that occur in the 'antisocial deviance' enacted by alienated young people who reject commonly accepted rules and expectations.

**해석** 다른 분야에서의 일탈과는 달리 스포츠에서의 일탈은 종종 규범과 기대에 대한 <u>아무런 의심 없는 수용과 극단적인 순응</u>을 수반한다. 예를 들어, 대부분의 북아메리카 인들은 미식축구 경기에 참여하는 것을 적극적 활동으로 간주한다. 젊은 사람들은 미식축구 선수로서 자신의 최고의 모습을 보이고, "팀에 '나'라는 존재는 없다"라는 말과 같은 슬로건으로 살아가도록 격려 받는다. 그들은 체중과 힘을 증가시켜서 좀 더 효과적으로 경기를 하고 팀의 성공에 기여하라고 격려 받는다. 젊은 사람들이 좀 더 몸집이 커지고 힘이 세어지라는 기대를 지나칠 정도로 수용하게 될 때, 그들이 경기장에서 미식축구 경기를 하는 것과 기술을 향상시키는 것에 지나칠 정도로 전념하여 근육을 형성하는 약물을 복용하게 될 때, 그들은 일탈하게 된다. 이러한 유형의 '과잉 행동 일탈'은 위험한 것이지만, 그것은 일반적으로 받아들여지는 규칙과 기대를 거부하는 소외된 젊은 사람들에 의해 이루어지는 '반사회적 일탈'에서 발생하는 역학과는 완전히 다른 사회적 역학에 근거한다.

① 피하려는 욕구의 긍정적 일탈
② 설립하는 데 있어서의 낭비된 노력과 자원
③ 독립되고 자유로워지려는 반사회적 일탈
④ 아무런 의심 없는 수용과 극단적인 순응

**어휘** setting ① 환경 ② 분야(=field) ③ 배경  deviance 일탈  *deviant 일탈의  norm 규범
see A as B A를 B라고 여기다, 간주하다  so that ① ~하기 위해서 ② 그래서
go too far 도가 지나치다, 도를 넘다  commit ① 저지르다 ② 전념[몰두]하다 ③ 다짐[약속]하다
overdo 지나치게 ~을 하다  ground ① 땅 ② 근거
dynamics (물리)역학  *dynamic 다이나믹한, 역동적인  antisocial 반사회적인
enact 행동하다, 행하다  alienate 멀어지게 하다, 소외시키다, 고립시키다  *alienation 소외, 고립
reject 거부[거절]하다  establish 세우다, 설립하다  extreme 극도(한)의  conformity 순응, 받아들임

**해설** 주어진 지문은 스포츠에서 일어나는 일탈행위를 미식축구 선수의 약물복용 사례로 설명하고 있다. 미식축구 선수들은 항상 최선을 다하고 팀을 위해 희생하라고 지도를 받고 이를 '의심 없이 수용(unquestioned acceptance)'하는데, 이에 '지나칠 정도로 순응(extreme conformity)'할 때 약물 복용이라는 일탈 행위를 저지를 수 있다는 내용의 글이므로 빈칸에 들어갈 말로 가장 적절한 것은 ④ '아무런 의심 없는 수용과 극단적인 순응'이다.

**정답**
22 ④

## 실전문제

**23** 다음 빈칸에 들어갈 말로 가장 적절한 것은?

What seems to annoy us in queues is seeing people get ahead. This is why, says Richard Larson, an authority on queues, any number of companies—from banks to fast-food chains—have switched from systems in which multiple lines feed multiple servers to a single, serpentine line. There's a theorem in queuing theory that says the average wait in either configuration is the same. Yet people prefer the single line, so much so that they have said they would be willing to wait in a longer line at Wendy's, where a single line is used, than in a shorter line at McDonald's, which uses multiple lines. Why? _____, says Larson. "If you have the single serpentine line, you're guaranteed first come, first served. If you have the multiple lines, you have what happens at McDonald's at lunchtime. You have the stress of joining a line with a high likelihood that somebody who's joined a queue next to you will get served before you. People get really irritated with that."

\* serpentine 구불구불한

① Service efficiency
② Time perception
③ Optical illusion
④ Social justice

## 실전 해설

**23**

What seems to annoy us in queues is seeing people get ahead. This is why, says Richard Larson, an authority on queues, any number of companies — from banks to fast-food chains — have switched from systems in which multiple lines feed multiple servers to a single, serpentine line. There's a theorem in queuing theory that says the average wait in either configuration is the same. Yet people prefer the single line, so much so that they have said they would be willing to wait in a longer line at Wendy's, where a single line is used, than in a shorter line at McDonald's, which uses multiple lines. Why? _____, says

*Main Idea : 한 줄 서기는 선착순을 의미하므로 누구에게나 공정하다.*

Larson. "If you have the single serpentine line, you're guaranteed first come, first served. If you have the multiple lines, you have what happens at McDonald's at lunchtime. You have the stress of joining a line with a high likelihood that somebody who's joined a queue next to you will get served before you. People get really irritated with that."

* serpentine 구불구불한

**해석** 줄에 서 있을 때 우리를 짜증나게 하는 것처럼 보이는 것은 사람들이 앞지르는 것을 보는 것이다. 이것이 은행에서부터 패스트푸드 체인점에 이르는 많은 회사들이 다수의 줄이 다수의 근무자를 제공하는 시스템에서 하나의 구불구불한 줄로 전환한 이유라고 줄서기 분야의 권위자인 Richard Larson은 말한다. 대기 행렬 이론에는 둘 중 어느 쪽 배열 형태에서든지 기다리는 평균 시간은 같다고 하는 법칙이 있다. 하지만 사람들은 한 개의 줄을 너무나 선호해서 다수의 줄을 사용하는 맥도날드의 짧은 줄보다 하나의 줄이 사용되는 웬디스의 긴 줄에서 기꺼이 기다릴 것이라고 말했다. 왜 그러한가? 사회적 공정성 때문이라고 Larson은 말한다. "만약 당신이 하나의 구불구불한 줄을 이용한다면, 당신은 선착순을 보장받는다. 만약 당신이 다수의 줄을 이용한다면, 당신은 점심시간에 맥도날드에서 일어나는 일을 경험한다. 당신은 옆줄에 서 있던 누군가가 당신보다 먼저 서비스를 받게 될 가능성이 매우 높은 줄에 서 있는 스트레스를 겪게 된다. 사람들은 그것에 정말 짜증이 나게 된다."
① 서비스 효율성
② 시간 인지
③ 착시 현상
④ 사회적 공정성

**어휘** annoy 짜증나게 하다, 귀찮게 하다  queue ① 줄 ② 줄서다  get ahead 앞서다
authority ① 권위 ② 권위자 ③ 당국  any number of 많은
switch from A to B A에서 B로 전환[이동]하다  multiple 많은, 다수의  feed 먹다, 먹이다
configuration 배열, 배치  be willing to ⓥ 기꺼이 ⓥ하다
guarantee ① 보장[확약]하다 ② 보장, 보증  first come, first served 선착순
likelihood 가능성  *likely 가능성 있는, 그럴싸한  efficiency 효율성, 능률
perception 인지, 인식  optical illusion 착시 (현상)  *optical 시각적인  *illusion 착각, 환상
recognition ① 알아봄, 인식 ② 인정, 승인  *recognize ① 알아보다, 인식하다 ② 인정[승인]하다
justice ① 정의 ② 공정함, 공평성

**해설** 주어진 지문은 줄서기의 선착순 개념 즉, 사회적 공정성을 설명하는 내용의 글이므로 빈칸에 들어가기에 가장 적절한 것은 ④ '사회적 공정성'이다.

**정답**
23 ④

## 실전문제

**24** 다음 글의 빈칸에 들어갈 말로 가장 적절한 것은?

The audience receives a sound signal entirely through the vibrations generated in the air, whereas in a singer some of the auditory stimulus is conducted to the ear through the singer's own bones. Since these two ways of transferring sound have quite different relative efficiencies at various frequencies, the overall quality of the sound will be quite different. You have probably experienced this when you have listened to your own voice, as on tape or through a public address system. It is easy to blame the 'sound of a stranger' for 'poor electronics,' but this is only partly justified. The major effect comes from the fact that you hear yourself differently from the way others hear you. This is one of the main reasons why even the most accomplished singers have to listen to the opinion of coaches and voice teachers as to 'how they sound,' whereas no concert violinist would have to do such a thing. To the violinist _____ to someone else standing nearby.

① the coaches are more helpful than they are
② the audience response is just as important as it is
③ playing sounds almost exactly the same as it does
④ the 'sound of a stranger' matters just as important it does

## 실전 해설

**24**

The audience receives a sound signal entirely through the vibrations generated in
↑ Two 개념: ① audience ② singer → 차이점 설명
the air, whereas in a singer some of the auditory stimulus is conducted to the ear through the singer's own bones. Since these two ways of transferring sound have quite different relative efficiencies at various frequencies, the overall quality of the sound will be quite different. You have probably experienced this when you have listened to your own voice, as on tape or through a public address system. It is easy to blame the 'sound of a stranger' for 'poor electronics,' but this is only partly justified. The major effect comes from the fact that you hear yourself differently from the way others hear you. This is one of the main reasons why even the most accomplished singers have to listen to the opinion of coaches and voice teachers as to 'how they sound,' whereas no concert violinist would have to do such a thing.

↑ audience과 같은 개념      ↑ audience과 같은 개념
To the violinist _____ to someone else standing nearby.

**해석** 청중은 소리신호를 공기에서 생성되는 진동에 의해서만 받는 반면에 가수들에게 청각 자극의 일부는 가수의 뼈를 통해 전도가 된다. 소리를 전달하는 두 방식이 다양한 주파수에서의 꽤 다른 상대적 효율성을 가지기 때문에 소리의 전반적인 질은 상당히 다를 것이다. 당신은 당신의 목소리를 테이프나 대중연설 체계를 통해 들었을 때 이러한 것을 경험했을 지도 모른다. '(내가 아닌) 낯선 사람의 소리'를 '형편없는 전자기기' 탓으로 돌리기 쉬우나 이것은 부분적으로만 정당화될 수 있다. 주된 결과는 당신이 당신의 목소리를 다른 사람이 당신의 목소리를 듣는 방식과는 다르게 듣는다는 것이다. 이것은 심지어 가장 뛰어난 가수가 '그들의 목소리가 어떻게 들리는지'에 대해 코치들이나 목소리 선생들의 의견을 묻는 이유 중에 하나이다. 반면에 콘서트 바이올린 연주자는 그런 일을 할 필요가 없을 것이다. 바이올린 연주자들에게 <u>연주하는 소리는 근처에 서 있는 다른 사람에게 들리는 것과 거의 정확하게 똑같이 들린다</u>.
① 코치는 근처에 서 있는 다른 사람에게 도움을 주는 것보다 더 도움이 된다
② 청중의 반응은 근처에 서 있는 다른 사람에게 중요한 만큼 중요하다
③ 연주하는 소리는 근처에 서 있는 다른 사람에게 들리는 것과 거의 정확하게 똑같이 들린다
④ 낯선 사람의 소리가 근처에 서 있는 다른 사람에게 중요한 만큼 중요하다

**어휘** audience 청중   entirely 전적으로, 완전히, 전부   signal 신호   vibration 진동
generate 발생시키다, 야기하다   whereas 반면에   auditory 청각의
stimulus 자극, 자극제 *stimuli (복수형)자극
conduct ① (열, 전기 등을) 전도하다, 옮기다 ② 수행하다 ③ 지휘하다   transfer 전송하다
relative ① 상대적인 ② 친척   frequency 주파수   overall 종합적인, 전체의
quality ① 질, 품질 ② 특성   probably 아마도   public address 대중 연설
blame A for B A를 B 때문에 비난하다   electronics 전자기기   partly 부분적으로
justify 정당화하다   major 주된, 주요한; 전공 *major in ~을 전공하다   accomplished 뛰어난
exactly 정확하게   matter 중요하다

**해설** two 개념(audience vs. singer)을 이용해야 한다. 빈칸에 있는 violinist는 audience의 입장이므로 violinist나 주변에 서있는 사람들(audience)은 같은 개념이다. 따라서 빈칸에 들어가기에 가장 적절한 것은 ③ '연주하는 소리는 근처에 서 있는 다른 사람에게 들리는 것과 거의 정확하게 똑같이 들린다'이다.

**정답**
24 ③

## 실전문제

**25** 다음 글의 빈칸에 들어갈 말로 가장 적절한 것은?

One of the main principles I follow when I draw outside is _____. I try to stay away from houses or barns that have unusual angles of the roof, or objects that look incorrect in size, perspective, or design. If the subject is confusing when you look at it, it will be more confusing when you attempt to draw it. I know a beautiful barn where the corners are not at right angles. No matter how many times I have drawn it, the perspective does not look right. If I were to make an accurate drawing of this barn and put it in a show, I'm sure I would get all kinds of criticism for my poor perspective. I would not be there to tell my critics that the barn is actually constructed this way. So, I stay away from subjects that do not look right to me.

① not to draw an object with imagination
② not to draw any objects that others have drawn
③ to convert inaccurate drawings into accurate ones
④ not to select a subject that is too difficult or odd

## 실전 해설

**25**

> ▸ Main Idea : 내 그림의 원칙은 혼란스러운 대상은 그리지 않는다.
> _____ : 집중해야 할 정보
>
> One of the main principles I follow when I draw outside is _____. I try to stay away from houses or barns that have unusual angles of the roof, or objects that look incorrect in size, perspective, or design. If the subject is confusing when you look at it, it will be more confusing when you attempt to draw it. I know a beautiful barn where the corners are not at right angles. No matter how many times I have drawn it, the perspective does not look right. If I were to make an accurate drawing of this barn and put it in a show, I'm sure I would get all kinds of criticism for my poor perspective. I would not be there to tell my critics that the barn is actually constructed this way. So, I stay away from subjects that do not look right to me.

**해석** 바깥에서 그림을 그릴 때 내가 따르는 중요한 원칙들 중 하나는 너무 어렵거나 이상한 대상은 선택하지 않는 것이다. 나는 특이한 각도의 지붕을 가지고 있는 집이나 헛간, 혹은 크기, 원근법, 혹은 디자인에서 부정확한 것처럼 보이는 물체는 멀리 하려고 한다. 어떤 대상을 쳐다볼 때 그것이 혼란스럽게 한다면, 그것을 그리려고 시도할 때는 더 혼란스러울 것이다. 나는 모서리 부분이 직각이지 않은 아름다운 헛간을 알고 있다. 아무리 많이 그것을 그렸지만, 원근법이 올바르지 않아 보였다. 만약 내가 이 헛간을 정확하게 그려서 그것을 전시회에 내 놓는다면, 나는 형편없는 원근법 때문에 모든 종류의 비난을 받게 될 거라고 확신을 한다. 나는 거기에 가서 그 헛간이 실제로 이런 식으로 건설되어 있다고 나를 비판하는 사람들에게 말하지는 않을 것이다. 그래서 나는 나에게 올바른 것처럼 보이지 않는 대상을 멀리 한다.

① 상상력으로 대상을 그리지 않는
② 다른 사람들이 그린 어떤 대상도 그리지 않는
③ 부정확한 그림을 정확한 그림으로 바꾸는
④ 너무 어렵거나 이상한 대상은 선택하지 않는

**어휘** principle 원리  stay away from ~을 멀리하다  barn 곳간, 헛간  unusual 이상한, 보통이 아닌  angle 각도  object 대상, 물건  incorrect 올바르지 않은, 부정확한  perspective 원근법  right angle 직각  *right 올바른  accurate 정확한  criticism 비판  critic 비평가  construct 건설하다

**해설** 주어진 지문은 그림을 그릴 때 특이하거나 부정확한 것처럼 보이는 물체는 멀리하려 한다는 내용의 글이므로 빈칸에 들어가기에 가장 적절한 것은 ④ '너무 어렵거나 이상한 대상은 선택하지 않는'이다.

**정답**
25 ④

## 기출문제

**01** 밑줄 친 부분에 들어갈 말로 가장 적절한 것을 고르시오. 2025. 국가직 9급

Active listening is an art, a skill and a discipline that takes _____ _____. To develop good listening skills, you need to understand what is involved in effective communication and develop the techniques to sit quietly and listen. This involves ignoring your own needs and focusing on the person speaking — a task made more difficult by the way the human brain works. When someone talks to you, your brain immediately begins processing the words, body language, tone, inflection and perceived meanings coming from the other person. Instead of hearing one noise, you hear two : the noise the other person is making and the noise in your own head. Unless you train yourself to remain vigilant, the brain usually ends up paying attention to the noise in your own head. That's where active listening techniques come into play. Hearing becomes listening only when you pay attention to what the person is saying and follow it very closely.

① a sense of autonomy
② a creative mindset
③ a high degree of self-control
④ an extroverted personality

## 기출 분석

**01**

> Active listening is an art, a skill and a discipline that takes _____.
> To develop good listening skills, you need to understand what is involved in effective communication and develop the techniques to sit quietly and listen. This involves ignoring your own needs and focusing on the person speaking — a task made more difficult by the way the human brain works. When someone talks to you, your brain immediately begins processing the words, body language, tone, inflection and perceived meanings coming from the other person. Instead of hearing one noise, you hear two: the noise the other person is making and the noise in your own head. Unless you train yourself to remain vigilant, the brain usually ends up paying attention to the noise in your own head. That's where active listening techniques come into play. Hearing becomes listening only when you pay attention to what the person is saying and follow it very closely.

**해석** 능동적 경청은 예술이자 기술이며 높은 수준의 자제력이 필요한 훈련이다. 좋은 경청 기술을 개발하려면 효과적인 의사소통에 무엇이 수반되는지를 이해하고 조용히 앉아서 상대의 말을 듣는 기술을 익혀야 한다. 이 과정은 자신의 욕구를 무시하고 말하는 사람에게 집중하는 것을 포함하는데, 이는 인간의 뇌가 작동하는 방식 때문에 더 어려워진다. 누군가가 당신에게 말을 걸어오면, 당신의 뇌는 곧바로 상대방의 말, 몸짓, 어조, 억양, 그리고 그에 따른 의미를 처리하기 시작한다. 당신은 한 가지 소리만 듣지 않고 두 가지 소리를 듣게 되는데, 그 두 가지 소리는 상대방이 내는 소리와 자기 머릿속에서 울리는 소리이다. 스스로 집중력을 유지하도록 훈련하지 않으면, 뇌는 대체로 자기 머릿속 소음에 결국 주의를 기울이게 된다. 바로 그 지점에서 적극적 경청 기술이 중요한 역할을 하게 된다. 그 사람이 말하는 것에 주의를 기울이고 아주 가까이 그것을 따라갈 때만 비로소 듣는 것(hearing)은 경청(listening)이 된다.

① 자율성의 감각
② 창의적인 사고방식
③ 높은 수준의 자제력
④ 외향적인 성격

**어휘** active 능동적인, 적극적인  discipline 훈련, 규율  involve 포함하다, 관련시키다
effective 효과적인  ignore 무시하다  immediately 즉시  process 처리하다  inflection 억양, 어조
perceive 인지하다  vigilant 집중하는, 경계하는, 방심하지 않는  end up ~ing 결국 ~하게 되다
come into play 중요한 역할을 하기 시작하다, 효과를 발휘 하다  autonomy 자율성, 자치
mindset 사고방식, 마음가짐  degree 정도, 수준  self-control 자기 통제력
extroverted 외향적인, 사교적인

**해설** 빈칸 완성의 처음 시작은 이 글이 무엇에 관한 글 (Main Idea)인가를 떠올리는 것이다. 주어진 지문은 적극적 '경청'을 위해서는 자신의 욕구를 억제하고 상대방에게 집중해야 한다는 내용의 글이므로 빈칸에 들어갈 말로 가장 적절한 것은 ③ '높은 수준의 자제력'이다

**정답**
01 ③

## 기출문제

**02** 밑줄 친 부분에 들어갈 말로 가장 적절한 것을 고르시오. 2025. 국가직 9급

> The holiday season is a time to give thanks, reflect on the past year, and spend time with family and friends. However, if you're not careful, it can also be a time you overspend on holiday purchases. People have an innate impulse to overspend, experts say. They are "wired" to be consumers. The short-term gratification of giving gifts to loved ones can eclipse the long-term focus that's needed to be good with money. That's where many people fall short. We can overspend because our long-term goals are much more abstract, and it actually requires us to do extra levels of cognitive processing to delay instant gratification. Additionally, consumers may feel _____ because they don't want to appear "cheap." Many companies also promote deals during the holidays that can encourage people to spend more than usual.

① a desire to work at overseas companies
② responsible for establishing their long-term goals
③ like limiting their spending during the holiday season
④ the social pressure to spend more than they might like

## 기출 분석

**02**
The holiday season is a time to give thanks, reflect on the past year, and spend time with family and friends. However, if you're not careful, it can also be a time you overspend on holiday purchases. People have an innate impulse to overspend, experts say. They are "wired" to be consumers. The short-term gratification of giving gifts to loved ones can eclipse the long-term focus that's needed to be good with money. That's where many people fall short. We can overspend because our long-term goals are much more abstract, and it actually requires us to do extra levels of cognitive processing to delay instant gratification. Additionally, consumers may feel _____ because they don't want to appear "cheap." Many companies also promote deals during the holidays that can encourage people to spend more than usual.

→ 논리의 방향이 같다.

**해석** 연휴 시즌은 감사를 나누고, 지난 한 해를 되돌아보며, 가족 및 친구들과 시간을 보내는 시기이다. 하지만 주의하지 않으면, 그것은 또한 연휴 쇼핑에 과소비를 하게 되는 시기가 될 수 있다. 전문가들은 사람들이 과소비에 대한 타고난 충동이 있다고 말한다. 사람들은 소비자가 되도록 "설계되어" 있다. 사랑하는 사람들에게 선물을 주는 단기적인 만족감은 돈을 잘 관리하는 데 필요한 장기적인 집중력을 가릴 수 있다. 바로 그 지점에서 많은 사람이 어려움을 겪는다. 우리는 장기적인 목표가 훨씬 더 추상적이고 즉각적인 만족을 미루기 위해서는 실제로 더 많은 수준의 인지적 노력이 필요하므로 과소비를 하게 되는 것이다. 게다가, 소비자들은 "인색해"보이고 싶지 않아서 <u>원하는 것보다 더 많이 소비해야 한다는 사회적 압박</u>을 느낄 수도 있다. 많은 기업 또한 연휴기간 동안 사람들로 하여금 평소보다 더 많이 소비하도록 유도하는 할인 행사를 홍보한다.
① 해외 기업에서 일하고자 하는 욕구
② 장기적 목표를 세울 책임
③ 연휴 시즌 동안 소비 제한을 원함
④ 원하는 것보다 더 많이 소비해야 한다는 사회적 압박

**어휘** reflect on 되돌아보다  overspend 과소비하다  purchase 구매  innate 타고난, 선천적인  impulse 충동, 자극  expert 전문가  wired ① 전선이 연결된 ② 타고난, 설계된  consumer 소비자  short-term 단기간의  gratification 만족감, 기쁨  eclipse 가리다, 희미하게 하다  long-term 장기간인  fall short 부족하다, 어려움을 겪다  abstract 추상적인  require 요구하다  cognitive 인식의, 인지적인  processing 처리, 가공  delay 미루다, 지연시키다  instant 즉각적인  additionally 게다가, 더욱이  appear ~처럼 보이다  cheap 인색한, 구두쇠 같은  promote 홍보하다  deal ① 거래, 계약 ② 할인행사  than usual 평소보다  desire 욕구, 욕망  overseas 해외의, 해외에서  establish 세우다, 설립하다  pressure 압박

**해설** 빈칸 완성은 문장과 문장 간 논리도 필요하다. 빈칸 다음 **because**를 이용해서 인과관계의 논리가 필요하다. because 다음 원인에 해당하는 '많은 기업이 사람들을 평소보다 더 많이 소비하도록 부추긴다'는 내용이 있으므로 이에 대한 결과가 빈칸에 있어야 한다. 따라서 문맥상 빈칸에 들어갈 말로 가장 적절한 것은 ④ '원하는 것보다 더 많이 소비해야 한다는 사회적 압박'이다.

**정답**
02 ④

## 기출문제

**03** 밑줄 친 부분에 들어갈 말로 가장 적절한 것을 고르시오. 2025. 지방직 9급

> A hunter-gatherer in the Stone Age knew how to make her own clothes, how to start a fire, how to hunt rabbits and how to escape lions. We think we know far more today, but as individuals, we actually know far less. We rely on the expertise of others for almost all our needs. In one humbling experiment, people were asked to evaluate how well they understood the workings of an ordinary zipper. Most people confidently replied that they understood zippers very well — after all, they use them all the time. They were then asked to describe in as much detail as possible all the steps involved in the zipper's operation. Most people had no idea. This is what Steven Sloman and Philip Fernbach have termed 'the knowledge illusion'. We think we know a lot, even though individually we know very little, because we treat knowledge _____ as if it were our own.

① from hands-on experiences
② in the minds of others
③ gained during education
④ learned through trial and error

## 기출 분석

03
A hunter-gatherer in the Stone Age knew how to make her own clothes, how to start a fire, how to hunt rabbits and how to escape lions. We think we know far more today, but as individuals, we actually know far less. We rely on the expertise of others for almost all our needs. In one humbling experiment, people were asked to evaluate how well they understood the workings of an ordinary zipper. Most people confidently replied that they understood zippers very well — after all, they use them all the time. They were then asked to describe in as much detail as possible all the steps involved in the zipper's operation. Most people had no idea. This is what Steven Sloman and Philip Fernbach have termed 'the knowledge illusion'. We think we know a lot, even though individually we know very little, because we treat knowledge _____ as if it were our own.

**해석** 석기시대의 수렵 채집인은 스스로 옷을 만들고, 불을 피우고, 토끼를 사냥하며, 사자를 피하는 방법을 알고 있었다. 오늘날 우리는 훨씬 더 많은 것을 알고 있다고 생각하지만, 실제로 개인으로서 우리가 아는 것은 훨씬 적다. 우리는 대부분의 필요를 (해결하기) 위해 타인의 전문 지식에 의존한다. 한 가지 겸손해지게 만드는 실험에서, 사람들은 일반적인 지퍼의 작동 원리를 얼마나 잘 이해하고 있는지 평가해 보라는 요청을 받았다. 대부분의 사람들은 어쨌든 그들이 그것을 항상 사용하기에 지퍼를 아주 잘 이해한다고 자신 있게 대답했다. 그들은 이어서 지퍼의 작동에 관련된 모든 과정을 가능한 한 자세히 설명해 보라는 요청을 받았다. 대부분의 사람들은 전혀 몰랐다. 이것이 Steven Sloman과 Philip Fernbach이 '지식의 환상'이라고 이름 붙인 것이다. 우리는 개인적으로는 매우 조금 알고 있음에도 불구하고 많은 것을 알고 있다고 생각하는데, 이는 우리가 <u>다른 사람들의 머릿속에 있는</u> 지식을 마치 우리 자신의 것인 양 여기기 때문이다

① 직접적인 경험에서 비롯된
② 다른 사람들의 머릿속에 있는
③ 교육을 받는 동안 얻은
④ 시행착오를 통해 배운

**어휘** hunter-gatherer 수렵 채집인  Stone Age 석기 시대  own 자신의  escape 탈출하다
rely on 의존하다  expertise 전문성  humbling 겸손하게 만드는  evaluate 평가하다
ordinary 평범한  confidently 자신 있게  reply 대답하다  describe 설명하다  step 단계
involve 포함하다  operation 작동  term (이름을) 붙이다  illusion 착각, 환상
treat 다루다, 대우하다, 대하다  as if 마치 ~인 것처럼

**해설** 주어진 지문은 사람들은 개인적으로 아는 것이 많지 않지만, 타인의 전문 지식에 의존하면서 그것을 마치 자신의 지식처럼 착각한다는 내용의 글이므로 빈칸에 들어갈 말로 가장 적절한 것은 ② '다른 사람들의 머릿속에 있는'이다.

정답
03 ②

## 기출문제

**04** 밑줄 친 부분에 들어갈 말로 적절한 것을 고르시오. 2024. 지방직 9급

> Javelin Research noticed that not all Millennials are currently in the same stage of life. While all Millennials were born around the turn of the century, some of them are still in early adulthood, wrestling with new careers and settling down. On the other hand, the older Millennials have a home and are building a family. You can imagine how having a child might change your interests and priorities, so for marketing purposes, it's useful to split this generation into Gen Y.1 and Gen Y.2. Not only are the two groups culturally different, but they're in vastly different phases of their financial life. The younger group is financial beginners, just starting to show their buying power. The latter group has a credit history, may have their first mortgage and is raising young children. The _____ in priorities and needs between Gen Y.1 and Gen Y.2 is vast.

① contrast
② reduction
③ repetition
④ ability

## 기출 분석

**04**

Javelin Research noticed that not all Millennials are currently in the same stage of life. While all Millennials were born around the turn of the century, some of them are still in early adulthood, wrestling with new careers and settling down. On the other hand, the older Millennials have a home and are building a family. You can imagine how having a child might change your interests and priorities, so for marketing purposes, it's useful to split this generation into Gen Y.1 and Gen Y.2. Not only are the two groups culturally different, but they're in vastly different phases of their financial life. The younger group is financial beginners, just starting to show their buying power. The latter group has a credit history, may have their first mortgage and is raising young children. The _____ in priorities and needs between Gen Y.1 and Gen Y.2 is vast.

**해석** Javelin Research는 모든 밀레니얼 세대가 현재 같은 삶의 단계에 있는 것은 아니라는 것을 알아 차렸다. 모든 밀레니얼 세대가 세기의 전환기에 태어났지만, 그중 일부는 아직 초기 성인 단계에서 새로운 직업과 씨름하며 자리를 잡아가고 있다. 반면에, 나이가 더 많은 밀레니얼 세대는 집이 있고 가정을 만들어가고 있다. 당신은 아이를 낳는 것이 당신의 관심사와 우선순위가 어떻게 달라질지 상상할 수 있고 그래서 마케팅 목적을 위해 이 세대를 Y.1 세대와 Y.2 세대로 나누는 것이 유용하다. 두 집단은 문화적으로 다를 뿐만 아니라 재정적으로 아주 다른 삶의 단계에 있다. 더 어린 집단은 재정 초보자들로서 이제 막 구매력을 발휘하기 시작한다. 후자 집단은 신용기록이 있고 첫 주택담보대출을 받았을 수도 있으며, 어린 자녀들을 키우고 있다. Y.1 세대와 Y.2 세대 간 우선순위와 필요의 <u>차이</u>는 아주 크다.
① 차이
② 감소
③ 반복
④ 능력

**어휘** notice 알아차리다  Millennial ① 천년의 ② 1980년대에서 1990년도에 태어난 사람들  currently 현재
stage 단계  turn 전환기  adulthood 성인기, 성년기  wrestle 씨름하다, 레슬링하다
career 직업, 경력  settle down 정착하다  on the other hand 반면에  priority 우선순위
split 나누다, 쪼개다  generation 세대  culturally 문화적으로  vastly 거대하게, 아주, 매우
phase ① 단계 ② 상, 모습  financial 재정상의, 재정적인  the latter 후자(의)
mortgage ① 담보대출 ② 저당 잡히다  vast 거대한  reduction 감소  repetition 반복

**해설** two 개념을 이용해야 한다. 주어진 지문은 Y.1 세대와 Y.2 세대 간의 차이점을 설명하고 있으므로 빈칸에 들어갈 말로 적절한 것은 ① '차이'이다.

04 ①

## 기출문제

**05** 밑줄 친 부분에 들어갈 말로 적절한 것을 고르시오. 2024. 지방직 9급

> Cost pressures in liberalized markets have different effects on existing and future hydropower schemes. Because of the cost structure, existing hydropower plants will always be able to earn a profit. Because the planning and construction of future hydropower schemes is not a short-term process, it is not a popular investment, in spite of low electricity generation costs. Most private investors would prefer to finance _____, leading to the paradoxical situation that although an existing hydropower plant seems to be a cash cow, nobody wants to invest in a new one. Where public shareholders/owners (states, cities, municipalities) are involved, the situation looks very different because they can see the importance of the security of supply and also appreciate long-term investments.

① more short-term technologies
② all high technology industries
③ the promotion of the public interest
④ the enhancement of electricity supply

## 기출 분석

**05**

Two 개념: ① 기존의 수력발전 ② 미래의 수력발전 → 차이점 설명

Cost pressures in liberalized markets have different effects on existing and future hydropower schemes. Because of the cost structure, existing hydropower plants will always be able to earn a profit. Because the planning and construction of future hydropower schemes is not a short-term process, it is not a popular investment, in spite of low electricity generation costs. Most private investors would prefer to finance _____, leading to the paradoxical situation that although an existing hydropower plant seems to be a cash cow, nobody wants to invest in a new one. Where public shareholders/owners (states, cities, municipalities) are involved, the situation looks very different because they can see the importance of the security of supply and also appreciate long-term investments.

**해석** 자유화된 시장에서의 비용 압력은 기존 및 미래의 수력발전 계획에 서로 다른 영향을 준다. 비용 구조 때문에 기존의 수력발전소는 항상 수익을 낼 수 있을 것이다. 미래 수력발전 계획에 대한 계획과 건설 계획은 단기간의 과정이 아니기 때문에 낮은 전력 생성 비용에도 불구하고 대중적인 투자는 아니다. 대부분의 민간 투자자들은 <u>더 단기간의 기술</u>에 자금을 대는 것을 선호하는데 이는 기존 수력발전소가 캐시 카우처럼 보이는 데도 불구하고 아무도 새로운 곳에 투자하지 않으려는 역설적인 상황을 초래한다. 공공 주주/소유주(주, 시, 지자체)가 참여하는 경우 그들은 공급 안정성의 중요성을 인식하고 장기적인 투자의 진가를 인정하기 때문에 상황은 매우 다르게 보인다.

① 더 단기간의 기술
② 모든 첨단 기술 산업
③ 공공 이익의 증진
④ 전력 공급의 강화

**어휘** pressure 압박  liberalized 자유화된  have effects on ~에 영향을 주다  existing 기존의
hydropower 수력발전  scheme 계획  structure 구조  existing 기존의  plant 발전소, 공장
earn 벌다, 얻다  profit 수익  construction 건설  short-term 단기간의  process 과정
popular 대중적인  investment 투자  in spite of ~에도 불구하고  electricity 전기, 전력
generation ① 세대 ② 발생, 생성  private ① 사적인 ② 민간의, 민영의
investor 투자자  *invest 투자하다  prefer 선호하다  finance ① 재원, 자금 ② 자금을 대다
lead to ~을 초래하다, 야기하다  paradoxical 역설적인  situation 상황
cash cow 캐시 카우, 고수익 사업[상품]  public 공적인, 공공의  shareholder 주주
municipality 지방 자치제, 지자체  involve ① 포함하다 ② 관계시키다 ③ 참여시키다
security 안전, 안정성  supply 공급(하다)  appreciate 진가를 인정하다, 중요시하다
promotion 증진, 향상  interest ① 흥미, 관심 ② 이익, 이자  enhancement 강화, 향상

**해설** two 개념(기존 vs. 미래)을 이용해야 한다. 기존의 수력발전은 수익을 낼 수 있고, 단기과정인데 반해 미래 수력 발전은 단기과정이 아니고 인기 있는 투자가 아니므로 문맥상 투자자들이 투자할 곳은 기존 수력발전이어야 한다. 선택지에 기존 수력발전을 설명하는 **short-term**(단기) **technologies**가 있으므로 빈칸에 들어가기에 가장 적절한 것은 ① '더 단기간의 기술'이다. 참고로 빈칸 다음 민간 투자자들(private investors)과는 달리 공공 주주들/소유주들(public shareholders/owners)은 공급 안정성(security of supply)과 장기적인 투자(long-term investments)를 중요하게 여긴다고 했고 선택지 ③ public interest와 ④ electricity supply는 모두 미래의 기술과 관련된 내용이므로 정답이 될 수 없다.

**정답**
05 ①

## 기출문제

**06** 밑줄 친 부분에 들어갈 말로 적절한 것을 고르시오. 2024. 국가직 9급

_____. Nearly every major politician hires media consultants and political experts to provide advice on how to appeal to the public. Virtually every major business and special-interest group has hired a lobbyist to take its concerns to Congress or to state and local governments. In nearly every community, activists try to persuade their fellow citizens on important policy issues. The workplace, too, has always been fertile ground for office politics and persuasion. One study estimates that general managers spend upwards of 80 % of their time in verbal communication — most of it with the intent of persuading their fellow employees. With the advent of the photocopying machine, a whole new medium for office persuasion was invented — the photocopied memo. The Pentagon alone copies an average of 350,000 pages a day, the equivalent of 1,000 novels.

① Business people should have good persuasion skills
② Persuasion shows up in almost every walk of life
③ You will encounter countless billboards and posters
④ Mass media campaigns are useful for the government

## 기출 분석

**06**

> Main Idea : 각계각층에서 설득이 나타난다.

_____. Nearly every major politician hires media consultants and political experts to provide advice on how to appeal to the public. Virtually every major business and special-interest group has hired a lobbyist to take its concerns to Congress or to state and local governments. In nearly every community, activists try to persuade their fellow citizens on important

> 나열의 시그널 : ① 정치가 ② 기업 ③ 활동가 ④ 직장

policy issues. The workplace, too, has always been fertile ground for office politics and persuasion. One study estimates that general managers spend upwards of 80 % of their time in verbal communication — most of it with the intent of persuading their fellow employees. With the advent of the photocopying machine, a whole new medium for office persuasion was invented — the photocopied memo. The Pentagon alone copies an average of 350,000 pages a day, the equivalent of 1,000 novels.

**해석** 설득은 거의 각계각층에서 나타난다. 거의 모든 주요 정치가들은 대중에게 어떻게 호소해야 하는지에 관한 조언을 제공하는 미디어 상담사와 정치적 전문가를 고용한다. 사실상 모든 주요 기업 및 특수 이익 단체는 자신들의 관심사를 의회나 주 정부 또는 지방 정부에 가져가기 위해 로비스트들을 고용해 왔다. 거의 모든 지역사회에서 활동가들은 중요한 정책 문제에 대해 동료 시민들을 설득하기 위해 노력한다. 직장 역시 언제나 사무실 정치와 설득 활동을 위한 비옥한 터전이 되어 왔다. 일반 관리자들은 업무 시간의 80% 이상을 언어적 의사소통에 소비하며 이 중 대부분은 동료 직원을 설득하기 위한 의도로 사용한다고 한 연구는 추정한다. 복사기의 출현으로 전 직원의 설득을 위한 완전히 새로운 매체, 즉 복사 메모가 발명되었다. 미국 국방부에서만 하루 평균 350,000페이지를 복사하는데, 이는 소설 1,000권과 맞먹는 분량이다.

① 기업인은 좋은 설득 기술을 가져야 한다
② 설득은 거의 각계각층에서 나타난다
③ 당신은 수많은 광고판이나 포스터와 마주칠 것이다
④ 대중 매체 캠페인은 정부에게 유용하다

**어휘** nearly 거의 major 주된, 주요한 politician 정치가 consultant 상담사, 컨설턴트 expert 전문가 provide 제공하다 appeal 호소하다 virtually 사실상 special-interest group 특수 이익 단체 hire 고용하다 concern 관심, 관심사 state 주 activist 활동가 persuade 설득하다 fellow 동료 policy 정책 workplace 직장 fertile 비옥한 persuasion 설득 estimate 추정하다, 추산하다 upwards 위쪽으로, 이상 verbal 언어적인, 말로 하는 intent 의도, 목적 advent 출현, 도래 photocopy 복사하다 whole ① 전체의 ② 완전한 medium 매체 invent 발명하다 Pentagon 미국 국방부 equivalent 동등한, 맞먹는 show up 나타나다, 등장하다 every walk of life 각계각층의 encounter 만나다, 마주치다 countless 수많은, 셀 수 없는 billboard 광고판 mass media 대중 매체

**해설** 빈칸 완성은 항상 이 글이 무엇에 관한 글인지를 떠올려야 한다. 주어진 지문은 사회의 여러 분야에서 흔히 이루어지고 있는 설득의 다양한 모습을 나타내는 내용의 글이므로 빈칸에 들어가기에 가장 적절한 것은 ② '설득은 거의 각계각층에서 나타난다'이다.

**정답**
06 ②

## 기출문제

**07** 밑줄 친 부분에 들어갈 말로 적절한 것을 고르시오. 2024. 국가직 9급

It is important to note that for adults, social interaction mainly occurs through the medium of language. Few native-speaker adults are willing to devote time to interacting with someone who does not speak the language, with the result that the adult foreigner will have little opportunity to engage in meaningful and extended language exchanges. In contrast, the young child is often readily accepted by other children, and even adults. For young children, language is not as essential to social interaction. So-called 'parallel play', for example, is common among young children. They can be content just to sit in each other's company speaking only occasionally and playing on their own. Adults rarely find themselves in situations where _____.

① language does not play a crucial role in social interaction
② their opinions are readily accepted by their colleagues
③ they are asked to speak another language
④ communication skills are highly required

## 기출 분석

**07**

It is important to note that for adults, social interaction mainly occurs through the medium of language. Few native-speaker adults are willing to devote time to interacting with someone who does not speak the language, with the result that the adult foreigner will have little opportunity to engage in meaningful and extended language exchanges. In contrast, the young child is often readily accepted by other children, and even adults. For young children, language is not as essential to social interaction. So-called 'parallel play', for example, is common among young children. They can be content just to sit in each other's company speaking only occasionally and playing on their own. Adults rarely find themselves in situations where _____.

> Two 개념: ① adults ② young children → 차이점 설명: 언어의 역할

**해석** 어른들에게 사회적 상호 작용은 주로 언어라는 매체를 통해 나타난다는 점에 주목하는 것이 중요하다. 모국어를 사용하는 어른들 중 그 언어를 사용하지 않는 사람과 교류하는 데 기꺼이 시간을 쏟는 사람은 거의 없으며, 그 결과 성인 외국인은 의미 있는 폭넓은 언어 교환에 참여할 기회가 거의 없을 것이다. 이와는 반대로 어린아이는 다른 아이들에게, 심지어 어른들에게도 쉽게 받아들여진다. 어린아이들에게 언어는 사회적 상호 작용을 하는 데 필수적이지는 않다. 예를 들어, 소위 '평행 놀이'는 어린아이들 사이에서 보편적이다. 그들은 서로 함께 앉아서 가끔씩만 말을 하고 스스로 노는 것만으로도 만족할 수 있다. 어른들은 사회적 상호 작용에서 언어가 결정적인 역할을 하지 않는 상황에 처하는 경우가 거의 없다.

① 사회적 상호 작용에서 언어가 결정적인 역할을 하지 않는
② 그들의 의견이 동료들에게 쉽게 받아들여지는
③ 다른 언어를 사용하도록 요청받는
④ 의사소통 능력이 매우 요구되는

**어휘** note 주목하다  interaction 상호 작용  mainly 주로  occur 나타나다  medium 매체
be willing to ⓥ 기꺼이 ⓥ하다  devote A to B A를 B하는 데 쏟다[몰두하다, 헌신하다]
interact with ~와 상호 작용하다  opportunity 기회  engage in ~에 참여하다
meaningful 의미 있는  extended 폭넓은, 확장된  exchange 교환  in contrast 이와는 반대로
readily 쉽게, 즉시  accept 받아들이다, 수락하다  essential 필수적인  so-called 소위
parallel 평행(선)  content 만족한  company 함께 있음  occasionally 가끔
rarely 거의 ~ 않는  situation 상황  play a role 역할을 하다  crucial 결정적인
colleague 동료  highly 아주, 매우  require 요구하다

**해설** two 개념(adults vs children)과 부정어(rarely)를 이용해야 한다. 주어진 지문은 어른들에게는 언어가 상호 작용을 하는 데 필수적 요소이고 아이들은 그렇지 않다는 내용의 글로 빈칸 앞에 부정어(rarely)가 있으므로 빈칸에 들어가기에 가장 적절한 것은 ① '사회적 상호 작용에서 언어가 결정적인 역할을 하지 않는'이다.

**정답**
07 ①

## 기출문제

**08** 밑줄 친 부분에 들어갈 말로 적절한 것을 고르시오. 2023. 지방직 9급

> We live in the age of anxiety. Because being anxious can be an uncomfortable and scary experience, we resort to conscious or unconscious strategies that help reduce anxiety in the moment — watching a movie or TV show, eating, video-game playing, and overworking. In addition, smartphones also provide a distraction any time of the day or night. Psychological research has shown that distractions serve as a common anxiety avoidance strategy. _____, however, these avoidance strategies make anxiety worse in the long run. Being anxious is like getting into quicksand — the more you fight it, the deeper you sink. Indeed, research strongly supports a well-known phrase that "What you resist, persists."

① Paradoxically
② Fortunately
③ Neutrally
④ Creative

## 기출 분석

**08**

We live in the age of anxiety. Because being anxious can be an uncomfortable and scary experience, we resort to conscious or unconscious strategies that help reduce anxiety in the moment — watching a movie or TV show, eating, video-game playing, and overworking. In addition, smartphones also provide a distraction any time of the day or night. Psychological research has shown that distractions serve as a common anxiety avoidance strategy. _____, however, these avoidance strategies make anxiety worse in the long run. Being anxious is like getting into quicksand — the more you fight it, the deeper you sink. Indeed, research strongly supports a well-known phrase that "What you resist, persists."

**해석** 우리는 불안의 시대에 살고 있다. 불안해하는 것은 불편하고 무서운 경험일 수 있기 때문에 우리는 영화나 TV쇼를 보고, 먹거나, 비디오 게임을 하고, 과로를 하는 등 순간의 불안을 줄이는 데 도움이 되는 의식 또는 무의식적인 전략들에 의존한다. 게다가, 스마트폰은 또한 하루 중 언제든지 주의를 산만하게 만들기도 한다. 심리학 연구는 주의를 산만하게 하는 것들이 일반적인 불안 회피 전략의 역할을 한다는 것을 보여주었다. 그러나 역설적으로, 이러한 회피 전략은 결국 불안을 악화시킨다. 불안해하는 것은 유사(流砂)에 빠지는 것과 같다. 즉, 그것과 싸우면 싸울수록 당신은 더 깊이 가라앉는다. 실제로, 연구는 "당신이 저항하는 것은 지속된다"라는 잘 알려진 문구를 강력하게 지지한다.

① 역설적으로
② 운 좋게도
③ 중립적으로
④ 창의적으로

**어휘** anxiety 불안, 걱정  scary 무서운  resort to ~에 의존하다  conscious 의식적인  overwork 과로하다  distraction 주의를 산만하게 하는 것  serve 역할을 하다  avoidance 회피  in the long run 결국  quicksand 유사(流砂: 바람이나 물에 의해 아래로 흘러내리는 모래. 사람이 들어가면 늪에 빠진 것처럼 헤어 나오지 못함)  sink 가라앉다  phrase 문구  resist 저항하다  persist 지속되다  paradoxically 역설적으로  fortunately 운 좋게도  neutrally 중립적으로  creatively 창의적으로

**해설** 불안과 그 회피 전략에 관한 글이다. 빈칸 앞에는 스마트폰과 같은 주의를 산만하게 하는 것들이 흔히 불안 회피 전략 역할을 한다는 내용이 있는데, 빈칸 뒤에는 역접 접속사 however와 더불어 그 회피 전략이 장기적으로는 불안을 악화시킨다는 상반되는 내용이 나오고 있다. 따라서 빈칸에 들어갈 말로 가장 적절한 것은 ① '역설적으로'이다.

08 ①

## 기출문제

**09** 밑줄 친 부분에 들어갈 말로 적절한 것을 고르시오. 2023. 지방직 9급

How many different ways do you get information? Some people might have six different kinds of communications to answer — text messages, voice mails, paper documents, regular mail, blog posts, messages on different online services. Each of these is a type of in-box, and each must be processed on a continuous basis. It's an endless process, but it doesn't have to be exhausting or stressful. Getting your information management down to a more manageable level and into a productive zone starts by _____. Every place you have to go to check your messages or to read your incoming information is an in-box, and the more you have, the harder it is to manage everything. Cut the number of in-boxes you have down to the smallest number possible for you still to function in the ways you need to.

① setting several goals at once
② immersing yourself in incoming information
③ minimizing the number of in-boxes you have
④ choosing information you are passionate about

## 기출 분석

**09**

How many different ways do you get information? Some people might have six different kinds of communications to answer — text messages, voice mails, paper documents, regular mail, blog posts, messages on different online services. Each of these is a type of in-box, and each must be processed on a continuous basis. It's an endless process, but it doesn't have to be exhausting or stressful. Getting your information management down to a more manageable level and into a productive zone starts by _____. Every place you have to go to check your messages or to read your incoming information is an in-box, and the more you have, the harder it is to manage everything. Cut the number of in-boxes you have down to the smallest number possible for you still to function in the ways you need to.

↳ Main Idea : 당신이 가진 수신함의 수를 최소화하라.

**해석** 얼마나 많은 다른 방법으로 당신은 정보를 얻는가? 어떤 사람들은 문자 메시지, 음성 메일, 종이 문서, 일반 우편, 블로그 게시물, 그리고 서로 다른 온라인 서비스의 메시지 등 6가지 서로 다른 종류의 통신수단에 답을 해야 할지도 모른다. 이것들 각각은 일종의 수신함의 유형이며, 연속적으로 처리되어야 한다. 그것은 끝이 없는 과정이지만, 지치거나 스트레스를 받을 필요는 없다. 당신의 정보 관리를 보다 더 관리하기 쉬운 수준으로 낮추고 생산적인 영역으로 전환하려면 <u>당신이 가진 수신함의 수를 최소화하는</u> 것으로 시작하면 된다. 당신이 메시지를 확인하거나 들어오는 정보를 읽으러 가야 하는 곳은 모두 수신함이며, 당신이 가진 것이 많을수록 모든 것을 관리하기가 더 어려워진다. 당신이 필요한 방식으로 계속 기능할 수 있도록 당신이 가진 수신함의 수를 최소한으로 줄여라.

① 한 번에 여러 목표를 설정하는
② 들어오는 정보에 몰두하는
③ 당신이 가진 수신함의 수를 최소화하는
④ 당신이 열정적인 정보를 선택하는

**어휘** text message 문자 메시지  in-box 수신함  process 처리하다, 가공하다
on a continuous basis 연속적으로  exhausting 지치는  get down 낮추다  zone 영역
cut down 줄이다  function 기능하다, 작동하다  immerse ① 담그다 ② 몰두하게 하다, 몰두하다
passionate 열정적인

**해설** 주어진 지문은 받은 정보를 수신함에 보관하는데, 이 수신함이 많으면 관리하기가 어려우니 가능한 한 이 수신함의 수를 줄이라는 내용의 글이므로 빈칸에 들어갈 말로 가장 적절한 것은 ③ '당신이 가진 수신함의 수를 최소화하는'이다.

**정답**
09 ③

## 기출문제

**10** 밑줄 친 부분에 들어갈 말로 적절한 것을 고르시오. 2023. 국가직 9급

Over the last fifty years, all major subdisciplines in psychology have become more and more isolated from each other as training becomes increasingly specialized and narrow in focus. As some psychologists have long argued, if the field of psychology is to mature and advance scientifically, its disparate parts (for example, neuroscience, developmental, cognitive, personality, and social) must become whole and integrated again. Science advances when distinct topics become theoretically and empirically integrated under simplifying theoretical frameworks. Psychology of science will encourage collaboration among psychologists from various sub-areas, helping the field achieve coherence rather than continued fragmentation. In this way, psychology of science might act as a template for psychology as a whole by integrating under one discipline all of the major fractions/factions within the field. It would be no small feat and of no small import if the psychology of science could become a model for the parent discipline on how to combine resources and study science _____.

① from a unified perspective
② in dynamic aspects
③ throughout history
④ with accurate evidence

## 기출 분석

**10**

Over the last fifty years, all major subdisciplines in psychology have become more and more isolated from each other as training becomes increasingly specialized and narrow in focus. As some psychologists have long argued, if the field of psychology is to mature and advance scientifically, its disparate parts (for example, neuroscience, developmental, cognitive, personality, and social) must become whole and integrated again. Science advances when distinct topics become theoretically and empirically integrated under simplifying theoretical frameworks. Psychology of science will encourage collaboration among psychologists from various sub-areas, helping the field achieve coherence rather than continued fragmentation. In this way, psychology of science might act as a template for psychology as a whole by integrating under one discipline all of the major fractions/factions within the field. It would be no small feat and of no small import if the psychology of science could become a model for the parent discipline on how to combine resources and study science _____.

**[해석]** 지난 50년 동안 심리학의 모든 주요한 하위 분야는 교육이 점점 더 특화되고 그 초점이 좁혀짐에 따라 서로 더욱더 고립되어 왔다. 일부 심리학자들이 오랫동안 주장해 온 것처럼, 만약 심리학 분야가 과학적으로 성숙해지고 발전하려면 그것의 이질적인 부분들(예를 들어, 신경과학, 발달, 인지, 성격, 사회 등)이 하나가 되고 다시 통합되어야 한다. 과학은 단순화라는 이론적 틀하에서 서로 다른 주제들이 이론적으로 그리고 경험적으로 통합될 때 발전한다. 과학 심리학은 다양한 하위영역의 심리학자 간의 협업을 장려하여 이 분야가 계속적인 분열보다는 일관성을 이룰 수 있도록 도울 것이다. 이러한 방식으로 과학 심리학은 심리학 분야의 모든 주요 부분/파벌을 하나의 학문으로 통합함으로써 전체 심리학에 대한 본보기가 될 수 있다. 만약 과학 심리학이 자원을 결합하는 방식 및 과학을 통합된 관점에서 연구하는 방법에 대한 모(母)학문의 모델이 될 수 있다면, 이는 결코 적지 않은 위업이며 그 중요도 또한 적지 않을 것이다.
① 통합된 관점에서 ② 역동적인 측면에서 ③ 역사를 통틀어 ④ 정확한 증거를 가지고

**[어휘]** major 주된, 주요한  subdiscipline 학문 분야의 하위 부분  psychology 심리학
isolated 고립된, 격리된  increasingly 점점 더  specialized 전문화된  narrow 좁은
mature 성숙해지다  advance 진보[발전]하다  disparate 이질적인, 다른  neuroscience 신경과학
cognitive 인지의, 인식의  distinct 다른, (뚜렷이) 구별되는  integrated 통합된
theoretically 이론적으로  empirically 경험적으로  simplify 단순화하다  framework 틀
collaboration 협력, 협업  sub-area 하위영역  field 분야  achieve 이루다, 성취하다
coherence 일관성  fragmentation 분열  template 본보기  fraction 부분, 분수
faction 파벌, 분파  feat 위업  import ① 수입(하다) ② 중요성, 중요도
parent discipline 모(母)학문  *discipline ① 규율, 훈육(하다) ② 지식분야, 학문, 학과목
unified 통합된  perspective 관점  dynamic 역동적인  aspects 측면
throughout ~의 전역에 걸쳐  accurate 정확한  evidence 증거

**[해설]** 빈칸 완성은 이 글이 무엇에 관한 글인가를 묻는다. 주어진 지문은 심리학의 하위 분야들 간 통합의 필요성과 이 과정에 있어서 과학 심리학이 통합의 중추적 역할을 해야 한다는 내용의 글이므로 빈칸에 들어갈 말로 가장 적절한 것은 ① '통합된 관점에서'이다.

**[정답]** 10 ①

## 기출문제

**11** 밑줄 친 부분에 들어갈 말로 가장 적절한 것은? 2022. 국가직 9급

> Scientists have long known that higher air temperatures are contributing to the surface melting on Greenland's ice sheet. But a new study has found another threat that has begun attacking the ice from below: Warm ocean water moving underneath the vast glaciers is causing them to melt even more quickly. The findings were published in the journal Nature Geoscience by researchers who studied one of the many "ice tongues" of the Nioghalvfjerdsfjorden Glacier in northeast Greenland. An ice tongue is a strip of ice that floats on the water without breaking off from the ice on land. The massive one these scientists studied is nearly 50 miles long. The survey revealed an underwater current more than a mile wide where warm water from the Atlantic Ocean is able to flow directly towards the glacier, bringing large amounts of heat into contact with the ice and _____ the glacier's melting.

① separating
② delaying
③ preventing
④ accelerating

## 기출 분석

**11**

Scientists have long known that higher air temperatures are contributing to the surface melting on Greenland's ice sheet. But a new study has found another threat that has begun attacking the ice from below: Warm ocean water moving underneath the vast glaciers is causing them to melt even more quickly. The findings were published in the journal Nature Geoscience by researchers who studied one of the many "ice tongues" of the Nioghalvfjerdsfjorden Glacier in northeast Greenland. An ice tongue is a strip of ice that floats on the water without breaking off from the ice on land. The massive one these scientists studied is nearly 50 miles long. The survey revealed an underwater current more than a mile wide where warm water from the Atlantic Ocean is able to flow directly towards the glacier, bringing large amounts of heat into contact with the ice and _____ the glacier's melting.

*Likeness(논리의 방향이 같다)를 이용해야 한다.*

**해석** 과학자들은 높은 기온이 그린란드 빙상의 표면이 녹는 것에 기여하고 있다는 사실을 오래 전부터 알고 있었다. 하지만 새로운 연구가 아래쪽에서부터 얼음을 공격하기 시작한 또 다른 위협을 발견했는데 이는 거대한 빙하 아래에서 이동하는 따뜻한 바닷물이 빙하를 훨씬 더 빨리 녹게 하고 있다는 것이다. 그 연구결과는 그린란드 북동부에 있는 빙하 79N(Nioghalvfjerdsfjorden Glacier)의 많은 "빙설" 중 하나를 연구한 연구자들에 의해 Nature Geoscience지에 실렸다. 빙설은 육지의 얼음에서 분리되지 않은 물 위를 떠다니는 얼음 조각이다. 이 과학자들이 연구한 그 어마어마한 빙설의 길이는 거의 50마일 정도이다. 그 조사는 대서양에서 나온 따뜻한 물이 빙하를 향해 직접 흐를 수 있어서 많은 양의 열기가 얼음과 접촉해서 빙하가 녹는 것을 <u>가속화시키는</u> 폭이 1마일 이상 되는 수중 해류를 발견하였다.

① 분리시키는
② 연기시키는
③ 예방하는
④ 가속화시키는

**어휘** air temperature 기온  contribute to ~에 기여하다  surface 표면  melt ① 녹다 ② 녹이다  ice sheet 빙상  threat 위협  attack 공격하다  underneath ~의 밑에, ~의 아래에  vast 거대한  glacier 빙하  finding 연구결과  ice tongue 빙설  strip 조각  reveal 드러내다  float (물에) 뜨다, 떠가다, 흘러가다  break off 분리되다, 갈라지다  massive 거대한, 어마어마한  current 흐름  separate 분리시키다, 나누다  accelerate 가속화하다

**해설** 주어진 지문은 빙하가 녹는 이유가 지구온난화가 아니라 대서양으로부터 흘러들어오는 따뜻한 수중해류 때문임을 밝히는 내용의 글이므로 빈칸에 들어가기에 가장 적절한 것은 ④ '가속화시키는'이다.

**정답**
11 ④

## 기출문제

**12** 밑줄 친 부분에 들어갈 말로 가장 적절한 것을 고르시오. 2021. 국가직 9급

> Social media, magazines and shop windows bombard people daily with things to buy, and British consumers are buying more clothes and shoes than ever before. Online shopping means it is easy for customers to buy without thinking, while major brands offer such cheap clothes that they can be treated like disposable items — worn two or three times and then thrown away. In Britain, the average person spends more than £ 1,000 on new clothes a year, which is around four percent of their income. That might not sound like much, but that figure hides two far more worrying trends for society and for the environment. First, a lot of that consumer spending is via credit cards. British people currently owe approximately £ 670 per adult to credit card companies. That's 66 percent of the average wardrobe budget. Also, not only are people spending money they don't have, they're using it to buy things _____. Britain throws away 300,000 tons of clothing a year, most of which goes into landfill sites.

① they don't need
② that are daily necessities
③ that will be soon recycled
④ they can hand down to others

## 기출 분석

**12**

: 집중해야 할 정보

Social media, magazines and shop windows bombard people daily with things to buy, and British consumers are buying more clothes and shoes than ever before. Online shopping means it is easy for customers to buy without thinking, while major brands offer such cheap clothes that they can be treated like disposable items — worn two or three times and then thrown away. In Britain, the average person spends more than £ 1,000 on new clothes a year, which is around four percent of their income. That might not sound like much, but that figure hides two far more worrying trends for society and for the environment. First (나열의 시그널), a lot of that consumer spending is via credit cards. British people currently owe approximately £ 670 per adult to credit card companies. That's 66 percent of the average wardrobe budget. Also (나열의 시그널), not only are people spending money they don't have, they're using it to buy things ＿＿＿＿＿＿＿＿. Britain throws away 300,000 tons of clothing a year, most of which goes into landfill sites.

↳ Main Idea: 쓸데없이 소비를 많이 한다.

**해석** 소셜 미디어, 잡지 그리고 상품 진열장은 매일 사람들에게 사야 할 물건들을 쏟아 내고 있으며, 영국의 소비자들은 이전 어느 때보다도 더 많은 옷과 신발을 사고 있다. 온라인 쇼핑은 고객들이 아무 생각 없이 쉽게 구매할 수 있다는 것을 의미하고 동시에 주요 브랜드들도 두세 번 입고 나서 버릴 수 있는 일회용품처럼 취급이 되는 값싼 옷을 제공한다. 영국에서, 보통 사람들은 일 년에 1천 파운드 이상을 새 옷을 사는 데 소비하는데, 이는 그들의 수입의 약 4%에 달한다. 4%가 많다고 여겨지진 않겠지만, 그 수치는 사회와 환경에 대한 훨씬 더 걱정스러운 두 가지 경향을 숨기고 있다. 첫째는, 많은 소비자 지출이 신용카드를 통해 이루어진다는 것이다. 영국인들은 현재 신용카드 회사에 성인 1인당 약 670파운드의 빚을 지고 있다. 이는 평균 옷 예산의 66%에 해당한다. 또한, 사람들은 가지고 있지 않은 돈을 쓸 뿐만 아니라, 그들이 필요하지 않은 물건을 사기 위해 돈을 사용하고 있다. 영국은 1년에 30만 톤의 의류를 버리고, 그 대부분은 쓰레기 매립지로 들어간다.
① 그들이 필요하지 않은
② 생필품인
③ 곧 재활용될
④ 그들이 타인에게 물려줄 수 있는

**어휘** bombard 쏟아 붓다, 쏟아 내다  treat 다루다, 취급하다  disposable 일회용의  throw away 내버리다  figure ① 인물 ② 모습, 형상 ③ 숫자, 수치  via ~을 경유하여, ~로  currently 현재  approximately 대략, 약  wardrobe 의상, 옷  landfill 쓰레기 매립지  daily necessities 생필품  hand over 물려주다

**해설** 빈칸 완성 문제의 처음 시작은 항상 이 글이 무엇에 관한 글인가를 떠올리는 것이다. 주어진 지문은 영국인들이 불필요한 것을 구매하는 데 돈을 낭비하고 있다는 내용의 글이므로 빈칸에 들어가기에 가장 적절한 것은 ① '그들이 필요하지 않은'이다.

**정답**
12 ①

### 김세현

**주요 약력**
- 현 박문각 공무원 영어 온라인, 오프라인 교수
- Eastern Michigan University 대학원 졸
- TESOL(영어교수법) 전공
- 전 EBS 영어 강사
- 전 Megastudy/Etoos/Skyedu 영어 강사
- 전 에듀윌 영어 강사

**주요 저서**

종합서
- 박문각 공무원 김세현 영어 All In One 기본서
- 박문각 공무원 김세현 영어 All In One VOCA
- 박문각 공무원 김세현 영어 전혀 다른 개념 문법
- 박문각 공무원 김세현 영어 전혀 다른 개념 독해
- EBS 완전 소중한 영문법
- EBS 이것이 진짜 리딩스킬이다

역서
- Longman 출판사 Reading Power 번역
- Longman 출판서 TOEIC/TOEFL 번역

---

## 김세현 영어 전혀 다른 개념 독해

**초판 인쇄** | 2025. 11. 10.  **초판 발행** | 2025. 11. 14.  **편저** | 김세현
**발행인** | 박 용  **발행처** | (주)박문각출판  **등록** | 2015년 4월 29일 제2019-000137호
**주소** | 06654 서울시 서초구 효령로 283 서경 B/D 4층  **팩스** | (02)584-2927
**전화** | 교재 문의 (02)6466-7202

저자와의 협의하에 인지생략

이 책의 무단 전재 또는 복제 행위를 금합니다.

정가 25,000원
ISBN 979-11-7519-361-1